BRITAIN'S WINNING FORMULA

Britain's Winning Formula

Achieving World Leadership in Motorsports

Martin Beck-Burridge
and
Jeremy Walton

First published 2000 by
MACMILLAN PRESS LTD
Houndmills, Basingstoke, Hampshire RG21 6XS
and London
Companies and representatives
throughout the world

ISBN 0–333–71270–6

A catalogue record for this book is available from the British Library.

This book is printed on paper suitable for recycling and made from fully managed and sustained forest sources.

10 9 8 7 6 5 4 3 2 1
09 08 07 06 05 04 03 02 01 00

Designed and formatted by
The Ascenders Partnership, Basingstoke
Illustrations by *Ascenders*

Printed and bound in Great Britain by
Creative Print & Design (Wales) Ltd, Ebbw Vale

Contents

Acknowledgements

THE authors gratefully thank their sponsors and the men and women of Britain's motorsport industry who supplied generous financial and practical support to this project whilst working to their usual rigorous race and rally schedules. They found the time to answer our numerous, frequently out-of-hours queries. They know who they are and we thank them all. A list of individuals would be invidious as their contributions were so wide-ranging. They are the essential elements in this fascinating and supremely successful industry.

Our special thanks to William Betts of PetroScience, Henley Management College MBA, for his extensive research assistance. Also to Nigel Geach of Sports Marketing Surveys for his time, and the statistics his organization generously provided. We are also grateful for the facilities of the Henley Centre for Automotive Studies. Other sources are acknowledged in the text.

Any errors or omissions are the authors' responsibility.

The authors gratefully acknowledge the assistance of Kodak who supplied all of the film used for the photographs in the plate sections of this book.

All of the photographs in the plate sections were taken on a Leica M6 camera and Leica lenses, supplied by Leica UK Limited.

MB-B is grateful for Leica's generous assistance.

Introduction

THE rate at which British owned car manufacturing companies have fallen into the hands of overseas owners had by 1999 left TVR, with an annual output c. 2000 specialist sports cars a year, as our largest wholly British owned supplier of private cars. It may well appear to the UK public that this single company upholds our sagging national automobile pride. However, this is simply not true as on the race and rally tracks of the world the contribution of British technology, engineers, aerodynamicists and designers is critical and pre-eminent.

In the premier World category for Grand Prix Formula One (F1) single seaters, United Kingdom Plc have been winners, on and off the race track, for the past forty years. Even the wealthiest opposition from Fiat-backed Ferrari of Italy has failed to dislodge the 'racer's edge' that Britain enjoys before a global TV audience; one measured by the hundred billion. Many times during this period Ferrari has shopped in Britain for personnel and parts and currently employs a British and British trained chief designer and head mechanic. In the early nineties they established a complete design and development facility in Britain to complete total racecar chassis designs.

However, the extensive pool of world leading technological excellence that is available in UK companies is applied with conspicuous success in more than just Grand Prix racing. The international market for the leading edges of automotive technology and design that these British specialist companies serve covers rallying, many different national and international single seat formulae, touring cars, concept vehicles, design studies and even vehicles for mass manufacturers. The customers that beat a path to their doors come from all over the world and include many of the major mass manufacturers and race teams who purchase high speed response, leading edge technology, extreme flexibility and some of the best automotive brains in the world.

From a survey undertaken in 1999 we estimate that the engineering core of the UK motorsports industry employed 50 000 people and returned an estimated

£1.6–£1.8 billion turnover. During the past decade several British motor racing companies have won the Queen's Award for Exports and the Queen's Award for Industry; some have won both.

Whilst Grand Prix racing is the highly visible tip of this engineering iceberg of expertise, Britain also accommodates three of the four teams that consistently win World Championship rallies, and is home to many teams contesting globally-televised touring car races. There is a host of events from international stadiums to the local field that are staged over each British weekend. It is this rich amateur heritage that has nurtured, and continues to nurture, the evolving reservoir of intellectual talent that is an essential element of the continued success of British professionals and their companies on the international scene.

Such is the importance now attached to the UK motor racing industry that it has its own trade organization: The Motorsport Industry Association (MIA). The UK motorsports industry itself has been the subject of extensive studies by organizations such as the IPPR (Institute for Public Policy Research), universities and university business schools. A stark contrast to such global, financial, intellectual and technological success is the fate of our mass manufacturing automobile industry.

Since the early 1960s the British automobile industry has been in decline, as its mass manufacturing enterprises failed and fell into the hands of foreign companies with the consequent decline in worldwide sales abilities. From 1945 to 1970 the British industry held a strong position in world markets, although one under constant threat from German, American, Continental European and latterly Japanese manufacturers.

Partly because of their undeveloped automobile industry and partly for strategic reasons the Japanese had not manufactured the car before the Second World War. They had concentrated on producing trucks. Even by 1951 Japan had still to mass-produce its first passenger car.

Despite allied devastation wrought on Japan's industrial base, by 1965 the re-emergence of Japan's industrial might had been so successful that their national automobile industry was already 40 per cent the size of Britains from a start of zero; they made no cars before 1950. Even the mighty American automobile manufacturers were not immune to the onslaught of Japanese production superiority. By the mid-1980s Japan had secured a devastating 27 per cent share of the American market, which prompted a massive restructuring of the once omnipotent American automobile industry.

Throughout the 1970s and 80s Japan's automobile industry expanded across the world. As their industry grew, so Britain's declined, along with much of our manufacturing industry. In the space of forty years the Japanese automobile industry has grown from one quarter the size of Britain's industry to more than

Table 1.1 **Passenger Car Production (000s)** | **GDP (billions $)**

	1965	1997	1998	1980	1998
Japan	696	7,950	8,056	1,045	4,958
USA	10,016	6060	11,636	2,467	8,111
Britain	1,722	1,670	1,745	534	1,288
France		2,060	2,595	686	1,394
Republic of Germany		4,650	4,806	810	2,353
Italy		1,631	1,608	463	1,145

Table 1.2 **Percentage Shares of UK Domestic Market**

	1973	1986	1997
BMC/BMW-Rover	31.9	15.6	9.0
Ford	22.6	25.8	18.3
GM	18.7	10.1	13.6
Fiat		3.0	4.1
Japan	5.6	11.2	14.2

seven times larger (including trucks). Today, although the Japanese economy has faltering the results of past success have been far reaching. The American industry has succeeded in a dramatic and probably sustainable turnaround, whilst the impact of Japan's startling export success and transplantation of production has been a major factor in the destruction of Britain's industry.

During the 1980s, Japanese industry launched a determined thrust into the European market place from manufacturing plants based in the United Kingdom. Japanese transplants such as Honda, Toyota and Nissan are now regarded as this nation's hope for the continued renaissance of our automobile mass production abilities. They also contribute to a worthwhile reduction of our continuing trade deficits.

Of Britain's £21.5 billion trade deficit on current account in 1988, over £4.97 billion can be traced to automobile imports with related parts increasing the deficit to over £6.8 billion. A reduction in the current account deficit in 1997 to £11.8 billion stemmed largely from the downturn in demand due to recession but also due to the increasing role of Japanese transplant exports. Britain's trade deficit in automobiles was £4.482 billion with related parts increasing that to over £6 billion.

Britain's automotive components industry has survived the bleak years of decline and now supplies European manufacturers and the new entrants with the parts that they need to comply with the EC requirements for European content. Foreign takeovers at Rover, Rolls Royce and Bentley, plus the increasing presence of Japanese manufacturing, have reduced the rapid decline in vehicle production. N.B. In June 1999 Rover Group's share of United Kingdom market had shrunk to 6.44 per cent. The continuing over-capacity in the European industry and worldwide leaves severe doubts as to need for the continued presence of such plants. Rover's plant at Longbridge has been under considerable financial pressures, happily resolved late summer 1999 by BMW and the British government. BMW plan to relaunch Rolls Royce from a new Greenfield site by 2003. It may well be as Madame Cresson the French Minister commented, that the continued prosperity of much of the European industry would appear to partially depend upon its ability to withstand the renewed competition from British-based manufacturing plants.

Germany and Japan remain dominant exporters in the world's mass-manufactured automobile market. The technical and design excellence of their manufactured products is a continuing reminder of their broad strengths. In America, Japan and Germany the industry has been one of the driving forces in other areas of technology such as Computer-Aided Design (CAD) and Manufacturing Systems (CADCAM). Inputs into the mainstream industry have also been evident within manufacturing, engine management systems, braking systems and new material technology. There are strong signs that the more advanced manufacturing and design systems used by the Japanese will now have a greater impact upon other industries.

The technological transfer from the British mass manufacturing industry is less evident. Past technical contributions of mass production automobile manufacturing activity in the United Kingdom have been relatively insignificant, judged by the number of patents taken out and the spin-offs into other areas of manufacturing production. In the motor sport industry change is evident, and Britain's smaller volume manufacturers are notably enterprising in their use of promising motorsport inspired technology for public sale.

The Rise of the UK Motor Racing Industry

Whilst the British have continually lost market share in the mass manufacture of automobiles, such setbacks have been offset by the enormous scientific and technical contribution of an almost unknown technological managerial and export success story: motorsports.

At the pinnacle of automotive technology Britain makes a major technical and engineering contribution to the motor racing and rallying industry, worldwide. Almost all of the world's premier automobile manufacturers from the USA, Italy, Germany, France and Japan draw upon UK technical and engineering expertise in this field.

Extensive international television coverage, and massive sponsorship by multi-national companies that are generally based outside Britain, either in mainland Europe, North and South America or the Pacific Rim means motor sports generate audiences of huge value to advertisers. In spite of the global following of millions of fans and therefore consumers, few outside the inner circles of the sport know there is an undercover secret within international motorsport.

Britain and British technological expertise, the majority located in a narrow corridor of excellence that stretches from Southampton to Derbyshire and thence out to East Anglia, dominates the world of motor racing manufacturing, design and development. This is true, regardless of whether the sport is Formula One Grand Prix racing, Formula 3000, the American Fedex CART series and for many lesser European and North American formulae.

Of the 22 cars on the grid at the start of most 1998 and 1999 Grand Prix, more than 20 featured design, manufacturing or development links to the United Kingdom. Statistically, seven constructors, providing 14 Formula One cars, are based in Britain and most of these come from Oxfordshire including Williams, Benetton and Arrows. The benchmark Grand Prix team of 1998, McLaren, are based in Surrey and that county was home to Tyrrell, which became British American Racing in 1999 and moved to Brackley, within ten miles of Silverstone. Also in Northamptonshire, Jordan chose Silverstone and Stewart Grand Prix (titled Jaguar Racing for 2000) are in nearby Milton Keynes.

In America's Fedex CART Championship premier league for single seaters, casually called Indycars, the UK export drive has been even more successful. Over 95 per cent of all the cars in that category had British chassis and engines created by British technologists for the 1998 season. Amongst 28 regular runners, some 22 Bicester built Reynards dominated the American formula, whilst the American entrepreneur Roger Penske has constructor premises in Poole, Dorset but bought Lola chassis in 1990.

Lola of Huntingdon have recently re-entered this America premier league formula, in which they once were the benchmarks, with encouraging results from a single entry. Even the turbocharged V8 engines engineering for America's most prestigious monopostos – featuring Northamptonshire-built engines from Cosworth and Ilmor, badged by Ford or Mercedes – were supplied in 1998 Britain for 19 of the 28 regular entrants in America's premier single seat category.

Britain's dominance in scientific, engineering, production and management skills in an industry that buys the very best talent is extraordinary. Many of these high tech, high-speed advertising billboards are a triumph of British managerial, scientific and engineering skills, even when the badge is foreign. In the most traditional of American of motor sports, stock car racing (NASCAR) the talents of Cosworth engineering have further improved the traditionally monstrous power outputs of domestic American V8 engines.

British talent has even been applied to the exalted name of Ferrari. The Ferrari Formula One car through the early seasons of the nineties was designed at their facility at Guildford under the direction of Englishman John Barnard. For 1997–9 Ferrari employed a British chief designer (Ross Brawn) and chief mechanic, both essential elements of the team's return to Championship form in 1998. Ferrari won their last World Constructors Championship in 1983 and their last World Driver's Champion was South African Jody Scheckter in 1979.

After many seasons of relative failure Ferrari decided to catch the English motorsport habit. Luca di Montezemolo (then the new president of Ferrari) made the momentous announcement at Monaco in 1992 that two Englishmen (John Barnard and Harvey Postlethwaite) would lead the design and manage the team respectively. Many Italians believed that desperation had set in. If so it was reasoned panic. Montezemolo added that 'in Italy we are cut away from the Silicon Valley of Formula One that has sprung up in England' (*Sunday Times* 6 September 1992).

Ferrari had been customers for British chassis manufacturing skills in the early seventies, having some prototype aluminium monocoque chassis constructed in Northamptonshire in a (subsequently successful) bid to counter the Cosworth V8-powered British horde. By the early nineties there was that complete design house based in Guildford. This facility was successfully charged with producing winning Ferrari racing chassis designs and much of the running gear outside the hallowed Ferrari engine itself. The V12 and subsequent V10 motors remained in Italy but with significant input from an ex-Honda engineer.

This contrasted with the accusation levelled at the British teams in the sixties and seventies by Ferrari's founder Enzo Ferrari, that the British were mere 'assemblatori', often translated as 'kit car assemblers'. The UK racing industry has always tried to utilize the best equipment for the job, rather than pursuing expensive in-house manufacture of every major component. Other 'Italian' teams such as Benetton are also located, designed and managed in Britain, although their significant financial backing comes from Italy.

In 1998 the probable minimum costs of running a winning Formula One team was £35 million per annum not including the costs of engines. To operate a solidly successful team such as Williams Grand Prix Engineering of Grove in Oxfordshire, who have won nine Formula One Constructors World Championships, one more than Ferrari, is likely to exceed this figure. Such excellence is sustained by a payroll of more than 300, a modern design and manufacturing complex (including a sophisticated wind tunnel to research the aerodynamic characteristics of half size models) and extensive CAD-supported manufacturing systems.

Williams' consistent success overcame initial and natural French xenophobia: France's major domestic manufacture Renault chose Williams to carry their engines back into Formula One. This was in spite of intense initial competition from the French based team Ligier, predecessor of the present Prost equipé.

Renault announced their withdrawal from Formula One in 1997 and Williams have worked hard to maintain their previous podium habitat in the interim with Mecachrome Supertec badged (ex-Renault) V10s. For 1999 Williams had to pay a reported £13 million per annum to continue supplies of the ex-Renault unit, whose sales rights had been acquired by ex-Benetton manager Flavio Briatore marketed under the Supertec label. This is interesting to students of Grand Prix finance, as the £13 million is simply to lease a supply of engines for race and test purposes over one season. We can appreciate the value of obtaining a free supply of engines direct from their manufacturer, especially as this route will also generate a more competitive power source. If British teams have a weakness in Grand Prix it is that dependence on French, German and Japanese major manufacturer funding to pursue their winning ways.

Today, BMW are not just investing in the Grand Prix ten cylinders that will power Williams in year 2000, but the Munich masters of Rover and the Rolls Royce trademark have transferred their motorsport activities (excluding engines engineering) to a magnificent purpose-built site, one local to Williams. That is a tremendous testimony to the seductive attractions of British motorsport manufacturers, suppliers and technologists, from one of Germany's renowned prestige automobile constructors.

The new Anglo-German alliance has already tackled Le Mans. It utilized Williams' chassis design, propelled by a majestic 6-litre BMW V12 (developed to win Le Mans in a 1995 McLaren). That Williams-BMW 1998 debut was notable for 6-hour pace, rather than 24-hour endurance but won the French classic in 1999.

Why Britain?

Why are the British so good at this demanding partnership of sport and technology? We will examine the origins of the present intellectual and technological supremacy in detail later. To discover some of the obvious answers you only have to return to the immediate post-war period, although some of the roots are obviously in the earliest days of motor racing.

In the period immediately after the war the British were seen as traditional losers – with a few conspicuous exceptions – in a sport dominated by the French founders, Italian innovators and the German's state-funded Grand Prix racing car benchmarks of the thirties. Post-war club racing in Britain on the old RAF airfields expanded rapidly through the fifties. It operated under benevolently innovative regulations overseen by the British RAC and developed by such innovative thinkers as the 750 Motor Club, the latter emphasizing engineering excellence at affordable cost.

Amongst 29 recognized graduates from this hard school of engineer-drivers were the pioneering provider of British-based IndyCar winners, Lotus founder Colin Chapman and the current production king of the premier American category, Adrian Reynard of the Bicester-based Reynard. Other graduates included Lola Cars founder Eric Broadley, Gordon Murray (South African designer of McLaren and Brabham Grand Prix winners) and Arthur Mallock, father to Ray Mallock and the Bedfordshire-based RML concern. RML constructed the 1998–9 British Touring Car Championship-winning (BTCC) Nissan touring cars.

The wartime innovative attitudes of engineering immediacy, innovation and 'can do' that prevailed in the military services tended to prevail in post-war British motorsports. This list is only a fraction of the pool of talent that existed, but from the late fifties onward Britain had motor racing design expertise in unparalleled depth. The UK still benefits from that 'can do' talent today. But talent and skill are not sufficient conditions for success on such a scale.

Fate seemed to step in with a number of fatal incidents in continental road races. Two accidents were particularly important in changing the attitudes to road racing on the Continent. After the disaster at Le Mans in 1955, Switzerland banned motorsports (legislation that remains today). Spain and Mexico banned motor racing completely and the French Government stopped the sport until the rules were revised later that year. The French and German Grand Prix were cancelled and the future of the Le Mans race was in the balance. The death of the Marquis de Portago in his Ferrari outside Mantua in the 1957 Mille Miglia effectively ended road racing on the Continent, although the Targa Florio in the more remote Sicilian landscape survived into the seventies.

The Mercedes Benz team withdrew from motor racing totally after the 1955 Le Mans incident and the disastrous state of fifties Italian economics, led a number of Continental companies, including Alfa Romeo, Lancia and Maserati, to withdraw from international racing. Simultaneously the British became more determined to *win* – rather than just 'Play the Game' within Grand Prix.

Tony Vandervell, owner of the high performance bearing company of that name, promised that the Vanwall cars made at his Acton and Maidenhead premises would beat Ferrari. Vandervell delivered success using the design talents of Colin Chapman and aerodynamicist Frank Costin, another 750 MC graduate.

The Vanwall team won the first Formula One World Constructor's Championship title for Britain in 1958: only Ferrari (eight Constructor titles) and Matra (one) interrupted the flow of UK-sourced titles to 1998. Williams alone have equalled all the overseas wins in this ultimate automotive technology contest, never mind the spoils accrued by McLaren (seven) and Lotus (seven).

Formula Junior racing for 500cc rear-engined cars in Britain prospered in the fifties, providing fertile ground for technical, regulatory and driver development. The rear engine principles utilised in the 500cc single seaters were subsequently to beat the best Continental opposition in Formula One Grand Prix, and the best in American racers, including those within the USA's Indianapolis backyard.

The revolution in small race car design, led by John Cooper, another graduate up from the 500cc ranks – and his innovative use of the Coventry Climax ex-water pump engine at the rear of a Grand Prix racing car – were crucial. The design that was to become the basis for all future racing car design was adopted by Cooper ahead of the pack: Australian Jack Brabham took the Formula One Grand Prix crown for a car constructed in Britain in 1959, and repeated the feat the following year. Subsequently Brabham himself would construct World Championship-winning Brabhams in Britain using Australian V8 motors and establish another strand in Britain's Grand Prix challenge.

The financial basis of teams was still somewhat uncertain and often rather tenuous. The vital commercial breakthrough for teams in the UK came via the partnership between Walter Hayes of Ford in Britain, Colin Chapman of Lotus, Mike (brother to Frank) Costin, plus Keith Duckworth of Cosworth.

Backed by the financial muscle of Ford and led by the strategic vision of Walter Hayes, Duckworth and the Cosworth team at Northampton created a bespoke engine for the Lotus 49. The Ford DFV (Double Four Valve) V8 was created for the Lotus but was to be available to all. Not only the most successful Grand Prix engine ever built, but also the most widely available – at a realistic price – to all comers. The availability of the engine to all was part of Ford's publicity strategy but it was to prove a dominant factor in Britain's Grand Prix future.

The unique design of the DFV unit, which used the motor as a weight saving, stressed, member of the chassis, removed the motor engineering headache from the constructor. Just as importantly suitable Formula One gearbox units – pioneered from a Volkswagen Beetle transaxle in lower powered categories and redesigned for increased power – subsequently became commercially available from proprietary suppliers such as Hewland at Maidenhead, rather than relying on ZF in Germany as was the initial case.

The commercial availability and the success of the engine provided British suppliers with demand in commercial volumes. The foundations were laid for Britain to become bespoke suppliers to the Grand Prix and allied trades of Fast Track motoring. But the structure's foundations were not yet complete.

Engineering genius Colin Chapman had been crucial in the development of the DFV and the combination of the DFV and the Lotus 49 (1967 season) was a formidable one. Chapman's brilliance did not end at the drawing board and one year later he brought non motor-trade sponsorship to motor sport with Gold Leaf Team Lotus; a direct result of lifting restrictions on sponsorship in the same year. The structure's foundations to a Formula One fortune were in place.

UK Motorsport confidence was boosted in the mid-seventies by Lord Hesketh who amazingly risked several millions of pounds (when the £ was worth 5.5DM as against 2.90DM today) to manufacture and develop the Hesketh Grand Prix car. It allowed James Hunt a platform to develop his driving abilities for his subsequently successful World Drivers Championship with McLaren in 1976.

Thirteen years later a further stage in the continuing development of the motor sport business was completed. The Formula One constructors appointed one Bernard 'Bernie' Ecclestone to lead their association, the Formula One Constructors Association (FOCA). Ecclestone delivered supremely professional business acumen to ensure a united front to negotiate with the circuit owners and advertisers worldwide. Only Ecclestone really understood that the fabulous financial future of this category lay in global TV rights and a hands-on-approach to any aspect that could conceivably effect the show, and therefore income.

The first Concorde agreement between FOCA led by Bernie Ecclestone and FISA in 1981 sealed the involvement of worldwide television coverage; thus establishing huge commercial involvement and the immense, secretive, financial basis of Grand Prix as global entertainment. Ecclestone's foresight in recognizing the future potential of an international sport has yet to yield the full multi-billion dollar flotation that the Grand Prix master seeks. This is partly because a European Commission is elaborately investigating possible Common Market regulation infringements, but it would be a brave individual who forecast anything other than untold financial rewards for the man who pioneered Grand Prix racing with electronic media in mind. The launch of the much heralded $1.4 billion 'Bernie Bond' has already occurred, although it has been hedged by certain safeguards.

Major Grand Prix team owners received an enormous bonus from Bernie Ecclestone's management of TV rights, income now estimated at £12 million per team per annum, instead of £1.1 million just two seasons ago.

The speed of response, innovative approach, commitment and entrepreneurial flair that epitomizes UK motorsport companies, has enabled some firms to build other innovative and equally radical aspects of their business. This could yet elevate the UK motor racing industry to further triumphs in mass manufacturing.

For example, the company founded by Tom Walkinshaw in 1975 – the TWR Group – expanded turnover by more than 300 per cent during the early nineties against fierce international competition. More importantly the Group's clients reads as a roll call of the automobile industry. The entrepreneurial flair of the founder has led the business into mainstream industry whilst retaining the speed, flexibility and 'can do' culture of racers. An astonishing 85 per cent of the TWR business is in road cars and just 15 per cent in racing cars.

In 1985 Walkinshaw convinced John Egan, then chairman of Jaguar Cars, that if TWR were given sufficient backing they would win the Le Mans 24 Hours. TWR delivered on that promise and the Walkinshaw Group continues to be commercially successful. Tom Walkinshaw would dearly love to achieve complementary Grand Prix success with the Arrows equipé. Perhaps the sale of part of that asset has provided an acceptable alternative; cash.

TWR-Jaguar track success in the eighties led directly to the development of the Jaguar XJ220 Supercar in the 1990s. This was the first road car built by the Group in a specially designed assembly facility at Bloxham, North Oxfordshire. The car was designed by TWR and built from local components manufactured in the factories that supply components to Formula One Grand Prix teams. Outsourcing has long been a part of Britain's motor sport suppliers.

In 1993 a similar TWR project was undertaken for Aston Martin Lagonda Limited, whose Chairman Walter Hayes, was determined that a more affordable new Aston Martin would attract sufficient buyers if it could be produced efficiently. All over the world TWR has worked in partnership with mass manufacturers, and in the cases of Jaguar, Aston Martin and Volvo a financial partnership has existed over a joint company to create and manufacture any joint ventures.

By early 1993 Walter Hayes' vision for Aston Martin had attracted substantial pre-production orders, the car having stolen the honours at the Geneva Motor Show. Other TWR Group commercial connections today include developing racing saloons for General Motors-Holden in Australia and Volvo in the UK, usually managing such race teams in the field. A fabulously rewarding contract with Nissan to win Le Mans was terminated after two promising – but not winning – assaults on the French classic at a reported cost £38 million.

The rewards are exceptionally high in Britain's motor racing business, but the clients – especially in Japan and Germany – see anything less than winning, as a failure to be punished. The honourable exception to prove the rule is the solid support Mercedes granted McLaren through uncharacteristic nineties seasons without wins. McLaren-Mercedes were rewarded by (mixed) dominance in the first part of the 1999 season, dominance that had media moaning that the silver and grey winners were 'boring'. A Ferrari Championship win could be seen as good for television and Grand Prix's image. This is not a level track!

TWR Group is now engaged in manufacturing high image Volvos in Sweden, such as the C70 coupé, alongside the leading TWR-Volvo British Touring Car Championship team (Rickard Rydell was the 1998 BTCC Champion). These developments were a calculated part of Volvo's marketing strategy to transform their rather staid image although Volvo have announced a cessation of their touring car efforts.

Such specialist manufacturing could be the first stage of a new trend in the partnership between the motor and motor sport industry. UK companies are already providing the design, development and manufacturing facilities for the production of specialist automobiles, concept cars and other marketing weapons. Speed of response, technological excellence, flexibility and design flair are advantages that UK motorsport related companies offer the giants.

Such thinking utilizes the technology and culture of the companies in the motorsport industry that has built up around Formula One. It also provides another outlet for the advanced technology and revenue to fund new innovations. Britain's Silicon Valley of Motor Sport – stretching approximately from Southampton in the south, north to Derby and embracing East Anglia – is the region with the necessary range and depth of specialist designers, component suppliers, engineers and technicians to support such activity.

That Ford found it more effective to sub-contract the design and development of a new Jaguar and Aston Martin to a small race-based company like TWR says a great deal about this industry. Sadly, few British companies have used this pool of technological talent and expertise. Nor does British industry, with notable exceptions such as ICI and HSBC banking, fund UK motorsports through sponsorship.

Simple emphasis on Grand Prix engine power is misleading, for multinational manufacturers use British racing teams for competitive chassis design, affordable precision engineering at speed and aerodynamic excellence. But this superlative engineering expertise would be valuable – but not unique – without the organizational culture that is driven by success and places no boundaries on work practices.

Formula One motor racing designers and technocrats have not yet taken over from the driver but they can make his job a lot easier, where regulations permit. British firms can provide such technology; electronics and associated racing software are UK strengths, and such knowledge is more difficult to replicate than a decade ago.

Foreign engine manufacturers such as General Motors (through its German, American and British divisions), BMW, Porsche, Ford, and Mercedes Benz have all utilized the race engineering excellence of British firms such as Cosworth (the world's largest manufacturer of racing engines) or Ilmor. Such mass production concerns and many more have been customers for Britannia's discrete motorsport engineering expertise.

Porsche's TAG engine (sourced at Porsche) turbocharged the McLaren Team to three Formula One World Drivers' Championships and two Constructors' Championships in the 1980. Then with Honda, McLaren dominated both championships in 1989-91. In 1992, 1993, 1996 and 1997 the Williams Team took both the Drivers' and Constructors' Championships with Renault engines, plus the Constructors Championship in 1994 and were runners up in both Championships in 1995. Such solid success attracts the best in the showroom to become clients on Britain's booming – and newer – industrial parks.

Williams also proved that they could win Championships at an additional discipline – touring cars – and received circa £5 million a year running Laguna Touring Cars for Renault GB between 1995 and 1999. Williams and Renault GB won four British touring car titles: that for manufacturers in 1995 and 1997. the Team title in 1997 and delivered the winning Renault for Alain Menu, 1997 Champion. Williams Touring Car Engineering employs over 60 people within separate premises at Didcot, and also had the initiative to attract significant sponsorship from outside the motor industry: Nescafé Blend 37.

Strength in Depth

There is a whole host of other companies that supply and build car chassis to the aspiring racing team worldwide or provide high level technical components to the racing car industry.

In 1997 it was suggested the UK motorsports industry employed over 50 000 people and returned an estimated £1.6 billion turnover with an export total of approximately 44 per cent (see IPPR Report). Several of the companies involved have already won the Queen's Award for Exports more than once. Lola and Reynard were Queen's Award for Export winners and are large-scale manufacturers of racing car chassis; Lola the sole source of chassis for the Formula One stepping stone category, Formula 3000. Reynard returned to Formula One Grand Prix within British American Racing during 1999.

In the manufacture and use of new materials such as carbon fibre and Kevlar composites, this British industry has a dominant world position, although our most high profile switch to this aerospace construction came through a McLaren Cars approach to Hercules Corporation in the USA: since then British teams have developed their own composite construction sites, usually in-house at major Grand Prix teams. When the Swiss-based Sauber team entered Formula One in 1993 they used DPS Composites Limited of Bookham in Surrey, a small (then six years old) British company, to manufacture a large number of carbon fibre and Kevlar components. The same concern supplied construction expertise in composites to Mercedes for sports racing in the late eighties.

Other British based and managed companies are too numerous to detail in this overview, but provide high technology components to motorsport concerns worldwide. Particularly successful are our transmission manufacturers including Hewland, Staffs Gears and Xtrac; whilst AP Racing at Leamington supply carbon fibre clutches and (as for Midlands-based Alcon) deliver astounding brakes to the biggest names in the business, as well as ambitious club racers.

Britain also has astonishing capabilities in electronic management systems and Zytek in Derby are particularly successful in commercially developing such skills. These skills have been promoted through a fascination with the high performance electric cars (development funds boosted by America's Don Panoz) and karting. Versatile Zytek also supply the mandatory V8 racing engine used in Formula 3000 Lolas.

British concerns also fabricate special steels or other exotic materials in mixes that meet motorsport's insatiable appetite for low weight and high strength. These come as anything from the fabled widget to hubs and shafts that must stand loads beyond 4G for two hours.

Those major overseas car manufacturers who use, or can afford to use, motorsports to help market their products are the winners of the earlier mass production car wars that Britain's automobile industry lost. Most studiously avoid trying to design their own chassis or even run their own team; and it isn't money that stops them.

The reality of competition often forces a change to a British chassis to achieve success. Honda has done this in the past in every level from Grand Prix to GT Racing. After the recent and tragic death of Harvey Postlethwaite, Honda has ended their campaign to build an entire Japanese based Grand Prix car from their British base in Slough. This was a devastating blow to their team, Britain's motorsport industry, and people involved in the sport. They have announced that they will now re-enter Formula One as an engine supplier only.

Porsche is the world's largest independent maker of pure sports cars and the most successful designer and manufacturer of sports racing cars with an unsurpassed record of wins. After several humiliating failures they assigned their 1989 Indycar project to the now defunct March organization and Porsche's last GP engine unit ran in a UK built Arrows chassis; albeit with no success. TWR Group provided the open sports car racing design that was powered by Porsche to win Le Mans 1996–7, ahead of the Porsche factory's own 911-based GT1 entries.

A large overseas customer for British bespoke motor racing technology has emerged as British American Tobacco decided to buy out a complete GP team (Tyrrell) with a budget to be measured out at £50 million a year. They entered Grand Prix in 1999 with their lead driver the 1997 World Champion Jacques Villeneuve, fresh from Williams, and a Reynard-designed Formula One car.

Racing carmakers spread throughout southern and eastern England such as

Lola, G-force, Van Diemen, Reynard and Ralt all serve a large number of different markets and formulae. These include Formula First, Formula Ford, Formula Atlantic, Formula 3000 (now a Lola-Zytek monopoly), Formula 3 and America's Indycar Series. Many of these companies echo the Formula One examples from Williams, McLaren and TWR, making motorsport or high performance contributions to the activities of major manufacturers.

The watching motorsport public – measured by the million on the annual RAC Rally of Great Britain – are usually unaware that they are cheering British engineering genius when the Japanese enjoy their considerable World Rally Championship success.

Subaru Imprezas for Scotland's 1995 World Champion, Colin McRae, were devised at Prodrive in Banbury. Mitsubishi Motors has a parallel engineering department beside the M1 at Rugby, that created winning Mitsubishis for multiple World Champion Tommi Makinen of Finland and England's Richard Burns. Just as in Formula One the engines are supplied from the factory, leaving Ralliart UK to focus on the rest of the car and event-winning management.

In the tough arena of global rallying thirty years of winning Ford Escorts have come from Britain. A new successor to the Escort, the Ford Focus, was rally engineered by Malcolm Wilson Motorsport at Millbrook, Bedfordshire months before showroom Focus sales commenced to debut on the 1999 Monte Carlo Rally. It proved a winner almost immediately.

Prodrive at Banbury (founded by David Richards who was Team Manager at Benetton Grand Prix for one year) is a remarkably versatile company, that engineers everything from competition components to complete cars. Prodrive won with BMW and Porsche, before rallying Subaru. In the 1998 season they produced competitive racing Honda Accords and in 1999 created and managed racing Ford Mondeo-Cosworth V6s.

Britain's Silicon Valley of Motor Racing

The pastoral and often genteel Home Counties of England from Surrey to Oxfordshire are the unlikely base for many of the companies that dominate this multimillion-pound, multi-national business. The Queen's Award for Industry has gone to several of the major motorsport concerns in this area, including Williams Grand Prix Engineering, the now defunct March Group and, in 1990, Reynard Racing Cars.

On 23 March 1993 the industry received some of the recognition it deserved when Eric Broadley, representing the motor racing industry, was presented with the Castrol/Institute of Motor Industry 1992 Gold Medal for services to road transport in the widest sense, by Prince Michael of Kent.

In 1994 a group of highly motivated individuals founded the Motorsport Industry Association (MIA), dedicated to furthering the interests of almost 150 motorsport related companies under the leadership of Chris Aylett.

The level of export earnings per employee is very high and according to our survey undertaken in 1999 the industry contributes well in excess of *£800 million a year to Britain's balance of payments and employs 50 000*, an estimated 30 000 of those particularly skilled in areas of high technology.

The dominance of these British companies in a worldwide industry, albeit a small one, is unparalleled in any other UK industry. Their positive balance of foreign earnings contrasts starkly with that of the domestic automobile industry as a whole, which recorded a deficit of over £6 billion in 1997. Such export-led performance has been won versus the fiercest international competition and without any Government funding.

The Formula One circus has become more powerful and international during the past few years, in spite of the controversy over tobacco advertising. Currently, computers and digital TV makes it possible for the cars and tracks to have country specific advertising, live. Each car and track can display live, simultaneous, but different computer-generated advertising. Such Grand Prix spectacle and immense televisual audience have required preliminary investment from Bernie Ecclestone, and increasing commitment from the Grand Prix teams.

McLaren record that their seasonal Formula One costs were £50 000 in 1968 (nearly £500 000 at today's values) and that they employed 25. In 1998 the counterpart figures were a racing budget in excess of £25 million and 250 employees, plus free engines. It is also on record that Williams Grand Prix Engineering required some £2.25 million a season as front runners in 1980, paying for Cosworth engines within that budget. For 1990 Williams drew on a £15 million budget, and then had free engines from Renault.

McLaren's free racing Mercedes-branded engines (created by Ilmor in Northampton) have a value of more than £220 000 each. Williams pay for their engines at present – c. £13 million in 1999 – and this accounts for much of the current wide difference in quoted budgets between these two equally determined and resource intensive operations.

The huge commitment of money and resources that is required has daunted even the mighty and successful Renault organization. They announced their withdrawal from the Grand Prix scene in 1997, although their V10 engine design and successors will be sold commercially to at least three teams and are currently powering Williams, Benetton and BAR.

Although Bernie Ecclestone has declared that grids will be full from 1999 onward, new manufacturers and teams are planned. Recent entrants include Ford and HSBC funded Stewart Grand Prix, who are in their second season with former triple World Champion Jackie Stewart's renowned financial acumen a vital component. As from June 1999 the Stewart team is owned by Ford who have reportedly paid some £100 million plus a £50 million per annum commitment for the privilege.

As detailed earlier, British American Tobacco purchased the Tyrrell Team and Jackie Stewart's 1969/71 and 1973 World Championship-winning Tyrrell equipé prepared for 1999, organized by Jacques Villeneuve's Manager Craig Pollock under the British American Racing Team.

We would also have expected Honda to re-appear from a British base although the cost and the tragic death of Harvey Postlethwaite has probably made it certain that they will only provide engines. The Volkswagen Group's recent shopping orgy should result in Grand Prix participation, possibly under the Audi brand with the possibility of other major manufacturers entering the circus as owners. Audi purchased the former Toyota motor racing works (TOMS) in Norfolk during 1998 and two divisions of Cosworth, selling a third (Cosworth Racing) to Ford for approximately £50 million. Ford has depended on Cosworth power for Grand Prix (Stewart, Tyrrell, Minardi in 1998), Touring cars (Mondeo) and World Championship rallying (Escort/ Focus).

On or off track, the pace for Britain's motorsport industry is hotter than ever. The race for supremacy remains a consistent commercial and competitive challenge: one worthy of minute examination, as we shall demonstrate.

Regulations for Individual Competitors, Safety for Spectators by the Thousand

Regulating for Success

BRITAIN'S post-war return to motor sport was welcomed by the public but Grand Prix success for Britain initially remained the rarity that it had been in the pre-war period. Although Britain had a broadly based establishment that encouraged grass roots racing and rallying to flourish, success was elusive. An inherent strength in design ingenuity and rule book interpretation to the maximum winning advantage did not instantly establish the British winning routine at the summit of international motor sport.

It would be impertinent to think that Britain's current pre-eminence in the racing and rallying business stems solely from the immediate post-war years, but it was in this period that the elements of the United Kingdom's present pre-eminent motor sport status was created.

Those outside Britain nominate our variety of race tracks (more than 60 permanent venues licensed in 1997, more than any other European country) and depth of weekend motor sport events as principle advantages enjoyed by UK Motor Racing Plc. Such diversity occurred against the elements, as even the most fervent patriot could not nominate our weather as on par with southern France or Italy for the regular enjoyment of outdoor sport.

Dogged British persistence by a number of key enthusiasts ensured that many wartime airfields (Silverstone, Snetterton, Goodwood and more) yielded their perimeter roads as rapid learning sites for equally numerous and enthusiastic demobbed servicemen, especially those with mechanical ingenuity developed during their military service.

The building of unique cars known as 'specials' was not the prerogative of the British. Any knowledge of Southern California's dazzling Hot Rod and custom habits would directly contradict that smug assumption. However, in the post-war period new motor cars were relatively expensive with the level of purchase tax at 33.3 per cent on ordinary cars and an extortionate 66.6 per cent on luxury models. This was all part of the drive for exports that the Chancellor of the Exchequer Sir Stafford Cripps exhorted manufacturers to satisfy. Even the price of rather popular cars such as the Ford Anglia was almost double that of pre-war prices, whilst petrol was also rationed, hire purchase was restricted and imports were banned. Manufacturers such as Lotus (the first) sold cars in kit form to overcome tax restrictions.

All these factors presented major problems for a generation of young men and women who had been transformed by their war experience into a generation familiar with machines on two, four (and many more) wheels, and complex aircraft. They had not only been taught to drive and maintain motor vehicles but fly and repair aircraft, the most sophisticated machines of the day. Their level of mechanical engineering skills were probably unsurpassed and the many motor clubs that were formed at this time, including the 750 Club, were an outlet for this frustrated expertise. The benevolent hand of the RAC was exceptionally important in monitoring regulations that enabled specials such as the 750s to race and compete.

This legacy continues today and Britain produces an amazing variety of low cost motor sport categories, as well as specialist low volume sports cars. The latter are now our only domestically produced passenger vehicles under full UK ownership. Many of these machines and purpose-built race cars can demand a level of mechanical ability that is at least on par with the constructor's driving talents.

The historical result was that even in the late 1940s there was an amazing variety of racing machinery assembled before huge crowds. The first British Grand Prix in 1948 at Silverstone, which was 'released by the Air Ministry for a trial period of 12 months', attracted over 100 000 people, warmly clad for the British autumn as that event was held in October rather than the subsequently traditional July. The spectators witnessed not just Grand Prix cars of all ages – Ferrari was then a newcomer whilst the majority of the then traditional British ERAs would have been more than ten years of age – but also an extremely important competition for 500cc motorcycle-engined single seaters.

This was an important and unique innovation, for this category bred not just the obvious wave of intensely competitive British drivers (18 year old Stirling Moss was on that 1948 grid) but also constructors who understood the advantages of rear engined racing cars. Then they were confined to the junior classes, but through the 1950s and into the early sixties they eventually transformed racing car design, and Britain's winning prospects. This applied both in the European Grand Prix establishment and American oval racing.

It was not simply in the appearance of revolutionary starter formulae designs which signalled the importance of this Grand Prix meeting. Obviously such a major event meant catering for the leading French and Italian Grand Prix teams, as well as the third of the field who used native ERA descendants from the thirties. This complexity plus the control of the huge crowds of spectators, required an experienced organization to provide the necessary safety precautions. This was in addition to attending to competitors' needs and overseeing the activities of voluntary marshals who are today recognized as amongst the best in the world.

Internationally, motor sports were and remain, under the control of the *Fédération Internationale de l'Automobile* (FIA), whose forerunner was established in 1904. The FIA title was established in 1946, but for the motor sporting world then the more important body was the *Commission Sportive Internationale* (CSI) of 1922–78, succeeded by *Fédération Interationale du Sport Automobile* (FISA). The last president (1991–3) of this organization was a British barrister and motor sports enthusiast, one Max Mosley.

The background to UK supremacy is not only about technology but pivots upon institutional influence. The accession of Max Mosley to the Presidency marked a very significant change in the influence of Britain in global auto-sporting politics after years of premier league motor sport government under French control.

Today the former British club racer and lawyer Max Mosley is perhaps the most powerful man in world motor sports. He holds the presidency of the FIA Motor Sports Council founded in the nineties (successors to FISA) and is an immensely powerful figure in the sport's development.

The Swiss-based FIA organization is supported by member national motor sport clubs from all over the world. In Britain the sport has historically been administered by the sporting division of the Royal Automobile Association (RAC), which gained its Royal title under the patronage of Edward VII in 1897, just two years after the French staged the world's first major motor race on the French public roads from Paris to Bordeaux and back.

The premier race billing title of Grand Prix was initially casually used as part of a 1901 motor sports week in Pau, France. The title Grand Prix only became truly significant in later years. Since 1950 every round of the World Championship has been a Grand Prix event, but Grand Prix were also the major events of pre-World War II races, including the European Championship. The title Grand Prix is now specifically used to denote those events that count towards the FIA Formula One world championship for drivers and constructors.

The RAC was recognized by the UK Government as the sole body to govern motor sports of all kinds in the UK and acted as the parent to many other clubs that sprang up in the UK. Today there are more than 700 motor clubs in Britain that are affiliated to the MSA (Motor Sport Association) RAC offspring, the unpaid foundations beneath the sheer number of events organized in Britain.

Before World War II the RAC were best known for running two Grand Prix in the twenties as well as organizing Britain's oldest motor race, the Tourist Trophy of 1905, a race title which is still promoted, albeit intermittently, today. The rapid development of the motor sport scene in the seventies and eighties and the continuous tensions between Continental and British constructors placed the RAC, or more particularly its sporting divisions (originally at posh Belgrave Square, now snuggling beside Heathrow Airport on a Colnbook industrial estate) under enormous pressure. The growing commercial importance of the British teams, circuit owners, constructors and competitors meant that they were increasingly determined that their needs would be met, particularly in the embryonic financial development decades of the seventies and eighties.

Hindsight confirms that RAC sporting organizations reacted positively to those requests and is now a very professional operation, far from its 1907 origins as a club for 163 wealthy gentlemen members. The stable, normally benign, influence of the RAC Motor Sport Division and its subsequent iterations (RAC MSA), have given British motor sports a governing body that allowed the sport in its many diverse forms to flourish with unusual vigour.

The big expansion in British motor sports came with the boom in purchasing power of the younger consumers in the sixties and seventies. A look through RAC/MSA statistics for competitions licences issued over a 30 year period tells us that nearly 22 000 were issued in 1967. Between then and 1977, licence numbers grew by some 30 per cent and approached the 30 000 barrier.

It was not all continuous growth thereafter and in the early eighties figures dropped back to the 27 000 level. It was not until 1986 that the total finally exceeded 30 000; over 32 000 licences (as confirmed by the MSA) were issued in 1998. Overall the number of people buying competition licences as opposed to the statistically similar number of licences issued, increased by a dramatic 44.8 per cent between 1967 and 1990.

A critically important aspect of the sport in Britain in this period was the relative ease of access for competitors through the levels of UK motor racing. The relatively inexpensive club racing categories such as the 750 Club were the first rung, followed by low cost single seater formula such as 1967's Formula Ford. We deal with the important role of technology development in detail in Chapters 6 and 9, but the adoption of a reliable mass production engine in a simple single seater chassis was vital at the club racing level, whilst the inspired idea of John Cooper to use a low cost water pump engine in a tubular space frame helped open the gates of international race experience and establishing a track record, for many aspirant World Champion drivers and constructors.

The popularity of road rallying, still today the branch of the sport that receives most MSA permits, swelled the number of competition licences further. In such events, in over 100 production cars, little modified from the showroom, participants would face a Saturday night, Sunday morning test of their two or three person crew to the limit of their navigational and driving abilities. This intense activity helped to grow a generation of extremely resourceful drivers and navigators that built on their fifties and sixties club experience, becoming international motor sport management personalities. In particular UK night rallying navigators proved particularly adept at international rally and race team management in the seventies and eighties.

During the self-styled 'Swinging Sixties', RAC-supervised motor sports of all categories and varieties exploded numerically. There were events such as autotests, sprints, hillclimbs and rallying (in those days on public roads or, subsequent specially timed stages on private/forestry grounds), onto autocross and rallycross. The RAC motor sport section was fundamental in devising regulations that were consistent with safety and the development of the sport's technological base. Even the effects of the 1974 fuel crisis and a temporary three-day week in Britain failed to put more than a hiccup on the UK's increasing zest for motor sports.

The RAC Motor Sports Division – as it then was – began to issue competition documentation publications by the thousand. By 1971 they were issuing their 'Blue Book' of regulations and a newspaper to a mailing list of 34 000!

Since the seventies, a major growth factor has been the intense adult and child support given to Karting as a natural path to single seater racing stardom. Given that an eight year old (yes, 8!) child can be granted a karting competition licence, and that many are driving with ferocious commitment long before they are teenagers, it is not surprising that such a large pool of native driving talent has developed in Britain. A depth of driving talent refreshed each new season by more wanting to follow the established Nigel Mansell route to the stars and money, supported by a Karting industry that is an important microcosm of the formula car race car construction business.

In 1997 the RAC/MSA was overseeing more than 4700 motor sport events annually, covering 22 differing disciplines. The competitors, team managers/owners and supporters provide an enormous 'home market' for the motor sport business. In addition there are more than 32 000 individuals who continue to hold competition licences which all helps to underpin Britain's status as a leading motor sports nation.

During the summer of 1998 the parent RAC organization went through enormous internal changes, and the sports division dropped the RAC section of its name, simply becoming the Motor Sport Association (MSA) from July of that year, thus recognizing a change in ownership of RAC Motoring Services.

'Motor Sport can be Dangerous'

Commercially attractive though MSA statistics have become – part of an industry where turnover is rated at £1.6 billion and total full/part-time employment at more than 100 000 – the parent motor sport body in Britain has always been charged with the task of setting practical safety standards, both for the watching public and participants. Thus the label on every spectator ticket, every programme and every official pass issued in the UK: 'Motor sport can be Dangerous', and it can ... .

At the close of 1997 MSA stated that, 'in the past ten years 29 competitors have died during the course of over 30,000 British events, and these include several drivers who died of natural causes whilst competing.' Every motor and kart racing competitor must undergo medical examinations and eye tests, the motor racing examination becoming more rigorous as the potential participant passes 40 and 45 years of age, particularly with regard to measuring heart beat and exercise performance.

The MSA further asserted, 'more dangerous sports in Britain include swimming, horse riding, air sports, climbing and fishing. In fact MSA authorized motor sport has varied between 11th and 13th in the Government's league of "Dangerous sports"'.

Assisting this fine record and providing very practical reassurance to every occupant of a competition car in the British Isles is the standard of volunteer marshals bred through motor club generations. These may be allotted any task from supervizing parking – critical to safety in forest rallying – to manning a key race track post with personnel to supply flag warnings and rescue the occupants of crashed vehicles.

The best known marshalling organization is the dedicated British Motor Racing Marshals Club (BMRMC). Their efforts, like those of other leading motor clubs who supply volunteer marshals, are assisted by a formalized structure of rescue training, including fire. British marshals are of such quality that their expertise is frequently demanded from overseas promoters. A select core of UK marshals is often imported to premier overseas events to boost the quality of marshalling.

Nobody at the MSA's Colnbrook HQ appears complacent about this surprising UK motor sports safety record. It has been the MSA that has been charged with the difficult job of balancing competitor eagerness to tackle public roads versus public interest in safety and rural peace. This denial of tempting tarmac to competitors has often brought harsh criticism of the RAC and its sporting divisions over the years, especially from the UK specialist motor sport press.

Britain differs from Continental Europe in that public road racing and rallying without strict average speeds has usually been forbidden to circuit racers and rally competitors alike. The only comparatively recent exceptions on the UK mainland were Birmingham's street races of 1986-89. These midland events demanded parliamentary co-operation and immense national and local political manoeuvring. They were well-supported at the time, but domestic sponsorship (from sources such as Halfords) dried up despite extensive TV coverage.

It has proved very difficult to re-open even UK tracks that have historic connections to the sport at the highest level such as Goodwood, once they have been the subject of restrictions. The Earl of March led a prolonged and ultimately successful campaign to re-open the Goodwood track for limited racing in 1998. It required considerable persistence and huge support to combat the strong local opposition from residents who, in many cases, live in houses that were built when the track was still used for 24 hour endurance races, or were adjacent to operational RAF airfields!

Road rallying in the UK was always strictly regulated, with heavy penalties handed out to rally clubs who transgressed 30 mph speed limits in their timed events on public road events. This was achieved by a number of rule book twists and interpretations on the 'Rules are Made to be Broken' theme, but all of these events are run on legitimate lines today, with an enhanced awareness of safety and environmental sensitivities.

Where an event is unrecognized by the MSA (such as local treasure hunts for under 12 cars), there can be trouble, but generally rallying has established itself as a respectable motor sport of great value to Britain. Road rallies co-exist alongside the special stage rallies that Britain imported from Scandinavia for the RAC Rallies of 1961 onward. These place a premium on high speed car control over loose and slippery off-public road surfaces. Special stage rallies are typically held over Forestry Commission Land, abandoned airfields or lonely tarmac trails that can be deemed private, such military roads over the Welsh Eppynt or Otterburn ranges.

Although motor racing, especially Grand Prix, dominates the headlines and TV time, it is actually motor rallying that is the most popular branch of participant motor sport in Britain, and road rallies remain the major home-brewed motor sport. The MSA authorized over 1000 rallies in every year since 1996, versus 251 (1996) and 323 (1997) motor race meetings.

Some 800 of those rallies were on public roads, just under 200 designated as special stage (private ground) events and under 100 were Historic Rallies. The latter branch is currently undergoing modest expansion due to the increasing affluence of the more mature enthusiasts, sponsorship from 'fashion' companies and an interested press.

There was bitterness amongst rally purists about public road rallying being 'driven off the road' in the seventies, when some 1500 road rally permits a year were issued. Yet there were long term international benefits to Britain from our restrictive attitude to public road motor sport.

Britain did not suffer the repercussions from politicians that inevitably followed the death of Italian spectators on the legendary *Mille Miglia* in 1957. Nor were we unlucky enough to suffer the wholesale slaughter that occurred at Le Mans 1955. Then a Mercedes racing driver and 83 spectators were slain as the factory sports racing car flew into the main start and finish enclosure of a circuit converted from public roads.

British motor sports have – often by good fortune – developed in a way that suits current concerns, including those involving protection of the environment.

The RAC and its MSA successors have not been popular with UK competitors whilst enforcing noise and fuel regulations, but the result has been a sport that can show a social conscience. Most racing cars are silenced to tight levels these days; thus the ludicrous spectacle of Dba noise meters being applied rigorously to the exhaust systems of all cars, from 500 horsepower V8 to 70 bhp one-make hatchback, at the archetypal British Club meeting at Donington. Meanwhile, commercial airliners from adjacent East Midlands Airport thunder overhead, drowning all instructions from official to competitors!

On public roads MSA permitted noise levels for competition cars are less than those for lorries. Politically Correct concerns over Forestry land use for rallying and repair of consequent damage are offset by competitors paying the Forestry Commission heavily for the privilege of using the land. UK motor rallying is the Forestry Commission's second largest income source; over £750 000 was collected within the entry fees for special stage rallies in 1997.

How much precious petrol (and a sip of diesel for the minority of rallying pioneers with turbo diesels) is used by British competitors?

Ignoring the fact that aviation spirit is a very differently refined fossil fuel, the MSA quote 'the petrol used in motor sport is insignificant. A Jumbo jet flying to Australia and back uses more fuel than all British motor sport competitors use in a year. If you include all spectators, football matches account for more petrol consumption than motor sport'. The MSA added, 'unleaded petrol is mandatory for many major British events, including the British Touring Car Championship and the British Rally Championship. All Karts must use unleaded fuel'.

Since the RAC and its MSA successors have successfully regulated the machinery and people sectors of British four wheel sports, it made sense that Britain would one day have an organization dedicated to building on the success of our motor racing hardware suppliers. Creators of complete cars, world class power trains, or the literal nuts bolts and rivets that hold such creations together, for all there is an organization to cater for their common good: the Motor sport Industry Association (MIA).

Former Lola (racing cars) Sales Manager Brian Sims was the first to form such an independent body, although the interests of the motor sport business are aired regularly within a separate committee of the London-based Society of Motor Manufacturers and Traders. Sims realized that a dedicated organization was needed to bond together such highly individual, creative and successful individuals as those who create racing cars and ancillary services.

In 1994 Sims created the MIA. A successful individual himself with an excellent record in raising sponsorship funds for major clients, it was no surprise when Brian Sims was himself recruited within a major sports agency working on Benetton Grand Prix business. Since November 1997 the MIA has been run by Chris Aylett and has evolved rapidly from the days 'when MIA funding was so low we could not buy a sandwich between us for a committee meetings', in the words of one associate.

In 1998 the MIA and its 70+ members affiliated to the Sports Industries Federation (SIF), an association with over 400 member companies. This move offered the MIA greater political influence and a number of important administrative benefits. The MIA moved into offices at Stoneleigh Park, Warwickshire and offers membership at 1998 costs between £205 and £1500 annually, depending on annual turnover.

MIA-member services in 1998 included:

- United motor sports industry lobbying voice to UK and European governments
- UK-based Department of Trade and Industry [DTI] supported Trade Missions
- Regular newsletter/Annual Achievement Awards Ceremony
- Technical symposiums/Educational conferences
- Promoting member achievements to Media
- Statistical industry information
- Insurance discounts
- Free audit to prepare for EU Competition Law
- Free 24 hour telephone legal advice service

By Autumn 1998 the MIA became a recognized body of real substance. Feedback to the authors was of a membership who felt that the MIA was serving a useful purpose, particularly in its political lobbying and DTI-supported trade missions. These have included missions to Malaysia and Sydney and in October 1998 the MIA sponsored the United Kingdom's representation to Japan for the

British Motor Show at Yokohama. Here 50 per cent of exhibition and travel costs were to be met by the DTI and over 150 000 people were expected to attend.

MIA Chief Executive Officer Chris Aylett set the organization and himself six highlighted targets to achieve in 1998 and is currently delivering on those promises. The MIA and its objective of 'one voice for an overlooked industry' seemed set for success.

Having examined forces that parented and developed UK Motor Sport Plc, let us examine the harsh post-war climate in which the principles of British technical success in motor sports evolved.

Hardware and the Evolution of Technology: from 1946 to the Benchmarks of the 1990s: the Cars and Components

Introduction

ESTABLISHING an industry to supply the needs of motor sport competitors was a natural progression that called for flexibility, ingenuity and a fearless disregard for bank statements. It took decades, and the beginnings were not auspicious.

> 'It is with genuine regret that we cannot include any British manufacturer amongst the great names who have featured so persistently in these pages, for the British motor industry has contributed almost nothing', wrote Rex Hays scathingly in the 1956 publication *The Vanishing Litres*.

That statement hints at the post-war despair created by Britain's international motor sporting record and the massive turnaround established by this small but often immensely profitable industry. This transformation has been achieved primarily through the smaller UK specialists – even now payrolls are unlikely to exceed 500 – who have contributed the most, although a number of larger organizations have helped to fuel the change.

It is important to acknowledge the debt owed to one giant in this racing and rallying revolution, Ford. Ford of Britain (a subsidiary of the world's second largest motor manufacturer) allied their shrewd investments in companies, rallying and racing to a strong marketing philosophy. But it was their investment in companies such as Cosworth that enabled Britain to monopolize the premier Grand Prix, and the highest levels of American single seater racing. Subsequently such British companies could sell their expertise in junior or feeder formulae with unmatched quantity and quality.

But not all UK Plc international achievements date to the post-war boom. Take a bow some earlier heroes, who recorded success against all the odds.

Vintage and veteran enthusiasts could rightly remind us that Britain constructed the first high speed banked track dedicated to motor racing at Brooklands in Surrey in 1907, complete with hills to test climbing ability and a then ultimate in high speed-banked-track. Brooklands spawned its own racing hardware specialists from providers of 'fishtail' exhausts to total car preparation and was a significant counter to the Continental motorsport monopoly until its effective closure in 1939, when its major role in the aviation industry was naturally paramount.

The 'Bentley Boys' dominated the world's most important sports car race the Le Mans 24 hours established 1923, winning the second race in 1924. The Bentleys boomed triumphantly through the 24-hour marathons of 1927–30, beating Mercedes on the way.

Grand Prix racing was initiated by the French in 1906 (also at Le Mans in the early twenties) and was traditionally dominated by France, Germany and Italy. Britain's first victory in a full-blooded Grand Prix occurred when Major (subsequently Sir) Henry Seagrave won the 1923 French Grand Prix at Strasbourg, in a Sunbeam. *A startling 31 years would elapse before a Briton would again win a Grand Prix race using a British car!* No wonder British race enthusiasts became so good at 'playing the game', excusing their absence from the winner's rostrums of Continental Europe.

A lesser Spanish Grand Prix success went to the same brave British Major and his now supercharged 140 bhp, six cylinder Sunbeam in 1924, surviving a tragic event that prompted the abandonment of riding mechanics in major races. That was deeply significant to the development of the modern Grand Prix car (and supporting monoposto formulae), leading to the single seater separation from all other categories of racing and rallying racing, all of which continued to offer – often theoretical – passenger accommodation. Only in current motor rallying is a passenger carried, and that is in the vital navigator/co-driver role which would be impossible for drivers to perform safely at current speeds, even assuming that most drivers could read a map.

The lack of winning British Grand Prix machinery forced Briton Richard Seaman to drive for Mercedes in the thirties to take his first, and tragically last, Grand Prix victory. Seaman's first post-race quote was: 'thank you. I only wish it had been a British car'.

The post-war Revival

The modern Grand Prix series of races for single seater racing cars built to the international Formula One specification, incorporating a World Championship for both drivers and constructors was inaugurated in 1950. Races for cars conforming to different Formula One technical specifications have been held in every subsequent season, with the exception of 1952–3. Then Grand Prix catered for Formula 2 single seaters.

Leading English Grand Prix drivers of the fifties, particularly Stirling Moss, Mike Hawthorn and Peter Collins were torn between patriotic outings in often unreliable/uncompetitive UK manufactured Formula One cars, and the lure of winning with Italian Ferraris and Maseratis, or Germany's Mercedes. Britain's first World Championship Grand Prix winner in 1953 and World Champion 1957 was Mike Hawthorn, who drove Ferraris to enter the history books.

However, change was coming. Even as Rex Hays was repeating the national angst about our general lack of international motor sport success, the Connaught company based at Send in Surrey, under the direction of Rodney Clarke and Mike Oliver were winning a Grand Prix. Not a World Championship qualifier, but on 23 October 1955 Tony Brooks and a Connaught powered by a normally aspirated 2.5 litre, four cylinder of 140 bhp, beat the best from Maserati. This momentous achievement, from a modest young man still in the throes of his final dentistry exams, emerged at the self-styled Syracuse Grand Prix of Sicily, the island off the 'toe' of southern Italy.

It was a portent of great things to come for Great Britain, but not for Connaught. The Connaught Company (established in 1947) failed to make a tenth birthday when building tycoon Kenneth McAlpine withdrew financial backing. Understandable, since McAlpine had been the sole source of finance for a successful project which had started simply as a provider of unique sports cars to support the McAlpine heir's racing ambitions.

Fortunately, there were others with more motoring business links that were prepared to bankroll the potential of British Grand Prix Racing Ltd.

The first and longest-lived (1950–79) of two mould-breaking post-war teams that were successful and competitive was the British Racing Motors (BRM) equipé. As is so often the case in this story there were a number of key individuals involved without whom BRM would not have existed.

Raymond Mays was the first entrepreneur to involve sponsorship in British motor racing on a large scale; at least on such a large scale for the period. To quote him;

> 'I believed, as the Italian and the Germans did, that the real fruits of a Grand Prix victory were not trophies and prize money, but the blazoning of the winning country's engineering genius. I believed that, when at last our National Anthem was played for the winner of the Grand Prix of Europe, the designers, craftsmen, mechanics and drivers responsible for victory would gain for Great Britain a thousandfold return on the vast expenditure of skill, sweat and money their effort would have cost.

Raymond Mays had developed and raced cars, including a season (1927) as a Mercedes works driver, before the war. In 1933 he established the English Racing Automobiles (ERA) company with generous financial backing from a friend (Humphrey Cook) and the technical abilities of an ex-RAF Cranwell cadet Peter Berthon. This company produced the single seater ERA racing car, a marque that is still extremely competitive in retrospective races.

The partnership between Mays and Berthon continued after the war as they set down their ideas for a post-war British designed and built racing car. Perhaps heralding the modern approach to the sponsorship of the sport, Mays set out to attract sufficient funds to build this testament to British engineering skills by writing a 'White Paper' to firms that specialized in different components; one firm for each component. The missive was sent on 2 March 1945 and by the following year Mays had raised some £25 000 in cash and a promise of £25 000 of constructive work, that in lieu of payment.

The crucial elements of the sponsorship were several early supporters who included Oliver Lucas of Lucas, Alfred Owen the head of Rubery Owen, Sir John Black head of the Standard Car Company, and many other top names from the companies of the day. By the end of the year Mays had 'sold' his idea to over 100 firms and at least one newspaper emphasized the significance of the project and the idea.

A leader article in *The Times* compared the importance of the influence of motor racing on the industry with the developments of the engines and aircraft for Schnieder Trophy air races of 1929 and 1931. A glamorously exaggerated stance, perhaps, but one which caught the imagination of many.

Berthon and Mays split their activities between designing the new car and gathering the essential lifeblood, financial support. Based at Eastgate House, Bourne in Lincolnshire, design work on the new BRM racing car started early in 1946 with Peter Berthon and an ex-ERA draughtsman Erich Richter working on the complex project.

At this stage the only money that had been received were the cheques for £1000 from Oliver Lucas and Rubery Owen! However, both were accompanied by the promise of a further £4000 worth of services and parts. By 1947 the British Motor Racing Research Trust estimated that the project would require £50 000 per year for five years.

The BRM organization was revised in July 1947 when the British Motor Racing Research Trust was formed. In the spirit of wartime Britain a national appeal had been launched. Thus, the main objective of the Trust was to handle the collection of monies from subscriptions, which were incoming from companies and the public. The name of the company to construct the car was changed from the original Automotive Developments Limited to British Racing Motors Limited, and its car was henceforth known as a BRM.

In a climate dominated by wartime priorities, the British Government was concerned about the use of materials. Licences were required for the supply of steel, aluminium, alloys and other high specification components. The then North Midland Regional Controller of the Ministry of Supply was particularly influential in helping Mays to gain access to the Government in the person of the Chancellor of the Exchequer, Sir Stafford Cripps. In spite of his exhortation to British industry to 'export or bust' the Chancellor gave his support to the project and promised that the Ministry of Supply would ensure that the BRM was given priority in materials.

This level of official UK interest in motor racing remains unprecedented. Even the voice of a contemporary *Times* leader column recorded its support for the project in emotive and dramatic terms. The article considered that the failure of British industry to produce a race winning Grand Prix car was a reflection of Britain's position as a declining industrial power and continued ...

> 'Failure in this undertaking must be as unthinkable as it was in the preparations for the Schneider Trophy races in 1929 and 1931'.

Was this an uncharacteristic overstatement? We think not. The BRM project fuelled the public imagination and was something of a beacon to thousands of people to whom the success of British engineering had been their life for the past six years, particularly those in the armed forces.

But the reality was that the astounding enthusiasm and energy of that BRM project team – Berthon, Mays and their colleagues – faced an awesome task. By the spring of 1947 the total complement at Bourne was around 30 people. As the design phase came to the end of its first cycle, the legendary Alfred Neubauer, manager of all Mercedes Benz racing activities, visited the Bourne factory. His views of the enterprise were perhaps more realistic than those hopes raised amongst the British public by leaders such as that from *The Times* , and certainly proved more accurate.

Neubauer commented to Raymond Mays that:

> 'I'd like to congratulate your people on the design. It is one of the finest designs I have ever seen or visualised. But you'll never get that motor to win races with your present small facilities.'

The point rapidly became clear to Mays as he and his team embarked upon the massive logistical problem of assembling the thousands of parts, being manufactured by over 200 of his 350 sponsoring firms. The complexity of the task was formidable as a multitude of components was being manufactured away from Bourne, the assembly base. Rather than manufacturing everything,

Mays and Berthon had simply gone to the best available suppliers. Outsourcing was the business method applied.

In this aspect alone the BRM project was prophetic, for Britain only hit the Grand Prix jackpot regularly, allowing global commercial success, when major items such as the engine and gearbox became sub-contractor responsibilities, a pattern that is followed by all but Ferrari in Grand Prix today.

The diversity of BRM suppliers and the lack of sophistication in their logistical and support systems meant that delivery schedules and therefore the assembly, proceeded sporadically. In the supercharger units alone there were 124 components that were designed, built and tested by Rolls Royce. More than 24 firms were sub-contracted to supply Derby based Rolls Royce with parts, and these had to be delivered to Rolls Royce, prior to assembly and test procedures.

The range of BRM suppliers revealed a roll call of the best in contemporary British manufacturing. Standard Motors were making the upper and lower crankcases and cylinder heads; Rubery Owen created the tubular chassis; David Brown machined gears; the clutch came from by Borg & Beck; whilst Girling were responsible for brakes. An early attempt at Just-in-Time production, under pressing post-war circumstances!

The scheduled BRM assembly programme of Berthon and Mays became more difficult to achieve, as the companies involved experienced rising demand for their products. This put considerable pressure on their production schedules: components for the BRM were often delayed in favour of more immediate revenue. One example is that Ferrari was then able to design and manufacture a major component in eight weeks; BRM's equivalent turn-round time was ten months to a year.

A partial solution to the scheduling problems was the establishment of a centralized progress office at the Rubery Owen works in Durleston. BRM manufacturing predicted the modern concepts of production technology used by the Japanese automobile industry, but BRM had no appropriate systems support, or the now ubiquitous computer.

The BRM was an expensive, technologically sophisticated machine with an engine and drive shaft layout of considerable complexity. The futuristic design contained 16 cylinders in two banks of eight, accommodated in cylinder blocks smaller than those within a baby 0.8 litre Austin Seven. The piston stroke was slightly less than the cylinder bore, reducing piston velocity and delivering a shrill 500bhp at 12,000 rpm. Leading edge Porsche front suspension and a De Dion pattern rear suspension, were BRM features of a low tubular chassis frame; one that housed the offset engine and – sloping down towards the rear of the car – allowed a low and streamlined shape.

There were severe teething troubles with the engine and other components, largely as a result of the power and complexity of the engine design. During the first half of 1950 the car suffered from severe misfiring problems, often resulting in extensive engine damage. As Neubauer had predicted these problems were both protracted and difficult to solve, imposing many sleepless nights on the small team at Bourne.

When Mercedes Benz had a problem with either parts or the technology, Neubauer was able to call upon the whole of the massive and well-funded Mercedes Benz organization. BRM relied upon a very small team and could only exhort their range of suppliers to do better without any obvious incentives.

Nevertheless the problematic BRM was scheduled to appear at Silverstone on 26 August 1950 for the *Daily Express* International Trophy Race. Disaster struck on the testing morning of 25 August.

During early testing both the cars' engines had a cracked cylinder number eight. Mays failed to convince the organizers or the Trust Committee that the car should not race. The third BRM was duly despatched and appeared on the Silverstone grid the next day. Before a large and optimistic crowd the starting flag fell: the BRM moved some two inches and stopped. The embarrassment of all British patriots can be imagined.

The crowd jeered The Great White Hope of British Motor Racing, but BRM persisted with wins in minor events. The most significant change came in 1953 when Sir Alfred Owen took over the whole project for that year. Under clear direction and with a single dedicated owner, the team slowly became serious contenders in the fifties and World Champions in the early sixties. Committees cannot and do not run successful race teams.

The individual who should be given maximum credit for taking Britain into Grand Prix Racing's Pole position – a benchmark for following generations – belongs to the Churchillian figure of Tony Vandervell, heir to Vandervell Products Ltd, bearing manufacturers.

Significantly, Vandervell was a world class company with an international perspective on business (their bearing business originated around a patented American design). The Vanwall race team was based at Acton, West London but their race engine development centre was at Maidenhead in Berkshire.

Leading German engineers swore that being forbidden Vandervell's legendary Thin Wall bearings in the immediate post-war period was a prime reason German competitors suffered initial durability failures and a comparative lack of high-rpm performance.

Tony Vandervell initiated his company's racing programme with a repainted Ferrari that was acquired in association with BRM, necessary to obtain the import clearances required in post-war Britain. That debutante was dubbed the 'Thinwall Special' in honour of the bearings used on that supercharged 1.5 litre

Ferrari. Bearings that were also supplied to the legendary Prancing Horse marque for a number of competition models.

Tony Vandervell took his own route to success. Rather than setting out to design a totally new car, Vandevell's team experimented with an existing product. Learning from the extensive modification and evolution of four Thinwall Specials (1949–52) based on Ferraris the team built up their experience and competence. They used a subsequent Cooper chassis for the Vanwall Special for the sixties, when it became apparent that the rear engine layout was the design future of Grand Prix. After some four seasons of development and learning the Vandervell backed team became creators of original Grand Prix Cars.

The Vandervell racing car quartet fielded in 1955-56 was technically important because Tony Vandervell predicted how some key aspects of Grand Prix would develop. He hired consultants of the calibre of Colin Chapman (founder of Lotus) and former De Havilland aerodynamicist Frank Costin. The former delivered unmatched strength to weight ratios within his chassis designs, whilst Frank Costin (brother of Cosworth co-founder Mike Costin) concentrated on effective 'tear drop' aerodynamics.

By 1957 the patriotically painted British Racing Green Vanwalls had become the finest Grand Prix cars of the final fifties seasons of the front engine era. They won two World Championship Grand Prix in that 1957 season, including the British event at Aintree; a fitting first Grand Prix win for a British car in the official Formula One World Championship series.

Even then, Vanwall had further heights to scale.

The first World Constructors' Championship went to the British team in 1958, and Vanwalls racked up nine World Championship race wins from the 1957 and 1958 seasons. Then the technical move to rear engines in 1959 coupled with the ill health of their patron and motivator Tony Vandervell conspired to dislodge Vanwall from the limelight.

The Vanwall team was disbanded in 1961 and Tony Vandervell died at just 68 years of age in 1967, the year that Vandervell Products Ltd was taken over by GKN. Tony Vandervell never revealed what it had cost to create a winning Grand Prix team, but we know his methods were closest to those of Ferrari in assuming responsibility for both chassis and engine manufacture, therefore his racing costs were considerably in excess of any British rival, with the possible exception of BRM.

The Vanwall racing cars, still gleaming in British Racing Green and including prototypes of rear engine layout, are beautifully preserved to this day. They are usually located in the Donington Park Collection outside Derby, courtesy of Britain's leading motor industry hardware supplier, GKN, who bought Vandervell Products in the aftermath of Tony Vandervell's death.

The Cooper Car Company and the Coventry Climax Engine

The beginnings of the commercial school of racing car design and construction had rather humbler origins than the heady atmosphere of post-war Formula One. Post-war club racing brought the aspiring amateur and the budding designer/manufacturer together in competition. Contact was direct and the aspiring racer was shown the worth of his hardware against the logic of the stopwatch.

The Cooper Car Company grew through the abundance of club racing that proved such a rich breeding ground for British driving and design talent in the decade after the war. Just as the BRM project had developed at an esoteric level, so did UK club racing. Cost considerations aside, one fundamental element that they had in common was the concept of buying components from those that made the best, regardless of origin.

The Cooper Car Company, the Surbiton, Surrey racers, graduated from the rear engine 500cc formula. The Cooper family created not just the commercially and competitively successful Mini Coopers, but also single seaters along similar rear engine principles to their early 500s, such track agility and affordability meeting the needs of more powerful categories. The pragmatic Cooper family would sell their straightforward – but effective – technology to private entrants, opening up British international winning opportunities on a scale that had not been seen since pre-war ERA.

How did a concern-making engine to power fire pumps become the backbone of the British Grand Prix onslaught?

In February 1950 Walter Hassan, an engineer with Jaguar cars, who had been instrumental in developing the XK120 sports car left the company and joined Coventry Climax, a company that built water pumps for fire engines. Shortly after the outbreak of the Korean War in 1950, the Government specified a new fire pump as part of their re-equipment programme. Working with ex-ERA engineer Harry Mundy, the two developed a small, lightweight, engine that exceeded the Ministry specification of 35bhp at 3,500rpm.

The Coventry Climax Company exhibited the engine at the Earls Court Motor Show in 1952 and as a result the company received enquiries from Colin Chapman at Lotus, John Cooper and Cyril Kieft, also a successful constructor of the period. The popular small sports car racing classes of the time were for engines of 1100 and 1500cc: the only small engines then available for racing were either modified Ford or MG units, which were expensive to modify and often unreliable.

By 1954 the first Climax racing engine was ready to be installed in differing chassis. As suppliers, Coventry Climax Company had, as Hassan put it:

'To be very careful about not having favourites to whom we would supply extra-special engines. This meant that as long as 'Joe Bloggs` had the right sort of money, he was entitled to the same engine, to the same specification, as those supplied to Colin Chapman, John Cooper or Stirling Moss'.

The Coventry Climax Company was extremely glad to have this association with motor racing as it provided excellent revenues and publicity, otherwise difficult to obtain for water pump engines! A total of 697 of the 'racing fire-pump' engines were built, several times more than any other engine previously sold exclusively for racing and a total only exceeded by more recent designs, particularly the Cosworth Grand Prix V8 families.

More sophisticated Coventry Climax engines intended solely for racing became commercially available to Grand Prix teams in the late fifties. Together with the Cooper chassis, these lightweight motors would deliver a new benchmark for Formula One that immediately delivered the 1959 and 1960 World Championships to Surbiton and Australian driver Sir Jack Brabham. The Climax V8 also proved effective in other chassis.

Lotus with Jim Clark won two more World Constructor titles for Britain in the sixties, the last of which was in 1965. Already Ferrari were beginning to feel the sea change in Formula One results, for British companies had won all but two of the annual constructor's titles since Vanwall inaugurated Britain's winning formula in 1958.

The phenomenal success of the Coventry Climax engines and Lotus, Cooper and Kieft racing cars was the true starting point of Britain's ability to sell racing cars and associated components to the rest of the world. The real significance was not just in the technology but in the trading philosophy. Previously, racing teams tried to retain all their hardware and knowledge for fear of losing a competitive advantage. It was not often that customers beat the works teams whether in Cooper or Lotus products, but it did happen and promoted the commercial and spectator appeal of motor racing.

During this early post-war period the huge interest in motor racing at club level in Britain meant that there was a ready market for the products of firms such as Lotus, Cooper, Coventry Climax and Kieft. But it was not only at the club level that the market operated, for there were a number of examples in the premier division.

The Rise of the British 'Garagiste' and Suppliers

The most memorable examples of the new 'level playing field' came from Lotus. Rob Walker's Lotus, prepared for Stirling Moss at Monaco 1961, performed the equivalent of a motor racing miracle and held off the entire pursuing Ferrari pack. Then Jo Siffert won the 1968 British Grand in a Lotus 49 Ford Cosworth V8, again in Rob Walker's tasteful dark blue and white striped livery.

The Vanwall Team had pioneered the Grand Prix winning track for British teams. Since 1958 the constructors' title has been won by English-based companies in every year except when Ferrari have taken the title (1961, 1964, 1976–7, 1979 and 1982–3). Otherwise there was a hybrid international title win for the Matra-Ford Cosworth V8 of 1969. Triple Matra/Tyrrell World Champion driver Jackie Stewart could argue that the Cosworth V8 was made in Northampton and the French Matra tended by the British team who subsequently created their own Tyrrell Fords in 1970. These cars provided the mount for Stewart's 1971 and 1973 World Driver titles and the 1971 Constructors' World Championship.

Complacency is the fuel of failure and in motor racing this is particularly true. Whilst Britain has been extremely successful in motor racing's Premier Division as chassis constructors and winning entrants, the last time a 'British engine' won the Formula One Constructors' Championship was 1981, when the Cosworth V8 powered Williams triumphed, although the 1998 champions McLaren used British (Ilmor) engines, albeit badged Mercedes .

Post 1981, British teams Williams and McLaren have taken all the Constructor titles, an exception being British- based Benetton who had Renault power in 1995. British Formula One success has relied on German (Tag-Porsche and Mercedes), Japanese (Honda) and French (Renault) finance technology, reflecting the true strength of mass production companies when it comes to motor racing.

What are the British supplier strengths that support our commercially sound performance in Grand Prix and other international formulae?

We will examine suppliers in individual detail later in the book, but some have been so fundamental to our progress at all levels that they deserve early recognition. It is critical to our understanding that motor sport manufacturing within an imaginary United Kingdom Plc is not just about a winning Williams or McLaren on global television.

The popular exhortation from the British Government to its weary post-war population to 'Export or Die', and the perceived needs of manufacturers to produce goods for foreign consumption, made motor racing a low priority that was officially regarded as rather frivolous. Even in the late nineties very senior motor sport officials revealed that British motor sport, in spite of its track record, suffers in the eyes of the UK establishment. 'Not quite the thing', especially in comparison with horse racing and other more traditional pastimes. It was not only Enzo Ferrari it seems who regarded Britain's teams and suppliers with disdain.

As we have seen Britons succeeded in spite of such narrow thinking in Grand Prix, but it was harder to fund other branches of the sport that were not regular headline winners. However, it is a fact that most of the estimated 600 plus British concerns involved in selling motor sport-related produce/services are involved outside Grand Prix, and export more than half their turnover. It is also a fact that several Grand Prix teams have been rewarded for their export successes.

Although the Vanwalls were the most patriotically painted and motivated winners for Britain in Grand Prix, they were NOT the most British in terms of hardware content. Amongst 88 listed suppliers known in 1975 the majority (78) operated from British bases, but there were significant exceptions at important development points, especially from Germany.

Aside from regularly racing on Robert Bosch fuel injection, Vanwall also took supplies, either routinely or at particular phases of development from a range of foreign companies. ZF supplied differentials, Fichtel & Sachs shock absorbers, Porsche supplied gearbox internals and patented synchronizers. Other suppliers included Mahle forged pistons within the winning British four cylinders, which ran to some 7500 rpm on later specification German valve springs.

Equally crucial to Vanwall's success was the contribution of Italy's tyre company Pirelli, mounted on Borrani wheels (fronts only in 1958) whilst the car had fuel tanks sourced in Italy, and American fuel pumps. Contrast those significant exceptions to the Vanwall 'British is Best' policy with the typical 'Kit Car' from the UK of 1968–81, the period when Ford Motor Company allowed supplies of their Ford-branded Cosworth DFV (Double Four Valve) V8 engine to reach beyond the initial exclusive 1967 Lotus contract.

Ford DFV: The Engine Legacy

From 1967 onward the existence of the Ford-funded Cosworth eight cylinder transformed Grand Prix racing. Despite the best efforts of France and Italy, the sheer affordability of that Ford branded engine which initially sold at £7500, allowed Formula One to develop into a superior Formula Ford. By 1979 only Ferrari, Alfa Romeo and Renault fielded Grand Prix cars without the ubiquitous DFV, which was supplied to nine teams (including Ligier in France) in 1979 and had amassed 125 GP victories twenty years ago.

The original Ford Cosworth deal involved Ford's Walter Hayes, Colin Chapman and Keith Duckworth, an ex-employee of Lotus and founder of Cosworth with Mike Costin. It led directly to the development of DFV and the Lotus 49, both significant Grand Prix milestones.

Ford agreed to fund the engine's development with £100 000 for the Grand Prix V8 and a further £40 000 for the earlier four cylinder FVA race and BDA road and race engines, the latter creating a family of inline fours that brought an enormous variety of racing and rallying success to Britain.

The Ford-funded Cosworth engines were all developed around the four valves per cylinder combustion chambers. The DFV Formula One engine was the most significant step toward routine British success at an international level. It freed designers from the major distraction of engines engineering and team managers from many of their engine budget worries.

Another vitally important innovation that came with the development of the DFV was the use of the engine as a stressed member to take on some of the duties that would have required more complexity [and weight] via separate subframes in then competitive contemporary rivals. According to Costin this was Duckworth's idea and certainly the car and engine were designed as a package. This car was truly the shape of the future and stressed engines of the most compact dimensions are now routine Formula One, though the field now prefers a vee of ten cylinders in the wake of Honda and Renault success.

The DFV continued to win in Grand Prix until overwhelmed by both turbocharging and Anglo-French FIA politics during the early eighties. But as late as 1994 Michael Schumacher drove a Benetton car with a redesigned Cosworth Ford V8 engine to wrest the driver's championship from the more powerful Renault V10 employed by Williams. In total Cosworth V8 racing engines have powered 174 Grand Prix winners, whilst the turbocharged [DFX and successors] family for American events has taken 12 Indianapolis 500s and uncounted premier league Indycar victories.

The Cosworth-Ford connection was probably even more significant in establishing a new core of British racing engine expertise. The DFV provided many of today's leading British engine specialists a living rebuilding it. About half a dozen specialists were authorized to carry out Cosworth routine rebuilds, as the pressure of 'must have' turn-around business became overwhelming for Cosworth in the seventies.

Just as Cosworth founding partners Mike Costin and Keith Duckworth had learned the practicalities of their craft first tuning, then creating complete competition engines (often from Ford), Cosworth thoroughbred racing engine knowledge seeped out to a wider ring of eager experts in the UK, who established their own concerns.

Whilst none have yet matched Cosworth commercial and competitive achievements, Cosworth has bred its own competitors. Mario Illien and Paul Morgan of Ilmor were former Cosworth employees who stayed in the Northampton region at Brixworth to establish a racing engine concern in 1985. One that now builds winning turbocharged V8s for America and V10s for Grand

Prix that carry a Mercedes badge, although the American turbocharged Illmor engines were supported by GM-Chevrolet initially.

Whatever the badge, Ilmor look most likely to challenge Cosworth's role as Britain's premier competition engine suppliers, leaving the Cosworth Ford branded V10 behind in the 1996-9 Formula 1 seasons. Ilmor recorded winning performances against everyone including Cosworth, in the American IRL and CART premier leagues. However, there is more depth to British engine builders in concerns such as TWR Arrows, where Brian Hart (formerly a Grand Prix and Formula 2 engine builder in his own right) has worked with that company's V10. There are also a large number of engine development specialists that we will discover in our next section, on the formulae outside Grand Prix.

Britain does have strength in depth in engines engineering even at Grand Prix level, but it is not enough to resist the big budget, mass manufacturers who currently monopolize the points-scoring positions (first six to finish) at 90 per cent of late nineties' Grand Prix. The exception, to prove the rule in 1998, was the Ilmor-created Mercedes V10 behind the winning McLarens. For the future, it may be that Cosworth Grand Prix winning fortunes will be rebuilt around Ford and Jaguar brand name ambitions, which exceed the points-scoring promise of three seasons with Stewart Grand Prix and the ten cylinder Zetec-R Cosworth.

Transmitting for Britain

Equally significant innovations (redeveloping the humble VW Beetle to finally meet the needs of Grand Prix racers) was the transaxle and gear set-output of Hewland Engineering. Of the nine Cosworth equipped racing teams in the 1979 season, seven cars used Hewland transmissions. Most were of the mainstay 5 speed FGA400 or FGB series, but the Berkshire based company (who moved to larger modern premises in 1997) was already working with Lotus and McLaren to provide 6-speed units.

The application of British engineering and transmission expertise did not end there, for Borg and Beck provided clutches to the whole of the 1979 grid (including Ferrari and Alfa Romeo) from a British base, whilst either Lockheed or Girling supplied brake systems for all the teams. The brake pads were supplied by Ferodo at Chapel en le Frith, the Yorkshire based Mintex company or, Dunlop (then British owned) for further friction material development.

Britain did not supply 100 per cent of every Grand Prix car in the seventies and early eighties, Ferrari, Alfa Romeo and Renault saw to that. But the dominance of the British supply base meant that it was often only in comparatively minor expenditure areas that overseas suppliers were used. For example Dutch Koni dampers were universal in 1979 and many engines used

Volkswagen production car radiators, or adaptations thereof, although Serck Radiators were also prominent.

The Supply Base Remains Strong

Britain does not enjoy the same dominance by value today, but remains a leading supplier to the Grand Prix circus of power trains, transmissions, carbon fibre/composite materials, brake and clutch components. The internationally competitive role of not just Cosworth Racing Limited (owned by Ford Motor Company as of October 1998) but others have usually benefited through the wide availability of the Cosworth V8.

In the 1997 season the Cosworth V10 racing engine was supplied to Stewart Grand Prix on an exclusive basis, but a less powerful version was also leased to Tyrrell and Minardi in 1998. Numerically and commercially therefore Cosworth continues to be successful and is doing good business for Britain, but breakaways at Ilmor engineered the Mercedes Benz engine that powered McLaren to the 1998 Constructor's title.

British transmission expertise continues to attract both UK and overseas-based teams. AP clutches and disc brake components were the most obvious components on many Grand Prix cars. Hewland and Xtrac are notable fabricators of gears; although often overlooked because the race teams themselves took the credit for the overall conception of now universal electro-hydraulic command systems for 6- and 7-speed transaxle units.

The big technical innovation in transmission technology in the 1998 season was in the use of lighter and potentially stronger carbon fibre (re-enforced by steel or titanium) gearbox casings for Stewart and Arrows. But new technology is not always reliable in the heat of racing and both UK based teams suffered varying degrees of unreliability. As a result Stewart Grand Prix designed both conventional metal and carbon fibre gearbox casings for 1999.

Ferrari pioneered the use of transverse gearbox location in their European Grand Prix cars of the seventies including the Ferrari 312T. Originally specified for its space-saving attractions versus the traditional longitudinal transaxle casings, only Williams of the major contenders used this transmission layout for 1998.

Britain's post-war start in the minefield of modern Grand Prix was a story of heroic but disastrous failure. From that early adversity grew a strong base of technology and expertise through which the sector has established a grip on Formula One. The teams, suppliers and individuals that devote their time and energies to this circus and the formulae that radiate beyond its televised glamour, continue to benchmark Britain as the nation that has the winning knack in terms of consistent success in this most difficult alliance between man and machine.

A World Beyond Grand Prix

Rallying: Isolated Territory Conquered for Major Manufacturers

IN the billion dollar World of Formula One, with an associated TV audience also measured by the billion, it is easy to forget that Grand Prix is simply the tip of FIA-sanctioned international motorsports. Not only is there a host of other F-prefixed single seater formula as stepping stones up the world class motor racing ladder (usually featuring an element of single source components these cost-conscious days) but we also acknowledge the influential enclosed cars of World Championship Rallying, sports and touring car racing.

The latter three categories feature visual ties to showroom cars and are often more important to a mass manufacturer than Grand Prix. The Monte Carlo rally is still a potent sales aid, and so is the whiff of Le Mans 24-hour sport-racing success. Touring cars have their own 24-hour international marathon (at Spa-Francorchamps, Belgium) and an increasing global TV audience for Australia's 'Great Race', The Bathurst 1000, another televisual event devoted to saloon car racing.

Here we investigate the historic and current essentials of these important motor sporting variations on a competitive theme, beginning with motor rallying.

Evolution of the WRC premier league

The World Rally Championship for Makes is the senior of two current World Championship titles, the more recent series reserved for Drivers. Established as a European Manufacturers' title in 1968, when it was won by Ford of Britain and their new Lotus Twin Cam-powered Escort, today the names on the Makes' title tend to be Japanese, although the engineering usually owes either major hardware (or a complete motorsport facility) to Britain.

Ford and their Escort also won a second outright championship in 1969 and fought hard for premier honours through waves of seventies Italian success until their last title with the obsolete rear drive Escort RS1800 (powered by a Cosworth engineered motor) in 1979. Most successful brand has been Italy's Fiat or Fiat-owned Lancia (14 titles), but since 1993 the winning brand has always been Japanese. Subaru-Prodrive were the most successful with three World Championships, whilst Toyota won two. Mitsubishi have just one Manufacturers' title to stack alongside the record-breaking 1996–8 hat trick so memorably scored by Tommi Makinen.

The younger title – naming a World Champion Driver – is an even more popular sales aid within rallying-aware car markets such as Scandinavia, France, Italy, Spain, Britain and the Asia Pacific region. There has only been a World Championship for rally drivers since 1978 and British success was traditionally along the same lines as pre-1957 Grand Prix: notable for its absence. That changed in 1995 when Scotland's Colin McRae overcame our abysmal record and heralded a wave of British drivers who occasionally overturn the traditional Finnish driver establishment in the late nineties.

However, most world rally titles have accrued to Juha Kankkunen of Finland (four), and the 1997-8 Drivers' titles also went to a Finn, Tommi Makinen. Yet rallysport remains truly international with champions having come from Britain, Germany, Sweden, Italy, Spain and France. Note that Germany was far more rally conscious when its national hero (Walter Rohrl) won the world title on several eighties occasions. Today German manufacturers tend to regard rallying as politically incorrect in today's united Germany, where the emphasis on pine forest preservation and ecological issues attracts strong political and public support.

Motor rallying earns less media coverage, especially TV, than its motor racing status equivalents, but manufacturers have learned more about their products and how to improve them for everyday conditions, than in any other branch of motorsports. Suspension that soaks up the worst of the bumps (promoting the use of low pressure gas dampers), effective lighting, screen heaters, proper wipers and washers, brakes that withstand Alpine descents, all owe their roots and rapid development to motor rallying.

Motor rallying is the true descendant of those pioneer motor races along the dusty dangerous roads of France and Continental Europe, for there was the need for a two-man crew, adverse terrain to conquer and a demand to set faster times than the competition. In essence current World Rally Championship (WRC) events (up to 16 of them spanning the globe and more than 15 000 miles) are still about beating both the opposition and a generally hostile environment, competing against the clock rather than racing wheel-to-wheel.

Today's turbocharged 4×4 permanent all-wheel drive rally machinery is as far removed from a 1903 GP Renault as a Stealth bomber has become from Bleriot's

Channel-hopping pioneer, but still it is the team within and outside the car that brings results. Results based on the fastest times over sections now timed to the tenth of a second. Such tests are usually referred to as Special Stages (prefixed SS on results), whilst the link sections to each test will be over public roads.

Therefore the competition rally cars must remain fully road legal, which is not a requirement in any major international racing category. In Britain, where most WRC cars were based, they will have to comply with the Construction & Use Regulations, right down to treaded tyres and rear lamp colours.

Britain created three of four regular World Championship contenders in 1998 with France's Peugeot set to join the fray in 1999, alongside Seat of Spain, Hyundai from Korea and Skoda from the Czech Republic.

The UK record in this mixed surface sport bears comparison with Grand Prix. We were not a natural cradle to the sport of racing through forests, as was the case in the Scandinavian countries, particularly Sweden and Finland. Nor was Britain home to classics like the Monte Carlo Rally or other Alpine terrain that provided a natural backdrop to test cars and crews to their extremes, against the watch.

However, Britons participated with success overseas, and the best were not necessarily male. Drivers such as Stirling Moss turned their hands to rallying with success in the Alps, but specialists such as Stirling's sister (Pat Moss-Carlson) in the brutal Healey 3000 succeeded in the toughest terrain. Pat was not just Stirling's sister and the wife of Sweden's greatest Saab rallyist (Eric Carlson), but a phenomenal driver (and a show jumper to Olympic standards) in her own right.

Pat Moss was hampered only by excessive modesty when promoting such incredible wins as the 1960 Rome-Sofia-Liège outright victory for BMC (now Rover) in a Sauna bath-on- wheels adorned by the Healey badge. It would be twenty years before another manufacturer, Audi in Germany, provided a genuinely talented woman with a car capable of winning world class events. Michele Mouton was entrusted with the flame-spitting beast of an automobile (Audi Quattro) and reaped the obvious publicity rewards when she won four World Championship rounds in 1981–82, and was runner up for the world title in 1982.

British males seizing fifties' success were Ian Appleyard (Jaguar), Ian Burgess (Ford) and Sidney Allard (using a Ford V8-powered sports car of his own manufacture). They proved capable of winning major continental classics, including Monte Carlo, The Tulip (Holland) and Britain's own RAC Rally. Ford of Britain also won the Monte Carlo Rally in the fifties but the driver was Dutchman, Maurice Gatsonides, ironically the subsequent inventor of the ubiquitous speed detection cameras nicknamed 'Gatsos'.

British rally navigators were reared on tricky UK map-reading events that demanded graduate mathematical brains, ingenuity, and an unusual degree of telepathy with the warped minds of organizers. Mix in an ability to organize a mobile office full of bulky maps and instructions whilst ignoring terrifying outside occurrences and it was not surprising that many British co-drivers eventually became team managers/owners. Their record includes representing companies as diverse as Toyota, Mitsubishi, Ford, Rover and Subaru.

Rallying calls for even more co-operative effort than racing as there are two crew within the car and the support/service team is an integral part of the way the sport developed. A sport that can attract millions from their firesides to face a November night in mid-winter Britain. The traditional UK closing round to the WRC series often decides the fate of the Championship for Drivers and the separate category of Manufacturers, thus witnessed by watching millions, the final audience figure boosted by regular BBC prime time evening coverage through the Midland-based Pebble Mill studios.

Current World Rally Championship events, held over closed special stage tests, traditionally derive most of their funding from manufacturers. Thus for similar reasons mass manufacturers support touring car racing: under their gaudy warpaint, the roofed saloons bear reminders of a showroom product.

Financial support outside the major manufacturers tends to be poor, the most obvious exception being Prodrive Subaru who enjoyed considerable support from British American Tobacco before that company opted for Grand Prix Racing for the 1999 season onward.

Most cars on the world stages are usually built to a fairly loosely interpreted WRC format, or the more tightly regulated 2-litre Kit category rules. This means the WRC cars featured permanent 4×4 with instant (usually dubbed 'Active') limited slip differential action to react to wheelspin, usually prompted by electronics and executed by a variety of highly developed front, rear and centre differentials.

Turbocharging of a 2-litre engine to 320 to 330 bhp has become the norm in WRC events, all the current engines of four cylinders with DOHC (Double Overhead Camshaft) operation of four valves per cylinder. The only engine that breaks the conventional inline four cylinder pattern is the flat four cylinder layout employed by Subaru, which has seen development periods in both Britain (Prodrive) and at the Japanese parent factory.

In 1998 both World titles were held by Tommi Makinen of Finland; the third successive year (1996–8) that Makinen has taken the title. As ever Makinen was driving a Mitsubishi created in England (Rugby) and Japan by a specialist sub-division of the company's engineering division, Ralliart. The Mitsubishi conformed to that WRC format in having turbocharging and 4×4, the motors built in Japan to yield something over 300 bhp with enormous pulling power (torque).

That is not a terribly high power per litre ability for a competition turbocharged engine – Audi exceeded 500 bhp in 1986 with a 2.1 litre turbo motor – but mandatory 34 mm air restrictors restrained power in this nineties' period. These regulations were prompted by the safety considerations that caused the Group B Supercars of the eighties from Audi, Ford, Peugeot, Lancia to be banned. Otherwise some 500 horsepower could have been easily available throughout the nineties and terminal speeds, all within feet of the bolder spectators, would have exceeded 130 mph.

Mitsubishi are the technical exception to the present WRC front running norm for they built their 1996–8 Mitsubishi Lancer Evos to earlier Group A regulations. These demand minimum production figures of 5000 per annum per each model, versus one car for homologation and enough components (including the body) to build a further 20 cars in WRC format. This offers manufacturers considerable savings in often unprofitable homologation runs that used to haunt the sport.

Despite the technical restrictions of Group A compared with WRC format, Mitsubishi report Group A is worthwhile for them in thousands of commercial sales of road replicas of their leading rally car. As of June 1998 Mitsubishi in Japan had sold 29 500 examples of the most recent Lancer Evo series III to V. The Evo V was rallied in 1998 by Mitsubishi Ralliart, and also badged Carisma GT for an identical car (driven by Briton Richard Burns) to gain commercial recognition in Britain.

There are some compensations in the competition regulations in that Mitsubishi can use the lightweight panels forbidden to WRC machines. Balanced by the fact that Subaru also sells replicas of its WRC machines commercially, both brands the subject of increasing grey (unofficial) imports to the UK in their highest performance specifications for sale to the public.

Such cars will typically cost £20 000–40 000 and have all the basic technical features of a 4×4 turbocharged WRC car. It is possible to order such cars with more sheer horsepower than the official factory competition car, because there is no need to fit the air restrictors required of international WRC-specification competition cars.

These unofficial imports are commercially interesting to demonstrate the immediate impact of rallying on showroom sales. Such Japanese high performers from Subaru and Mitsubishi are pure production offerings from Japan and hit a market formerly dominated by Ford of Britain.

In their turn, Ford learned from the earlier example of the sales popularity of the Mini Coopers, which earned their worldwide reputation through rallying, particularly a trio of victories (and a disqualification) within Monte Carlo Rallies of the sixties. Ford applied the lesson with a commercial vengeance from the sixties to the nineties in sales of Cortina GT, Lotus Cortina, Escort RS and Sierra/Escort Cosworth RS types.

At their best such specialist cars exceeded 25 000 sales at premium prices, adding to the prestige of more lowly members of the same model families. Ford came out of that sector with the pressure created by Britain's extraordinary stolen car crime rate and consequent pressure of high insurance rates in the early- and mid-nineties.

Ford branding will support the total change to the Focus as the basis of future rallying, rather than Escort. Ford are currently expected to re-enter the high performance arena for customers. The initial Ford re-entry model was the Cosworth branded showroom version of the Focus, as displayed at the US Auto Show in 1999 and expected to lead to a showroom 200 bhp front drive Cosworth or Focus R by Year 2000.

Aside from Mitsubishi and their Group A format Evolutions, WRC cars of 1998 were branded Ford Escort WRC, Toyota Corolla WRC and Subaru WRC Impreza. All had British competition bases, save Toyota, which nevertheless featured some British components. Most notably the 6-speed Xtrac gearbox (with unique design features to a TTE specification) and Alcon disc brakes.

The Japanese giant chose Cologne in Germany in the seventies as its competition car preparation site. Initially privately owned by former World class rally winning driver Ove Anderson of Sweden, the team gathered a multinational team of specialists (some ex-Ford of Britain technicians and administrators) under the branding of Toyota Team Europe (TTE).

The TTE site (adjacent to the main German Toyota import HQ) is the biggest competition operation in Europe in terms of employees and technical resources, a comparatively compact team of 16 engineers assigned to the initial CAD design of Toyota's current WRC challenger.

TTE also had the 1998–9 capability to compete effectively at the Le Mans sports car classic in a racing GT1 car created at Cologne and run by TTE. This is a massively effective operation, its World Championship-gathering abilities in the nineties only blunted by a scandal over an illegal turbocharger unit on their previous World Championship-winning Celica coupé that resulted in TTE being banned and fined heavily for contravening FIA regulations.

The FIA forced TTE to sit out a season, but the company took a longer break before returning to instant winning form with a brand new WRC design based upon its best-selling Corolla. The Corolla choice was a Toyota management/TTE decision, which made more commercial and competitive sense than the low volume Celica, a squat coupe that was not the easiest car to adapt to the demands of rough road rallying and optimum vision.

To prove that Britain will not have her way unopposed in future WRC events France's Peugeot also entered the 1999 WRC ranks. As former multiple WRC Champion constructors of the eighties with the 205T16, they were taken extremely seriously. Peugeot's welcome participation presented another stiff foreign factory-based challenge to the existing establishment of British-based specialists working for the big mass-production names.

The Front drive format

The second major grouping to be found on both the world and national stages – where WRC cars are outlawed from winning major prestige titles such as the French or British Rally Championships – are more closely related to showroom cars. Technically, they depend on a front drive formula, as does every modern hatchback bar the BMW Compact, and non-turbocharged, 2-litre, 4-cylinder engines, again items found in most mass-market brochures.

The more radically engineered examples – with wide or narrow tracks and aerodynamic/wheelarch bodywork stretches to match, are labelled Kit Cars. Their predecessors, now falling out of international rallying favour, were simply called 2-litre Formula and corresponded to a rally equivalent of SuperTouring racing, clothed in showroom bodies with significant engineering alterations (requiring a £140 000 price tag in the UK for a 1997 rallying Golf, rather than a showroom £17 000).

Technical changes in both categories include replacement 6- or 7-speed sequential gearboxes, unique transmission shafts, gears and bearings, massive brakes (around 14 inches diameter). In addition a body strength multiplied by a factor ten times more than that of the 1997 production equivalent, and an engine yielding around 115 bhp more than the public offering. It is also worth noting that 2-litre gearboxes (and associated high value transmission components) for all but Skoda came from UK sources, and that exception was originated around a popular UK design.

Leading Kit/2-litre contenders, that will typically taken in a couple of WRC rounds, as well as the thriving National Championship programmes of Britain, France or Scandinavia are as follows.

- **Renault Mégane Maxi** The French-built machines won all three British Championship categories in 1998. Ironically Renault did not compete with official factory entries in their own French series, leaving Peugeot to dominate at home in 1998.

  The 280bhp 16-valve engines were prepared in France but the 7-speed sequential gearbox was from FFD/Ricardo in Coventry. Only one team technocrat in 1998 was from Britain, senior engineer Andy Thorne, and a former member of both Mazda and Ford at Boreham rally teams.
- **Seat Ibiza GTI Evo** The Spanish company has dominated the 2-litre division of the Kit Car/2-litre category within WRC taking the WRC class title for the seasons 1996–98 inclusive. Now have larger ambitions for the

Cordoba 4×4 turbo car chasing outright WRC victories from 1999 onward.

The 2-litres front drive Ibizas were prepared and maintained by Cupra Sport in Daventy, UK for British events. Winner of the 1998 Ladies' Award and runner-up for the UK national title in 1998.

- **Volkswagen GTI 16 valve** Prepared by SBG of Daventry for British events, a 16-valve GTI won the Manufacturers' section of British Rally Championship, 1997 and was third in both Driver and Manufacturer sections of 1998. The 16v used Lehman of Liechtenstein engines but 6-speed transmissions came from Gemini Developments in the UK Midlands.

  For 1999 onward Volkswagen themselves decided to take over the competition operation and dropped SBG. However Volkswagen created a 'Daughter Company' in Wellingborough, Northamptonshire, investing in Britain in a similar purpose-built manner (albeit at a fraction of the cost) as BMW at Williams Grand Prix Engineering.

  Designated Volkswagen Motorsport GB this interesting operation had Volkswagen GB and Germany personnel on its board and was charged with making any Volkswagen presence in the World Rally Championship effective.

  A long overdue change to current Golf body and 20-valve engine did not happen (as planned) in 1998 but was a key requirement for 1999, when two Golf GTI 20v 2-litres were scheduled to contest the premier British series and selected WRC rounds within the Kit Car Category.

- **Ford Escort RS2000** Now obsolete, originally developed by former Ford Motorsport technician Gordon Spooner in Essex and taken into Kit Car format by Ford at nearby Boreham for 1997–8 with much promise but no budget.

  A regular UK 2-litre winner whilst driven by Gwyndaf Evans (to close of 1997), but lost direction and finance after Evans defected to Seat for 1998. It then became obvious that Ford Motor Company wanted Focus in the later nineties, leaving nothing but privateer demand for the obsolete Escort.

- **Skoda Octavia 20v Kit** Prepared in native Czechoslovakia but used British inspiration for 6-speed gearbox and AP triple plate clutch/ differential assembled with expertise from Prodrive at Banbury, who also supplied transmission components, including active differentials to Seat for their Cordoba WRC project.

  Handicapped by excess weight (290 kg over limit) and 30 horsepower deficit, the Octavia was simply designed to give the Czech team a 1998 taste of life beyond rallying their faithful Felicias, and some prediction of the body demands that would be placed on the Octavia for in-house preparation.

Incidentally Skoda are no joke in modern motor rallying. On their last 27 visits to Britain's tough RAC/Network Q WRC qualifier the Czechs (armed usually only with 1.2 or 1.3 litres within the rear engine Estelles or front drive Felicas) scored 26 class wins.

- **Hyundai Coupé 2.0i** Re-prepared by MSD (Motor Sport Developments) at Milton Keynes for 1997 RAC Rally after an Asian preliminary programme with Australian input. MSD campaigned the coupé again in 1998, hindered by 80 Kg excess weight and 30 horsepower less than their best rivals in the 2-litre category.

  Now confirmed as future WRC contenders and undertaking an expanded programme at the Milton Keynes base of MSD (Motor Sport Developments), the only spanner in their competition ambitions could be the Asian financial crisis. However, a Briton was seconded to look after Motorsport amongst many other global Public Relations issues at Hyundai's Korean HQ, so the team should always be assured of a sympathetic ear in times of woe.

  MSD was founded by former GM Opel and Vauxhall rally technician David Whitehead and is as versatile as many bigger outfits. MSD has also constructed, entered and raced in the SuperTouring category on behalf of Honda (Accord) and Peugeot (406) during the mid- and late-nineties. They also represented Vauxhall in the one-make Vectra series (1997–8) as well as developing the basis for special high performance editions of the Vectra that proved very popular in short showroom runs (c. 200) during 1997–8 under the practical engineering leadership of David Gray.

  In yet another versatile engineering and entrepreneurial move Whitehead also masterminded an MSD team tasked with the creation of a new Russian rally car, one based on a model that had yet to be delivered to the showrooms. Top marks for initiative!
- **Nissan Sunny GTi Kit,** created by Nissan Motorsport Europe at Didcot, Oxfordshire. Nissan driver Mark Higgins was the winner of the 1997 British Rally Championship for Drivers, bringing the Nissan score in the UK title hunt to a brace of championships in three seasons: excellent for such a vaguely focused effort.

  Nissan motorsport engineering was perhaps the most internationally sourced company one could cite in the 1996–8 period. Mechanically the Sunny and the Almera broke little new 2-litre front drive competition ground, allying reliable JECS electronic injection engines (c. 265 bhp in 1997) with an NME modified 6-speed sequential gearbox sourced from Ricardo/FFD.

  The suspension on the Sunny series was unusual in employing German Eibach springing with Japanese Kabaya damping. Together with a direct

Yokohama tyre contract it was obvious that excellent handling was a major Nissan Motorsport attribute in a wider variety of conditions than major rivals could offer. The Nissan Motorsport braking system was also slightly different in 1997, deploying the UK independent company Alcon's discs at the rear whilst Italy's big Brembo units slowed the 960 kg Nissan from the front.

But in 1999 Higgins drove for Volkswagen in the British premier league series and the Nissan rally programme was shelved in yet another erratic weave of managerial magic; Why? The Nissan Almera GTi hatchback (and its Sunny-branded predecessor) for British and occasional overseas programme was obviously technically effective, but politics within Nissan terminated the more adventurous WRC programme in late 1998, much to the disappointment of Didcot-based rally manager Dave Whittock.

As for so many other Nissan programmes in the past (right up to Le Mans with TWR), one has to question company commitment to a consistent motorsport programme. It has to be emphasized that the situation was made more difficult in 1997–8 by the Japanese parent company's obvious sales difficulties at home and within the recession ravaged Asia Pacific Rim.

- **Peugeot 306 Maxi** Prepared by the factory in France and multiple winner of their National Championship this car proved capable of setting faster times than WRC cars on some (Spain, Corsica and Monte Carlo) tarmac-surface qualifying events in 1997–8. Majority French content, but the Wokingham-originated Xtrac 7-speed sequential gearbox was a notable 1996–8 exception.

Such Kit cars (particularly the Peugeot 306) were developed to such an advanced specification (unhindered by air restrictors), and allowed a minimum weight of just 960 kg that they proved faster than the 1230 kg WRC cars over dryer tarmac tests. Thus, one has to remember that full blown WRC turbo 4×4 cars are built with the 80 per cent loose surface events in their series as a priority, not the 20 per cent of tarmac sections that see French-based Peugeot-Citroen and Renault field such rapid specialist front drive machines.

The French front drive lightweights are often compared to racing saloons, but they actually enjoy freer regulations in some respects: i.e. they are not required to run the 8500 rpm engine rev-limiters that are mandatory in SuperTouring. Since higher rpm generate more power, it is only the demands for some semblance of road flexibility on link sections that keeps the most radical French chargers from handsomely exceeding 300 bhp with their 9500 rpm abilities and comparative flyweights.

As it is the power to weight ratio of a top flight Peugeot or Renault in tarmac trim equated to 320 bhp a ton, whereas the heavier WRC cars with little more power generated c. 275 horsepower a ton in 1998.

There should have been a traction advantage for 4×4 to offset this, but under some conditions the wide tyres and low weight allowed the front drive brigade to contribute to the faster times recorded on some WRC events from 1997 onward. Despite the embarrassment of the premier league – the Formula 1 of rallying if you like – being temporarily outperformed by the junior aspirants (equating F3000), there was no sign of regulation changes from the appropriate FIA sporting commission to compensate the WRC entrants and enhance their speed until year 2000.

Those are the main 2-litre front runners internationally and their UK content. What of the major league suppliers?

Purveying Parts and Professionalism Globally

Unlike motor racing, the Americans relegated rallying to club status for many years, so there was not the potential mass market for British rally specialists that existed in motor racing. Despite this market limitation, a look through the 1997 specifications of the four leading WRC turbo cars revealed that they all used British gearboxes.

These were all sequential units from Xtrac, bar the Subaru 1995–97 WRC Championship winners in which Prodrive parented a 6-speed unit. One that also proved popular for further development in 1997–8 Seat and Skoda WRC challengers, along with 4×4 hardware sourced at Prodrive, as well as continuing with their own in-house developments for Subaru.

Xtrac were the suppliers of four leading teams amongst ten brands seen in 1997 WRC events. Whilst FFD-Ricardo, the descendant of the old Harry Ferguson transmission empire, equalled Xtrac at four teams supplied with 6- or 7-speed units, all of them with 2-litre front drive layouts. Finally Hewland supplied one team Seat's Cupra Sport organisations in Spain and the UK with a 6-speed sequential for the Ibiza. The Seat had the best 2-litre success rate of all and Seat won the 2-litre division of the WRC from 1966–8.

Whilst UK concerns also monopolized the supply of transmissions, Britain's other hardware supply success story was from Alcon of Coventry. Alcon supplied their disc brakes to Subaru, Toyota and Renault amongst major teams, plus rear discs only (in 1997) to Peugeot and Nissan.

From Great Britain Motorsport Plc's viewpoint note that from 1996 onward three British companies prepared and entered World Championship Rallies on behalf of three amongst the four major WRC teams. This was set to change as newcomers from France (Peugeot), Spain (Seat) and Korea (Hyundai) joined the WRC series in 1999 onward, but still UK content remained high, especially in the case of Hyundai with the primary WRC centre located at MSD, Milton Keynes.

Banbury in Oxfordshire is home to World Championship rallying Subarus (Prodrive Engineering) whilst Mitsubishi Industries entrust their Rugby-based Ralliart UK parallel engineering team with the creation of a competitive rally car and the organization needed to field it on a World Championship event. Exceptions include Mitsubishi engines and associated electronics prepared in Japan and shipped on a rota.

Mitsubishi is an interesting case study. Part of the gigantic Japanese Mitsubishi Heavy Industries conglomerate, Mitsubishi Ralliart previously contented itself with divisional World Championships in a 1995-7 clean sweep of the lower Group N (showroom) categories. As the Evo-coded series of Lancers and Carismas gained competitive strength, the Japanese parent company's management became more interested in outright WRC victories/championships. They started to supply a suitable financial and engineering budget to allow their partners in Britain to achieve more ambitious goals.

Ford learned that in-house rally preparation with a unionised workforce and the inevitable rates of overtime on such rugged events was not an economic proposition. Shattered by a budget reportedly 'in excess of that for Grand Prix racing' Ford management reluctantly abandoned more than 30 years' tradition and shifted preparation from its traditional Boreham, Essex airfield site.

The job went to sub-contractor Malcolm Wilson Motorsport (immediately re-named M-Sport) to field re-engineered (to WRC format) Escort Cosworths from 1997 Monte Carlo Rally onward, subsequently Ford Focus from 1999.

That concludes our introduction to the key events and players in the creation of the current World Rally Championship. Now, we detail Britain's principal motorsport service providers in the top leagues of the World Rally Championship.

Prodrive

Prodrive at Banbury is a multi-activity engineering organization employing around 385 during 1997–8. The company was born out of a marketing consultancy for Rothmans in rallying and retains exceptional marketing, organizational and administrative skills. This versatility makes Prodrive suitable for manufacturers wanting complete car competition origination and fabrication; most smaller components are assigned to further UK sub-contractors. But the company's exceptional managerial and marketing abilities enable Prodrive to enter and run those vehicles on events with a strong element of marketing expertise to draw on to extract further value from any programme.

Prodrive's WRC record in recent years is better than any empty mission statement: three World Rally Championships for constructors (1995–6–7) and one Championship driver (1995, Colin McRae). In 1998 British-based Mitsubishi-Ralliart (GB) scooped the silverware pool, but Prodrive Subaru still won world class events in their last year under British American Tobacco (BAT) colours and sponsorship.

- *Current Rally Car:* Subaru Impreza WRC 4×4 turbo.
- *Principle UK hardware suppliers:* In-house assembly and design includes AP carbon fibre clutches, Hewland gears for the Prodrive-designed 6-speed, Alcon disc brakes.
- *Key managerial personnel:* David Richards founder and majority shareholder, owner. The former World Rally Championship-winning Navigator also managed the Benetton Grand Prix Team for a 12-month period in 1997-8 and brought back an outside perspective on Prodrive that proved valuable.

Other Prodrive directors with smaller stakes in the privately owned company (David Richards owns 'more than 50 per cent' of the available equity), are co-founder and first employee Ian Parry, who is now the commercial director. David Lapworth, Managing Director to Prodrive Motorsport Division is responsible for many other Prodrive engineering activities, inside and outside motor sports. Hugh Chamberlain is the Marketing Director.

M-Sport

M-Sport represents the Ford Motor Company in WRC events. The company grew from Malcolm Wilson Motorsport (MWM), which was an established independent commercial operation in the sale of Ford rallying parts and cars in Cumbria.

Originally MWM was established in the wake of Wilson's rally driving success. Malcolm was British Champion in 1994 with an Escort Cosworth and was so respected for his car development abilities (honed over years in every Ford from Anglia to Focus) that Wilson completed most of the factory test driving duties on earlier eighties and nineties motorsport Fords.

Today M-Sport is the division contracted to Ford Motorsport, employing 78 in 1998. 'Up to twenty' of those personnel were required at Millbrook Proving

Ground, Bedfordshire, for six months of 1998 to develop the 1999 Ford WRC challenger based on the Focus.

M-Sport has been the Ford-contracted representatives in WRC since the start of the 1997 season. They built and entered the obsolete Escort Cosworth to the World Rally Championship (WRC) format for 1997–8 with intermittent success. The Ford Escort's last WRC win was recorded in September 1997 when Carlos Sainz of Spain led Finn Juha Kankkunen to a Ford -12 on the Rally Indonesia. Unfortunately for Ford who had spotted his talent back in the eighties, the Spaniard returned to Toyota for 1998.

Created by former Porsche engineer John Wheeler, the WRC Escort remained a good car, truly a pioneer amongst purpose-built competitors for the nineties. This Escort mongrel was mated with a Sierra and featured that bigger car's unique longitudinal-mounted Cosworth turbo engine.

The Escort RS Cosworth was the last winning Ford to be created and built at Boreham, prior to the M-Sport switch in 1997. It was also part of a 1992–96 Ford showroom line, heading the company's performance offerings as Escort RS Cosworth, but sales and therefore production did not match those of previous Sierra 4×4 Cosworth-branded derivatives (c. 7100 versus 12,250 manufactured respectively) owing to British social conditions.

The Escort finished its final factory outing on Britain's November 1998 WRC qualifying event in second (Juha Kankkunen) and third position (Bruno Thiry of Belgium), marking the last time that Ford used the Escort badge in a 30-year motor sports span. For 1999 an M Sport association with Ford in Britain using resources at the Dunton Engineering Centre, plus the Cologne Wind Tunnel and Ford Motorsport (for homologation) at Boreham Airfield, designed, developed and tested the Ford Focus World Rally Car hatchback, under the leadership of Guenther Steiner, an Italian from the German-speaking area of Merano.

Managerial approval was given for the Focus WRC programme in January 1998, with its planned debut in the January 1999 Monte Carlo Rally. The Focus made its public running debut with Malcolm Wilson at the wheel in November 1998 and was an immediate WRC event winner (Safari and Portugal) when driven by ex-Prodrive and Subaru Champion Colin McRae in 1999.

A vestigial trade-only Ford parts sales operation remains in Cumbria awaiting a move with the rest of M-Sport to a magnificent 115-acre site developed from an old hospital complex. One developed with much friendly advice and access to the TWR premises at Broadstone, to help Wilson arrange the necessary high tech facilities sympathetically within an area of outstanding natural beauty.

- *Current Rally Car:* Ford Focus WRC 4×4 turbo
- *Major UK hardware suppliers:* Mountune Zetec 2-litre turbo engine rated at 300 bhp at 6500 rpm, with mandatory FIA 34 mm air restrictor. Unique

Garrett turbocharger sourced in Los Angeles, but Garrett also has a UK presence at Skelmersdale, Lancs. Reportedly 550Nm of torque generated by 4000 rpm, some ten per cent more than the Cosworth Escort delivered. A reported ability sustain 7500 rpm is attributed to the purpose-built turbocharging and UK-sourced Pectel electronic engine management systems. Also from the UK: Xtrac 6-speed sequential gearbox and advanced traction control systems featuring electro-hydraulic active differential operation. Titanium is used for foot pedals, steering rack and wheel hubs.

A Focus showroom body is claimed to be 15 per cent stiffer in torsion than an Escort. Installing some 45 metres of hand-crafted steel tubing to supply rollover cage and body integrity allowed Ford and M-Sport to quote a boost in body stiffness in WRC format amounting to 30 per cent stiffer, in favour of Focus.

- *Key managerial personnel:* Founder and owner Malcolm Wilson is a former British Rally Champion. Guenther Steiner: WRC Focus Project Manager, and Marc Amblard, Chief Engineer. Martin Whitaker: Director, Ford Motorsport.

Ralliart UK Ltd

Ralliart UK Ltd founded and operated for former 'Marathon Man' London–Sydney winner Andrew Cowan. The rugged Scottish farmer won that 1968 epic in a Hillman Hunter (*née* Rootes Group, now absorbed by France's PSA), but Cowan's durable managerial and driving talents also attracted support from Mercedes and Mitsubishi. Cowan enjoyed international motorsport success as a long distance rally/marathon competitor for both Japanese and German brands.

Ralliart at Rugby functions with approximately 62 employees (1998–9) to fabricate and field WRC versions of Mitsubishi saloons. Only the engines engineering remained in Japan during the successful 1997–8 seasons. However, Mitsubishi runs parallel engineering programmes at home to monitor progress through constant global computer links. Much of the Evo's original success attributable to former Chief Engineer Roland Lloyd, who joined Ricardo/FFD for 1997.

Ralliart had no commercial function during 1997–8 and was not permitted to sell parts or cars to the public, but other branches of Ralliart (notably Germany) were permitted to trade with the public, so that attitude could change.

Initially chronically under-funded, and therefore forced to miss many championship rounds, Mitsubishi now tackles a full WRC programme with two Group A, evolutionary developments of their 4-door Lancer/Carisma lines. The results have been spectacular with Tommi Makinen of Finland winning the WRC title for drivers in 1996–8 and Mitsubishi Ralliart securing the coveted Manufacturers' WRC title in a 1998 Championship double.

- *Current Rally Car:* Mitsubishi Lancer/Carisma Evo series of Group A, format to compete in WRC with the usual 4×4 and turbocharging features.
- *Major UK hardware suppliers:* Xtrac gearbox and other differential gears and control systems. Over 1100 man-hours devoted to creating each body with integral safety cage construction from Midlands-based labour force.
- *Key managerial personnel:* Founder/concession owner Andrew Cowan won the London Sydney Marathon 1970 and is also an active Scottish farmer from the Duns district that produced Lotus Grand Prix Legend and double World Champion, Jim Clark. Phil Short is a former world class co-driver and the Team Manager. Chief Engineer was Bernard Lindauer.

5

Touring Cars: a Main Event

From Supporting Cast to Prime Time TV Star

WHEREAS Germany, the USA and Australia viewed touring car (alias saloon or stock car) racing as the finest post-war fare, the English, as ever, took their time. Finally the UK transformed a dowdy support act into a global TV money-spinner. But it took an Australian to make it happen.

So far as British competition car and component manufacturers were concerned, premier league touring car racing was simplified in the nineties. You either prepared outline mass production (*see:* Rules of Admission, p. 68) 2-litre saloons to the FIA Super Touring formula, or you were unlikely to be involved at an international level.

In 1999 Britain it was obvious that the global impact of 2-litre Super Touring had waned after a remarkable decade in which up to 13 of the world's leading mass manufacturers had been tempted into the arena. UK specialists awaited proposed new overseas formulae to see if any of them attracted a sufficient cross-section of manufacturers or privateers to make a touring category a more worthwhile business proposition than BTCC. Or would the BTCC in Year 2000 format, a heavily revised category aimed at reducing costs by a minimum ten per cent, make more commercial sense?

Touring car racing evolved in Britain during the fifties as a supporting (usually dubbed 'saloon car') event beside major races such as the British Grand Prix; events in which amateur saloon car racers met factory-backed professionals and could still win. By 1958 a formal championship was established by the enterprising British Racing & Sports Car Club (BRSCC) with four capacity classes. That was settled with a unique run-off between two competitors who had tied on points. Thus the first National British Saloon Car Racing Championship driver was 'Gentleman' Jack Sears in a large factory (BMC)-supported Austin A105 six-cylinder saloon, although overall race wins still went the way of Jaguar. For the fifties and the opening years of the sixties, a Jaguar was the winning choice. The Coventry factory would supply high performance equipment commercially whilst retaining the absolute best for their contracted saloon car drivers, who were usually single seater professionals such as Stirling Moss topping up their incomes.

In his last year of professional racing (1961) Stirling Moss filed a taxable income, after he had paid all travelling and associated expenses for tackling 57 varied events most of them outside Grand Prix, of £8000; equivalent to £150 000 in 1999 values. Today there is not a professional (as opposed to paying driver) Formula 1 pilot on the grid who performs in more than 16 Grand Prix per annum or who takes less than a £1 million annually. The equivalent of Moss, Michael Schumacher generates in excess of $20 million annually in driver retainer fees alone to say nothing of his sponsorship income from endorsements.

Austin and Ford followed Jaguar's saloon car racing example. The big technical difference was that these mass producers without in-house sporting pedigree searched for small specialists with a talent for extracting the racing best from their unlikely showroom offerings. Often as not the proprietor of the specialist tuning company would have been an outstanding engineer-driver and the beginnings of a business that would lead to the multi-million pound BTCC (British Touring Car Championship) were established. The same principles also applied to rallying (*see* preceding chapter) and the founder-director of the biggest competition operation in Europe (Toyota Team Europe, Cologne) was a Swede who drove for major British, Italian and French enterprises at World Championship standard before establishing TTE.

Before the UK Touring Car Championship could become the plausible playing field of Super Touring today, it had to suffer decades of under-promoted obscurity as a sideshow to single seater events. Press and public confusion centred upon its multiple-class system (based on engine displacements). This allowed tiny 1-litre cars at the rear to win their class and therefore to frequently win the overall British title. Individual races were won outright by bigger capacity cars to the bewilderment of onlookers and the delight of a few partisan insiders.

In 1961 American Grand Prix hero Dan Gurney dramatically demonstrated that a 7-litre Chevrolet Impala could be more or less dragged off the street to set a pace beyond that of even the best 3.8 litre Jaguars. At this time Chevrolet proprietors General Motors were famous for *not* participating in motor racing, so it was the ambitiously sporting Ford Motor Co. who re-learned that 'cubic capacity' wins lesson in Europe.

Ford imported a variety of large Galaxies, allegedly compact Falcons and for the later sixties, their commercially and competitively successful Mustang Pony cars. They ruled the British – and occasionally European – roost with their comparatively large V8 engines. Not unnaturally the natives grew restless and outlawed large American sedans via a 3.6 litre cubic capacity limit. Thus was the British series dominated from 1974 into the eighties by modified 3-litre Ford Capris, 2-litre Triumph Dolomites and, in the eighties by smaller capacity V8 Rovers of a convenient 3.5 litres.

However, a capacity class system was retained, allowing the Japanese Toyotas to score their first major impact on European Championship racing in England. Inevitably small capacity Minis also continued collecting silverware for an unfeasibly long period as British rules were manipulated to keep the ailing BMC and its BLMC/BLMH successors interested in the category that only Ford dominated overall.

Primarily because the cars were so radically uprated for racing in the later sixties, comparatively humble saloon car racing cost more than was healthy for a large and competitive field. Every key aspect that could influence track performance would be purpose-built and Britain established an early lead in this field. Americans were domestically orientated, investing in their traditional Stock category from NASCAR with emphasis on 200 mph speedways, or in racing their Pony cars whilst the market was strong; roughly from 1966–1970 in the SCCA Trans Am category.

In continental Europe the emphasis was on racing saloons with strong and visible links to the production product. Leading contenders such as Mercedes, BMW and Alfa Romeo were caught off guard when the British started competing with such contradictory devices as hand-built racing saloons, dedicated from start to finish to setting the quickest lap times over shorter distances than Continental Europeans tackled.

Europe's biggest one hour- to 24-hour races emphasized endurance and were collected together as the European Touring Car Championship ETCC, which spanned 1963–88. The first winner was a German in a Jaguar, Peter Nocker and the last an Italian in a BMW. Thus, the ETCC featured appropriately Common Market results, which unfortunately and frequently turned sour over the vexed question of regulations to suit widely disparate technical specifications amongst contemporary rivals. The FIA international sporting authority (then in Paris) abandoned the ETCC in 1988. The FIA also tried a World Championship for Touring Cars (WTCC) in 1987, but that was even worse tempered as, in the opening round, the first seven cars were disqualified! Subsequently touring cars had occasional World Cup weekends of racing from leading national teams (1993–5 inclusive) and these went the way of Ford, twice and Audi in 1995.

Radical saloon car re-engineering allowed UK specialists to flourish and through the seventies such skills were exported directly to Continental Europe, notably Germany and the USA. For example, the considerable amount of work that Cosworth carried out on Ford competition engines to power outlines from the sixties Cortina to the nineties Mondeo often found itself exploited overseas.

General Motors in the USA and Germany became a big fan of Cosworth in Northampton. GM deployed Cosworth expertise to produce four valve per cylinder heads, plus alloy castings. GM also improved the competitiveness of their NASCAR V8s against their only domestic NASCAR rival: Ford. More prestigiously, Cosworth's capability with aluminium castings (including a patented casting process that raised quality to unique heights) attracted support from Mercedes Benz.

Despite media outrage at home in Germany at the 1983 announcement of the prototype Mercedes 190E 2.3/16, Mercedes stuck with Cosworth. British manufactured DOHC 16-valve heads for the thousands of production Mercedes 2.3/16s followed, as well as heads, for the logical 2.5/16 evolution. Valuable business!

Britain began to look at cheaper saloon car racing formulae. During the 1970s various production based classes matured from a series of experimental handicap events (reflecting how saloon cars had first managed to compete on a class-levelling basis). These catered for the arresting spectacle of the tiniest Fiat blob racing in the wake of the most luxurious Rolls Royce limousine. Such informality could not be permitted in a serious British Championship, a pity for the crowds loved it, even if they were baffled as to who had won! So other routes were devised. These embraced the first one-make racing series for mass production machines such as the Mini, Escort or Renault 5.

These one-make series attracted massive support from their manufacturers and were heavily promoted for short periods. However, the enduring idea of everyone racing the same brand of car, which has had implications for single seater racing, has persisted. Low cost series for Minis were viable more than 30 years after the first series was organized.

Renault still invest major capital in the support of major league one-make races across Europe, the latest showcasing the unlikely combination of the minimal Clio hatchback and a mid-engined V6 of some 285 racing horsepower. The reward for manufacturer is that eye-catching Clio hybrids will attract major TV coverage and interest the public in a Renault Clio rather than any one of twenty other global rivals.

Within mixed-marque saloon car racing there was an original thought in 1972. The British clubs tried a series based on racing by list price. An interesting experiment that failed to catch the public's loyalty when the ugliest Moskvich ran away with all the major prizes! In the USA, Germany and Australia racing cars with tin roofs and showroom links were the main attraction of the largest race meetings; one capable of drawing in more than a quarter of a million spectators.

The American NASCAR series was established in 1948 and is now one of the USA's biggest spectator sports regulars, setting new records for sell-out attendance every season. In the late nineties the situation was that you had to book a year ahead to attend most NASCAR events. Special occasions, such as Florida's Daytona 500, had 'Full House' signs up at least a year before each edition.

In terms of TV audiences around the World, NASCAR is not quite so awesome. The American series, which far outdraws single seaters domestically, is beaten for automotive TV audience in many countries outside the US by Grand Prix, British Touring Car Racing or World Rally Championship screen time. Most coverage is routed via satellite, especially Eurosport or cable. But when a major terrestrial channel does decide to televise a Grand Prix live its audience will often dwarf that of the non terrestrial channels, especially in Britain where BBC/ITV deliver by the million in the late nineties versus thousands for satellite and cable.

The most sophisticated televised saloon car racing coverage, now frequently imitated and emulated, came from Australia. Sydney's Channel 7 station introduced the lightweight revolving camera into the sport, plus in-car live links that allowed a Prime Minister to chat on air with a leading race driver, as he headed their premier event (Bathurst 1000), only for the driver to suffer car failure. Amazingly for Australia's cliché image, the driver's language was not just a succession of beeps and set a fine example to sports personalities everywhere.

In terms of global TV audience Bathurst became significant, so it is worth noting that its recent promotion as a 2-litre race and its associated TV deals has been the responsibility of the same TOCA organization that runs the British series (*see*: *Who are TOCA?* below)

Who are TOCA? And who watches their show?

The TOCA initials are not deeply significant; they simply sounded enough like the Formula One Constructors Association (FOCA) initials to persuade co-founder Alan Gow into purchasing an off-the-shelf company in Britain. One that would administer and promote the UK BTCC series from 1992 onward under a licence granted by the Government-recognized Motor Sport Association, then the RAC MSA, today simply MSA.

Then as now, the BTCC catered for 2-litre, 4-and 5-door saloons measuring at least 4.2 metres long and produced in volumes beyond 25 000 per annum. There have been significant changes in race and technical formats over the seasons, including a major technical shake-up scheduled for Year 2000 with the aim of reducing costs by 'at least 10 per cent'.

TOCA is responsible for all aspects of series administration and promotion, but directly and primarily only employs 'less than six people' including Chief Executive Officer Alan Gow: others with specialist skills are sub-contracted over shorter periods, as required. Expatriate Australian Gow, a former employee at Andy Rouse engineering (then creators of leading Ford competition cars) loved saloon car racing, understood how it could be promoted into a main event, and enthused others with his vision. Today TOCA claims over 1.945 billion TV viewers annually around the globe, including 32 Chinese stations accounting for 700 million. TOCA developed an association with BBC Grandstand as the TV bedrock on which such astonishing viewing figures were founded.

In 1993 the BBC was showing under three hours of BTCC coverage annually, but since the Corporation lost Grand Prix rights to ITV that BTCC figure escalated to 15 hours in 1998. This reflected the brave step of allowing live BBC coverage of three BTCC race meetings, full length, instead of edited film highlights.

The majority of the meetings were enticingly covered by the controlled and sharply edited film coverage emanating from London Specialists BHP (Barrie Hinchliffe Productions) Ltd. BHP staked their claim to being Britain's leading exponent of motorsport TV and film action back to 1970s coverage of what became World Championship rallies, before moving into BTCC coverage for the 1980s and 1990s.

The biggest single British BTCC audiences are drawn by the Saturday or Sunday BBC Grandstand broadcasts, which typically average over 2 million viewers. For TOCA the real marketing clout came through the 100 terrestrial and satellite/cable TV stations that broadcast BTCC coverage in 120 countries during 1998.

That is far from the end of TOCA income/promotional ability. Aside from print media valued at £20 million in UK coverage for 1997 (double that of 1998) there was an official BTCC web site attracting 5.4 million hits that year, plus a TOCA-authorized Playstation video game which exceeded 1.2 million sales in 1998. A second edition (TOCA 2) was launched in November 1998.

Spectator attendance at BTCC events was at record levels in 1998 when both Silverstone and Brands Hatch recorded crowd figures in excess of 35 000 at the gate, typically paying a minimum of £16 to £18 for basic admission passes. That meant a minimum of £560 000 gate money to be split between the most successful circuits and TOCA.

Who was the typical TOCA event spectator?

According to Sports Marketing Surveys working the crowd at Brands Hatch in August 1998, the majority were male; no surprises there. Women were well represented and bought more of some sponsor products – notably Nescafé Blend 37 and Kaliber low alcohol beers – than their male counterparts. Most likely age was over 35 years, categorized as C1 for 47 per cent of males and 59 per cent of females.

The surprise was that most females claimed to be in the £30 000 to £39 000 income brackets (22 per cent), while the biggest income sector (19 per cent) amongst males reported £20 000 to £24 999 although another 18 per cent of males also fell within the £30 000 to £39 000 sector. 14 per cent of men answered the survey with income figures beyond £60 000 with 11 per cent of females in the same top questionnaire bracket.

Other TOCA income sources included a long term (1993-2000) title sponsorship deal from the weekly classified advertising magazine *Auto Trader* as well as significant registration fees associated with the championship contenders.

Co-founders of TOCA included David Richards, Chairman and majority owner at Prodrive; Dave Cook contemporary creator of Vauxhall-branded racing cars, and the aforementioned Andy Rouse. Also present at the start of 2-litre BTCC was Vic Lee, an extremely successful entrant of BMW cars in the 1991-2 UK series under the VLM banner, winning the title in both seasons. Lee was subsequently convicted and jailed for drug smuggling offences committed in 1992 and released in 1998, re-establishing his career at lower levels of Motorsports in 1999.

Until the 1991 launch of the British Touring Car Championship (BTCC) for just one 2-litre class, saloon car racing was the poor relation in Britain. It had always attracted some BBC TV and specialist print media support, but its myriad engine capacity classes usually produced a champion in a smaller capacity car, one consistently hidden in the bustling pack. Not an easy sport to comprehend for the public or mass circulation media.

When the RAC MSA assigned the rights to run and promote BTCC qualifying events to Alan Gow's TOCA organization in Warwick from the second year onward of the 2-litre formula, the results were spectacular. Gow clearly understood (possibly from the importance attached to touring car racing his native Australia) that consistent television coverage and broadly framed regulations, would lure more mass manufacturers to spend at record levels.

Gow succeeded even beyond his own dreams, but we should salute the ingenuity and initiative of the other wise men who framed Super Touring rules that would appeal to the broadest cross-section of motor manufacturers.

At its 1997–8 peak, the BTCC was capable of attracting eight manufacturers (13 around the world) and such popular regulations were behind counterpart series in Germany, Japan, France, Belgium, Australia, Scandinavia (particularly Sweden), South Africa, the Czech Republic, Spain, Italy and Portugal.

Most of those 11 countries modified or dropped the Super Touring concept in the later nineties to suit national needs. Yet the 2-litre category remained viable in five of those 11 countries for 1998: Germany, Italy, Australia, South East Asia and the Czech Republic. Judging by the vigour with which Alan Gow launched technical cost-cutting initiatives for Year 2000, the BTCC bedrock to 2-litre racing retains a strong future far into the Millennium.

The premier German National series, Deutsche Rennmeisterschaft colloquially known as the DTM, evolved from decades of confrontations between BMW and Ford in the 1970s. Subsequently it became a three cornered show with Porsche scoring most outright victories in the later 1970s and early 1980s.

From there DTM flowered a domestic battle royal between BMW, Audi and Mercedes. When BMW and Audi withdrew by the close of 1992, the DTM was poorly supported with Mercedes centre stage, because few other European teams could afford the increasing technology costs. The DTM transformed (briefly) into ITC format (International Touring Car) concept of the mid-nineties. But this was also insufficiently backed by the manufacturers (Mercedes, GM-Opel and Alfa Romeo) to attract wider support. Now, the 2-litre Super Touring format was attracting more Media (especially TV) coverage. The ITC series collapsed at the close of 1996 and both Alfa Romeo and Opel operated Super Touring teams as 1997–8 marketing replacements in the German Super Tourenwagen /STW ADAC-organized Championship for 2-litres.

A 1998 STW battle developed between BMW, represented by Schnitzer of Freilassing and still using some UK development inputs from the 1996-7 McLaren engineering co-operation deal, and Peugeot. They fought for the 1998 driver's title, resolved in favour of BMW's Johnny Cecotto plus a three-cornered manufacturers' dispute between GM-Opel, BMW and Peugeot. This allowed GM-Opel a championship title after the most intense and expensive manufacturer effort seen in 1998 STW.

Unfortunately STW, the strongest 2-litre series outside Britain between 1995–8, looked in danger of collapsing beyond 1999, a blow to the many British suppliers involved. Audi and BMW home teams stopped direct domestic involvement for the 1998 season, basically because they had expensively higher international motorsport ambitions. Following Nissan Deutchland's withdrawal from the STW 1998 series, like Honda using British specialists to construct the cars used in Germany, only Honda and GM-Opel were committed to the 1999 STW. The brief span of popularity for STW (Super Touring Wagen) was exhausted, with Germany looking for new saloon car racing formulae as we closed for press.

Ironically one of the biggest supporters of STW, GM-Opel, had created major interest in a replacement rear drive/400bhp formula for Year 2000. Opel demonstrated how the Astra coupé could look in a prototype constructed for display at the company's annual 1998–9 motorsport conference by Ray Mallock Ltd (RML) of Britain.

Germany's British Implants.

Ford's superiority over BMW in the sixties and seventies, on BMW's home tracks, owed much to British specialists, particularly Ford competition personnel and engine building expertise from Cosworth and the now defunct Harry Weslake organization of Rye, Sussex. Ford and their sub-contractors transplanted homologation expertise (the international recognition process through the FIA parent body for any car that a manufacturer will use internationally) from ultra special versions of the 1968–70 rally and race Escort into the more suitable (for racing) 1970–74 Capris.

The European Mustang imitation with British Weslake V6 motors swept all before it in both the European Touring Car Championship (ETCC) of 1971–2 and the DTM domestic championship. Then in May 1972, key personnel at Ford Motorsport in Cologne defected to BMW to establish BMW Motorsport GmbH, taking with them these valuable British lessons and a respect for UK motorsport methods.

BMW beat Ford in Europe throughout the remainder of the seventies, though interest in the premier ETCC series waxed and waned. Now the wheel has turned full circle with BMW creating a British Motorsport base alongside Williams Grand Prix Engineering. This centre will tackle all but the hallowed engines engineering motorsport tasks. Motor engineering remaining in Munich, along with BMW's commercial M-brand operations.

At its best the ETCC featured Ford and BMW joined by Volvo and Tom Walkinshaw Racing TWR, racing versions of the Jaguar XJ-s and Rover V8. This added welcome variety to the previous duopoly of Ford v. BMW results, both Jaguar and Volvo winning a title apiece.

For British hardware suppliers, TWR's success was significant, attracting GM-Holden of Australia to become TWR customers through a separate SVO facility established in Australia which creates special V8 racers and road cars for that market. TWR's performance also attracted Volvo of Sweden's respect, and they became 1994–99 TWR customers when they returned to saloon car racing in nineties Britain. Subsequently Volvo became further involved in partnership deals with TWR that produced a rather different breed of sporting showroom Volvo, such as the elegant C70 coupé before the Ford take-over that was announced in January 1999.

Back in 1986–88 both BMW and Ford brought two new race weapons, the M3 and Sierra RS Cosworth, to fight for both ETCC and World Touring Car Championships: the latter lasted one year only (1987), for the manufacturers cheated too much to police effectively! Finally the ETCC series was terminated in 1988 and touring car racing has been administered by the FIA on the basis that it should remain of National Championship status, rather than an a full international competition category.

Exceptions included the FIA World Cup (Ford won twice with Mondeo-Cosworth in 1993–4, Audi in 1995 with their Quattro A4). The Bathurst 1000 in Australia has always attracted a sprinkling of overseas competitors,

Rules of Admission: BTCC

The rules which have attracted such a broad cross section of the world's mass manufacturers to participate in FIA Super Touring (based on the original 1990 2-litre BTCC concept) have simple basic elements that provide split-second equality between an enormous variety of manufacturers. The key technical requirements (as of 1998) were:

- The body to be not less than 4.2 metres long and produced in a volume not less than 25 000 units annually.
- Engine to measure no more than 2000 cc, no more than 6 cylinders and electronically limited to 8500 rpm. Basic annual production volumes, not less than 2500.
- Limited aerodynamic additions to the showroom body
- Weight differential operate on a minimum 975 kg for the front drive majority and plus 25 kg for rear drive (BMW).

particularly from Britain. TWR inevitably contested Bathurst and won with Jaguar, but more recently Bathurst turned to Super Touring format which saw BMW just beat out Audi in 1997 and TWR-Volvo victorious in 1998.

The hardiest European annual event has proved the Spa-Francorchamps 24-hour race, which turned from a pre-war sports car event into one for touring cars in 1964. Unfortunately BMW, particularly their sub-contracted squads from Schnitzer in Germany or Bigazzi in Italy, have proved too good for the future of the event. BMW scored their 20th victory at the Belgian classic in 1998 but Peugot took a decisive 1-2-3 victory in 1999.

The Super Touring Manufacturers

We now cover major motor manufacturers and how they have been represented in the Super Touring events of the nineties, with any major British supplier interests.

Alphabetically the majors were:

Audi Sport

The Ingolstadt based offspring of Volkswagen Group ran one of the few in-house factory efforts. They achieved global domination in 1996 with their unique 4×4 Quattro transmission system, winning a record seven national championships. Not winners when forced by an FIA ruling to adopt front drive for 1998.

Little British hardware involved, besides Alcon brakes, and AP carbon clutch and a Castrol oil contract for the A4, but the BTCC cars were run out of a UK base at Buckingham with consequent employment benefits between 1996–98. An Audi Sport UK base was established in September 1995 funded with serious support from Audi UK marketing measured in million pound units and employment peaked around 20 engineers and technicians in July 1997.

Audi first contested 2-litre/Super Touring events with their 80 Quattro, then (1995) switched to the A4 Quattro. From 1998 onward the Quattro 4×4 system was banned by FIA (as were their unique 5-valve per cylinder engines). Factory efforts wilted with substantially the same A4 running gear in two wheeldrive format for 1998, and Audi withdrew to concentrate on 1999 sports car racing (see Chapter 7). In Britain, Audi were winners of all three BTCC championships (driver, manufacturer, team) in 1996, runners-up in drivers' series, 1997. Forced to adopt front drive in 1998 Audi Sport UK struggled to finish in the top three. There have been no German factory-financed entries since 1998.

Whilst developing their 1999 R8 Le Mans sports car (with assistance from the Norfolk-based ex-TOMS facility they purchased in 1998), Audi AG funded technical touring car development by ROC in France and representation by Abt in the 1998 German Championship, but results were unsatisfactory.

Approximate 1997 BTCC budget: £5 million

Alfa Romeo

Perhaps the most emotive name in motor racing after pre-war glory and the association with Enzo Ferrari. Alfa Romeo was accidentally involved in Super Touring as a factory when most of the budget had been spent supporting the ultra-expensive German and subsequent ITC high tech series.

Technically, Alfa Romeo competes from national or in-house resources. The current 156 was aerodynamically and structurally (claimed to be stronger than a Formula 1 chassis) enhanced with the aid of CAD resources at owners Fiat's central research facility.

From its 300 bhp engine (managed by Magneti Marelli) to the Brembo brakes and OZ cast magnesium wheels this is the epitome of an 'Italian Job'. However, as for most teams, tyres come from Michelin France and the sequential 6-speed transmission from Xtrac in the UK.

Back in 1994 Britain a brace of Alfa Romeo 155 TS saloons proved BTCC winners for the factory team operating using a unique truck transportation and rota system of cars and personnel direct from the team's competition HQ (Alfa Corse) in Milan. The 155 was a winner domestically and in Spain when run in winged 'Silverstone' special edition format, a specification partially echoed by a limited edition showroom special of the same name sold in Britain. The 155 was competed by Prodrive at Banbury in 1995 BTCC without success, but set a new UK allcomers record for the number of accidents per competition mile covered.

Subsequent 156 has not yet raced in the UK, despite assurances that it would be appearing in a couple of guest 1998 races. The home team won the 1998 Italian Super Touring title against strong opposition from obsolete BMW 320 and front drive Audi A4.

Approximate 1994 BTCC budget: In excess of £4 million. Quoted price to a German team of a single racing factory Alfa Romeo 156 for 1998 was $400 000 (£242 240). This compares with the quarter million routinely quoted for front running BTCC factory racing cars.

BMW

One of the founding teams in 2-litre BTCC, and a company with the strongest British competition and commercial links – BMW traditionally contested touring car racing as a core value amongst its showroom selling points, a policy reviewed and diminished from 1998 onward.

Aside from the consultancy agreement with McLaren, British hardware suppliers AP Automotive (brakes/clutches) and Australia's Holinger (gearboxes) have been consistent BMW suppliers in touring car events.

Technically BMW differed from 90 per cent of its 2-litre rivals in having rear wheel drive and – because this was the layout that held a traditional track racing advantage – the company carried a variety of weight penalties through its racing career with the 3 Series. Despite this handicap the BMW Touring Car record is unmatched for longevity and success (particularly in endurance events), culminating in the 1997 FIA Touring Car World Cup, a title secured in recognition of the number of individual national titles won by the BMW 320i.

Today every BMW-backed 2-litre touring car commitment has been terminated in favour of Grand Prix and international sports car racing (both with British partner: Williams). BMW last raced touring cars as a factory operation in Britain during 1996 having established a UK record that included a hattrick of the inaugural BTCC titles (1991–3).

Since that withdrawal, BMW raced on an arms-length basis with the previous (E36 coded) 3 Series in Germany and Italy, winning the 1998 German title and giving Alfa Romeo a tough time in Italy.

During 1998 it became evident that – for the first time since the sixties – BMW would not commit factory resources to touring car racing. The result was that the E46 current 3 Series has not been developed as a 2-litre factory-backed racer.

Instead BMW Motorsport from their Garching Munich customer department offer a less prestigious showroom category 320i six cylinder development. Via BMW North America an extensive GT-linked USA racing programme witnessed six cylinder (M3) variants gradually overhaul and then dominate production and race track rivals such as Porsche, albeit a Porsche effort not on the same professional level as BMW deploy in the USA, their largest export market.

BMW's commitment to Britain is high profile through its ownership of the Rover Group and the brave 1995–7 establishment of a pioneer BMW Motorsport Ltd in the UK. All this makes it ironic that they have not raced in the BTCC since 1996.

Williams will not assist BMW on 2-litre touring car programmes, although 2-litre engineering had been within BMW Motorsport's 1996–7 deal with McLaren Cars. Then BMW had assigned all works outside the engine bay to McLaren, who concentrated on the technical development of GT and touring car programmes with BMW Motorsport power, resulting in an expensive but significant gain in success, most pronounced in GT Racing (*see* Chapter 7).

Ford

Another Touring car stalwart and traditional track adversary for BMW in Europe, Ford Motor Company (after years in dominating outright results with the turbocharged Sierra Cosworth variants) was slow to become involved in 2-litre Super Touring.

Nearly two seasons had passed before a brave marketing man within Ford of Britain put his signature to a multi-million pound programme that would see the Mondeo redeveloped around a Mazda/Ford-source aluminium V6, one that was engineered by Cosworth to produce class-leading power.

Assembled and developed by Andy Rouse Engineering in Coventry, the Mondeo was initially as big a success as previous competition Ford saloons. Then Ford Motorsport and the tiers of mediocre middle management moneymen, bloated by success, lost a sense of direction.

After two successive world titles and winning pace throughout 1993–4 British seasons, the Mondeo became uncompetitive during 1995. Diversions such as a 4×4 platform for German events coupled with both 4 and 5-door bodywork emphasized an expensive and unsuccessful period of Ford management in 2-litre motorsport, ignoring the fact that chassis technology was overtaking their Cosworth power advantages.

Ford began an apparently eternal search for a new Mondeo racing partner to take them to their accustomed success rates in the UK, but Ford exited the German STW, post-1995. To date this Mondeo partnership search has seen Ford racing Mondeos built in Germany (1996, Wolf Racing and Schubel), redesigned by a division of Reynard during 1996–8 (who also tackled the Chrysler Corporation's Stratus for Super Touring) and run by West Surrey Racing through 1996–8.

In desperation Ford hurled dollars at the Mondeo to elevate its racing profile. Ford of Britain hired former World and Cart/Indycar champion Nigel Mansell to drive the Mondeo three times in 1998 BTCC: once it nearly brought a victory, but for the rest of the time the Mansell-Mondeo alliance was notable for a soundtrack of fracturing body panels and electronic cash transfers assigning ever larger sums to an apparently uncontrollable project.

Although Prodrive has been selected for 1999 BTCC and beyond, Cosworth have remained the engine suppliers throughout. It was Cosworth and Schubel who developed an ingenious driveshaft through the vee of the motor as a solution to the problem of mounting the engine earthwards to compete with its other front drive rivals in lowering the centre of gravity and therefore enhancing cornering speeds.

Prodrive relinquished a two season association with Honda (1997–8) to prepare Ford Mondeo-Cosworths from 1999. Great things are expected of one of the most expensive programmes seen in British touring car racing, with former Champion Alain Menu purchased from Renault-Williams for 1999 to lead their anticipated revival, this first win achieved in August 1999.

Estimated 1998 BTCC budget, including WSR, Cosworth, Reynard consultancy and purchasing fees, plus Mansell's driving fees on top of two contracted drivers: c. £8 million.

GM-Opel & Vauxhall

For British purposes this means Vauxhall branding. For Germany and virtually any market outside Australia (Holden) the company concerned is the German-based Opel arm of General Motors. The product raced in Super Touring has been the Vectra, but Opel and Vauxhall arrived at this commonality by very different routes and retained national autonomy on features such as engine and body preparation into the late nineties.

As you would expect of co-founders (with BMW) of the 2-litre division (then within the main BTCC multi-class system of the late eighties), Vauxhall racing saloons are primarily British products. Only in 1998 did GM buying power prevail in the provision of a common engine supplier for British and German programmes. Spiess were nominated in place of Swindon Racing Engines, a supplier who had served Vauxhall well for more than ten years, including the Vauxhall Cavalier 1995 BTCC title with John Cleland.

The switch to the Vectra in 1996 was difficult after the well-proven Cavalier. For the Cavalier had utilized a known 16v power train inherited from a 2-litre Vauxhall Astra, class winner in the 1989 BTCC. For Vauxhall the racing change was a matter of adapting existing Cavalier drive train technology to the Vectra, swapping to the effective Ray Mallock Racing (RML) preparation company from Dave Cook Racing for the 1996 season.

Vauxhall has not redeveloped into a leading force in BTCC since 1995 and their dissatisfaction showed in a rather clumsy change over from RML to the newly formed Triple 888 concern for the 1997–9 seasons. A subsidiary 1997–99 Vectra a one-make series based on the 2.5 litre V6 as a 210 bhp supporting act to the main TOCA run BTCC, had an equally chequered career.

Initially established and run by Motor Sport Developments (MSD) constructing 24 such trainers for aspirant BTCC drivers and teams, the Vectra SRi failed to provide the ladder of opportunity anticipated. Logic dictated that in 1999 responsibility for maintaining and constructing this Vectra support act with its marketing ramifications for the slower selling V6 lines would also be transferred to Triple 888 as well.

Over in Germany Opel won the 1998 Manufacturers' Championship, a better performance than the British counterpart operation. However, BMW (winners of the STW series for drivers) were not registered and the Opel success was largely scored on strength of numbers versus chief adversaries Peugeot with a two-car équipe. In Germany, a four car squad of Vectras contested the 1998 STW series and the cars were prepared and entered in that country by two principal teams.

High value UK content in German Opels was confined to the Xtrac gearbox. This contrasted with the Nissan Europe approach who in 1998 used RML assembly and preparation for both Britain and Germany.

UK BTCC Vauxhall budget in 1998: £5 million.

Honda

One of the most successful names in recent motor racing history Honda has impeccable British credentials through their Swindon manufacturing plant. UK bases have been used for an assortment of rallying, production racing and Super Touring projects besides the higher profile GP collaborations with McLaren and Williams, in the eighties and early nineties.

For Super Touring events Honda uses the Accord in Europe. Essentially the European racing operation was directed from Reading and Chiswick offices and also utilized initial British preparation bases. A central motorsport co-ordinator established 1996–7 Accord Super Touring programmes in Britain, Belgium and Germany.

The Accord was always competitive enough to win individual races. Most experts think the Honda is technically the best base for the Super Touring formula, having a low and wide stance, one of the most powerful engines, plus all round double wishbone suspension. Yet championship success has been elusive in the major British and German arenas, whilst Belgium has now switched over to a cheaper and less prestigious formula that is contested by non-factory teams (Honda's Integra R wins in this category).

In Britain preparation, development and racing duties have been assigned to a number of top-notch teams: MSD (1995–6); Prodrive (1997–8) and West Surrey Racing (WSR) from 1999 onward; the BTCC Accords constructed for 1999 onward by Fosstech in Yorkshire. The constantly changing search for a perfect partner reflects Honda dissatisfaction with track success attained versus the suitability of its product. Honda engine preparation has remained primarily with one supplier: Neil Brown Racing Engines in Lincolnshire. Brown is backed up by the might of the Honda R&D centre on occasion and secondary programmes that were by Mugen-Honda in Japanese touring car classes.

Honda was distracted with a major commitment to re-enter Grand Prix with a test team facility established at Bracknell, Berks in the winter of 1998–9. The Super Touring programmes of Britain and Germany (where the cars are constructed and developed by JAS Engineering) are set to continue at least until Honda finds the success it deserves.

BTCC Budget 1998: c. £4 million.

Nissan

Nissan Motor Sports Europe (NME), is a Didcot based arm to Nissan's once-sprawling motorsports empire which curtailed its rallying and Le Mans ambitions in favour of the proven success of the BTCC in the closing months of 1998. Even the German parallel touring car race programme (STW) was axed; a reflection of the problems Nissan faced in its market vulnerability through billion dollar losses and accumulated domestic debts, factors that forced through a 37 per cent shareholding alliance with Renault.

The successful BTCC assault in 1998 was a different affair to Nissan's previous (1992–4) attacks on the same series. These were conducted through the non-factory Janspeed concern in Salisbury, Wiltshire. Janspeed prepared every aspect of the Primera eGT including the engine. That approach had patchy success, the Janspeed Nissans finished 1-2 at the 1993 British GP support event, but were often inconsistent elsewhere. Janspeed heir Keith Odor was killed contesting a German STW event in 1995, Nissan having withdrawn from the BTCC at the close of 1994.

The trek back to competitive form came with the NME Didcot-based managerial skills of 1969 BTCC champion Alec Poole and the use of some outstanding sub-contractors. The major factor was hiring Ray Mallock Motorsport Ltd (RML) at leading edge (opened by Lord Hesketh in mid-1995) Wellingborough premises. The Northamptonshire concern were commissioned to design, fabricate, assemble and enter the reworked Primeras from the 1996 BTCC onward, and they were supported in a cost-sharing measure by the German-based (Keke) Rosberg team. Rosberg fielded Primeras (with much less success) in the STW German series, 1997-8, before central Japanese management stopped STW funds.

RML proved a sound BTCC preparation move as they had excellent, resources and motorsport skills in depth. RML employees and management had contested an unusual variety of motorsports, emphasized by the parallel programmes with GM-Vauxhall/Opel in the creation and assembly of GM rally cars in a separate factory (on the same Northants site) to that of Nissan. RML had already demonstrated the capability to take a basically competitive car like the Vauxhall Cavalier and turn it into a BTCC champion's mount in 1995.

Other key sub contractors included Engine Developments Ltd (EDL) at Rugby, best known for their work on the Yamaha GP unit and the long-term engineering skills of founder John Judd. During a winning 1998 season Nissan also used motors from IES International Engine Services Ltd in Witham, Essex, headed by former Ford and Cosworth engineer Graham Dale-Jones.

These engine transplants seemed to spice up the overall race pace. A tactic occasionally echoed in earlier times when the Japanese factories would send development engines to UK competitors. In general, as with Japanese brands in rallying, the British seemed able to supply the most competitive and durable power units when faced with a tight set of regulations.

The 1998–99 BTCC seasons, netted Nissan two Manufacturers' titles, one that they promoted earnestly through national press advertising and motor show exhibits with a vigour that put previous BTCC title-winners to shame.

BTCC Budget 1998: under £4 million, including significant contributions from Vodaphone to top up major expenditure from Nissan UK.

Peugeot

Infamous in Britain for not winning a BTCC race during their 1992–8 participation period, the only participating manufacturer not to score a solitary win, Peugeot meant more in Germany. From 1996–8 the factory-fresh French team were front three runners in Germany, versus Audi, BMW and GM-Opel. The invading Peugeot 406 driven by Laurent Aiello (at Nissan in Britain by 1999) beat all the powerful German home teams in 2-litre STW to become outright German Champions of 1997.

Why the form difference in two ostensibly identical racing 2-litre Peugeots?

Away from the corporate Lion emblems, the 406s for Britain and Germany differed fundamentally and had important lessons for the UK Touring Car business. It confirmed we have no divine right to win and that indomitable spirit is just one ingredient in a winning team: one that will not, on its own, beat cash and resources.

Coventry-based Peugeot Sport exhibited a UK history for pulling off David and Goliath wins in rallying and racing, using a fraction of rival budgets and a maximum of in-house resources. The team's earlier programme with the previous 405 model was largely conducted on this basis, using consultancy help from Richard Longman (another former BTCC champion driver) at Christchurch in Bournemouth.

Peugeot Sport UK had been starved of funds to the point at which they were the only ones rebuilding engines and other major components at test track sessions. The speedier and more expensive BTCC norm had become to replace complete engines or other important hardware with entire assemblies, a Grand Prix lesson from the late sixties onward to lower formulae.

Peugeot Sport in the UK tried to operate on a million pound budget when the top BTCC rival teams had two to three times that amount. It was 1996 and the advent of the 406 before Peugeot in Britain had a chance to enjoy a trebled budget and sub-contracted car design, creation and preparation services. These came from MSD (Motor Sport Developments) at Milton Keynes who held on to the business of creating and fielding the £200 000 plus racing 406s from 1997–8, when Peugeot withdrew (as they did from the far more successful German programme) from the BTCC.

Peugeot came close to winning pace, indeed unlucky not to win on several occasions, but motor racing is as unforgiving as any other professional sport. Without wins, any increased funding (c. £3 million) behind the British programme was doomed. Aside from tight funding, what were the technical differences between the British and French approach to the same 2-litre task?

The British edition of 406 drew very little from the French winning formula and this seemed attributable to the infamous engineering philosophy of 'Not Invented Here'. The British chassis featured engineering alternatives to the French methods, plus the fact that the British team could not afford to do things the parent factory way, especially being unable to secure a supply of the fabulous Pipo sub-contracted motors. These had put Peugeot Sport France on a par with anything the German factories could bring to their 1996–8 battles, developing from a 300 bhp unit in 1996 to one of 320 bhp in 1998. That was an expensive and laborious 20bhp bonus to be achieved under the same tightly regulated Super Touring formula.

Both sides did agree on some major British suppliers. Xtrac supplied a six speed sequential gearbox on both sides of the channel, whilst Alcon in Coventry were listed suppliers to the French (at least for rear disc brakes) and AP Racing supplied both front and rear disc brakes for the UK Peugeot 406. The British used their own ideas in body construction and suspension via the input of Mike Pilbeam Racing Designs at Bourne in Lincolnshire. Pilbeam are known for hillclimb championship single seaters, but a loyal collaboration period with MSD on other projects, including Honda and Vauxhall products, ensured their presence at Peugeot's UK 406 gestation.

The Anglo-French Peugeot attitude contrasted with the Renault UK-funded assault on the BTCC, which was to yield manufacturer, team and driver titles. The Renault-Williams touring cars showed what could be done with maximum co-operation on both sides of the channel, given superior funding. Yet the most important element in that Anglo-French Renault racing success was the co-operation the Williams name unlocked. A lesson for us all in the UK; one reinforced by the contrasting success of the Renault UK-Williams alliance to that of Peugeot Sport UK.

BTCC budget 1998: £3.5 million.

Renault

Originally represented by an Anglo-French technical consortium that fielded the unsuitable R19 (albeit a wet weather winner on outstanding Michelin tyres) and an earlier rendition of the Laguna, Renault changed tack dramatically.

Renault UK funded a unique approach to the fabled Williams Grand Prix team. Williams set up a separate touring car team in November 1994, which remained huddled in the shadow of Didcot's dominant cooling towers. The Williams GP team relocated to Grove in the same county during 1995.

Renault UK and WTCE did not enjoy totally unfussed progress to championship excellence in 1997. In the 1996-Williams-Renault Laguna era, they rode through a terribly tricky diplomatic period when it was obvious that the Laguna could win in Britain regularly with Alain Menu driving, just so long as the engine did not explode, which happened on too many occasions.

That dirty linen was obvious for the Media to see, but Williams and their competitive personnel managed to keep a diplomatic decency over frequent engine failures: drivers controlled their tempers and the on-record comment. During the 1996–7 winter the relationship was rebuilt and Sodemo supplied reliable, powerful 2-litre units that led the other Renault Williams alliance into a clean sweep of the 1997 BTCC titles. A lesson in how to keep a winning multinational team together that was never learned over at Peugeot.

Titled Williams Touring Car Engineering (WTCE) the team scored on immediate and consistent 1995–7 front running pace. French-speaking Swiss driver Alain Menu based himself in Oxfordshire and was second in the series 1995–6, won outright in 1997. The Williams Renault Dealer Racing team (employing 65 by 1998) scooped Manufacturer Awards for Renault in 1996–7 and maintained a competitive, rather than dominant, pace through 1998 winning no major award. A reflection of that 1998 form was the defection of star driver Menu to Ford and Prodrive for 1999.

Major UK suppliers abounded in the Super Touring Laguna, which raced only in Britain from 1995–9, not France or Germany as might have been expected. There was an exceptional trip to Australia's Bathurst extravaganza in 1997. The assembly and unique WTCE design and creation of the complete Lagunas is such a British affair that it is easier to spot the obvious exceptions such as the Sodemo engines, Eibach suspension springs or Italian OZ wheels and Michelin tyres.

Even in citing Magneti Marelli cockpit instrumentation as an overseas supplier you are on dangerous ground, because Williams GP evolved this digital system originally and WTCE adapted its multiple readout functions to suit the Laguna. Similarly, the six sequential gears are made by Hewland (a 1998 exception to the Xtrac monopoly) but their design, casing and sequential gearshift are all engineered by WTCE. More straightforward are the AP Racing components, including the popular 6-piston callipers, massive 378 mm front discs, smaller 4-piston rear discs and the 5.5 inch carbon fibre clutch. WTCE was closed at the end of the 1999 season, Williams and more recent partners BMW having alternative ambitions.

BTCC Budget 1998: Over £6 million in direct funding but significant backing from Nescafé Blend 37 marked the first major non-automotive sponsor in BTCC and allowed one of the most generous racing budgets to be found during 1998–9.

TWR-Volvo

Originally signed to a three year contract from the 1994 BTCC season onward, TWR (Tom Walkinshaw Racing) have represented Volvo Car Corporation of Sweden with flair over an extended 1994-9 period, their relationship in BTCC terminated by Ford, post takeover.

TWR and Volvo started with the novelty of racing an 850 estate (yes, a yellow Labrador and Wellingtons were occasionally faked to attract yet more publicity) which shrewdly distracted attention from the steep learning curve both parties pursued in putting the boxy and spacious 850 (now V70) onto the pace of their BTCC rivals. The estate gimmick was raced just in 1994, but that was not the only individual technicality. Across the engine bay beat the only five-cylinder motor in international motor racing. Initially Volvo applied more manufacturing skills than was usual in this kind of manufacturer/sub-contractor relationship, constructing some test bodies and creating a base line for race engine modification.

From 1995 onward TWR-Volvo became much more effective challengers. They fielded the 850 saloon variant in 1995–6 and it really should have won the BTCC title in just its second season, for Rickard Rydell exhibited such blistering practice lap speeds that he claimed pole position a record 13 times, but only converted those to victory on six occasions. That left Rydell and TWR-Volvo third in the series, a result they repeated in the last season of racing the 850. For 1996 was the season the Germans came to BTCC and finished first (Audi/Frank Biela) and second (BMW/Jo Winkelhock) neither German conforming to the front drive norm that Volvo deployed

For 1997 TWR-Volvo and their freshly converted (ex-Post Office) base at Leafield Oxfordshire (also home to the Arrows Grand Prix team) had a new Volvo to field, the S40. The smallest offering of the Volvo range was equipped with the 850's five-cylinder running gear and much was expected in its 1997 début season. Unfortunately, during the off-season key engineering talent John Gentry (designer) and Dave Kelly (chief race engineer) were poached for the fledgling Triple 888 GM-Vauxhall camp and this reduced the effectiveness of the TWR team for a short period.

The TWR-Volvo S40 performed just slivers below expectations for loyal and talented star driver Rickard Rydell. Since winning margins are so tightly packed in the BTCC, these key personnel departures made some difference to the TWR-Volvo team's early 1997 performance. The predicted acquisition of the BTCC title (which TWR promised to the Gothenberg manufacturer within three years of the programme's start) was not delivered in that fourth year.

A fifth season in the UK made the championship difference. In 1998 the S40 and Rydell alliance raced to their BTCC title win. However, it was far from the quickest car on every occasion, and Nissan finished with the commercially useful Manufacturers' BTCC title to promote after the strongest of years with their Primera.

Factory-funded Volvos resisted the rumoured expansion into the counterpart German series, but the older TWR-Volvo designs were shipped to Australia and Sweden at the close of recent racing seasons, where they have performed competitively against Audis and BMWs since 1996.

As this is another British-based effort from creation to racing entries, UK content is higher than you might expect from the nameplate. The motor is not further sub-contracted to an outside specialist but appears to be a co-operative effort between TWR's strong resources at Kidlington (where more than 30 are employed purely on engine engineering under the leadership of the ex-Cosworth guru, Geoff Goddard) and Volvo's inevitably larger facilities. The engine management system is British from Zytek at Derby and the high value six-speed gearbox and transaxle is sourced at the almost inevitable Xtrac.

However S40 race brakes are by Brembo in Italy, the dampers were by Ohlins of Sweden for many seasons (a Japanese substitute was engineered in 1998), whilst the wheels came from BBS in Germany and the tyres (as was almost universal in 1997 BTCC) came from Michelin. Thus we have no cause for British complacency here and it was interesting to see that Ford ownership ceased British racing activities for 'Safety First' Volvo post 1999.

BTCC Budget 1998: Over £6 million.

Conclusion

The path from the support event to a major source of wealth, revenue and marketing advantage for the largest industry in the world is one which has parallels in the rise of the power and popularity of Formula One. The development of television coverage, the use of effective marketing expertise and the money derived from mass manufacturers have been vital in the evolution of this sport/business. BTCC in future will be less stable in 2000 with 1999-announced withdrawals from Renault and Volvo reducing manufacturer support to four likely companies: Ford, Honda, GM-Vauxhall and (possibly)Nissan.

The Thoroughbreds: Formula Single Seaters

Introduction

DEDICATED racing cars are the British export forte; some single seaters are made in numbers that exceed those of specialist showroom vehicles. We trace the evolution of a vigorous business, one that is fuelled by ambition at every level.

By definition, this is a chapter that deals with multiple class racing, that introduces us to categories from single seat trainers such as Formula Ford to half million dollar American formula cars for league division 1, which often feature British power-trains (engine and transmissions) as well. All are purpose-built racing cars operating within tightly drawn regulations and customers who demand winning values at equally competitive cost. We have not listed every category in which the British supply men and materials but have highlighted those of the greatest commercial impact.

Britain's majority presence across such a wide spectrum is remarkable, but not unchallenged. Only Italy, France, Japan and America produce such pedigree formula racers in remotely competitive opposition. However, the kind of export impact that Dallara of Italy has in Worldwide Formula 3, demonstrates that Britain does not always rule the tarmac. We can expect both Swift in the USA and Mygale in France to give the United Kingdom industry frequent reminders of this fact at the highest and lowest levels.

The Formula in Brief

International Single Seat Formula cars

- **CART-organized Champ Cars, USA** is the premier league of American single seat racing which is presently backed and named after the Fedex

Corporation and is a leading market for many UK concerns. The formula is currently predominantly British Reynard chassis and Xtrac transmissions, plus sub-contract composite and metal fabrication activity from Galmer Engineering, major engine engineering from Cosworth and Ilmor, with PI Research at Cambridge adding their electronics expertise to many front runners and Lola staging a 1999 comeback to form.

- **Indy Racing League, USA** is a comparatively new category that was set up on old enmities created back in USAC days. This now runs in opposition to the CART/Champ Cars Championship and gains strength through holding the blue riband event in American racing, the Indy 500. British supplier interest is strong through consultancy on engines and chassis engineering supplied by TWR, G-Force and Galmer.
- **Formula 3000, European Grand Prix-supporting category** is currently over-subscribed with 21 teams and 42 drivers chasing 26 grid places at the opening 1999 round. The regulations are set to impose a limit of 30 cars qualifying in Year 2000. Britain is the principal hardware (power train, chassis and tyres) supplier to the category, with a 1999 sales potential of £11.3 million.
- **Formula 3, European nursery formula** is traditionally regarded as the embryo professional driver's route to the top but this role has now been weakened by equally powerful one-make formulae and dwarfed by the success of F3000 as the apprenticeship to Formula One. Dominated by Italian Dallara concern after many years of British mastery and strongest at National Championship levels in Britain and Germany, with prestige events at Monaco and Macau still attracting large and competitive grids.

National or One-Make Formula:

- **Indy Lights, USA** is the major feeder formula to bigger things in the USA since 1986 and open to bids from chassis and engine manufacturers for Year 2001 on fixed formula contracts. Presently supplied by Lola (UK) and GM (USA). Series owned by CART since 1998.
- **Barber-Dodge, USA** is a starter formula which pioneered the leasing principle in single seat racing chassis.
- **Formula Ford** is a worldwide category with three primary engine sizes, FF2000 2-litre formula with major market in the USA. FF1600 the long running 1.6 litre push-rod entry level is truly global; whilst 1.8 litre Formula Ford Zetec is best supported in Britain. Most chassis supplies originate in Britain, but the French constructor Mygale were 1998 UK Champions.
- **Formula Vauxhall** was a high profile UK based 1.6 litre supporting act

to the British Touring Car Championship. Notable for frenetic racing, the youth of drivers and sole category suppliers Van Diemen, Vauxhall, Hewland gearboxes and Avon tyres.

- **Formula Renault** is a primarily Anglo-French formula with an additional German national title in 1999. High profile expenditure within the TOCA touring car package at all UK events. Most chassis are French or Italian made by Mygale or Tatuus. A one make formula from Year 2000 aimed at cost cutting, with the contract expected to go to Tatuus in Italy.
- **Formula Palmer Audi, UK** has turbo-charged Audi engines from a Liechtenstein specialist with UK modifications, within in UK-supplied Van Diemen chassis. British National category which is set to go European in Year 2000 with possible GP support role thereafter.

The Categories

CART/Champ Cars are popular, but the primary US motorsport attractions in terms of TV and spectators, remain a domestic series based on Detroit V8 lore; NASCAR for stock car racing tracks, ovals or road race courses, versus straight line drag racing over the traditional quarter mile. British companies have been involved in component supply to such categories, but major British exports derive from comparatively unpopular single seater categories, where the UK has a successful pedigree of more than 35 years.

Rewind to the early sixties and uncover a sport sanctioned and operated by the feudal methods of USAC (United States Auto Club). Although US racing had opened its doors to outsiders in the 1920s and 1930s it remained isolated. 'Poppa' Moss, Stirling's father, finished eleventh in the 1925 Indy 500 and both Auto Union and Mercedes sent winning works teams to the United States in the 1930s. However, by the sixties single seat racing in the USA racing was set in a rigid and introverted, format.

There was a front engine rear drive upright single seater norm contested primarily by American drivers, Offenhauser 4-cylinder engines and crude single seater chassis. A time warp had occurred and outsiders were unwelcome. Given that US prize money and sponsorship exceeded the rewards of European constructors (who would not benefit from widespread sponsorship for another decade), a successful invasion of the American premier league could be financially worthwhile. British based teams exported the mid-engined, lightweight, single-seater technology that had recently overturned the European establishment, with considerable benefits to the beleaguered UK balance of payments for the remainder of the century.

The pioneers again included Australia's Jack Brabham and the Surrey-based

Cooper Car Company, but their initial efforts were less successful than Lotus. Colin Chapman and his East Anglian équipe had the benefit of the unmatched driving talent of Jim Clark and growing commercial links with Ford Motor Company, who wanted to overwhelm the US Offenhauser establishment as part of the Ford Global Total Performance programme.

Aptly, British racing's breakthrough into the USA accompanied other glamorous British export earners as the Beatles pop music era was in full swing. The United Kingdom pop music industry was also to bestow longer-term benefits to the UK economy. In August 1963 Jim Clark scored the first British USAC win recorded in post-war competition, Clark piloting a Lotus Ford at Milwaukee, deep in heartland America. The USA authorities were not delighted and there were many rearguard actions to be fought before the Indianapolis 500, jewel in the USAC crown, was won by the Clark/Lotus-Ford alliance in May 1965. American home teams climbed aboard the fragile new British bandwagon to such effect that half (nine of eighteen) USAC races were won with British sourced chassis (either Lotus or Brabham) in 1965.

The immediate commercial beneficiary was Brabham as Lotus concentrated on its factory programme with Ford. Lotus had always sold competition cars to customers, initially through Lotus Components and then Lotus Racing. However, in 1971 major league Indycars were not part of the Lotus sales scheme, but they did sell American V8-propelled Formula 5000 single seaters amongst the six alternative (including Formula 3 and Formula Ford 1600) Lotus Racing products. Group Lotus regarded Lotus Racing as a financial loser. After a spectacular public disagreement with Lotus founder Colin Chapman, Lotus Racing Managing Director Michael Warner resigned and the division closed in 1971. Even so Lotus Racing made more than 72 cars in that terminal season, including 35 low cost Formula Fords. Subsequently, another Lotus customer legend, the two-seater Lotus Seven, was sold off and the manufacturing rights transferred to Caterham Cars in 1973. Caterham still run a very profitable business today based on Lotus technical principles but with many detail developments, some 25 years later.

The most significant and enduring British racing car exporter to the USA entered the results lists in May 1966. Graham Hill won the Indianapolis 500 in a Lola. It was this Huntingdon based company which links the 1960s to the 1990s, despite some lurid financial intermissions occasioned by an aborted Grand Prix assault.

In 1978 a new American organizational and promotional body called CART (Championship Auto Racing Teams Inc.) was founded by team owners and entrepreneurs Roger Penske and Pat Patrick. The CART organization broke away from the 21-man USAC board of control and ran its own racing series from March 1979 onward. This schism was vital to British interests, because the entrenched attitudes of the USAC establishment were removed and exports gradually grew in a more prosperous series based on the needs of sponsors, spectators and the media, particularly television.

The CART series put the older series in the shade, but old enmities burned bright as the USA single seat championships moved through a number of names including the popular nickname, Indycar. Today Indycar, as the American's premier league single seat racing series, acknowledges its roots in the 1999 title Fedex Championship Series. The title Indycar is now inaccurate as the 1996 American motor car racing revolution saw the Indianapolis circuit owner Tony George and the USAC authorities on the same side of the fence with their Independent Racing League (IRL). This series was generally a poor relation to the Champ cars, but with the emotional pull of the annual Indy 500 event within its otherwise undistinguished calendar and an increasing number of former Champ/CART stars participating in IRL races, it survived.

IRL cars do not represent the kind of dollar earnings found in CART/Champ cars for British enterprise. The major IRL beneficiary is G-Force technologies in West Sussex with chassis and metal manufacturing capabilities in the UK, representation in the USA and Japan. Sharing the contract with Dallara of Italy, G-Force has held the contract for making a control formula composite chassis for IRL use three seasons since 1996. Similarly in Japan G-Force shared chassis supplier roles with Reynard and Lola for Japan's pre-1999 national F3000 series (see Formula 3000). Just to add to the confusion there is another UK company called G-force operating from Aylesbury, but this exists primarily to race and supply hardware for Porsches and the G refers to owner John Greasley.

Engineering and Transmission Engineering

Financially, power-train engineering is more important to Britain than the higher profile chassis-making activities of concerns such as Reynard or Lola. Reynard do a magnificent job in controlling a major category against the best opposition in the world, but the revenue to be derived from engines and transmission hardware, whenever Britain can gain a share of the action, is financially impressive. For example Reynard had a 1998 turnover of £33 million, whereas the engines and transmission specialists, agglomerating Ilmor, Cosworth, Xtrac and Hewland, revealed a substantial combined turnover of £151 million in 1998. Not all of that derives from CART in the USA as all these organizations have significant presence in other Formula, but CART is a key component in the finances of that UK quartet. Those four hardware suppliers also account for 1201 vital highly skilled jobs and a small number of part time or short term-contract workers, versus 230 at Reynard who utilize up to 23 part-time or contract workers.

One of the most important companies in the industry in terms of turnover and global presence is the Tom Walkinshaw Racing Group; TWR Group. They employed 1314 in 1997 and had an independently audited turnover of £155 million. By 1999 internal reports indicated more than 2400 employed on TWR projects around the world and a total Group turnover of £370 million, but these had not been ratified. What we do know is that TWR have found alliances with major manufacturers from Mazda and Jaguar yesterday to GM in Australia under the Holden brand and Volvo in Sweden, alliances that boost TWR employment and turnover figures far beyond any other company that has a motor racing core. In 1999 TWR reckoned that only '10-15 per cent' of their income derived from motorsports. TWR do not supply American CART teams, although they do list IRL amongst six categories with TWR development involvement, through race development of the engines. Such winning IRL racing engines are of American GM origins not European and are branded Aurora (Oldsmobile), which meant that TWR could claim credit for their role in powering the winner of the 1996 Indy 500.

Cosworth for Ford in Formula One and CART, plus the performances of Ilmor Engineering in dominating 1998 Grand Prix with McLaren West Mercedes and their competitive ability in the Fedex CART events (also as Mercedes), shows the British can compete in racing engines engineering, given sufficient budget. Sadly, the complete lack of British presence in mass manufacturing automobile company ownership reduces UK opportunities to demonstrate that Britain excels at the ultimate level of motor engineering.

CART has utilized British power sources, usually with attendant UK transmission systems for many years, since Cosworth redeveloped their Grand Prix DFV V8 for the CART championship, at first as a turbo-charged conversion and secondly as a unique DFX family of engines to meet American regulations and conditions. This 2.85 litre lightweight thoroughbred soon established its worth, winning three times in 1976 for the Parnelli team and driver Al Unser. Cosworth Engineering's racing in America was a commercial venture and the same applied to associated Hewland transmissions. Their continued success led to the subsequent future profitable participation of British power-train engineering in CART events. This continues in the nineties not only through Cosworth's latest turbo-charged V8s, but also the turbo-charged Mercedes-Ilmor eight cylinder and transmission systems from Xtrac.

Ilmor, founded in 1984 by former Cosworth employees Mario Illien and Paul Morgan was, almost, immediately successful. Not just in powering the winning car in the American series for five sequential years from 1989–93, but also in making the right alliances with major manufacturers to badge their engines and increase income from Blue Chip sources. The Chevrolet division of General Motors were Ilmor's first such customers and powered a series of winning Dorset-built Penske chassis.

In November 1993 Mercedes took a 25 per cent stake in Ilmor and the right to rebadge different racing engines such as a V10 for Formula One and the turbo-charged V8 for CART Champ Car racing, leading to championship success on both sides of the Atlantic. West McLaren Mercedes dominated the 1998 World Formula 1 series with an Ilmor unit producing over 750 bhp from 3 litres. In the USA Ilmor supplied four teams (eight cars) with their Mercedes badged power plant winning nine races, breaking an Ilmor winning drought of 1995–8. In 1999 Ilmor supplied engines for seven leading cars, Penske having cut back to a single entry that season, and won the opening event of the year. Thus ensuring that British engines engineering remained on the pace despite significant Honda and Toyota opposition.

British Chassis Suppliers

Fortune favoured British commercial racing car manufacturing interests within what became CART/ Champ Cars. Lola and March dominated the eighties but McLaren were earlier and equally effective operators on the American scene. Famous through domination of the Can Am Sports racing series, McLaren starting winning USAC races with American Drake-Offenhauser power in 1972; they continued as major British suppliers and exporters of chassis until 1979.

McLaren in 1999 is devoted to Formula One as a manufacturing and employment activity and does not supply single seat racing cars to outside teams or individuals. As at October 1997 McLaren International Ltd employed 212 personnel and had a turnover of £58.1 million. This makes an interesting comparison with those now making their primary living from selling racing cars and their power-trains, or the TWR Group's progression into major collaborations with volume manufacturers through design and technical consultancy and co-production.

Whilst Roger Penske established a British operation at Poole Dorset to construct his winning cars, this was a self-centred team operation rather than a commercial venture. It was important on a prestige basis that a co-founder of the CART organization finally decided 'British is Best' for his needs, but the major source of commercially supplied chassis came from Lola and March. The latter won their first CART event in late 1981 and the March team contested the series until their demise in the nineties.

On the chassis engineering side Lola and March were the biggest players in the eighties, indeed by 1984 no other chassis brand was capable of winning in the 16 race CART season. March continued to progress and by their 1986 American zenith the Bicester marque won all but three of a total of 17 CART races. Before March Engineering's unfortunate closure in 1990 after twenty one years of business, the company had established not just a solid US record of success but had also produced hundreds of formula racing cars in Formula 3, 2 and Grand Prix Formula One. All of these chassis were sold on a commercial basis, which was a first for a British company.

In America March engineered some profitable, but competitively unsuccessful CART race engineering deals with engine supplies and backing from Alfa Romeo and Porsche. The failure of Porsche's CART campaign was particularly high profile, as this was a company associated with competition success. Therefore the recriminations that followed their failure to win did the March reputation as much harm as earlier customers, who were not satisfied with the quality of March chassis manufacture.

Ironically, a British company that had never manufactured an Indy or Champ car that was also based in Bicester, bid for the remains of March Engineering, which by then owned the formerly successful Formula 3 commercial manufacturers, Ralt. That company was Reynard and they continued to fly the British flag in American racing, entering Champ Cars in 1994 with their traditional winning debut. This was an astonishing achievement, for Lola were represented by the cream of winning drivers and had 20 chassis at the opening 1994 round at Australia's Surfers Paradise, whereas Reynard had six chassis. America's Michael Andretti scored the début win for the Chip Ganassi team who had backed Adrian Reynard when others would not. Reynard appeared in the top positions regularly, whether powered by Cosworth or Ilmor V8s.

However, in that first season Reynard won three times, Lola just once and the purpose-built factory Penske slammed them both with a crushing 12 Champ Car victories. An answer to Penske would be found and for both Penske and Lola it would mean trouble. Reynard with Gilles Villeneuve and a Ford-Cosworth V8 Xtrac power-train set the 1995 season pace in Reynard's second season.

For French Canadian Jacques Villeneuve the 1995 American Championship and Indianapolis 500 win were CV credentials to 1996 employment at Williams Grand Prix. For Reynard they were the keys to becoming the establishment suppliers to the Fedex Champ Car series. As we stated earlier, Reynard turned this 1995 title and subsequent US Championship wins of 1996–8, to commercial gold. During 1997 Reynard produced and sold 38 Champ Cars, whilst in the 1998 season they sold 43. Interviewed by the authors in 1999, Reynard director Rick Gorne spoke of a deliberate easing in numbers supplied to the American market by 'weeding out some of the less competitive teams'. A difficult decision since these rolling chassis (the complete car minus an engine) sell for around

$550 000 each including the vital back up spares package ($486 000 without). America, including the supply of $50 000 Indy Lights cars (*see* Indy Lights, below) *accounts for more than half Reynard's £33 million turnover*.

At the 1998 peak Reynard and their North American associates had supplied 22 of 28 chassis seen regularly in the premier league. British engine builders Cosworth and Ilmor accounted for 19 of those 28 engines, usually with a British sourced Xtrac transmission.

In 1999 the Japanese power-train opposition had hardened with Honda supplying engines for eight chassis (including the competitive Scot Dario Franchitti's Reynard) and Toyota supported four entries. As has been the case in 95 percent of the categories they have contested since entering motor racing in the sixties, it was Honda who offered the most clearly competitive engine. Indeed in 1997 it looked as though Honda were set on the kind of domination they exhibited in Formula One with Williams and McLaren, for they propelled the first three drivers home in that season's CART Championship chase.

Our interview, at the beginning of 1999 preceded the first CART race of that season and another win for Reynard with an Ilmor Mercedes power pack. Although Reynard expected fewer new chassis to be sold in the USA in 1999, the 28 car grid was dominated by the marque, with no less than 22 born in Bicester. They were competing against two American-made Swifts and one example of the Lola and Penske marks, the latter a shadow of its former three car grandeur in the earlier nineties; Penske scored its last championship title win in 1994. As the season developed four Swifts were seen and were making their presence felt in the top ten, so the British marque should not be complacent as Swift won on their 1997 début in the CART/Champ Cars category. A measure of British (read Reynard of late) domination in the most prestigious American single seater category was that the Californian Swift concern, not the same company that manufacture effective Formula Ford in the UK but with shared origins, had *scored the first victory for an American chassis in 14 years!*

However, there are warning signs that America's premier league will not continue to pay the price of dominant British technology on a yearly basis. Major Champ Car team owner Derrick Walker said in April 1999 'the situation has changed a bit in the last few years, in that today's chassis are evolutionary rather than revolutionary. That means there is less need to go out and buy brand new cars at the beginning of every season, especially for new teams'. 'We're probably the only racing series in the world which literally throws away £25 million worth of chassis at the end of each season. The cars just go straight in the dustbin. That's ridiculous.' concluded the owner of Walker. There is now provisional agreement amongst the leading teams to freeze chassis design in Year 2000.

Worldwide Single Seater Formula with UK Connections

Formula 3000

The 1985 replacement formula for FIA Formula 2 single seaters, aimed at providing the last stop en route to a Formula One career, Formula 3000 withstood many years of economic pressure to lower costs. Now it is the senior single seater category to use a mandatory engine, chassis and tyre choice. However, there were discussions in 1999 aimed at Formula One imposing a V10 compulsory engine layout in Grand Prix. Thus reflecting the reality that every engine in the current 3 litre category is of this layout and has been since Ferrari dropped its V12 in 1996 and Ford the customer Cosworth V8.

F3000 moved to all British hardware in 1996 and the change has contained costs bringing a tough but fair playing field for ambitious drivers and teams. They will budget an initial £270 000 per car in UK hardware before any track time has been logged and around £750 000 to run a typical two car team over a season.

There were 42 F3000 cars, engine and tyre sets trying to race in 1999. That meant a potential market of £11.34 million for Lola, Zytek, Hewland and Avon tyres to share at the season start, although not every team would have brand new equipment each season.

Despite the fact that the East Anglian team of David Sears (Super Nova) had won the F3000 title three times in the four years prior to the 1999 season, British drivers were notable for their absence. There were just four UK drivers on the 1999 grid and one of those had won his drive through becoming 1998 Formula Palmer Audi Champion. None were with the crack Sears outfit which was possibly a reflection of the rather high admission price. It is a fact that with honourable and rare exceptions, major British companies are notoriously averse to backing their home teams and talents in motorsports.

F3000 survived many crisis seasons until the mid-nineties switch to a mandatory chassis and engine (Lola and Zytek) from Britain and a control formula tyre from Avon slashed costs. Until 1998 there was also a national F3000 Championship in Japan, chiefly disputed by Reynard and Lola. This category was replaced by Formula Nippon, which we describe in our postscript.

Britain was a successful supplier in the preceding Formula 2 alliances between March chassis and BMW power; alternatively Ralt and Honda provided many titles. Thus a trio of British chassis manufacturers originally dominated F3000 in the eighties, Lola, Ralt and March. As their fortunes waxed and waned, a fourth UK contender entered with its customary debut winning impact; Reynard took pole again.

Sport or business? Both, as we can see from the advertising at the 1997 British Grand Prix at Silverstone. Behind this global attraction, beats the commercial heart to the British motorsport industry.

Familiar sight in the late 1990s, with Michael Schumacher atop the 1997 British Grand Prix podium, but what was not quite so obvious was that the RAC paid to title sponsor the GP they created following the commercial take-over of their motoring services division.

Seen on a 1999 historic display at the British industry's most important annual (Autosport) show. The Gold Leaf livery and Ford-backed Cosworth V8 engine revolutionised British commercial and competitive interests in Grand Prix from 1967 onwards.

The 1996 Ford and Cosworth alliance behind the 3-litre Zetec-R GP motor was not immediately successful in the manner of the DFV, its first season served with the Swiss Sauber équipe. For 1997–9 the V10 was front line equipment for the Stewart SF-Fords and developed into a lightweight, compact, front runner. By September 1999 it had equalled the 800 bhp of the opposition and won a Grand Prix for the final Stewart GP team season.

Reynard Indycar seen in 1999 Bicester production. The Oxfordshire company continued to dominate American Fedex CART Championship races, but Lola came back from isolated entries to competitive form so that even Roger Penske was forced to buy British rather than run a single Dorset-built Penske chassis. The re-financed American Swift company have provided winners in CART category and should ensure the UK suppliers do not become complacent.

The 1999 Stewart SF – Ford Zetec R GP car undergoes rig testing at the Milton Keynes headquarters facility. Every aspect – down to the dummy driver – is simulated to save restricted – and expensive – track testing time. This livery will change to Jaguar for the 2000 season as the team will from then on be known as the Jaguar Formula One team.

Resources of technology at Reynard.

Computer test centre and rig at Stewart Grand Prix.

The Ford Focus was rapidly developed into a World Rally Championship contender by a small sub-contract team based at the GM-owned Millbrook Proving Ground in Bedfordshire.

Centre of attention. Ford Focus WRC challenger is unveiled in November 1998 at Ford R&D headquarters for Britain in Dunton, Essex. The purpose-built Ford used a turbocharged Mountune Zetec engine from local suppliers at Maldon and won the toughest WRC event in the calendar (Africa's Safari) in its 1999 debut season.

The 1995–9 association between TWR and Volvo Car Corporation in the British Touring Car Championship typified by Kelvin Burt in the 1996 Volvo 850. The link lasted until Ford bought Volvo. Lead TWR-Volvo driver and 1998 BTCC Champion Rickard Rydell was transferred to the Ford Mondeo SuperTeam for year 2000.

Formula Ford accounts for the biggest production runs in Britain. The market leader is East Anglia's Van Diemen – now owned by an American group – but French Mygales and smaller scale British opposition offer winning competition.

Formula Palmer stand, 1999 Racing Car Show.

Reynard's past and the foundation of the company.

Historic and current engine building room belonging to Cosworth at St James Mill Road, Northampton. Currently it is used to assemble the winning Ford-branded Cosworth XD turbocharged engines for American CART Championship racing, although the company also have a rebuild facility in Torrance, California.

Audi Le Mans action with the R&D type that secured third and fourth on a reliable debut. The company invested in British-based construction resources in East Anglia and ran an unsuccessful R8C coupé through Audi Sport UK. Audi also invested in 1930s competition Auto Unions to celebrate their heritage, created/restored in association with Crosthwaite & Gardiner in Sussex.

By the time of Reynard's 1988 debut the balance of power was already shifting in UK Formula car manufacture. Because Reynard had effectively challenged Ralt's traditional Formula 3 dominance, that company's annual output had fallen from 80 to 35 Formula 3 cars per annum. Ralt desperately needed a commercial result in F3000. The decision by two drivers to withdraw their promised £400 000 sponsorship funds just prior to the start of the 1988 season, so weakened Ralt that it was not long before it was absorbed by March.

Ralt had a considerable reputation for quality that March lacked and Ralt's outstanding commercial design operated in Formula 3 where March was no longer effective. However March, having gone public at just under £15 million on the UK stock market in 1986 became involved in two less successful transatlantic projects for two manufacturers, namely Fiat owned Alfa Romeo and Porsche. These high profile failures (particularly Porsche) damaged March's most profitable sales market, that for American Champ cars.

By 1989 March Plc, run by professional managers rather than professional racers, was on its knees, unable to pay the wages bill. Reynard's Formula 3000 success, only Lola now commercially rivalled its profitable record in the category, made it quite feasible that the 1976 established Reynard would buy the 1969 founded former Grand Prix regulars March, and get Ralt into the bargain.

Reynard was unable to buy March-Ralt and continued fighting Lola in Formula 3000 until 1996. Then, to the surprise of many including Reynard who had been technical consultants on many aspects of the one chassis, one engine replacement F3000, the FIA picked Lola as the sole chassis supplier, an arrangement that continues until the close of 2001. According to sources at Reynard Lola undercut them on the fixed price composite tube chassis for F3000, reducing profits in favour of the advantages of fixed production run security that can be crucial in business survival. At the time the ex-works chassis cost was quoted at £53 000 for Lola and £70 000 at Reynard.

The latter was almost half what teams had been paying when there was a choice of F3000 chassis, because of the overheads of race car development on the usual 'what it takes' basis, rather than a commercial decision that's only possible in a monopoly. Some three years later the cost of a Lola chassis neared £70 000 but there seems little doubt that the teams are happy with this as it is not the majority of their annual budgets of £325 000 to £350 000 per car. It is also relevant to note that Lola supplied their T96/50 chassis between 1996–8, superseded by a more expensive and advanced chassis for 1999–2001 the B99/50.

There was also a surprise in the compulsory engine choice for 1996–2001, as Honda faded from the F3000 scene in pursuit of Formula One glory (their engine for F3000 was a British co-developed Judd unit from Rugby), in the face of more consistent Cosworth V8 success. The latter was a cost-conscious, regulated V8 brother to the Grand Prix unit, which helped Zytek in Derby to earn a pedigree in the category.

Initially they supplied Cosworth customer V8s, then associated with Mugen Honda. By 1992 they had developed their Zytek KV motor, still the standard F3000 power plant in 1999 but manufactured at their Repton, Greenfield site. As for a Bentley turbo R and Aston Martin DB7, Zytek's own electronic engine management system is also a feature of the KV eight cylinder unit. Zytek was the first to supply an EMS (Electronic Management System) to a Formula One team and has more recently pioneered hybrid electro-petrol V8-powered racing motors in association with Panoz and their 1998 Q9 project (see Chapter 7). Today, Zytek from Derby and Repton continue competition supplies of such EMS controllers to Arrows Grand Prix V10s and other categories of motor sport, including touring cars.

Today such business has yielded a company with an annual turnover of £8 million, of which 70 per cent comes from motor sport and some 60 per cent represents exports. There are 90 employees and the new Repton site south of Derby, was built in 1997–8. This is a development displaying much in-house engineering ingenuity including items such as leading edge technology of new engine test cells with immense ecological sensitivity, as a necessary planning permission bonus. The F3000 magnesium and aluminium alloy Zytek V8 of 3 litres is available to teams on a rotating lease basis only, costing £27 500 per engine in 1998 with most competitive teams leasing two or three engines per car. The KV develops a comparatively restrained 505 bhp at 8800 rpm; nearly 300 bhp and a full 8000 rpm short of a full blooded GP unit built and maintained regardless of cost. The KV also has an unusually long 2000 mile service interval for a pedigree competition engine.

Such serviceability is appreciated by all concerned in F3000 for its contribution to reduced costs and coupled with performance reliability. A seasoned F3000 observer commented in 1999 that he could only recall one engine failure occurring since the one make Zytek was adopted. That is a telling testimony in a sport where explosive performance is not always a complimentary term.

PS: *Formula Nippon* The 1999 designated replacement for F3000 in Japan was an ambitious category with Formula One regulations sitting around a single mandatory engine supplied by Mugen-Honda. Principal British interests came packaged alongside a Reynard with 13 such cars supplied for the new Japanese formula by Spring 1999. Lola were also represented in this category and the two British concerns controlled the top nine finishing positions in the opening round, all but two of those finishers from Reynard.

Formula 3

This is the rarity amongst international status/single seater formula, for Britannia no longer rules the tarmac. The philosophy behind Formula 3 (F3) is to act as a professional stepping stone for drivers on the way to Formula One. Some very talented and perhaps lucky pilots have driven directly from F3 into Grand Prix racing. The current norm is a one make category/F3 season and then F3000. One make categories have as much power as 210 bhp F3, indeed turbo charged Formula Palmer Audi has more. The chasm between 200–250 bhp apprentice Formulae and the 800 bhp level in Formula One and Champ Cars is judged too big a gap to jump. So the 500 bhp F3000 with its clear links back to earlier Grand Prix technology, is now the more logical last rung on the ladder to the top.

Today's F3 cars are very sophisticated miniature racing cars that demand minute understanding of their teams to release adhesive cornering capabilities from their stiffly constructed carbon fibre chassis, plus specialist driving techniques for their air restricted, low rpm, 2-litre engines. The cost of proving your talent in this Grand Prix waiting room is exorbitant compared to one-make categories at roughly double Formula Renault, triple Formula Palmer Audi.

However, if a driver truly wants to scale the peaks of Formula One and earn those multi-million dollar cheques, then F3 can be worth the £300 000 required to participate with a top line professional équipe. For example the Paul Stewart Racing équipes have dominated the influential British Formula 3 series with a win rate of six out of seven UK F3 titles in the seasons preceding 1999. Drivers who went through the Stewart Racing 'Ladder of Opportunity' would obviously have a good chance of future employment at Stewart Grand Prix, or their rivals.

Formula 3 is one of few categories where the grip of the car is more than capable of transmitting the power available. This requires the teams and their drivers to use their abilities to adapt the car's cornering abilities most precisely to each circuit, using a combination of fine mechanical and aerodynamic adjustments. The British series is a seasonal benchmark session for overseas drivers to make their name against the best Britain can provide, but Germany has an equally effective F3 championship.

The days when Ralt and then Reynard provided the majority of chassis dramatically ended during the 1993 season. Italy's Dallara concern although unsuccessful in Formula One, had targeted British Formula 3 in 1993 and started to win, despite the initial presence of only two chassis. Customers followed swiftly, dumping their Reynards in mid-season as the Dallaras proved consistently faster, thanks to superior aerodynamics. That vital aerodynamic superiority was a function of Dallara owning their own wind tunnel, common in Formula 1 but then a rarity in lesser formulae. Dallara spent more expensive labour in aerodynamic development than was economic for Reynard in a customer supply formula.

It was a bloody dent in the nose of British racing car manufacturing, for an overseas manufacturer had come to Britain and overturned the established order. It showed that we do not have a God given right to the racing car business of the world and that it can be literally a matter of weeks, less than half a dozen racing weekends, in which the tide turns and a manufacturer loses their principal racing car market.

Reynard had made a record 100 plus Formula 3 cars in a year and had won the Blue Riband British, German and Japanese Championships. Yet they were forced to abandon the category they had contested with the traditional winning début since 1985 at the close of the 1993 season. This quiet 1993 revolution established a 1994 monopoly for Dallara that remained during the 1999 season, when the opening rounds of the British series contained only Dallaras on the 17 car grid. That was a lot of potential profit and revenue for Britain's racing car business to lose and leave untapped. One man, Steve Ward at the reconstituted Ralt in Witney, Oxfordshire was trying to redress the balance at the time of writing, with a revolutionary gearbox concept in a new Ralt F3.

Currently a tiny business with '4.5 employees', it looked impossible for Ward/Ralt to turn the clock back. This prompted us to wonder what if Great Britain Plc should support a Ralt revival, or any Reynard quest to reconquer their former F3 market? Perhaps with tax credits in the Reynard case or affordable access to facilities such as wind tunnels for Ralt? The question is, would such support be successful? Or simply preferable to watching another UK-owned manufacturing business disappear along the burnished slope that has swallowed so much British owned manufacturing ability?

The current F3 situation is made worse for the UK by the fact that not one had an all-British engine source. There is a preparation/maintenance specialist for the numerically most common Mugen-Hondas based in the UK, which is Neil Brown's Lincolnshire concern. Other engine makers represented on that 1999 UK F3 grid were TOMS Toyota and General Motors, Opel by Speiss in Germany, and Renault. This professional team uses engines from Sodemo of France, although the Promatecme (French) team has been based at Silverstone for several seasons and spends one of the most generous budgets in British Formula 3 to the benefit of UK plc.

One Make Formulae

This category is often sub-divided on the basis of the principal engine supplier, but other backers are appearing. Even when a name such as Audi appears in a formula name, such as Formula Palmer in 1998–9, the manufacturer did not provide major finance and technical support. The healthiest categories are those which are self-financing, or that have prospered even when the major manufacturer has withdrawn/reduced support.

The supreme example here is Formula Ford. Although heavily supported by Ford from the mid-nineties onward and backed by the British arm of that global corporation in the sixties, Formula Ford survived for many years on its own merits, with low cost spectacular racing. That is the mark of a vital category and one that will provide a decent living for the UK motorsports business.

Subsidiary American Single Seater Formula

Indy Lights

Roger Bailey, former Tyrrell Grand Prix employee in the Jackie Stewart era, is a man who has seen most things in motor racing and found the technical answers to a multitude of problems. His long and interesting journey through motor racing has so far included Formula One, three years running the factory BMW turbo 4 cylinder racing saloons versus 6-cylinder Porsches in America among many others. This expatriate Briton does not bathe in nostalgia. Instead he runs the biggest American single seater racing series outside CART/IRL series. A single seater formula designed to feed drivers and teams on to the premier league using the same tracks. Indy Lights provides business that has significantly benefited UK single seater chassis manufacturers March (1986–92) and subsequently Lola from 1993–99.

Now President and chief operating officer of American Racing Series Inc, the experienced Bailey guides the PPG Dayton Indy Lights Championship from offices in Troy, Michigan. The recent series have been good economic news for Britain plc, with 1998 Lola chassis prices running at $142 000 (£86 060 at prevailing exchange rates) and Hewland gearboxes employed on these 190 mph 'trainers'. The series organisers also order over $500 000 (£300 303) worth of spares annually. The engines are leased from the American automotive giant General Motors at $48 000 (£29 090), who supply the 4.2 litre V6 base that is modified to extract 425 bhp. These engines have a 7400 rpm limit that reduces maintenance to periodic overhauls every 500 miles, comparatively long, low cost intervals by racing standards. Bailey reckons that total cost per car in Indy Lights should be budgeted around $190 000 (£115 151) including the Indy Lights rebuild of a leased engine and outright purchase of the Lola chassis, quoted previously.

This significant American one make series has had a relationship with British suppliers since 1986, but our January 1999 interviews were conducted against a backdrop of bids to establish suppliers to the formula effective Year 2001 onward. As you would expect, American domestic manufacturers and Continental European companies realize the commercial worth of such transatlantic business and the competition will not stand still.

Lola naturally attempted to retain their monopoly, but were initially up against America's Swift and Eagle constructors and the Italians who destroyed Britain's hold on Formula 3, Dallara. No decision had been made by August 1999, but the rivals were now Lola versus Reynard and the Japanese company, Dome. Roger Bailey frankly admitted that the future of the formula was now, 'dependent on the engine supplier we can find for the future. We have looked all over the place, Europe, Japan and the States, but finding a supplier interested in supporting a second tier, feeder, category is not easy'.

Bailey added: 'Back in 1986 there was not so much racing choice in American single seater formula racing and it was easier for us to become established. Today that choice exists plus the fact that racing in America is dominated by the enormous distances and thus travel/accommodation costs must be part of any national racing budget. I believe we may have to do more to control the costs of testing to be competitive with other formulae,' he concluded.

Roger Bailey spoke warmly of the British racing car business, particularly Lola under Martin Birrane's recent ownership and the service it offers. He told the authors in January 1998, 'I still think Britain provides good quality at affordable prices. The UK has the infrastructure to support this repeatable quality with amazing delivery times. I have seen no evidence of British standards dropping. I still think it is a world benchmark for the racing car construction business.' These words are frank and interesting as they are from an external competitor; long may they prove true.

Barber-Dodge

Another American category in which a British supplier is dominant and currently only supplier, is Reynard. This one make category was a pioneer in providing racing equipment on a lease basis and now operates as Barber-Dodge. As the name implies the 300 bhp V6 power unit is supplied by the Dodge division of DaimlerChrysler and former driver/racing school proprietor Skip Barber created the category in the eighties, when Saab of Sweden were the power providers.

This lease formula was good business for Reynard with 40 such cars built by 1999, when the ex-factory price without engine was $50 000 (£30 303) per rolling chassis. Although Barber-Dodge is only an entry point to a professional level, rewards are high. In 1997 the prize fund stood at $100 000 (£60 606) for the winner with an additional $50 000 (£30 303) provided in the form of an engine lease deal for the Indy Lights category.

Formula Atlantic

This was a category that did not sustain its initial promises in the Europe of the 1970s when it featured the Ford-Cosworth BDA engine. However, Formula Atlantic has retained its attraction in the USA where it has flourished and honed Grand Prix drivers, including Gilles Villeneuve and his son Jacques.

Now the power comes from Toyota and the series is formally known as the Toyota Atlantic Championship. In 1997 most chassis came from Ralt which was purchased from March in April 1994 and is now solely owned by former British rally driver Steve Ward. The Ralts had reigned supreme in the US Atlantic category from 1993–7 and 20 new Ralts were shipped to the States from 1994 to early 1999.

Unfortunately for Britain and Ralt, Carl Hass the successful US entrepreneur who marketed Lola successfully before ending that business relationship after more than 20 years co-operation, bought into the American Swift company in 1998. One of the side-effects of that Carl Hass deal, aside from Swift having more resources to challenge Reynard in the CART Champ Car events of the late nineties, was that Hass established Swift as the sole supplier for a new Atlantic car to be run from Year 2000 onward. Effectively that meant the end of the US Atlantic market for Steve Ward's Ralt and he sold the last Ralt Atlantic racing spares as a job lot for a fraction of their retail value.

Thus another category was lost to British enterprise.

Formula Ford 2000

Extinct as a primary graduate formula in eighties Europe but still a popular UK club racing category, Formula Ford 2000 remained extremely competitive in the USA throughout the nineteen nineties. As the name implies it was a grown up cousin for graduates of Formula Ford 1600. Ford commercial interest waned when the 2-litre, single overhead camshaft 'Pinto' engine became obsolete, after years of service in products as varied as the Transit van, various Cortinas, Capris and in its final car iteration, the Sierra.

Commercially and competitively Van Diemen, who supplied the first six finishers in the final Championship table, dominated the 1997 Formula Ford 2000 season in the USA. In June 1999 Van Diemen responded to our survey nominating the USA as 'our largest market'. Obviously, FF2000 played a critical role in Van Diemen's total annual output of 'approximately 140 units' as they listed 45 Formula Ford 2000's for America, as the largest single model type made up to April 1999.

Reynard and their 1987-licensed constructor, Fulmar Competition Services (FCS), manufactured 329 of the winning Reynard FF2000 design with 210 being assembled at Reynard. The majority of the production was in the 1980s and many were exported to the USA. Production of this obsolete design ceased in 1990.

Subsidiary European Single Seater Formulae

Formula Ford

Just as the Ford Model T started many generations on their motoring lives, so Formula Ford has been the birthplace of many successful Grand Prix careers. Not just for racing drivers, as leading designers such as Rory Byrne of Toleman, Benetton and Ferrari proved his draughtsmanship at this level. As did Adrian Reynard with his unequalled success as a designer/driver in Formula Ford 1600 (FF1600) and Formula Ford 2000 (FF2000). The latter single seater, overhead camshaft, Ford powered designs assisted one Ayrton da Silva Senna emerge as a unique talent, to startle UK opponents. This success preceding his becoming a multiple Formula One World Champion driver and one of the greatest drivers the world has ever seen.

Established in 1967 as the answer to a Brands Hatch racing school's prayer for a more durable racing car in the hands of the general public, Formula Ford has prospered in Britain for more than 30 years. In 1990 Ford estimated that over 9000 of the Ford powered single seater cars had been constructed. This means that these spindly trainers, for track use only, had outsold the public showroom efforts of many specialists, or limited runs of mass production machines, such as Ford's own first edition Escort RS Turbo.

Overseas, Formula Ford has featured in over 20 countries. Its success depends on how hard local manufacturers, or those with a regional sales interest, push to dislodge or submerge this comparatively cheap (motorsports are always expensive) but effective formula. Perhaps its biggest success is in luring so many overseas drivers to come and spend their racing budgets competing in Britain to establish their names. In 1999 this would cost in excess of £90 000 for a year with a professional équipe.

The first race for Formula Ford was held at the Brands Hatch circuit on 2 July 1967. Ironically the field was troubled by gearbox failures from a Renault transaxle gearbox never intended for racing. The Jim Russell Racing organization which today is a multi-national company with branches all over the world and a £1.6 million turnover, chose to ignore the pioneering Lotus-Renault marque, introducing its customers to the now ubiquitous Hewland gearbox. This gear box proved a far more reliable component within the £999 Birmingham built Alexis Formula Ford chassis and engine assembly and proved the foundation of one of the 'names' in this industry, one Michael (Mike) Hewland and the company he founded, Hewland Engineering. A 4-speed Hewland gearbox was still mandatory as the category raced into the nineties.

Today, the principles of a low cost tubular frame, bodywork with no aerodynamic aids and controlled tyre choice alongside a variety of mass production Ford power units, still mated to Hewland gearboxes, retain the economy of this formula. Ford engines from the original 1500cc Cortina GT and the traditional 1600cc pushrod, crossflow unit are used in national and club championship racing, with the 1800cc series unit based on the double overhead camshaft Zetec engine for international and major national series.

Engine power escalated from approximately 75 in the sixties to around 150bhp in the nineties under tightly worded regulations designed to cut cost and equalize power. Nevertheless, engine specialists have bred alongside the Ford formulae; amongst the long-lived and successful companies, were Minister in Kent who propelled many future Grand Prix stars in their Formula Ford days. Minister built or rebuilt over 300 motors in a year, with a total workforce of less than 20 in 1989. Amongst their 1999 rivals are equally durable Scholar at Stowmarket in East Anglia and the more recently successful Solus Racing Engines Ltd, not far away at Bishops Stortford.

Today Van Diemen are the elder statesmen chassis constructors of Formula Ford. Van Diemen became suppliers in three main categories, which were analysed in 1999 as FF2000 for the USA with 45 chassis manufactured; FF1600 for world markets 25 manufactured and, senior league Formula Ford Zetec with 30 made. The remainder of Van Diemen production is accounted for by other categories, including a Ford powered sports racer the S2000 that was a more popular category in the eighties, and the starter category Formula First, a beginner's primary formula created by Brand Hatch Circuits for 1986.

Van Diemen's seniority or successful pedigree is no guarantee of winning, as waves of fresh competitors surface every year. They may succeed in dislodging 'The Tasmanian Demons' temporarily, but the Norfolk organization has remained an important regional employer in this primarily rural area for more than 25 years. In 1999 Van Diemen employed 40 people full time, four on contractual/seasonal work patterns and two part-timers. They made 'approximately 145 cars a year, the majority to Formula Ford specifications'.

In the 1998–9 British racing season, major Formula Ford contests saw three British based concerns face serious foreign opposition. Van Diemen had to face the 99 British race winners Ray and Swift, the latter then moving from Plymouth to premises at Castle Combe, Wiltshire. The established British manufacturers fought on home tarmac against the invading French Mygale cars.

Ominously Mygale managed to secure both the British Championship and Formula Ford festival major prizes in 1998, although only four such chassis were fielded in Britain in 1998 against the Van Diemen horde. These French winners were usually prepared and entered through Haywood Race Preparations in Staffordshire and Mygale had orders for five new Formula Ford chassis and two rebuilt machines at the start of 1999.

Swift were also something of underdogs and their history bears examination, because it explains some of the cycles that change the face of racing car construction so thoroughly and frequently. There are presently no trading links between the Swift racers that provide speed if not numbers opposition to Reynard in the American CART Fedex Champ Cars category and the recently much changed Swift Racing Car Constructors at Castle Combe. Managing Director Allen Cooper recalled, ' having recently taken over the Swift concern at Plymouth we are still in the throes of change but we build about 18 cars a year with a staff that will be around 15 when we have settled in. Presently we supply complete cars for Formula Ford-Zetec and Formula Ford 1600, but the irony lies in our supply of FF2000 cars to the USA. For it was from America that the Swift name came to Britain, back when the rights to the American Swift Formula Ford car were acquired in this country during the seventies. So the wheel has gone full circle.'

Compared to Van Diemen both Swift and Mygale are minnows, for the East Anglians have built Formula Fords by the hundred in their boom years, since being established by Ralph Firman and Ross Ambrose in 1973. Ambrose left and much of Van Diemen's subsequent success is due to the expertize and imagination of chassis designer David Baldwin.

In the eighties it was not uncommon for Van Diemen to make hundreds of Formula Fords per season. But things are tougher in the late nineties and realist Ralph Firman, who once worked for brother-in-law Jim Russell's Racing School Formula Fords, knows that his order book will only remain healthy so long as he can keep the comparative Minnows at bay. Since 1997 that ambition has looked tougher by the season and America's Don Panoz acquired Van Diemen during 1999, along with Sussex-based G-force.

Formula Palmer Audi

Founded in the winter of 1997–8 by former Grand Prix driver and BBC commentator Dr Jonathan Palmer, FPA (Formula Palmer Audi) was an audacious move that has resulted in an immensely successful commercial operation that supports its unique lease package presentation.

After just one season of racing for the 1.8 litre turbo-charged single seaters, Jonathan Palmer was able to report a group turnover of £8 million and the employment of 85 full time and 100 part-timers. In 1991 the former Grand Prix driver had established the business Palmer PromoSport that provided 'event days' and hospitality at major events such as Grand Prix. In Britain Promosport accents driving high performance cars, a separate operation that continues in a parallel operation from its earlier Bruntingthorpe home in Leicestershire.

Dr Jonathan Palmer had always planned that the racing formulae and his other business should have a permanent base and the establishment of massive facilities at an old RAF base at Thurleigh Airfield, Bedford expected to be fully operational by August 1999. Prior to that date impressive workshops had been established, their massive 30 000 sq ft looking under-utilized with 30 FPA cars under preparation and some of the corporate toys resting. But that is only the beginning of Palmer accommodation, for his seven transporters can simply drive into the covered caverns of this facility!

FPA was besieged by technical problems in the opening 1998 rounds, but these simply underlined the fast response abilities of the UK motorsport industry. The Van Diemen chassis had to be adapted when the recommended specialist Liechtenstein Audi engine supplier delivered units that fouled the engine bay. Then it was discovered that the imported specialist-modified Audi engines would not perform reliably or manageably deliver their power, never mind tolerate the planned overboosted power surges. So Mountune in Essex, best known for the Ford work including the winning Focus WRC and Pectel, also with Ford rallying links, reprogrammed engine computer management and redesigned the intake system in weeks to release the full potential of these engines. From mid-1998 onward they yielded a European one-make high of more than 250 bhp, with a brief overboost facility that released extra passing ability for maximum excitement.

The basic attractions of FPA were an all in lease cost of £85 000 for each of 24 drivers in 1998, to cover complete participation in the inaugural season, plus guaranteed equality of equipment and outstanding on and off circuit promotion/hospitality back-up. Finally, the championship prize was more worthwhile than rival series in providing a F3000 drive with a leading team Astromega in 1999, for 1998 Champion Justin Wilson.

Leasing had been utilized in American one-make racing previously with Barber Dodge and the major Indy Lights series working on a leased engine, also featured in European F3000, and a bought chassis amortized over four years if the buyer wanted. In the UK the alternative training championships were structured on the traditional basis of buying a car or buying a drive from a professional team, subject to sufficient lap speed being displayed in pre-season testing.

From the competitor's viewpoint in 1998, this meant an FPA driver could get started on a £20 000 deposit, paying the £65 000 balance in instalments, a more convenient method for sponsor's cashflow. At the 1 October 1997 launch of FPA, Jonathan Palmer quoted the following prices for participation in established British single seater championships. They are the maximum prices, valid only as FPA delivered a professional and equal back up for their immediate full grid of competitors. The table below provides some overall comparisons of the costs of campaigning the 1998 season between different formula.

Table 6.1 **Some Overall Comparisons of Campaigning Costs in 1998**

Formula Vauxhall Junior	£85 000
Formula Ford, Zetec	£90 000
Formula Vauxhall Snr	£110 000
Formula Renault	£145 000
Formula 3	£300 000

The 1998 season was certainly a commercial and competitive success and 1999 began with equal enthusiasm for a now proven formula. The organizers signalled that FPA was ready to move into an additional European series for Year 2000. It was possible that Volkswagen Audi Group's ambitious motorsports plans might include Grand Prix beyond the Millennium, giving FPA a further useful life as a logical starter point in any single seater promotional plans. Whatever happens in Germany, Dr Palmer has shown a degree of skilful surgical precision in the businesslike manner in which he has analysed what ambitious drivers/customers need, and provided it at a price they can apparently afford.

Formula Vauxhall-Opel

This category ran for ten years until General Motors terminated their financial support at the close of 1998, but the formula continued on a low-key basis in 1999. As a driver training formula its simplistic tube frame and powerful 16-valve/2-litre Vauxhall engine has proved an extremely effective package. The 1998 World Champion Mika Hakinen made his name in this formula, as did 1998 Le Mans winner Alan McNish. This formula also provided decent revenue for many British suppliers, including Cosworth who were responsible for the original 16-valve engine, Hewland Mk9 5-speed gearbox and leading constructors Reynard and Lotus.

The involvement of the Lotus organization was a matter of company politics. GM owned a majority of Lotus shares in the late eighties as the formula was being created; GM relinquished their interests in the early nineties. GM was convinced that the Lotus name would be beneficial in marketing the fledgling formula. In fact Adrian Reynard was responsible for designing the monocoque, aluminium honeycomb chassis with magnesium alloy bulkheads and steel rollover cage. His company created the car with an eye to rapid production in the summer, which is often a slack period for race car factories.

Reynard received a three-year contract from GM to make these single seaters, subsequently extended by a year. It was good business; with just over 200 of the 155 mph monopostos made by the close of 1991. In fact 1988 was such a good production year for Reynard with 241 racers manufactured that it stands as an unsurpassed volume, but in this racing car-building business, as in mass manufacturing, volume is not a profits warranty.

In 1999 Reynard was larger than ever with turnover at £33 million in 1998, yet making fewer than 100 cars annually. But those cars were for premier price international categories, including their technical engineering partnership in BAR Formula One.

What of Formula Vauxhall Opel? After GM pulled the finance, renamed series were run in Britain and Europe for the large number of remaining cars under the names Europa Cup (UK) and EFDA (the previous European organizing company) Euro series titles.

Formula Vauxhall

Initiated in 1991 as Formula Vauxhall Junior, pitched as a prestigious showcase for the best of the young driving talent emerging particularly from the karting apprenticeships. This flyweight single seater category with its 1600c Vauxhall/Opel Tigra engine of 145bhp was renamed simply Formula Vauxhall for 1999. For more than five years it, together with Formula Renault and Formula Ford, has been promoted as part of the support acts to the official TOCA Touring Car weekends.

The 425 kilogram (935 lb) machines of box tube construction utilize only Hewland gearboxes and Avon tyres and are all are supplied by Van Diemen. Twenty-one of these cars were on the grid early in 1991 aiming for a £12 000 Championship cash prize, with a Formula 3000 test day promised to the champion. The series is promoted through the professional talents of East Anglian based company Media Matters. They employ five full timers on this series and four other clients, to create a turnover of £370 000 per annum. Television coverage is provided through satellite and is particularly important to overseas drivers who will be spending £65 000 to £85 000 a year to participate via UK professional teams. The series is supported at the tracks by Vauxhall's expensive but effective Vauxhall Village with its hospitality and media areas also available to the one-make Vectra touring car series that Vauxhall have supported since 1997. Vauxhall withdrew such support for both Vectras and F/Vauxhall at the end of 1999, when both categories lost their TOCA-support status.

Vauxhall underwrote racing that earned warm critical reviews for its frequent changes in race positions, overtaking manoeuvres guaranteed to provoke the 'ooh' and 'ah' factor that is an essential, but often missing, ingredient in so much motor racing. Although the earlier 2-litre Vauxhall-Opel categories roamed across Europe this series is currently confined to the UK. The outstanding quality of the drivers is a feature of Formula Vauxhall, for the first Champion was Dario Franchitti, now earning an excellent living in CART Champ Cars.

Formula Renault

This series enjoyed high status in Britain, through supporting the TOCA touring car package presentation; see also *Formula Vauxhall*. Formula Renault was not a French formula either in its hardware or its concept. French Mygale and Italian Tatuus, with many ex-Dallara staff, developed the winning 1999 hardware to function with 2-litre Renault power. It was not always a French preserve and more than half-a-dozen British-based companies contested Formula Renault in the early days. More recently Swift suffered bloody noses when they tried to break the Franco-Italian establishment in 1997 and this could have been a contributory factor in the restructuring of this previously successful Formula Ford outfit in 1999.

Best for Britain were the specialist engine rebuilding services and the supply of items like dry sump lubrication and rack and pinion steering components from the Titan Motorsport and Manufacturing Company at St Neots in East Anglia.

The primary British trading benefits in Formula Renault come from a healthy series with British based teams including the Mygale/Haywood alliance, spending record one-make category budgets of £110 000 to £145 000 in 1999, depending on team and the extent of their overseas travel. The hardware subsequently featured Hewland gearboxes instead of the original adapted Renault production unit, and many British engine specialists, including Formula Ford exponents Solus. All applied their blueprint rebuild technology in this category at costs in the £10 000 region. Such revenue will be denied to the UK in Year 2000 when new 1180 bhp/16-valve Renault Laguna engines will be sealed. Specialist blueprinting for power will not be allowed, saving upwards of £10 000 on an annual racing budget.

Renault Sport is trying to halve the costs of their category, from £40 000 per race-ready car to £20 000 in Year 2000. They will employ composite chassis technology instead of tubular frames, but as noted this work is not likely to come to the UK. Tatuus in Italy are the most likely beneficiaries.

7

A Sporting Chance: Sports and Grand Touring Cars

Foreign Domination?

FROM the Bentley Boys and their deep pockets to today's multi million pound assaults on Le Mans and other classic endurance races, the British have always been sports car competitors. Today it's tougher than ever to export such knowledge, but significant German, American and Japanese teams do depend on UK expertise, although rather secretively.

Whilst the UK has an honourable record in sports car racing which is typified by Le Mans wins from the 1920s Bentley Boys to the 1980s TWR Jaguars, this is currently the UK's weakest international motorsport area. Le Mans and the American national series aside, closed coupé (GT1 and 2) racing and that for open prototypes, went through upheavals in the nineties.

Mercedes, through their German AMG operation, dominated to such an extent in the 1998 FIA GT series that they won every race bar Le Mans. This total domination was a factor in Porsche's sabbatical from the sport in 1999. However, sports and GT categories world-wide struggled for popularity outside the Le Mans classic, failing to gain the spectator, sponsor and TV support that is vital to modern motorsports. Essentially, the problems of sports prototype GT car racing have been similar to those of touring cars namely, how many technical links should the racers have to the car a customer can buy? Domination by one marque determined to push grey areas of necessarily indecisive regulations that were formed in a bid to attract the widest spread of manufacturers to support this branch of the sport, are equally hard to overcome. These manufacturers have often won international titles against insignificant opposition.

Britain has an extraordinarily successful Le Mans track record through Jaguar in post-war years, and the UK acted as host/co-creators to the GT40 Fords that overthrew Ferrari's grip on world sports car events of the sixties. In the nineties Britain has supplied the base for BMW sports racing activities since 1995, with the McLaren-BMW until 1997 and then Williams-BMW in 1998-99. Subsequently Britain has become the home base to the Audi coupe section of the company's R8 coupé for their GT racing programme including Le Mans in 1999.

British motorsport companies have also been host or design consultant to many of the Japanese efforts to win Le Mans. It remains a curiosity of motor sporting life that the Japanese had won Le Mans only once prior to 1999, and that was with the generally under funded Mazda team using an obsolete British March chassis.

The true aristocrats of long distance International Championship events for sports or GT cars have tended to be German. Aside from the obvious Porsche and Mercedes eras, there have been less obvious German alliances that have shown the pace to win at Le Mans, including Cologne-based Toyota and their GT1, which led Le Mans to within an hour and twenty minutes of the 1998 finish. The British compensation was the presence of lady engineer and aerodynamicist Joanna Moss within the multi-national Toyota Team Europe.

More prosaically, Porsche-powered race cars have won Le Mans a record 16 times, thirteen times factory-built entries, since their first outright win in 1969. The battle for the 1998 FIA World Championship for GT1 cars was effectively fought between Schwabian regional manufacturers Mercedes and Porsche, this time Mercedes doing the winning. Except that is for the pinnacle of Le Mans, the victor's garland going to a factory-built Porsche 911. Although the race car bore little relationship to the road car of the same name, save the principle of a flat six engine, albeit mid rather than rear-mounted.

For two decades from 1970 to 1990, Porsche were the major winners in varying GT classes regulated by the FIA. Usually, Porsche ensured that even major groups such as Fiat-Lancia and Ford made no lasting impact on their domain although both Tom Walkinshaw Racing's Jaguars and Mercedes interrupted Zuffenhausen's inexorable victories. The TWR Jaguar was the most consistent winner, but Porsche continued to be successful at Le Mans, sometimes by accidents such as the provision of a TWR carbon composite chassis originally intended for another manufacturer! This was mated with a Porsche engine and scored two consecutive Le Mans wins in 1996–7.

When a McLaren BMW F1, converted from the exotic £627 000 Gordon Murray road car design, won Le Mans on its 1995 début there was renewed competition at Le Mans but it did not spill over into the often poorly supported rounds of the official FIA GT Championship. Both Porsche and Mercedes looked at the converted McLaren BMW and deliberated that a proper sports racing formula car with major inputs from single seater technology would do a job better, even if the rules were framed with the requirement to produce sufficient numbers to homologate a road car.

The Anglo-German McLaren BMWs and their representative privateer teams were soon eclipsed by such factory efforts, but McLaren BMW almost wrested the 1997 FIA Championship from Mercedes' grip. Indeed they led much of the season after they resorted to their factory Schnitzer team and a lot more of the McLaren racing influence.

The BMW factory racing enterprise could not stay with McLaren, because of that Formula One team's Mercedes alliance. Therefore, when BMW moved their motorsport activities other than engines engineering to Britain, the Williams Grand Prix company gained a sports car racing alliance with the Bavarian manufacturer, in addition to the anticipated Grand Prix partnership. You can read how that developed as we investigate UK-influenced international sports racing teams that follow.

Audi Sport

Not an obvious candidate for British input, Audi Sport of Ingolstadt is actually the front house assembly and entrant organization for the prestige car manufacturer Audi owned by Volkswagen Group. This organization first made a motorsport impact with the in-house rallying 4×4 turbo Quattro. This car revolutionized the established rear wheel drive order and delivered Audi an appropriate Quattro quartet of world rally titles.

Unsatisfied with safety and publicity, particularly minimal TV coverage and home market political opposition to forest rallying on environmental grounds, Audi withdrew from rough road rallying in 1987 and concentrated on motor racing. Until the close of 1997 they were able to use their unique and radical Quattro 4×4 transmissions in a variety of turbocharged and normally aspirated racing saloon cars in successful USA campaigns, but had more obvious production links in Europe.

British input was initially minimal, confined to braking systems particularly through Alcon in Tamworth, Staffordshire, clutch components or Castrol oil contracts, until the winter of 1995/6. Then Audi decided on a worldwide push with their Quattro A4 racing saloon and set up a UK base in Buckingham entitled, Audi Sport UK. This very effective liaison brought a clean sweep of 1996 driver and manufacturer team titles to the Anglo-German alliance in the UK. This was one of seven country titles swept up by Audi in national saloon car racing.

Audi Sport staged a spirited runner-up performance in the 1997 BTCC. They had a less satisfactory season in 1998, when the international authority the FIA, outlawed all wheel drive designs in touring cars categories. Once the all wheel design was outlawed in Formula One and GT Le Mans formulae, Audi knew that they faced the loss of a unique selling point and a competitive edge in international motorsports from 1998 onward. The Ingolstadt factory chose to challenge for Le Mans victory in 1999 and beyond, whilst continuing to investigate Formula 1 beyond the Millennium. Audi Chairman Dr Franz Josef Paefagen told us in Berlin in 1998 that should Audi decide to opt for Formula One in the future they would make the complete car. This prediction is potentially very bad news for British motorsport engineering.

As the harsh realities of progressing their Le Mans programme developed in the late nineties, it was soon obvious that Britain will be a principal partner in any future Audi motorsport programmes. This will be an involvement stretching far beyond the six-speed sequential gearbox designed by Ricardo FFD of Coventry, which is common to both Audi R8 designs. Such a growth came through the Le Mans Audi challengers R8R (open Roadster) and R8C (closed Coupé) for the 1999 season and the dialogue between Ingolstadt and Audi Sport UK. On examination of the twin turbo V8 racer supply chain, one soon realizes that Audi's 1998 purchase of the ex-Toyota TOMS racing car facility in Norfolk for an undisclosed sum, was far more significant than the same company's accidental (a by-product of the Volkswagen Bentley take-over) acquisition of Cosworth in Northampton.

Following that deal, Audi swiftly sold Cosworth Racing on to Ford for a reported £50 million; according to Cosworth's declared turnover for 1998. The Cosworth divisions Audi retained were primarily concerned with road car manufacture, although the specialist casting technology obviously had some overlaps with Cosworth manufacture of racing engines for Ford, even after the take-over.

Audi renamed TOMS Racing Team Norfolk (RTN), and with it Audi acquired the race car fabrication abilities in carbon fibres and composites, plus the expertise and intellectual capital of their 30-strong staff. It was not long before significant British input was making its impact in the manufacture of chassis components for the Audi R8R. Then it was announced that the overall design lead had and would continue to come from British veteran (30 years from BRM Formula One to TWR Jaguar and Nissan sports cars), Tony Southgate.

The R8R was presented to the press in 1998 in the winter slush of Berlin. The car was bloodied in competition at Sebring, Florida in that State's traditional sunshine. In March 1999 Audi raced head-to-head with BMW's Williams engineered opposition (*see* page 110), which was in its second year of operation with a well-tested and advanced chassis. Although both the Audi open cars finished they were not fast enough; an alternative would be needed if the company was to have a realistic chance of achieving the declared objective of a début win at Le Mans.

Then came the formal announcement of the poorly kept secret that Audi would field a closed Coupé R8C version of the same car (turbo V8, six speed sequential change gearbox, shared rear suspension) at Le Mans 1999. Audi

Sport UK was charged with creating and running the unique R8C, a totally different external design to the original open Audi R8R. It was an expensive belt and braces, open and shut, approach to the great French race, one unique amongst major manufacturers in recent years. The employment of two teams, one in Britain the other in Germany, asserted more about Audi's immediate commitment to outstanding track performance than any amount of public relations' presentations could ever achieve.

Theoretically, the closed and elongated coupé design would be faster, especially along the straight, where sleeker body and lower aerodynamic drag factor were complimented by Le Mans regulations that allowed another 10–15 bhp beyond 600 bhp, via larger air intakes and increased turbocharger boost. Unfortunately, some of that theoretical engineering advantage was lost by the tiny timescale allowed to field the R8C from Britain. Neither R8C finished, but trhe German R8Rs were third and fourth.

Tony Southgate remained the overall design influence on the coupe, especially upon aerodynamics which were the product of 40 per cent scale model work in a Swiss wind tunnel; whereas the open R8R, was the aerodynamic child of working with the French Fondmetal establishment and its former Renault Sport management. Both R8 racing designs would only be cosmetically modified by Audi's imperative to build in as many reminders of their road cars as possible, particularly the recently released Audi TT showroom coupé.

Another British designer, Peter Elleray who detailed the complete R8C project, supported Tony Southgate. This was based on the composite production skills of an increased 40-strong racing team at Norfolk (RTN), under the leadership of the same Japanese manager who had operated the TOMS' facility from its 1992 inception. The Audi racing coupé was approved, conceived, constructed and ran its first trials within six months which was an astonishing testament to the reflexes of the British based motorsport business, especially those of the dedicated multi-national staff at Racing Team Norfolk, who saw very little but artificial light burning throughout that winter.

By contrast the parent company's open R8R sports racer was on a longer schedule, project approval granted in Autumn 1997, first trials on the company test track at Neustadt around 11 months later and the project formally announced in October 1998. That allowed further intensive testing to continue until the car's March 1999 race début in Florida, followed by further test mileage (much of it on the southern French Le Castellet circuit) before taking part in the May public time trials, allowing pre-qualification for Le Mans in June 1999. It was confirmed in March 1999 that Audi Sport UK would run the R8C at that year's Le Mans, whereas the open car would be entered and operated by previous Porsche-powered winning entrants, Joest Racing from a German base.

Accidentally, Audi allowed German and British racing ideologies to be perfectly contrasted and many clichés proven. The measured German approach did bring traditional Teutonic reliability on the first public appearances of the R8R. The British last gasp initiative, necessary because Audi in Germany delayed the start point on the closed coupé by one year, suffered some erratic early outings, including the loss of a door for the first chassis on at least two occasions. But it allowed Audi the chance of competing with favourites Toyota and Mercedes, who both had closed coupé designs only for the 1999 Le Mans.

Fuelled by huge international sporting and commercial ambitions, Audi and BMW made massive investments in their 1998–9 sports car racing programmes. *A total estimated investment of some £50 million, with at least 30 per cent of that investment directly spent in the UK.* This statistic included the Audi purchase of TOMS Toyota in East Anglia and boosting employment from 30 to 40 technocrats to create the R8C and run it from Buckingham based Audi Sport UK. It does not include running the final year of Audi A4 touring cars in Britain so you can add in £5 million for that enterprise, 75 per cent spent directly in the UK. Now add BMW Motorsport's construction of Oxfordshire premises with a 60-strong payroll (over 90 per cent British) and calculate costs for 1999 BMW Motorsport gearboxes from Xtrac and Audi's associated investment in Britain's Ricardo FFD for their input on the transmissions of both open and closed Audis.

The authors are probably just skimming the surface of what was really spent in Britain in the 1998–9 period, but we have included the Williams Grand Prix chassis adapted from Renault V10 to BMW V10 operation. Ask the Audi board in Germany about all this UK expenditure and they might well counter that the flow was not only one way. As we have said, we believe Ford in Britain had to pay Audi more than £50 million for the racing division of Cosworth engineering that Audi, almost accidentally, acquired as a by-product of the Volkswagen Group's 1998 purchase of Rolls Royce Bentley and the Cosworth Group, from Vickers Plc.

BMW Motorsport

Now based in Britain for their sports and Grand Prix programmes, excluding engine development which remains in Munich, BMW Motorsport have a long history of Anglo German chassis and race car engineering alliances. These stretch back to the alliance with March of Bicester in 1973 Formula 2 and racing purchases from Lola, that began in the mid sixties.

In 1995–7 BMW Motorsport worked with McLaren on both their sports racing programme (confusingly based on the McLaren F1 3-seater showroom supercar with BMW V12 power) and further chassis and aerodynamic development of their 3 Series touring cars. BMW emphasized their 1999 commitment to continued engine engineering in Germany, through a new Munich BMW competition engine preparation site employing 130 people. They would produce the 3 litre V10 Grand Prix engine and the continued supply of 6 litre sports racing V12s from Munich to Britain for the winning Williams 1999 Le Mans contender, the LMR.

BMW Motorsport Ltd, the 1996 offshoot of a proud Bavarian parent has now turned the wheel full circle by setting up a separate £5 million facility adjacent to Williams Grand Prix Engineering at Grove, Oxfordshire. The first product of that union was the 1998 LMP V12, an open sports car designed by Williams and rapidly developed through the new facility by BMW Motorsport Ltd. A brace of LMPs ran at Le Mans in 1998, retiring prematurely after just four hours when the wheel bearing seals failed. Both BMW machines were retired on safety grounds by chief designer/engineer Graham Russell, who had previously been best known in Britain for his work on the winning Williams Renault Laguna touring cars.

As further evidence of the 'can do' philosophy of Britain's motorsport industry, the 60 strong Williams team at Grove delivered the 1998 racing machines in a matter of months. Originally the LMP project was approved in July 1997, but there were the usual big car company delays whilst corporate men fiddled with non-functional aspects of the design to brand the car with BMW styling and badge cues. The delays resulted in little preliminary testing and some serious quality problems and a subsequent quietly desperate period of getting the revised LMPs constructed in a series of 16 hour days. Nevertheless the cars qualified sixth and twelfth at the 1998 Le Mans race and one showed third place promise in its abbreviated race.

For the 1999 season the BMW and Williams alliance had much more time, with their 1998 LMP taking six months to put together as they revitalized the LMP V12 project around a totally new chassis coded V12 LMR. Again the recipe was a large 6 litre BMW V12 that has been raced since the McLaren-BMW's 1995 Le Mans winning début. This was installed within a British carbon fibre composite chassis, allied to carbon fibre disc brakes. Extensive durability testing and added Williams-BMW pace on an air-restricted 580 bhp made them formidable performers in 1999, although BMW felt themselves handicapped by rules that favoured the majority of its turbocharged rivals.

The alliance's winning record opened with victory at Sebring, USA during March 1999, demonstrating a pace that was seconds beyond either the indigenous Riley & Scott Ford V8s or the open Audi R8Rs. However, both Audis finished this preliminary encounter in third and fifth places, whilst BMW finished one of three cars (one of the 1998 development LMPs was revamped privately and run by Britain's David Price team for former German banker Thomas Bscher) owing to accidents.

Le Mans 1999 saw Williams support BMW Motorsport and their chosen Schnitzer racing team in fielding two works V12 LMRs, backed by the Price run privateer versions of the 1998 LMP. Therefore, a trio of German prestige marques including Mercedes, BMW and Audi, two with obvious British links, clashed in a field that also featured Toyota (Cologne), but not traditional Le Mans winners Porsche. The Anglo-German BMW triumphed.

Meanwhile, the Williams BMW Grand Prix engine test programme commenced with track tests from April 1999 onward, conducted by BMW Motorsport using Jorg Muller as the driver and a 1998 Williams Grand Prix chassis. From Year 2000 onward the alliance will race under the Williams BMW banner. So the only public Williams BMW racing co-operation seen in advance of the Millennium was the sports-racing Anglo-German alliance.

Whatever the Le Mans result in 1999, British motorsport engineering was bound to feel the financial benefit of the Audi and BMW programmes. Both centred on winning Le Mans and American racing programmes for the open versions of their sports prototypes, to boost exports in their most important overseas market.

Chrysler Motorsports

The enormous 8 litre, V10 powered Chrysler Viper in its striped working suit, strikes onlookers as the essence of an American racing car, its brutal power so flagrantly displayed in long distance competition. In fact these cars are European in their racing origins. These production based machines run by Oreca from a French base, depended on at least 30 sets of lightweight carbon fibre and Kevlar body panels constructed by Reynard in Britain. Just part of a racing improvement schedule as they grew ever further from their showroom specifications, in a 1995–9 sports and GT development. The Chrysler funded (Dodge branded for the USA) racing schedule was based on the official FIA international series of the period. The related development programme enabled the Vipers to grow from underdeveloped brutes that could be embarrassed by privately run Porsche 911s, into GT2 class champions and then the dominant contenders of a revised 1999 FIA series that eliminated former front runners from Porsche and Mercedes.

The Viper body deal reflected another working relationship between Reynard and Chrysler in 1996-7, with Reynard designing a racing version of the Dodge Stratus touring car. This was successfully raced, winning the American 2-litre title in 1997. But when the US series was abandoned because of poor support this part of the Reynard Chrysler co-operation ceased. However, Reynard also enjoyed providing high profile motor show concept cars, for what was Chrysler Corporation (now DaimlerChrysler) and later extended this activity with show and one off running prototypes for Ford. So the benefits of the Chrysler racing programmes were not confined to the track for Reynard in the UK.

Although a British team, Chamberlain, fielded such Chryslers on a privateer basis the works Chrysler Motorsports équipe was run by the immensely able Team Oreca from southern France. Oreca also held the rights to construct all customer Vipers, including those for an American club racing specification [ACR] as well as the full-blooded sequential gearchange FIA racers [GTS-R]. Chrysler Vipers won the FIA GT2 Championship in 1998, with British works Viper driver Justin Bell taking the title for FIA GT2 Drivers in 1997. At press time Viper V10s led the FIA 1999 GT championship outright, the faster GT1 sports racing cars having been barred at the close of 1998, following the Mercedes clean sweep of results.

TWR-Nissan GT1 Le Mans, 1997–8

Developed in a physically separated small team, with under 40 regular personnel dedicated to building Nissan a Le Mans winner at Broadstone Manor, Oxfordshire, this Anglo-Japanese project represented a rare failure for the TWR Group in the eyes of contemporary media. Journalists expected TWR to match their achievements of winning Le Mans for Jaguar in 1998–90. Nissan did not commit to an anticipated third year to build on the third place and the reliability achieved at Le Mans 1998 by the TWR-Nissan R390 GT1 design, which also achieved fifth in category on its 1997 Le Mans début; when it had set the fastest pre-qualifying time.

The two year programme reportedly accounted for a $38 million (c. £24.5 million) budget from Nissan to TWR, but subsequent 1999 investigations revealed £20 million spent over two years. This included development of a separate road car – then required by the regulations – and a truncated development period for the racing Nissan, which ran the Japanese company's twin turbo V8 engine.

On the latest audited accounts we hold for the TWR Group those of 1997, it is fair to say that the Nissan Le Mans deal assisted the company in its financial progress. Turnover escalated from the 1996 figure of £144 million to £155 million in 1997 and declared annual profits escalating from £4.3 to £5.1 million, in the same period. However, we acknowledge that the core of TWR business has now changed and Nissan was the largest and most recent motor racing deal completed by TWR outside Formula One. TWR in 1999 show less and less dependence on motorsports and more reliance on their co-manufacturing deals. These extend to companies such as Aston Martin (the DB7 with more than 2000 engines made) and with far more long term significance and size, their 51 per cent majority holding in the joint manufacturing company TWR has established with Volvo. The first TWR-Volvo product, the 1998 C70 has been commercially and critically welcomed in establishing a presence in the profitable sporting coupé market for Volvo.

Subsequently, Nissan split their efforts for Le Mans 1999. The turbocharged V8 motors remained of factory origin and were supplied ready to install, as in the TWR era. Britain Plc did retain a large chunk of Nissan Motorsport business, as G-Force Composites in West Sussex manufactured the carbon composite chassis of Nissan's 1999 newcomer.

Lister Cars

An international project for 1996–7 and a regular sight in the thriving British domestic BRDC Championship of 1997–9, Lister was an ambitious project of incredible complexity on tiny resources. Most famously and inventively allied with Newcastle United Football Club, therefore supported at Le Mans 1997 by a black and white 'Toon Army', Lister driving force Lawrence Pearce deserved more in the way of results for his aggressive and inventive approach to GT1 success on a minimalist budget. The latter estimated beneath a million pounds for Le Mans, at a time when factories expected to spend over £10 million on a successful multiple-car entry.

Powered by a variety of in-house developed Jaguar V12 motors, the Listers usually proved quick enough to match many more well funded names, but lacked long race durability. Out of the international arena in 1998, Lister contested the FIA GT series in 1999 with encouraging speed, but was not a major commercial supplier of competition components or complete cars other than their factory effort, at press time.

Lola

Once regarded as the only choice in British sports car racing, Lola have been through all the reversals of fortune that mark any leading constructor in such a fickle sport as motor racing. These remarks are also relevant to Lola fortunes in CART/Champ Cars in the USA and Formula 3000 pre-1996. Following the humiliating failure of the Lola Formula One project in 1997, Lola had to be completely restructured in 1998 under the leadership of Martin Birrane, a former racing driver and an effective entrepreneur with an original financial base in property development.

Lola's return to sports car racing, or more correctly manufacturing an open chassis suitable for European and American use with a wide variety of engines, did not really make a public impact until 1999. Then the B98/10 sports racing car in open configuration was ready to race to Le Mans or other endurance events. Dubbed B98/11, the carbon composite design was initially engineered with the 4-litre BMW V8, a customer engine designed for American racing with no UK connections or a 5-litre V8 Ford in mind. Lola designed a 6-speed sequential transmission and Hewland manufactured unique components to suit.

The Lola's début in the April 1999 European International Sports Racing Series, facing a squad of now obsolete Ferrari 333 SPs, was almost the stuff of Lola legends dating back to when founder Eric Broadley was *the* British commercial racing chassis establishment. Racing at Monza, the emotional heart of the Italian road racing, the Lola and its British developed Judd V10 racing engine of Grand Prix heritage proved exceptionally rapid, building up a dominant lead before retirement. The Lola performed well in Le Mans qualifying and American 1998 tests with alternative power units installed. It looked to have a bright commercial future over a three year design life, although direct opposition came from Reynard and their 2KQ Chassis for year 2000.

Lotus GT1, 1995–7

Perhaps the best known brand in British sports motoring, Lotus has not enjoyed a happy and profitable presence in the European sports car racing arena of the nineties. In America however there was sustained success in the late eighties and early nineties for the turbocharged Esprit in production based American series, for a factory team that successfully dented Porsche 911 and Chevrolet Corvette dominance in this arena.

Unfortunately, like the Lotus Grand Prix team, Lotus sports racing activities devolved outside the main car making facility at Hethel so that the producers of the commercially successful Elise were unable to build any logical links with the racing team. The racing team had occupied the old Ketteringham Hall site of the GP team after Lotus Grand Prix collapsed in the 1994–5 winter.

Utilizing mainly Dutch funding and drivers, V8 variants of the Elise, initially used a Lotus based engine, then a Chevrolet unit that proved erratic and unreliable. Sentiment aside, there was really no link back to 1957–71, when Lotus was a major commercial supplier of sports racing cars and associated hardware through Lotus Components Racing. Under its Asian ownership, the financial group that also has a majority holding in Proton, Lotus Cars and the Lotus Engineering Group are prospering at their Hethel HQ. It is perfectly possible that the solid sales success of the Elise running at over 3000 per annum in 1999, may yet propel the marque back into the sports racing limelight.

There has already been a one-make racing series for the Elise in Italy from 1998 and the factory engineers have developed a wide range of equipment that has dual road and track use. So whilst we must mark Lotus as temporarily absent from an obvious area of motorsports, their future prospects are brighter than ever.

Marcos

The Wiltshire based Marcos organization has recovered from a lackadaisical eighties, in a father and son family operation with the marque literally racing back to glory in the nineties. One of the few smaller operations (they employ 50 people) to sell road cars on a commercial scale and compete in racing successfully, Marcos took their basic Rover aluminium V8 engined LM600 design from a British BRDC class winner into FIA international competition with a larger Chevrolet power plant.

For 1999 the marque was represented in the FIA International GT class by the LM600 and factory backed owner/driver Cor Euser with ex-Lotus co-driver Mike Hezemans; both driver and owner from Holland. Marcos had commercially distinguished itself by selling over 15 cars a year for a Dutch one make racing series, for the less radical Mantis model during 1998–9.

Panoz

At least three leading British motorsport companies Reynard, DPS Composites Ltd and Zytek were integral to the flamboyant American Panoz projects. Not the most obvious of companies for a book focused on British motorsport business achievements. However, the Atlanta based Panoz outfit with their front-mounted Ford America V8 powertrains and Xtrac 6-speed rear gearbox transaxles were the design creation of the British company Reynard Special Vehicle Projects (RSVP) in 1996.

Surrey-based DPS Composites constructed much of the carbon fibre composites with DPS co-founder David Price entering and operating the cars on both sides of the Atlantic, a service he also performed for the 1998 Williams BMW LMP owned by Thomas Bscher, in 1999. On occasion Britain did not take all the Panoz business 'in-field', as a French concern DAMS also entered and raced the Panoz successfully.

Eponymous owner Don Panoz and his pharmaceutical business are the epitome of the American dream, accompanied by Panoz ownership of several leading road racing tracks and his enthusiastic promotion of Le Mans rules for American sports car racing. In spite of his American heritage he came to Reynard in Oxfordshire to create what is currently the world's only front engine, rear drive design racing at such a senior level of motorsports, discounting the similarly configured Chrysler Viper, although that machine was converted from a showroom design.

Ready to race at Le Mans in 1997, the Panoz featured composite construction with a rear transaxle and monster 6 to 6.9-litre Ford competition versions of their mass production V8 in their heavily scalloped prows. Originally the shape was going to be simply that of the limited production 4.6-litre production cousin, but

Reynard adopted their usual leading edge aerodynamic philosophy to the unique layout and the car became a contender at Le Mans. That was backed by an extensive programme of American events through 1997–8 as a GT1 rival to Porsche and others.

Capable of winning in shorter American events, the Panoz bred another distinctive offspring with British roots. This was a hybrid V8 electric powered Panoz GTR-Q9, with the lightweight electronic provision of more than 150 bhp from the separate motor, one energized by the regenerative braking system developed in association with F3000 engine suppliers, Zytek in Derbyshire. The Panoz GTR-Q9 hybrid was underdeveloped and late to appear before Le Mans pre-qualifying 1998. Whilst the conventional petrol fuelled Panoz GTR made the necessary qualifying times comfortably although sandwiched by a pair of TWR-Nissans, the Hybrid was just over 15 seconds slower than the fastest Porsche in the GT1 class and therefore did not get a race.

The pioneering Panoz, with the somewhat macabre nickname 'Sparky', continued to be developed by Zytek and Panoz Motor Sports and proved reliable enough to finish 12th in the 1998 Petite Le Mans event held over ten hours at Road Atlanta in autumn. Contemporary reports indicated that the additional battery pack weight accounted for some 100 kg of the 160 kg surplus generated by the innovative electronics.

The hybrid Q9 was a bold effort and typical of both adventurous Panoz and British ingenuity under the leadership of Don Gibson at Zytek. One could see a possible commercial avenue in Zytek's development of an electric Lotus Elise for public road use in 200 bhp format. This was the project that inspired Don Panoz to instigate the racing programme after he saw the show Lotus Zytek constructed for the American SAE Congress in Detroit earlier in 1997.

The authors have personal experience of this intriguing low noise and emissions sports Lotus, travelling in a second prototype that followed the original show car and was demonstrated to us in spring 1998. This is a true electric car, qualifying under California's zero emissions regulations, that is totally unlike the racing Panoz GTR-Q9, for the prototype Elise has no petrol or other internal combustion power. Even more impressive is that the whining Elise generates silent standing start performance that eerily delivers 0-60 mph faster than a Porsche Boxster!

There were no obvious backers prepared to expand on the Elise's promising beginning, but Zytek had sold some very high performance Karts, with their environmentally aware power packs allowing use in circumstances (indoors and adjacent to quiet areas) that would obviously not be appropriate for conventional petrol powered karts. As to the Panoz Q9 project, it was expected to return to the tracks later in 1999 but not at Le Mans, where Panoz qualified an open top Spider version of the front engine design with exceptional speed.

Changing the Rules: Management, Business and Sponsorship

Introduction

TELEVISION through the BBC was an immediate companion for an amazing cross-section of British motorsports in the fifties and sixties. However, it was not until the eighties and nineties that TV became the terrestrial and satellite link that unlocked both a global audience, large amounts of multi-national corporate cash and, subsequently, TV cash. In addition to the continuing expansion of worldwide motorsport as well as the television coverage, there is the often overlooked role of print media in British motorsport prowess. This part of the story also involves the determination, influence and intelligence of two men who have probably had the most fundamental role in the post war development of the sport.

Television is an ever-hungry glutton for spectacle and colour but, before they will beat a path to your door you have to have a spectacle to offer. That spectacle and the organization behind it, is the reason for the material success of the modern motor racing formulae, in particular Formula One and are the first part of the story. In fact it should be understood that this organization of the spectacle that is motor racing lies at the heart of the development of the cluster of engineering excellence that thrives off motor racing in the United Kingdom. One would not exist without the other but, more importantly, the constant development that has and continues to generate technological superiority would not have survived nor thrive without the spectacle and the organization that creates it. The spectacle generates the TV cash that creates the sponsorship money; the cash feeds the engineering.

However, when the story of the transformation of motor sport began in the 1970s Formula One was not the premier category, nor was it the most well organized or popular category of motor sport. The Formula One team owners were primarily independent and entrepreneurial characters that had little interest in the wider organization of the sport, except as it directly effected their racing.

But the world was changing and becoming more global, linked by television and a modern business culture. There was little doubt that the sport needed a new philosophy, a new organization and some new people to take it forward.

The Beginnings are Established

During the immediate post war decades the sport was a somewhat loosely organized, rather haphazard activity; often an enthusiast's adventure. The organizers of the races were never able to guarantee the numbers or types of cars on the grid, or which drivers would appear. The advertising at each circuit was the responsibility of the circuit owners and the main sponsors were almost always automotive suppliers. The money involved was relatively small as the amounts earned by the leading drivers of the fifties, sixties and seventies show. We have already discussed the massive post-war contribution of personalities such as Tony Vandervell, Raymond Mays, Peter Berthon and many others. Many of these devotees used either personal or personal corporate money to develop their racing experience and added such depth to the pool of engineering and driver excellence that a foundation for the industry developed.

In these early post-war decades, corporate contributions often came through the determined and passionate efforts of people such as Raymond Mays whose personal charm and persistence pulled the money for the BRM project out of the corporate pockets of post-war British industrialists. Although the project was started and sold as an opportunity to 'sell' the excellence of British industry the contributing companies had very little idea or opportunity to capitalize on their investment. The concept of corporate marketing was largely a closed and arcane mystery to the companies involved and, of course, commercial television was but a vision.

Drivers and team owners were less well rewarded and rather more diverse in their interests and activities, than they are today. Although Colin Chapman floated his company in 1968 making himself a millionaire in the process, he was an exception. Bruce McLaren's organization did not produce road cars and Chapman's organization was unique in the spread of its activities from Formula One, other formulae, and consultancy to road cars. Jack Brabham also created a financially successful organization but the rewards available now are of a different order of magnitude than in the 1970s.

The organization of the sport was also very different with drivers such as Moss, Clark, Fangio, Hawthorn *et al.* all driving many different types of racing cars in many different formulae. In 1962, the last year of his racing life, Stirling Moss drove in 57 races whilst today's Formula One driver would probably only drive in the sixteen rounds of the World Championship. The legendary Jim Clark was killed in an accident on 7 April 1968, in a Formula 2 race at Hockenheim in

Germany; a current Formula One driver would not be competing at this level. Their financial returns were also less and in 1961 Moss was probably the highest paid driver in the world as he had achieved success for Mercedes Benz in sports cars and Grand Prix. In that year his gross income was said to be £32 750 out of which he had to pay all of his expenses. Moss is reported as saying that his disposable income was approximately £5000. Jim Clark was in a similar position, although his earnings were greater and he encountered considerable problems in achieving a reasonable tax position. Clark was one of the first drivers to move abroad for tax purposes, albeit reluctantly. Today very few top drivers live anywhere but Monaco.

In the immediate post-war period (*see* Chapter 1) the dominance of the pre-war manufacturers' marques such as Mercedes Benz, Alfa Romeo, Maserati and Ferrari waned. The proprietary chassis fabricators such as Cooper (their earlier success faded, Cooper ceased trading in 1968), Lola, Brabham, Lotus, McLaren and then March all made contributions to the demise of the unique cars produced by the 'great pre-war names'. Throughout the 1960s these companies produced chassis for Formulae One, 2, 3 and many sports cars. Formula 3 was a massive market in Britain and mainland Europe, with the latter alone accounting for nearly one hundred cars being sold in Europe in the years of the late 1960s. Although Lotus was a successful player in the early years of this new industry the most successful was the company run by the Australian world Champion, Jack Brabham.

These successful chassis fabricators, plus the remarkable Cosworth Ford DFV engine which, after 1967 was sold to anyone with the necessary funds, turned the fabrication of racing cars into a business. As a matter of fact it was also Colin Chapman who managed to persuade Ford to invest in the enterprise to build the engine; Ford now own Cosworth Racing, the company that built it.

The opportunity for competitors and team principals to purchase a potentially winning chassis and engine combination, was part of the vital changes needed to transform the sport into a business. There was another vital ingredient that had to be added to the mixture and it was Colin Chapman who seized the opportunity with the lifting of restrictions on advertising sponsorship on the cars. The John Player Tobacco Company sponsored the 1968 Lotus 49 and the car was painted in the red and white of their new brand of cigarettes, Gold Leaf. Modern corporate sponsorship of motor racing was born and modern sponsors and teams are imitating this initiative by Colin Chapman of Lotus. It was 1970 before the next Grand Prix sponsor arrived; Yardley for BRM in 1970. Chapman was a commercial as well as a technological innovator in Europe, learning his sponsorship craft from earlier sixties participation in the more commercially aware American racing scene.

Proprietary chassis and engine availability, sponsorship from both automotive suppliers and tobacco manufacturers and the number of tracks available worldwide, were the key elements that transformed the rules of the game and enabled the last stage to take place. But the period of change had been more than twenty years. The next phase of change would take half as long and involve more business reorganization than engineering or racing technology; it was nothing less than the transformation of a business.

The Development of an Organized Spectacle

The People

In his foreword to the story of March Engineering (*March; the Grand Prix and Indy Cars* by Alan Henry, 1989) a company he started with Robin Herd, Alan Rees and Graham Coaker, Max Mosley said;

> 'Some rounds of the 1969 World Championship had only 13 cars. All this changed in 1970, with ten March Formula One cars built and usually five or six of them on the grid. In addition, everyone could see there was nothing magic about Formula 1 – if we could start in September with an empty shed and no money yet be on the front row of the grid the following March, so could they.'

The importance of the point Max Mosley makes, the success of the Cooper Company's cars throughout the early fifties and sixties, the successes of Lola, McLaren, Brabham and others including March chassis and the DFV engine, changed some of the rules of the game. Prior to these events, everyone believed that either exotic genius or more likely, large corporations of the mighty automobile industry, were necessary requirements to producing a successful chassis and race engine; certainly the latter came from the large corporations. March had started their operation in a small garage in Twyford in 1969 just as the large motor companies were withdrawing from their previously intensive and financially large involvement in motor racing and as the Ford Cosworth DFV became available.

However, regardless of the success that March, Lola, Lotus, Brabham, Cooper or any of the others competing in the 1960s had generated, the sport was still a somewhat haphazard spectacle. There was no discipline amongst the teams to provide cars at every round of the championship and the individual events were not organized in any co-ordinated manner. The modern Formula One constructors' and drivers' championship, which started in 1950, provided a definitive focus for drivers and teams alike, but it lacked organization. The schedule of races around the world was established and the first race of the new championship was held at Silverstone on 13 May 1950. However, the circuits used did change regularly, there were no rules governing the number of events that each participant had to enter, and the venues offered variable facilities.

This rather eclectic and slightly anarchic situation continued until the early 1970s when several events started the process of reorganizing the sport. In 1969 Bernie Ecclestone offered to help establish a new Formula One Team with Jochen Rindt and Robin Herd, each having 45 per cent of the equity. The plan did not come to fruition, but the March Team did with the quartet of Max Mosley, Alan Rees, Graham Coaker and Robin Herd. By 1970 the March Team had entered Formula One with the major sponsorship of the oil additive company STP. This gave the urbane, intelligent and extremely shrewd Max Mosley a place on the Formula One Constructors' Association, FOCA. One of the essential people and elements, on which the transformation of motor racing in general and Formula One in particular would depend, was in place.

Max Mosley is the barrister son of Sir Oswald Mosley and a man of exceptional determination and intelligence. The authors had an extended interview with Max Mosley in June 1998, when we discussed the business of Formula One in particular and the business of motor racing in general, for several hours. Mosley's enthusiasm and fervour for this sport and business was apparent and transcends the commitment of the merely dedicated businessman or barrister, although it is sometimes masked by this urbane Englishman albeit a truly cosmopolitan one. Amongst the many points of discussion was the development of the sport from the late 1960s. Mosley made it very clear that the sport's organization was not an accident, but the vision of one Bernie Ecclestone.

In 1957 Bernie Ecclestone had purchased the assets of Connaught Engineering at auction, but after the deaths Stuart Lewis-Evans and the remarkable Archie Scott-Brown at Spa in 1959, he withdrew from racing. In 1969 he was, amongst his other business interests, running Colin Chapman's Formula 2 team and, in view of his offer to Robin Herd was obviously interested in returning to the sport with a Formula One team. The opportunity arrived in 1970 when he purchased an interest in Motor Racing Developments, the Brabham Team, from Ron Tauranac.

In October 1971 Ecclestone purchased the Brabham team outright from the designer and part owner Ron Tauranac. After Tuaranac's departure Ecclestone is reputed to have said,

> 'The most important thing for anyone in business is to be able to make decisions quickly ... This means that the top job is a one-man job. If there are two top men a lot of time is wasted just trying to agree.' (Eric Dymock, 1980)

The same issue occurred when the Ford/Fiat merger was discussed in the 1980s and 1990s; Trotman and Agnelli could not agree who was to be head of the merged corporation. Ecclestone's influence on the future of Formula One had begun as he now had a seat in the Formula One Constructors Association. More importantly another person and crucial element on which the transformation of the business was to be based was in place. The changes did not take long to start but it was to be a long, eleven-year haul.

Throughout the following seven years the Fédération Internationale du Sport and the Formula One Constructors Association moved into a position where they often in conflict. Jean-Marie Balestre was the main spokesman for the FISA as head of the CSI committee. Throughout this period Max Mosley and Bernie Ecclestone represented the Formula One Constructors' Association on the FISA Formula One Commission and negotiated with Balestre and the other members. Balestre was an important figure in the ensuing period of the transformation of the manner in which this sport and business was conducted. Balestre was clear in wanting to wrest the commercial control of the sport back into the grasp of FISA and by the end of 1977 the antipathy between the two parties was clear. In 1978 Balestre was elected President of FISA and the lines of the future were drawn.

The Organization

The long series of crucial events which transformed the business of Formula One started early in the 1972 season and were subsequently exacerbated by the oil crisis of that decade. At the Monaco Grand Prix in 1972 the Formula One Constructors clashed with the International Sporting Commission (the CSI) over the number of cars on the grid, although in reality there were a number of other issues festering. The new commercialism had increased the number of teams and there were a total of 25 cars available, whilst the AC de Monaco had raised the number on the grid from 16 to 18, leaving seven cars out. The constructors decided to make a stand and negotiated the Geneva Agreement that established a set payment to each team and guaranteed a full grid for each race.

The Constructors were also unhappy about certain changes in the technical regulations governing the size and structure of fuel tanks and making pit stops compulsory. The matter of deformable fuel tanks was not in dispute, but compulsory pit stops were. Furthermore the real issue, money, did not surface until October 1972. The circuit owners were represented by an organization called Grand Prix International and the Constructors had issued a demand for increased appearance money, raising the fee for each team to appear to £103 000. The GPI and the CSI had a more or less common membership base and in this instance they worked closely together in an attempt to resist the demands of the Constructors, responding to FOCA with an offer of £53 000.

It seems certain that by the end of 1972 the root causes of the decade of disputes between the Formula One Constructors' Association had been planted, and by the end of the year, it was a stand off. The early rounds of the 1973 season's championship were due to start in January and Argentina, Brazil and South Africa all pleaded special cases and when the circus arrived at Montjuich Park in Spain for the first of the European races the die was cast. The drivers and cars already in the running for the Championships would remain in contention. The three members of FOCA's finance committee Max Mosley, Bernie Ecclestone and Phil Kerr had ignored the GPI and negotiated with individual circuit owners; they were not about to give up the golden egg of Formula One. FOCA's organization had taken the initiative by refusing to be drawn into negotiations and the CSI and GPI were on the defensive. But the season did not run smoothly

There were several fatal accidents that 1973 season including the deaths of Roger Williamson at Zandvoort and François Cevert during practice at Watkins Glen. The latter tragedy was followed by Jackie Stewart's retirement. The safety campaigns led by the Grand Prix Drivers' Association had only partially improved the safety conditions at the tracks, including the safety barriers. At Zolder the drivers failed to stop the race in spite of their conviction that the circuit was unsafe.

The spectre of the oil crisis loomed over the world economy and the reality of the three-day week in Britain tended to focus people's minds, so the conflict between the powers in motor racing was suspended, for a time. As the 1974 season started the problems facing the circus did not diminish the commercial interest and financial support it received. The sponsor cash encouraged more entrants and more commercial sponsors supported more teams. In spite of all the difficulties and a continuing toll of fatal accidents, including the deaths of Peter Revson in practice at Kyalami and Helmuth Koinigg on the guard rail at Watkins Glen, the circus thrived.

1975 was an important milestone in this third phase of events that changed the face of Formula One. The battle between the CSI, FOCA and the GPI flared as the GPDA lost the battle with the team owners at the Spanish Grand Prix. Whilst the drivers began to work under the umbrella of FOCA, CSI proved to be an almost spent force in this dispute so the team owners made their position very clear to the drivers. In spite of the death of four people when a barrier failed and a car went over it into the crowd the racing went on. The barriers failed yet again. The Constructors then cancelled the Canadian Grand Prix, yet another example of the inadequacies of the CSI.

By the end of the 1975 season a deal had been worked out between the CSI and FOCA that effectively formed the basis for the governance of the circus for the next decade. The deal involved a 26-car grid (still in existence) and an arrangement where the race organizers paid a set and rising fee for each race. FOCA was then responsible for allocating the money to the individual teams. The CSI set up a special Formula One committee including representatives from FOCA to undertake the government of the circus. To quote Eric Dymock who wrote in 1980 'Having subdued the drivers FOCA now proceeded to subdue the CSI'. But the arrangements were not yet settled and a further seven years of uneasy and unsettled progress commenced.

However, Bernie Ecclestone and the FOCA organization had effectively taken the initiative from the CSI, Balestre and therefore FISA. Ecclestone had basically cleaned up the whole process of staging a Formula One race and in the process made the lives of the team owners easier and more lucrative at the same time; improving their value equation in modern business speak. He had negotiated a deal with FOCA where they contracted his own commercial organization to organize the shipment of the equipment and cars, the race calendar, the race track facilities including advertising and television rights, in return for a fixed fee. Effectively, Ecclestone's organization became the promoters of the circus acting on behalf of the teams and most importantly, the sport's commercial director. Television was still a haphazard affair with most companies wanting to be paid to broadcast races.

Mosley was very clear that by 1977 the situation had reached a pivotal point, when the expense of putting on a Grand Prix was a major issue for the circuit owners, who had become somewhat nervous of the last minute cancellations that seemed to occur for little reason. He also made it very clear that at least one circuit group had offered the Grand Prix directly to FOCA, rather than run risks of the uncertainty. This could have meant that the mainly British based constructors would have been running a separate (rival) set of races. However, the drivers' licences would then have been revoked by FISA probably preventing them from participation in any motor sport. The period between 1977 and the crisis of 1980 when there was a distinct possibility that this would happen, was yet another period when the need for some drastic changes was made clear.

The number of sponsors increased along with the wealth of the sport and the people in it. The sponsors ranged from tobacco companies to automotive product makers, perfume and toiletry manufacturers, toy companies, a bank and a manufacturer of audio-visual equipment. But these companies were still the mainstay of the sport and the sponsorship money whilst lucrative was not yet magnified by the wealth of global television. Besides, there were a few changes in the management of the sport that had to be put in place.

The struggles between the constructors and the established international body that controlled motorsport, the Fédération Internationale de l'Automobile (FIA) and in particular its subsidiary body the Fédération Internationale du Sport Automobile (FISA) had become something of a saga, with Ecclestone and Jean-Marie Balestre the lead characters. The latter, who was elected President of FISA in 1978, was a man who certainly did not suffer fools gladly and whose reputation as a somewhat brittle personality seems justified. In the antipathy which existed between the members of FISA and FOCA during the 1970s and early 1980s there are many occasions when it appears that personalities were as important as the issues involved.

The feud that had simmered on throughout the 1970s had reached a turning point and it was essential that the situation was stabilized and the means for extending rather destructive and petty issues eradicated. According to Gerard Crombac's fascinating book on Colin Chapman after the débâcle of the Spanish Grand Prix at Jarama, Balestre arranged to meet Chapman at Le Mans in an attempt to resolve the issues. An extraordinary agreement was reached which involved Chapman taking over as President of FOCA and Balestre would ensure that FISA would agree to 'rescind the skirt ban in favour of a tyre width restriction', which Chapman was convinced would have the same effect; shades of 1998! In addition Balestre would help Chapman to heal the rift between the 'grandee' Formula One constructors Ferrari, Renault and Alfa Romeo and the others. But Chapman was essentially a racer and not the sort of character to play the role that Bernie Ecclestone had played so successfully for FOCA. Furthermore, he also agreed with the stand Ecclestone had taken and he was not one of the 'grandees'. By the time he had returned to Norfolk he had apparently changed his mind.

Ecclestone was clearly in the position he had always claimed was necessary for successful management, at least as far as FOCA was concerned;

> 'The most important thing for anyone in business is to be able to make decisions quickly ... This means that the top job is a one-man job.'

The confidence that all the team owners had and continue to have in one Bernard Ecclestone is completely justified and as the team owners realized, their role was to produce the cars and the spectacle. Managing that is difficult enough so leave the management of the presentation of the spectacle to others.

One example of the obsession with power that characterized the FISA/FOCA conflict, is the occasion in 1980 when Balestre issued an edict that all drivers had to attend a mandatory pre-race briefing on pain of fines. Several drivers had failed to attend the briefings at the Belgian or Monaco Grand Prix and at the Spanish GP at Jarama FISA announced that any drivers who had not paid their fines would not be allowed to practise and therefore not race. There followed a split between the members of the organising committee who sided with FOCA and the drivers, probably because the organizers had offered to pay the fines, but Balestre refused to be moved. After some futile attempts at negotiations Balestre announced that the Spanish GP would not count towards the Championships, at which point the Renault, Ferrari and Alfa Romeo teams who had supported FISA withdrew. FOCA then announced that they would not take part in the French Grand Prix.

The dispute between the two factions simmered on with arguments about sliding skirts and other regulations and the responses became somewhat theatrical on both sides. The obvious (?) compromise of FISA dealing with the regulations and FOCA dealing with the money and commercial aspects, appeared to be impossible. Firstly, because bad regulations would put huge amounts of money, existing and potential sponsors and the ability to provide the racing spectacle, at risk. Secondly, the authors think it highly probable that Balestre was determined that the commercial aspects of the sport would be taken back by the FIA. These matters were certainly at the forefront of FOCA's thinking in relation to the turbo charged engines. These were very much more expensive than naturally aspirated engines such as the Ford DFV and there was a danger that teams without access to factory engines would be uncompetitive and at financial risk. Regulations were and are a fundamental part of the commercial base of the sport, in the same way as governmental regulations effect industry, only more so.

The issue of conflict between money and sport was clearly not going to go away. Indeed, the purists who wish that it had never surfaced are really wishing for a world that was never there. In a 1908 issue of *Autocar* a correspondent wrote, 'There are no more races', referring to the fact that the intense rivalry between the British, French, Italian, German and American manufacturers was dominating the fixing of the regulations to favour one type or another. Races may not have been 'fixed' but regulations certainly were, and the issue in the 1980s was to ensure safety, provide a spectacle and to ensure the numbers on the grid. The stakes were always high and money, power and prestige had always been a part of this sport, probably the most commercial of the century. Before the First World War it was the manufacturers in Europe and America who were trying to dominate; in Europe before the Second World War it was intense nationalistic rivalry, war by another means. Then in the 1980s the competitive lines were drawn between the largely British based fabricators, dubbed by Enzo Ferrari as mere 'assemblatori' and the mass manufacturers of mainland Europe such as Renault and Ferrari. The latter had effectively been owned by Fiat since 1969 and the competitors merely followed the same path: war by another name, motor racing.

The 1981 Concorde Agreement

Perhaps the first sign of potential agreement was when Balestre seemed to comprehend that FISA had disregarded its responsibility to bring in regulations in a manner that ensured that they were capable of implementation. Their attempts to expel the ground effect principle failed through the ingenuity of the designers, in particular Gordon Murray.

The television issue was an important aspect of the Concorde Agreement of 1981 and probably a major factor in encouraging the protagonists to settle the dispute and get on with the game. In November 1980 Bernie Ecclestone raised the spectre of a separate race series when he announced that FOCA would run its own events under the auspices of a new organization to be called the World Federation of Motor Sport. But the GPI (the race organizers), many of the sponsors (tyre companies in particular) lined up against FOCA; Goodyear hinted that they would withdraw from racing altogether. It was apparent that the sponsors and many of the suppliers did not want to see motor racing becoming like boxing, with a plethora of championships. It was probably never really a possibility anyway because of huge costs involved in setting up one race, let alone a series.

Therefore, although Balestre was effectively in a corner so was everyone else. In addition it seems very doubtful that the TV companies would have been supportive of any breakaway series either. Whilst since he had become President of FISA in 1978, Balestre had always wanted the commercial rights of the Formula One Grand Prix Circus to come under FISA' s control, he realized that this was not to be.

The representatives of FISA and FOCA attended a meeting in January 1981 at the heart of Italian motor racing, Maranello, Italy. The home of Enzo Ferrari and the red racing cars, certainly represented a man and a marque that has had an enormous influence on motor sport. At this meeting the Concorde Agreement of 1981 was signed. The agreement effectively split the running of the sport into the matter of financial negotiations for the race series and the regulations governing the technical aspects of the races and racing cars. FISA was the acknowledged authority on all aspects of the technical rules governing the races and the cars whilst FOCA would be responsible for the financial aspects.

Under the Concorde Agreement of 1981 Balestre effectively leased the TV rights to FOCA as the contract acknowledges that the FIA owns the TV rights to Grand Prix races, forever. The actual contract was with FOCA, not with Ecclestone who was effectively sub-contracted through his own company to provide the commercial management of Formula One. Ecclestone had effectively devised the means of managing the regulatory and commercial aspects of the sport and Balestre eventually made him a Vice President of the FIA, which gave Ecclestone an ideal opportunity to work with rather than through the members of the FIA governing committees. It also meant that many members were able to see Ecclestone in action and to know the man. In the light of the next stage of these events some may have regretted that action.

In spite of their closer working relationship, in the ensuing decade the acrimony between Balestre and Ecclestone surfaced a number of times and the combination of their personal relationship and the difficulties of running the complex business did not make life easy for either man. When March pulled out of Formula One and eventually out of business Mosley continued to work in the business as a freelance consultant. Amongst others Mosley developed a sound knowledge of the workings of the FIA and certain views as to the manner in which it was being run. The organization was, in common with many similar organizations in other sports, run by a number of talented and well meaning people who were amateurs in a period when sport was professional reality. He and others thought that he could not only do it better but that he had the flair and ability to reorganize its methods and structure.

The FIA members and others had seen the results of the acrimony that the relationship between Balestre and the Formula One Constructors' Association created, as did circuit owners who often bore the brunt of the disagreements. Furthermore, the FIA were very well aware that a large proportion of their income came from the TV rights and other fees generated by the efforts of Ecclestone and emanating directly from the Formula One circus. In 1986, with the organized support of Bernie Ecclestone and many of the Formula One owners and a large number of the 143 clubs from 117 countries who were members of the FIA, Max Mosley stood for President against Jean-Marie Balestre.

The Englishman surprised no one, except perhaps Balestre, when he won the election very convincingly. As he said to us in 1998, he took his time to make a careful assessment of the style, structure and operational relationships of the FIA. The situation did not fill the then forty-six years old barrister – a man with a strong reputation for clarity and order in all things – with either confidence, or an easy mind. This was somewhat surprising to us in view of the fact that he had worked closely with Ecclestone during the seventies and early eighties developing the structure of decision making and relationships between FOCA and the FIA. Nevertheless, he did not let the past prevent him from setting about the restructuring and reorganization in a very focused and methodical manner.

He was concerned with a number of issues but identified three as the crucially bad aspects of the contractual relationships between the FIA and FOCA. Under the 1981 Concorde Agreement the FIA had a legally loose and untidy contract with the Formula One Constructors Association which, as Mosley pointed out, was a changing group of teams that did not and by definition could not, be a stable group. Secondly, the very source of the FIA's income was Bernard Ecclestone's own organization and the FIA had no contract with that at all. Finally, the very basis of the circus and therefore of the income, was the teams that were members of FOCA. Teams came and went and the contract for the teams to attend each of the season's races with two cars was therefore dependent upon the group's consistency, and yet the group changed repeatedly. This situation was not tidy or legally tolerable for this barrister of motor sport.

The already close relationship that Mosley and Ecclestone had formed, plus the high degree of mutual respect that they had for each other's different but complimentary abilities, was an important factor in the next round of the industry's transformation. In effect Mosley was simply recognizing the reality that the teams were already paying Ecclestone and that meant that he was allocating the funds from the TV companies, circuit owners and others to the teams in a formula that has never been transparent. In addition Mosley was convinced that by dealing directly with the man who had developed the vision of the spectacle, and knew how to ensure that the teams and the circuits delivered it, he would be ensuring the vital income stream for the FIA.

In an article in *Business* in January 1999 Mosley is quoted as saying 'There was a kind of constantly changing bunch of contractual partners, and the man with the real money was hiding behind them. We had to have a contract with Bernie and he was more and more the man with the money – it seemed to me that we needed a contract with Bernie and also with the teams, because of their own actions. If we had a contract with Bernie then it wouldn't matter whether the teams came and went and which teams were there or not.'

These events came to a head in the latter part of 1994 at a meeting of the Senate of the FIA, a part of the organization that had been established on the recommendation Ecclestone with Balestre as Chairman. Over the following two years the situation was resolved except as far as the competition laws of the European Union were concerned. The outcome was that Ecclestone would assume the contractual responsibility and he did, with a fifteen-year contract for the TV rights. Television in the post-1980s has made the organization that Bernie Ecclestone created and put in place into a massively successful money machine. Whilst the role of FOCA is vital to the business, at the very centre of the business is the FIA Senate and then Ecclestone's own company that is contracted to run the commercial aspects of Formula One on a 15-year contract.

The arrangement did not receive the total approval of all of the Formula One teams, as some of the members of FOCA took the view that the massive (and increasingly huge) television revenues that Formula One generated were essentially theirs! Not a view that Mosley has any sympathy with, as he sticks to the law and the spirit of the original agreement signed in 1981. As he said to us 'The vision is Bernie's and he has generated the TV interests and knows how manage them'. In addition there was no one else who knew television, worldwide promotion and the business of motor racing. The new contract with Bernie Ecclestone's company succeeded the defunct Concorde Agreement. There was another aspect of the FIA's strategy in giving Ecclestone the extended agreement, the FIA's desire to see a more structured corporate entity in place that would provide a continuous executive management of the commercial side of the sport. The fact that they were correct in being concerned about continuity was confirmed in June 1999.

Bernie Ecclestone was born in 1931 and is currently sixty-eight years old: in June 1999 he underwent heart by-pass surgery from which he looks set to make a full recovery. Nevertheless, given the importance of the issues involved, the increasingly rapid growth of the revenues and the importance of those revenues to the financial health of the FIA, their prudence is logical. But the deal had another twist yet to come.

In 1996 Ecclestone started to work on the flotation of a bond based on the increasing revenues earned by his company, a revenue stream that was now guaranteed for ten years. These bonds are a relatively new financial instrument that has been developed to provide people or organizations such as writers, musicians (or inventors with important patents) with a secure and regular income stream, with the opportunity to raise capital sums based on that income stream.

Ecclestone approached several financial institutions and by the end of 1996 Salamon Brothers had agreed to float the bond for a total of $2 billion. This prompted the FIA to offer to increase the period of Ecclestone's television rights by a further ten years in exchange for 10 per cent of the bond. Salamon Brothers attempted to float the bond in 1998, the two year gap being due to the internal wrangling over the allocation of the TV revenues to the teams; but the float failed. Further attempts to float the bond were met with considerable market scepticism, and even when Morgan Stanley came alongside the issue was ill received and failed to proceed.

Then, in May 1999 the bond was at last given a rating by the top four agencies (rating is an essential prerequisite to issue) through the combined efforts of both banks plus the assistance of the WestDeutsche Landesbank. More importantly, the latter bank persuaded Ecclestone and the FIA to accept that the bond's period be reduced from 20 to ten years and a reduction in the issue value of $600 000, making the issue price $1.4 billion. However, the market is still somewhat unsure of the bond's real value, although it has been issued on the Luxembourg Stock Exchange. The shadow of the European Commission's Competition Directorate who announced their preliminary findings on the contracts in June 1999, after a two-year inquiry, still hangs over the deal;

> 'The inquiry concludes that Mr Ecclestone broke the EU competition law when he obtained exclusive television broadcasting rights to world motor racing events. European Commission insiders said that the contracts – against which a $1.4 billion (£880 million) Formula One bond issue was secured – would have to be renegotiated if the initial findings of a Commission investigation were confirmed.'
>
> *Financial Times*, 30 June 1999.

This problem will continue to haunt the bond's future, unless the European Commission's Competition Directorate and the Commissioner Karel van Miert can be convinced to withdraw their objections to the contract, which was probably awarded to Ecclestone's company without any semblance of competitive tendering. We suspect that this dispute will run for some time to come, as it seems to be in the nature of such things. The contract has been in place for some five years and the Commission's response to the documentation submitted by the FIA which, at Mosley's request, included all of the contracts that Ecclestone has with the individual television companies, has been a long time coming. The FIA was also criticized in the report, as it was claimed that it had 'abused its dominant hold over motor racing to restrict competition' *Financial Times*, 30 June 1999. The FIA has recently moved its offices from Paris to Geneva, outside the jurisdiction of the Commission, although according to Mosley, for reasons unconnected with this dispute.

There is little doubt that Ecclestone's influence on this industry (a very much smaller stage) has been at least as great as the Robber Barons of Rockerfeller, Ford, Carnegie *et al*., had on the structure of America's industrial sector at the turn of the century. Furthermore, the impact of his contribution has still to be assessed and such an assessment will have to await the final outcome of the changes chronicled above. However, the authors are convinced that the world of Formula One and of motor racing in general has been irrevocably changed by the business genius of Bernie Ecclestone and his influence has definitely been a major element in the success of the British motorsport industry. Britain has few enough of such talents for them to be ignored or to go unrewarded.

The Impact of Television

At our interview with Mosley he made the analogy between Formula One and a TV soap that took place over a season. The characters and the plot changing constantly but within the clear and regular parameters of the story line. Furthermore, the attraction of motor racing in general and Formula One in particular is that sponsors are provided with a seamless season of events, unlike football, Wimbledon, cricket or rugby. These sports are also rather less complex or expensive to stage and do not involve the huge logistical effort of transporting several tons of high tech equipment across thousands of miles sixteen or seventeen times a year. Indeed, the model of Formula One and the extensive reorganization of its management and presentation to the world, is one which is now being followed by other sports including football and rugby, with athletics just coming out of the past.

Whilst there were many real issues of dispute between FISA and FOCA during the contentious years of the late 1970s there were also a number of issues about power; who was to run the sport? It was also apparent to all of the parties concerned that the interests of the spectacle, therefore the sport and the business, had to be of paramount concern to to everyone involved. Furthermore, the scope of the business and the money involved had developed under the management expertise of FOCA, very clearly led by Bernie Ecclestone and aided by Max Mosley. The promoters, working with the power of global television, had taken the initiative away from the international federation that had traditionally managed and organized the sport.

Effectively the Grand Prix series and much of motor sport has become the joint property of the promoters and the traditional organizers, because of the impact of television money, the sponsorship of global corporations and the TV viewer, all of whom are now more important than the trackside spectator. In the future the impact of digital television will probably bypass any of the problems created by the ban on tobacco advertising. Moreover, as is shown by the statistics presented in Tables 8.1 and 8.2, tobacco advertising was some 11.8 per cent of the total team sponsorship in 1999, down from 12.5 per cent in 1993 (8.8 per cent in 1998). This contrasted by tobacco's gain in circuit advertising in the same period when the number of companies rose from one to three and the percentage rose from 4.3 per cent to 7.1 per cent, presumably because of differing national rules. However, tobacco companies such as Marlboro and British American Tobacco remain large players in the support of the sport.

Table 8.1 **Team Sponsorship – Primary Sponsors: 1993 F1 Season**

Industry	No. of sponsors	Share %
Motor	31	55.4
Tobacco	7	12.5
Industrial	5	8.9
Clothing	4	7.1
IT	3	5.4
Drink	1	1.8
FMCG	1	1.8
Electrical	1	1.8
Photographic	1	1.8
Machinery	1	1.8
Tourism	1	1.8
Grand total	**56**	**100.0**

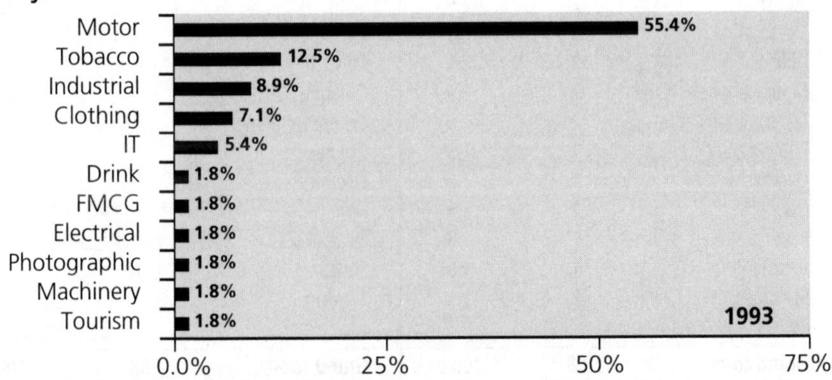

FISA made several attempts in the early 1980s to use the pull of the crowd to encourage the TV companies to pay for the privilege of televising the Grand Prix season. Max Mosley recounted the story of how Ecclestone managed to get an agreement from the European Broadcasting Union to show all of the rounds and originate the TV coverage. Therefore, there was one supplier and one fee, but the EBU's agreement was subject to certain conditions, including the proper presentation of all trackside advertising so that it did not interfere with the camera coverage. Another issue related to the previous organizers for the TV coverage that was, in effect, the French company Elf. That tended to result in somewhat biased advertising that did not endear other companies to the medium nor encourage them to pay reasonable sums for the privilege of appearing alongside the Elf logo. The new agreement effectively ensured that the advertising and exposure would be in accordance with the sponsorship programme.

At the time of the Concorde Agreement of 1981 the total television audience of Formula One was spread over a total of 44 countries and estimated at some 12 million; but what 12 millions? By 1987 the audience had grown and the total TV rights income was some $5 million of which the FIA would have received approximately $1.5 million. By the beginning of

Table 8.2 **Team Sponsorship – Primary Sponsors: 1998/1999 F1 Seasons**

	(1998)			(1999)	
Industry	No./sponsors	Share %		No./sponsors	Share %
Motor	19	27.9	Motor	18	26.5
Tobacco	6	8.8	Tobacco	8	11.8
Clothing	5	7.4	FMCG	7	10.3
Financial	4	5.9	Telecommunication	7	10.3
Drink3	4.4	2	Financial	5	7.4
FMCG	3	4.4	IT	5	7.4
Computer games	3	4.4	Clothing	3	4.4
Industrial	2	2.9	Drink	2	2.9
Electrical	2	2.9	Industrial	2	2.9
Airline	2	2.9	TV	2	2.9
Mobile phone	2	2.9	Catering	1	1.5
Telecommunication	2	2.9	Computer games	1	1.5
Photographic	1	1.5	Courier	1	1.5
Ceramics	1	1.5	Electronics	1	1.5
Courier	1	1.5	Film	1	1.5
Inline skates	1	1.5	Inline skates	1	1.5
Jewellery	1	1.5	Stationery	1	1.5
Stationery	1	1.5	Tourism	1	1.5
TV 1	1.5	2			
Grand total	**68**	**100.0**	**Grand total**	**68**	**100.0**

Table 8.2 (continued) Industry 1998/1999 F1 Seasons

Industry	1998	1999
Motor	27.9%	26.5%
IT	11.8%	7.4%
Tobacco	8.8%	11.8%
Clothing	7.4%	4.4%
Financial	5.9%	7.4%
Computer games	4.4%	1.5%
Drink	4.4%	2.9%
FMCG	4.4%	10.3%
Airline	2.9%	
Electrical	2.9%	
Electronics		1.5%
Industrial	2.9%	2.9%
Mobile phone	2.9%	
Telecommunication	2.9%	10.3%
TV	2.9%	
Other	10.3%	12%

0.0% 10% 20% 30% 40%

the 1990s the total annual TV audience worldwide was estimated at 17.6 billion in 144 countries which had increased to more than 50 billion in 202 countries 1999 (source FIA). This huge global audience attracts the sponsorship (advertising) spend of many companies that are not linking themselves with the teams or the sport because of motor racing. They are looking for relationships that will enhance their own brand awareness and generate the level of exposure that cannot be achieved in other ways, except by even greater expenditure. The growth of television audiences is shown in Tables 8.3–8.5 below.

Table 8.3 **Formula One Fans Tune In ... in Record Numbers Growth of Global Television Audience**

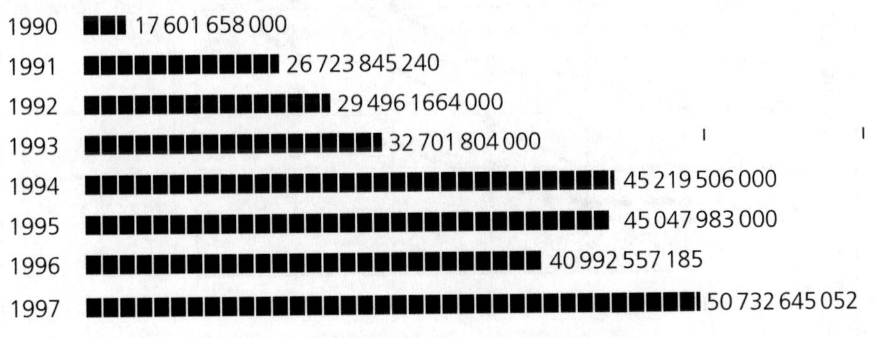

Year	Audience
1990	17 601 658 000
1991	26 723 845 240
1992	29 496 1664 000
1993	32 701 804 000
1994	45 219 506 000
1995	45 047 983 000
1996	40 992 557 185
1997	50 732 645 052

Source: Fédération Internationale de l'Automobile

Table 8.4 **All Formula One Audiences by Year**

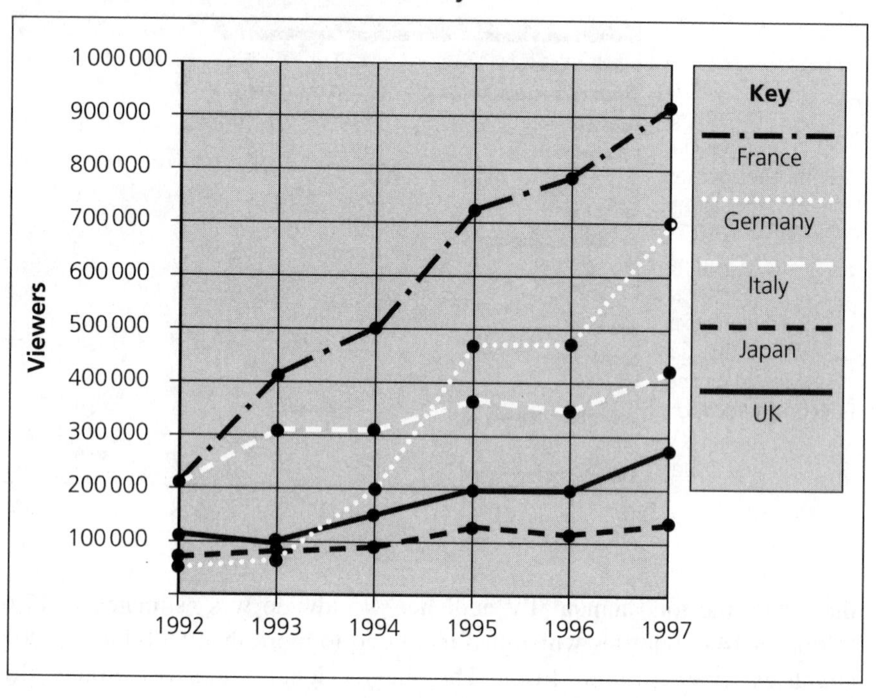

Table 8.5 **Specific Formula One Audiences by Year**

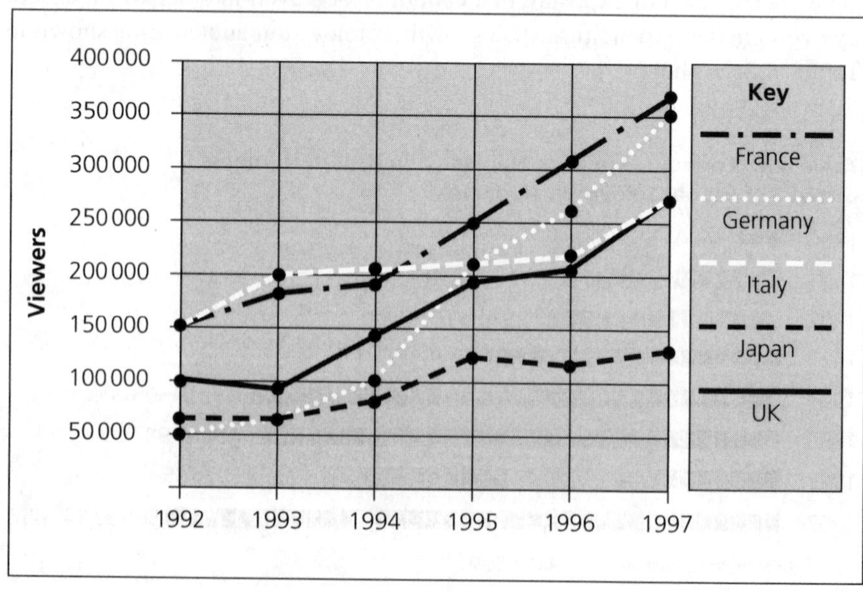

The philosophy that Raymond Mays used to sell the idea of assisting BRM to success when he was trawling the corporate offices of Britain's engineering companies, is still essentially what drives these relationships. Now, the companies have the opportunity to place their brand image before the largest single audience of sport in the world. Sponsors make the relationship because the image of Formula One is appropriate to the company's aspirations and products. Finally, the companies who pay for the sponsorship take a great deal of trouble to utilize the relationship by using the sponsorship to enhance their advertising campaigns and the image of their products. Finally, the organizations involved sometimes actually design products that carry the brand names of the teams concerned. The team names are themselves becoming 'brand names' in their own right.

The Formula One organization that is Ecclestone's creation has proved a model that others, including the Touring Car promoters (TOCA), have followed. In 1998 the worldwide television audience that followed the British Touring Car Championship was nearly 2 billion and more than 1.2 billion of that number were viewing from Asia and the Pacific Rim (source TOCA). TOCA, run by the Australian Alan Gow, is the only major area of motor-sport that is not run by the committee of FISA. The FIA are responsible for the World Rally Championship and provide that global sport with the regulatory backing.

The Prodrive company run by the ex-world Rally Championship co-driver David Richards and his co-director Ian Parry is an exceptionally professional and profitable organization that has a turnover in excess of £47 million. The marketing element of their business has always been at the forefront of their philosophy. They have been so successful in the management stakes that David Richards was put in charge of the Benetton Formula One team until it became clear that he would not be given the necessary executive freedom. This company also lives and dies by the success of their marketing but they are slightly different from a pure race team in that they also act as automotive engineering consultants to a number of companies. They are also developing special cars that will carry the Prodrive badge in the same way that Fords often carried the Cosworth badge; it is all about product differentiation and branding.

All the companies and teams involved in the sponsorship of the motorsports have one thing in common; the reach of global television to some extent increasingly defines their market place. Tables 8.6–8.11 detail the sponsors by team and by circuits in the seasons 1993 and 1998 respectively. The data clearly demonstrates that the spread of companies involved has increased between 1993 and 1998, particularly as far as circuit advertising is concerned but also as the types of companies supporting Formula One teams. Moreover, the companies involved are no longer confined to tobacco companies and five teams in the 1998 season had no tobacco sponsorship, albeit circuit advertisers recorded

Table 8.6 **1993 Sponsors by Team**

Team	Sponsor	Sector
Benetton	BENETTON	Clothing
	CAMEL	Tobacco
	ELF	Motor
	FORD	Motor
	SULA SUGARFREE	FMCG
BMS	AGIP	Motor
	CHESTERFIELD	Tobacco
Ferrari	AGIP	Motor
	FIAT	Motor
	MAGNETI MARELLI	Motor
	MARLBORO	Tobacco
	PIONEER	IT
Footwork	BP	Motor
	FOOTWORK	Motor
	JAPAN	Tourism
	TOSHIBA	IT
Jordan	ARISCO	Motor
	DIAVIA	Motor
	PERAR (Ball valves)	Motor
	SASOL	Motor
	UNIPART	Motor
Larrousse	CHRYSLER	Motor
	ELF	Motor
	LARROUSSE	Motor
	ZANUSSI	Electrical
Ligier	ELF	Motor
	GITANES BLONDES	Tobacco
	MAGNETI MARELLI	Motor
	RENAULT	Motor
Lotus	CASTROL	Motor
	HITACHI	Machinery
	KOMAT'SU	Industrial
	LOCTITE	Industrial
	SHIONOGI	Industrial
McLaren	BOSS	Clothing
	COURTAULDS	Clothing
	KENWOOD	IT
	MARLBORO	Tobacco
	SHELL	Motor
Minardi	AGIP	Motor
	BETA	Motor
	COCIF	Industrial
	MERCATONE	Industrial
	MINARDI	Motor
Sauber	ELF	Motor
	LIQUI MOLY	Motor
	MERCEDES	Motor
Tyrrell	BP	Motor
	CABIN	Tobacco
	CALBEE	Clothing
	YAMAHA	Motor
Williams	CAMEL	Tobacco
	CANON	Photographic
	ELF	Motor
	LABATT'S	Drink
	RENAULT	Motor

Table 8.7 **1998 Sponsors by Team**

Team	Sponsor	Sector
Arrows	DANKA	IT
	IXION	IT
	PARMALAT	FMCG
	ZEPTER	IT
Benetton	AGIP	Motor
	AKAI	Electrical
	BENETTON	Clothing
	D2	Mobile phone
	FEDEX	Courier
	KOREAN AIR	Airline
	MILD SEVEN	Tobacco
	PI.SA	Ceramics
Ferrari	ASPREY	Jewelery
	FIAT	Motor
	MAGNETI MARELLI	Motor
	MARLBORO	Tobacco
	SHELL	Motor
	TELECOM ITALIA	Telecommunication
Jordan	BENSON & HEDGES	Tobacco
	G DE Z	Financial
	NATWEST	Financial
	PEARL	Financial
	PLAYSTATION	Computer games
	REPSOL	Motor
	S. OLIVER	Clothing
McLaren	BOSS	Clothing
	COMPUTER ASSOCIATES	IT
	FINLANDIA	Drink
	KENWOOD	IT
	LOCTITE	Industrial
	MERCEDES	Motor
	MOBIL 1	Motor
	SCHWEPPES	FMCG
	SIEMENS	IT
	SUN	IT
	WARSTEINER	Drink
	WEST	Tobacco
Minardi	FONDMETAL	Motor
	MTA	Electrical
	ROCES	Inline skates
Prost	AGFA	Photographic
	ALCATEL	Mobile phone
	BIC	Stationery
	CANAL+	TV
	GAULOISES	Tobacco
	PEUGEOT	Motor
	PLAYSTATION	Computer games
	TOTAL	Motor
Sauber	PETRONAS	Motor
	PLAYSTATION	Computer games
	RED BULL	FMCG
Stewart	FORD	Motor
	HSBC	Financial
	LEAR	Aeronautical
	MCI	Telecommunication
	TEXACO	Motor
Tyrrell	BROTHER	Industrial
	EUROPEAN	Airline
	FORD	Motor
	MORSE	IT
	PIAA	Motor
	YKK	Clothing
Williams	AP LOCKHEED	Motor
	CASTROL	Motor
	FALKE	Clothing
	SONAX	Motor
	VELTINS	Drink
	WINFIELD	Tobacco

Table 8.8 **Circuit Advertisers: 1993 F1 Season**

Industry	No. of sponsors	Share %
Motor	10	43.5
Drink	3	13.0
IT	3	13.0
Tourism	2	8.7
Electrical	1	4.3
Newspaper	1	4.3
Ski equipment	1	4.3
Tobacco	1	4.3
White goods	1	4.3
Grand total	23	100.0

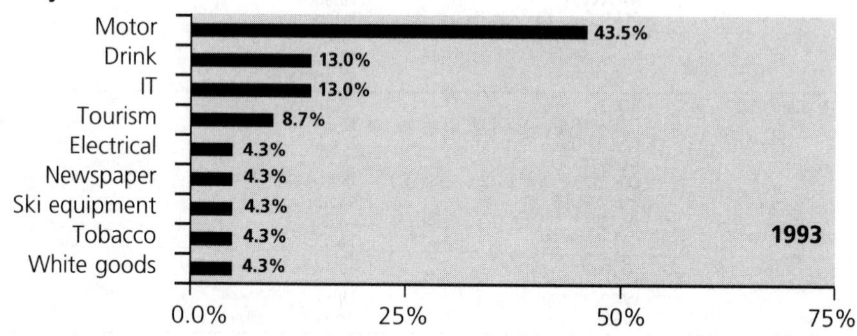

gains in both the number of tobacco companies participating and their percentage of total circuit advertising (see Tables 8.8 and 8.9).

The markets that these companies/sponsors were and are fighting for are global and multi-cultural, transcending national and regional boundaries. Companies provide the sponsorship money to the constructors but television and that now means ITV as far as the Formula One circus is concerned in the UK, provides more money. More importantly television advertising is the main incentive for the involvement of the sponsors of the sport. Each of the Formula One constructors who are signed up members of the circus receives a guaranteed income of between £5.8 and £14.4 million per season. However, it has taken Bernie Ecclestone and the Formula One Constructors' Association more than a quarter of a century to achieve such relative financial stability.

TV income is additional to the sponsors that individual teams attract and the television companies pay the vast sums because they are drawn by the magnet of the huge global audiences. These are the customers that consume their advertisers' products and it is the advertising income, or a part of it, that the TV companies use to fuel the motorsport spectacle. More particularly the advertisers are looking for specific audiences in terms of age, socio-economic group and gender. Whilst the popularity of motorsport has grown around the world the profile of the TV audience has changed. The Formula One audience in particular is no longer simply the 'petrolheads' as it has become one of the most glamorous and prestigious sports in the calendar.

Advertisers are looking for sports/attractions that provide them with an audience of customers or potential customers in specific socio-economic groups, ages and gender profiles. In Western Europe football and Formula One audiences have a similar male/female split, with Formula One audiences 63 per cent/37 per cent, but this has altered significantly during the past decade when the split was 80 per cent/20 per cent. However Formula One audiences have a significantly higher socio-economic profile and are slightly older, than football. Whilst athletics and ice-skating have the highest levels of female viewers, the audience for figure skating is significantly older. Golf is the one sport that has a higher socio-economic profile than motorsport but the audience tends to be significantly older and smaller; see Table 8.12. Tables 8.13A and 8.13B show that to some extent the popularity of the sport feeds upon itself; as the audience grows so does the coverage.

Television's Continued Importance

However, all of this televisual commercial and economic attraction is traded and, like any other valuable commodity the price depends on the scarcity and the urgency of demand; the demands of the global companies for market positioning is fierce. Their demand for markets has provided the huge stream of cash that has rolled into motorsport in general and Formula One in particular, a stream of cash that has literally been generated by the structure and the spectacle created by Ecclestone. Even the TV companies are not immune from the hot house of competition and, just like the teams that race on the track, momentary hesitation or lack of concentration can be disastrous. Just such a salutary lesson was handed out to the British Broadcasting Corporation at the end of the 1995 season.

The BBC had been the pioneers that had carefully nurtured the televising of the fledgling Grand Prix spectacle since early 1980s and one man had been responsible for that dedication; Jonathan Martin. But on 13 December 1995 he received a telephone call from the one man who the sport has recognized as knowing the TV business and its relationship with motorsport: Bernie Ecclestone. The conversation was short and to the point. Ecclestone told Martin

Table 8.9 **Circuit Advertisers: 1998 F1 Season**

Industry	No. of sponsors	Share %
Motor	10	23.8
Drink	7	16.7
Financial	5	11.9
IT	4	9.5
Tourism	4	9.5
Tobacco	3	7.1
Airline	2	4.8
Mobile phones	2	4.8
Coffee	1	2.4
FMCG	1	2.4
Media	1	2.4
Supermarket	1	2.4
TV	1	2.4
Grand total	42	100.0

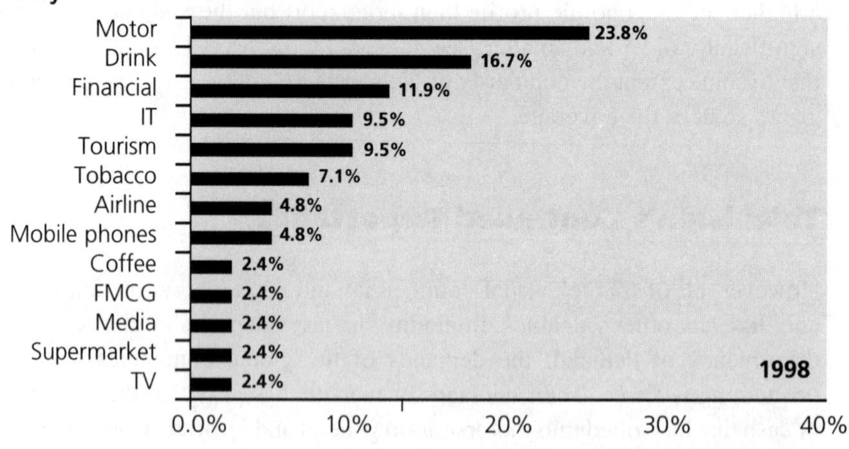

that he had sold the United Kingdom television broadcasting rights of the Formula One circus to Independent Television for £65 million. The answer that Martin reportedly gave was predictable, 'Bernie, it would have been nice to have been able to put in a competitive bid'. Ecclestone's response is not so predictable unless and you would be in a minority, you knew Ecclestone well. 'Unless you have been cheating me all these years Jonathan, there is no way that you could possibly pay what they are paying, so there was no point in talking to you about it' (*Financial Mail* on Sunday 1 November 1999). The report in the *Financial Mail* on Sunday stated that one of the ITV executives involved in the negotiations, Andrew Chown, said 'Normally I deal with committees and

Table 8.10 **Circuit Advertisers: 1993**

ALFA ROMEO	Motor	NORDICA	Ski equipment
CAMPARI	Drink	OLIVETTI	IT
CANDY	White goods	OPEL	Motor
CHAMPION	Motor	PANASONIC	Electrical
ESSO	Motor	PIRELLI	Motor
EURODISNEY	Tourism	PLAYER'S	Tobacco
FOSTER'S	Drink	Q8	Motor
FUJI	IT	SAMOA	Tourism
GOODYEAR	Motor	TAG HEUER	IT
IP	Motor	THE EUROPEAN	Newspaper
MOBIL	Motor	VAUXHALL	Motor
MOLSON	Drink		

Table 8.11 **Circuit Advertisers: 1998**

ABN AMRO BANK	Financial	HSBC	Financial
AGIP	Motor	LA CAIXA	Financial
AIR CANADA	Airline	MAGNETI MARELLI	Motor
AMP	Financial	MARLBORO	Tobacco
AREXONS	Motor	MASTERCARD	Financial
AUSTRALIA	Tourism	MELBOURNE	Tourism
BOB'S	Motor	MOBIL 1	Motor
BRIDGESTONE	Motor	MOLSON DRY	Drink
CAMPARI	Drink	NICE–MATIN	Media
CANADA	Tourism	PLAYER'S	Tobacco
CASINO	Supermarket	QUANTAS	Airline
CELLEIR DES DAUPHINS	Drink	QUEBEC	Tourism
CHAMPION	Motor	RAC	Motor
COCA COLA	FMCG	SELENIA	Coffee
CONTINENTAL	Motor	SHELL	Motor
CYNAR	Drink	SIEMENS	IT
D2	Mobile phones	SUN	IT
FINLANDIA	Drink	TAG HEUER	it
FOSTER'S	Drink	TELESP CELLULAR	Mobile phones
GAULOISES	Tobacco	WARSTEINER	Drink
GLOBO	TV	ZEPTER	IT

Table 8.12 **Formula One TV Viewer Demographics**

		Viewed 10+OP's	Support Team	Men	Women	6–14	15–34	38–49	50+	Upper	Middle	Lower
Western Europe	France	33%	57%	61%	39%	7%	22%	22%	49%	39%	41%	20%
	Germany	47%	46%	65%	35%	5%	35%	21%	40%	51%	38%	11%
	Italy	28%	72%	66%	34%	6%	31%	30%	33%	34%	49%	17%
	UK	54%	41%	62%	38%	9%	27%	25%	39%	46%	24%	30%
Central Europe	Czech. Rep			69%	31%	9%	24%	27%	40%	11%	22%	67%
	Hungary	38%	44%	59%	41%	10%	27%	24%	39%	11%	26%	66%
	Poland			58%	42%	12%	35%	34%	19%	36%	35%	29%
	Russia			71%	29%	11%	28%	26%	35%			
Asia	China			58%	42%	17%	39%	25%	19%			
	Indonesia			57%	43%	21%	39%	20%	20%			
	Japan	19%	38%	66%	34%	4%	47%	35%	14%			
	Philippines			57%	43%	21%	44%	19%	16%			
	Thailand			55%	45%	22%	44%	19%	15%			
South America	Argentina	18%	67%	58%	42%	9%	31%	28%	32%			
	Mexico	15%	27%	57%	43%	23%	42%	20%	15%	19%	21%	66%

Other Sport Viewer Demographics

Sporting Events	Men	Woman	4–15	16–34	35+	AB	C1	C2	DE
Football	62.9%	37.1%	10.6%	25.8%	63.6%	16.9%	26.6%	23.7%	32.8%
Athletics	53.2%	46.8%	8.8%	19.1%	72.1%	18.6%	26.6%	22.4%	32.4%
Golf	59.0%	41.0%	4.7%	14.9%	80.4%	20.5%	28.2%	21.3%	30.0%
Ice Hockey	53.7%	46.3%	12.5%	33.0%	54.5%	18.4%	20.4%	40.8%	20.4%
Skiing	51.0%	49.0%	8.6%	17.2%	74.2%	20.7%	27.5%	19.8%	32.1%
Figure Skating	44.4%	55.6%	7.5%	12.8%	79.6%	19.2%	28.8%	19.6%	32.4%

Table 8.13A **Formula One – The Growth: TV Coverage**

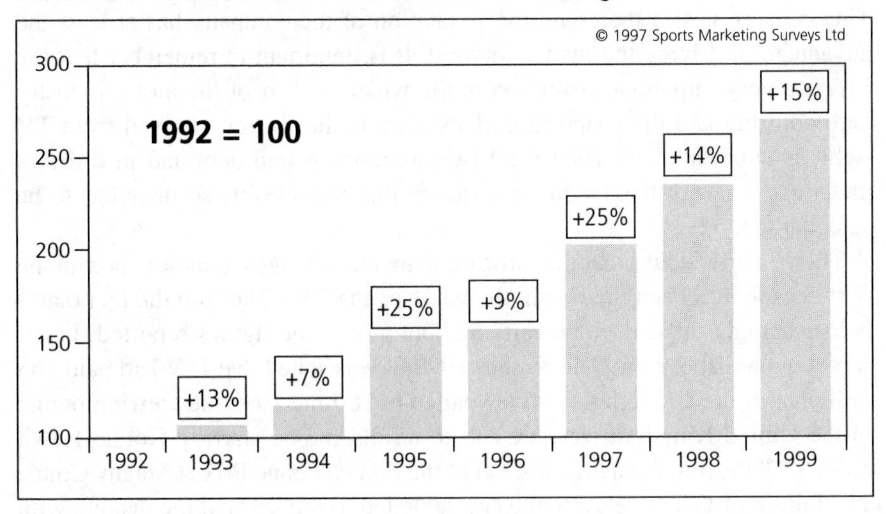

Table 8.13B **Formula One – The Growth: TV Audience**

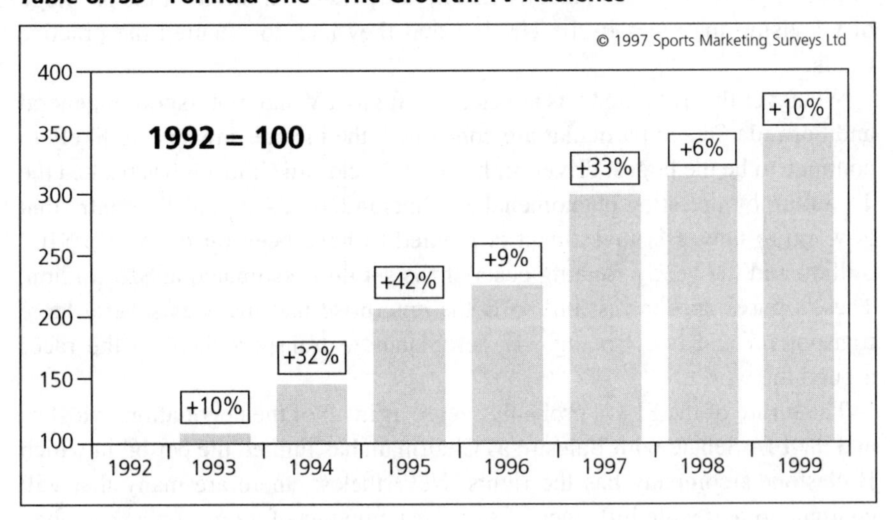

various levels of authority. With Formula One it is just Bernie Ecclestone – full stop'.

The story is interesting for three reasons. Firstly, the fact that it illustrates the continued trust and respect that the Formula One Constructors and the Fédération Internationale de l'Automobile have for Ecclestone's commercial and business acumen. Secondly, it is a classic example of the negotiating skill and blunt honesty of the man. Thirdly, it also suggests that the FIA's desire for an executive structure for the business Ecclestone runs, has yet to be fulfilled. This concern is still there and the flotatation of the company has at least the advantage of driving the matter forward. It is important to remember that the FIA is a very important institution in the wider context of the motor industry and motoring and the proportion of its income that is now derived from TV rights is substantial. In 1987 the FIA was running into debt and in order to undertake its work the TV income stream that provides its security has to be safeguarded.

There is little doubt that the most fundamental changes in motor sport in the past decade, has been the rise in the value of the TV rights and the fact that it is increasingly difficult to be certain about any of the figures reported. In the report quoted above on 1 November 1999, it was stated that ITV had paid £65 millions for the UK rights for five years. On 26 June 1999 the viewing public in the United Kingdom were treated to an old movie starring Goldie Hawn rather than the timed practice session of the French Grand Prix at Magny Cours. The failure of ITV to televise the spectacle led to reports that the dispute with the 'bosses of Formula One' (*Sunday Times*, 27 June 1999) was to blame. Further reports suggested that ITV had in fact paid £80 million for the privilege of televising the races in the UK but that they had not secured the practice rights.

Whatever the truth the facts are clear, as far as TV and motorsport in general and Formula One in particular are concerned, the income streams are likely to continue to be the largest driver of the sport. Ecclestone himself has backed the TV future by investing phenomenal amounts in the new digital TV centre that is working now. His investment is reputed to have been up to (over?) $100 million and the yearly running costs of the set up is estimated at $20 million. These figures appear vast but so is the enterprise that includes several large transporters and two Boeing 747 aeroplanes to transport them to the races around the world.

The future of the FIA is probably secure as in all of the negotiations Mosley, and the FIA Senate with Balestre as Chairman, has limited the period in which Ecclestone's company has the rights. Nevertheless, there are many that will continue to regret the influence of such vast amounts of money on a sport that, to the minds and hearts of many in the United Kingdom, was something of a modern gladiatorial battle. A battle in which their cavalier heroes such as Dick Seaman, Raymond Mays, John Cooper, Mike Hawthorn, Stirling Moss, Colin Chapman and Jim Clark took on the world and won.

The fact is that this is now a multi-billion pound global business in which Britain has retained the technological and managerial lead, through the re-structuring brought about by a number of brilliant individualists. But it would be a travesty if the contribution of the one man, who laid the financial and organizational foundations for the teams and companies to lead in the technology and management of this sport, were not to be recognized. A travesty probably led by the British antipathy towards the creation of new wealth, an antipathy that may well lead to our future failure in many other areas.

Constructors, Customers and Suppliers: Interactions of Technologies and Hardware

Vision without Action is a Daydream
Action Without Vision is a Nightmare
JAPANESE PROVERB

Introduction: The Scope of the Market

MOTORSPORT, viewed as a market, is highly segmented. The segments, or formulae (Formula One, Formula 3000, Formula Ford, Touring Cars, Rally Cars etc.), are differentiated via the application of sporting regulations. These regulations constrain or dictate all aspects of competition – the product, permitted technologies, geographic scope and promotion. It follows that the costs of competing and barriers to entry, are strongly influenced by these regulations.

While this book takes an overview of the Motor Sport Industry in the United Kingdom this chapter focuses on a selection of constructors in major formulae and their associated suppliers. We shall also consider the scope of the industry as a whole, and the dispersion of the constructors in Formula One, Formula 3000, plus other single seat formulae, rally and touring cars in association with suppliers of hardware and components and major volume manufacturer's race operations.

There are a number of important regulatory considerations that apply to the industry and the different formulae. Formula One represents the pinnacle of automotive technology primarily because it is an 'open' formula. Competing teams, often regarded as entrepreneurial lead users, attract best of breed suppliers and technology partners, along with the best of available engineering and managerial talen. These cars must conform to a set of regulations, but the regulations do not dictate or constrain the choice of component suppliers.

Other single seat Formula classifications (notably Formula 3000) prescribe the use of a standard car and there are a number of chassis suppliers who dominate the sector. These cars must conform to a set of regulations that do restrict the choice of component suppliers.

Motor racing, from Formula One through Touring and Rally cars down through the different single seat formulae, is the subject of constant media attention which generates the lifeblood of the industry; sponsorship money. This has led to an enormous quantity of written material, detailing the statements and actions of key industry players. This archive of material provides a rich source of raw data for analysis and study.

In this manner is the industry divided into sectors and into markets, suppliers, contractors and customers. The ultimate end product consumer is the spectator who provides the reason for the involvement of the sponsor. In turn, the sponsor purchases the space on the cars, billboards around the tracks and, indirectly, the global television exposure. Television is the oxygen of this industry and the factor that fans the flames of the marketing people in the multi-national/global companies that fund this industry, particularly within the upper echelons.

The global reach of Formula One and other motorsport categories is the reason for companies providing sponsorship and TV viewing time. However, the spectacle has also been 'tailored' in many ways to enhance its TV value. Although TV income is additional to the sponsors that individual teams attract it is now the life blood of the sport and the viewers are the customers of the sponsoring companies. They imitate an initiative taken by Colin Chapman of Lotus when he persuaded the tobacco company, John Player to livery the Lotus 49 in the Gold Leaf colours for 1968. It was not until 1970 that the next Grand Prix sponsor arrived; Yardley for BRM in 1970. Chapman was a commercial as well as a technological innovator.

Geographic Innovation and the Scope of the Industry

We make no apology for limiting the scope of this study to the industry within Britain. In contrast to the well-documented decline and acquisition of Britain's volume car producers, the motor sport sector in Britain has enjoyed continued growth for the last fifty years and been internationally dominant for the past thirty.

This chapter examines part of the commercial extent of British domination in this market and the relevance of an agglomeration of world class teams and suppliers in Britain's motor sport cluster, a region 'centred around Oxfordshire and stretching in an arc through into East Anglia and down into Surrey' (Henry *et al.*, 1996). In order to explore the links between motor sport and associated industries, and the flow of technology throughout the resultant network of companies we shall also explore:

- The nature of the motor sport industry and market in Britain, including analysis of stakeholders, supplier relationships and supply chains.
- Innovation and radicalism within the motor racing environment. Does the motor racing environment promote the creation of new technologies, or does it rely more on the incremental improvement of existing technology?
- The part that associated industries play in innovation, or continuous improvement. How can associated industries benefit from technologies developed within the motor sport industry?

Technological Innovation and the Scope of the Industry

Twiss and Goodridge (1989) assert 'no technology has unlimited potential. Eventually its advance will be constrained by a physical limit'. The rate of advance of technology through innovation can be seen as analogous to the growth in a market as it approaches saturation, following a classic 'S curve'.

As a technology approaches maturity, there is less scope for radical improvement. Fawn and Foxall (1992) expand this theory, by treating technological innovation as an evolutionary process. Their work suggests that within embryonic markets 'competition is especially strong in the area of technological development where there is much trial and error, rapid change and competition among the new entrants to match and exceed each other's performance'. In a maturing market, they contend that 'technological and marketing knowledge is pervasive and competitive advantage lies in the

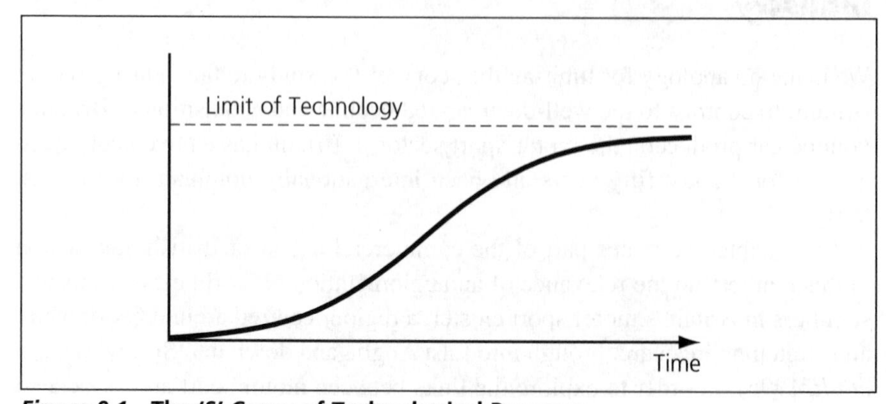

Figure 9.1 **The 'S' Curve of Technological Progress**

incremental improvement of productive and marketing operations'.

Although it is certainly characterized by rapid change and fierce competition, Formula One is hardly an embryonic market. In our opinion, it is best thought of as a maturing entertainment industry. According to the work of Fawn and Foxall (1992), we can anticipate that 'the dynamics of improvements introduced at different times by different manufacturers will cause a continuing pressure for incremental product improvement'.

It has proved difficult to derive an independent estimate of the turnover of the motor sport industry in Britain. Financial information is not publicly available and a substantial number of suppliers also act as contractors to other industries (notably the aerospace and defence industries). However, it is reasonable to assume that all Formula One constructors operate on an annual budget of between £30 million and £100 million, the latter is Ferrari's estimated budget for 1998, quoted in *Hotten* (1998).

Turning to the value of British motor sport companies, a recent spate of acquisitions has provided some indications of value. Major financial institutions are taking equity stakes in Formula One constructors, bringing City money into an industry traditionally financed by tobacco sponsorship. Stewart Grand Prix gained support from the HSBC as an initial sponsor and Warburg, Pincus, the venture capital firm, has taken a 40 per cent stake in Jordan for an investment of $60 million (*The Times*, 17 November 1998). Morgan Grenfell Private Equity has taken a major stake in TWR Arrows (valuing the company at £110 million, *Autosport*, 14 January 1999). In the most recent acquisition Ford have taken ownership of Stewart Grand Prix for an estimated £100 millions plus a further £50 millions annual level of support. Perhaps this is the shape of things to come?

The Distribution of the Industry

The overall distribution of the motor sport and race car construction industry, and in particular the significance of Motor Sport Valley, is regularly cited as important to the way in which technology is created and (consciously or inadvertently) disseminated. By way of example, as already mentioned, Henry *et al.* (1996) cites the British Motor Sport Industry as an example of a 'new industrial space' that is responsible for technological innovation.

The benefits of location, external architectures and networks are all well documented (Kay, 1993; Porter, 1990). Kay (1993) suggests that 'external architecture is found where firms share knowledge, or establish fast response times, on the basis of a series of relational contracts between or among them'. Porter (1990 and 1998) notes the tendency for powerful firms within an industry to be found within the same country or region, a phenomenon he terms 'clustering' and attributes to the importance of technical factors. Kay (1993) believes that Porter overstates the importance of technical factors, postulating instead that architecture and access to scarce resources are fundamental to such agglomerations. However, in more recent work Porter emphasizes the totality of 'clusters' in the sense that all ancillary services such as marketing are specific to the cluster (Porter 1998).

There are striking parallels. Aston and Williams (1996) suggest, between the development of Motor Sport Valley in Britain and that of Silicon Valley in the United States. In both instances, they contend, development can be traced back to a talented group of amateurs sharing information in a self-help network and finding solutions to technical problems that were both cheap and efficient.

The interest in this new industrial space does, however, present its own problems. It is apparent that existing literature (Northamptonshire County Council, 1997; Henry and Pinch, 1997; Milan, 1995) focuses on the agglomeration of teams and suppliers within Motor Sport Valley, to the detriment of analysis of other parts of Britain. Such a limited focus is understandable, given the apparent conflation of markets and industries. However, in order to attain an overview of the capabilities of motor sport companies in Britain as a whole, a more comprehensive study is first required.

The *Autosport Directory* (1998) was selected as the most up-to-date and complete repository of information relating to motorsport suppliers and constructors. It provides contact information, along with the capabilities of each company. Based on information taken from this directory, Table 9.1 sets out a capability inventory. Figure 9.4 then graphically presents this capability inventory, showing the concentration of motorsport capability within Britain, segmented by county.

Motor Sport Valley is commonly defined as the combination of the West Midlands, Northamptonshire, Oxfordshire and Surrey. Using this as a working definition, then analysis presented in Table 9.1 suggests that the valley contains less than 25 per cent of Britain's motor sport engineering capability. In other words, there appears to be only a limited agglomeration of capability within Motor Sport Valley; the 'Valley' is wider than suggested by others. Figure 9.3 presents the location of Formula One constructors, showing a clear geographical agglomeration whereby the majority of constructors are situated in Motor Sport Valley.

By way of contrast, Figure 9.4 presents the location of F3000 teams. This reveals no agglomeration, though several teams are located close to major racing circuits (Silverstone in Northamptonshire and Snetterton in Norfolk). The authors would suggest that the key reason why F3000 teams do not cluster is that they don't manufacture components, or contract independently with suppliers to manufacture components for them. F3000 teams rely on a few common suppliers – F3000 is a control formula where technical aspects of the car are prescribed by the formula regulations.

The agglomeration of Formula One teams does not, however, imply a similar agglomeration of suppliers. Table 9.5 illustrates the point that major suppliers to Formula One are geographically dispersed; only two (AP Racing and ATL Fuel Cells) are located within Motor Sport Valley (as defined above), and the majority are based outside of Britain. However, it is important to emphasize that Formula One teams design and build up to 80 per cent of the cars' components apart from engines. This research demonstrates that there is an agglomeration of Formula One constructors but that there are no parallels with either other formulae (such as F3000), and that it is not shared by suppliers to the industry. It also suggests that the reasons underlying the agglomeration of Formula One constructors in Motor Sport Valley require further investigation.

Technology and Innovation: The Importance and Commercial Basis of Technology Transfer

However, the simple economic benefits, important as they are do not provide a sufficiently broad or realistic assessment of the important linkages between industries that help to drive economic development and growth. Industries literally feed off one another and the extent to which this industry has spawned companies and growth is considerable. The TWR Group with a turnover in excess of £370 million is a company that has its roots in motor racing and still earns approximately 15 per cent of its revenue from the sport or related activities; but whose total revenue does not appear in surveys. There are numerous technological transfers between companies in this industry and other industries.

Twiss and Goodridge (1989) suggest that technology 'is the application of scientific knowledge to serve the needs of society or individuals', suggesting that technologies targeted at a defined market will achieve greater success. Roberts (1988) expands on the notion that technology entails the application of scientific knowledge, when he offers the following definition of technology:

> 'Technology is the understanding and application of scientific knowledge, technical information, know-how, critical materials, unique manufacturing equipment, end products, and test equipment essential to research, develop, produce and use state-of-the-art items or systems.'

Loveridge (1994) has little to add to these definitions, but does stress the importance of tacit routines and knowledge (cliché: 'We know more than we can say'). Tacit routines, he suggests, often relate to the specific organizational system in which they arise and can contribute to an organization's unique

Table 9.1 **Motor Sport Capability in Britain**

	Avon	Bedfordshire	Berkshire	Buckinghamshire	Cambridgeshire	Cheshire	Cleveland	Clwyd	Cornwall	Cumbria	Derbyshire	Devon	Dorset	Essex	Fife
Aerofoils					1						3		2		
Alloy Products	1			1	1										
Axles															
Bearings		1			2			1							
Body Shells					3	2					1			1	
Brake Systems	1	2		1		2						3		1	
Carburettors / Fuel Injection	1	1	1			1	2	1	1			3	1		1
Castings					1	1								1	
Consultancies	5	4	3	5	5	1					2	1	3	7	
Cylinder Head & Block															
Telemetry		3			3	1					1		2	1	
Designers	3		1	1	3	1				1		3		5	
Differentials	1		1			1								1	
Dynamometers	1	1	1	1		1								2	
Engine Components	3	4	2	1	3	4							1	2	
Engine Management														1	
Engine Manufacturers	1	3	5	6	3	6	1	1	1		1	1	1	14	
Engineering Components		1			1	2			1					1	
Engineering Services	1	2	2	4	1	4	1				3	1	3	3	
Exhausts	2	1	2		2	5	1	2			2	3		2	1
Foundries											1				
Fuel Injection				1					1						
Fuel Tanks				1		1		1			1			2	
Gearbox Specialists	1	2	4		1								1	3	
Glass / Carbon Fibre			1	1	4	3					3	1	1	1	
Hoses and Fittings	2	1	3	1		1			1		1	3		1	
Ignition Systems		3		2		1		1				1		1	
Lamps and Lights					1	1				1					
Oil and Fuel	1		2		1			1	1		1			3	
Oil Tanks											1			1	
One Make Specialists											3		3	2	
Propshafts		1													
Quick Release Fittings			1					1				1			
Race and Rally Preparation	1	9	4	8	4	13				5	5	6	6	13	1
Race Car Construction	1		5	2	8	6				1	2	3	3	5	
Radiators															
Rod Ends			1		1			1					1		
Roll Cages	1				2			1							
Rolling Roads	1	2		1	1	7			1		1	3	3		
Seat Belts and Harnesses	2	1	1		1	1		1						2	
Seats			1			1		1			1		1	3	
Spherical Joints			2		3			1							
Suspension and Steering	2	3	2		5			1			1	3	1	7	
Tyre Companies		1	1	1		2								2	
Wheel Manufacturers				1		3								1	
Wind Tunnels		1											1		
Wings											2		2		
Wiring		1													
Totals	**32**	**48**	**46**	**40**	**63**	**77**	**5**	**15**	**7**	**8**	**37**	**36**	**36**	**89**	**3**
Percentage of Total	**1.5**	**2.2**	**2.1**	**1.9**	**2.9**	**3.6**	**0.2**	**0.7**	**0.3**	**0.4**	**1.7**	**1.7**	**1.7**	**4.2**	**0.1**

Total Capability 2141 (distinct capabilities held by Motor Sport firms in Britain)
Percentage in Valley 22.7%

Table 9.1 (continued) **Motor Sport Capability in Britain**

	Glamorganshire	Gloucestershire	Gwent	Hampshire	Herefordshire	Hertfordshire	Kent	Lancashire	Leicestershire	Lincolnshire	London	Merseyside	Middlesex	Norfolk	Northamptonshire
Aerofoils				2					1		1			1	1
Alloy Products						1		1			3				6
Axles		1		1		1									1
Bearings		1		1		1			1	1			1		3
Body Shells				3		1	4				1				1
Brake Systems	1	2	1	1		2	1	1	3		2				4
Carburettors / Fuel Injection	2	1		1		1	2	3	2		4		1	1	3
Castings						1	3	1			2				2
Consultancies		4	1	5		8	8	4	4	1	9		5	3	6
Cylinder Head & Block										1	1				
Telemetry				1			3				2		3	3	3
Designers	2	2				2	4	2	2	1	4	1			7
Differentials		2		1			1				1		1		1
Dynamometers		1		3			2		1					3	3
Engine Components		6		6	1	2	9	2	2	3	5		6	1	3
Engine Management								1		1					1
Engine Manufacturers	2	5		10	1	2	14	5	7	2	8	1	7	3	23
Engineering Components	1	1		2		1	1		1	2	4		3	1	5
Engineering Services		3		1		2	2	3			1		3	1	
Exhausts	1			3	1	2	2	3			5	1	1		2
Foundries							1								1
Fuel Injection		1				1			1				1		2
Fuel Tanks				1			2				1				1
Gearbox Specialists		2					3	1	1		1		1		3
Glass / Carbon Fibre		1		3			1			1				2	3
Hoses and Fittings	1	2				2	1	2		1	1		2	1	3
Ignition Systems		3						1	1		3		2	1	2
Lamps and Lights				1											1
Oil and Fuel		1		2		2	2			3	10	1	1		1
Oil Tanks							1				1	1			4
One Make Specialists	1	1		1		3	7	2		1	6	1	3	2	
Propshafts								1							
Quick Release Fittings		1				1	1								1
Race and Rally Preparation	1	3		9	1	8	16	9	10	5	7	2	3	7	14
Race Car Construction		1		2		1	6	3	2	4	2	1	4	6	14
Radiators							1		1				1		3
Rod Ends		2				1	1		1	1					2
Roll Cages					1					1	1				4
Rolling Roads	1	1		4		1	2	3			3		2	1	
Seat Belts and Harnesses				4		1	2				3				3
Seats				2	1		1				2				1
Spherical Joints		1				1		1	1						1
Suspension and Steering		4		2		1	1	4	4	3	2		1	1	8
Tyre Companies				2		3	2	1			2		1		2
Wheel Manufacturers				2		1	7		1		1				
Wind Tunnels				1							1			1	
Wings				1							1			1	
Wiring	3						1	1					1	3	1
Totals	**16**	**53**	**2**	**78**	**6**	**53**	**116**	**54**	**47**	**33**	**101**	**9**	**54**	**43**	**156**
Percentage of Total	**0.7**	**2.5**	**0.1**	**3.6**	**0.3**	**2.5**	**5.4**	**2.5**	**2.2**	**1.5**	**4.7**	**0.4**	**2.5**	**2.0**	**7.3**

Total Capability 2141 (distinct capabilities held by Motor Sport firms in Britain)
Percentage in Valley 22.7%

***Table 9.1 (continued)* Motor Sport Capability in Britain**

	Nottinghamshire	Oxfordshire	Shropshire	Somerset	Staffordshire	Suffolk	Surrey	Sussex	Tyne and Wear	Warwickshire	West Midlands	Wiltshire	Worcestershire	Yorkshire
Aerofoils		3					2	1						
Alloy Products			3			1	3	4	1	1	1			
Axles							1				1		2	2
Bearings			1		1		2	1			2		1	1
Body Shells		2		1			4	2		1		1	1	2
Brake Systems		2			4		2			3	3		5	2
Carburettors / Fuel Injection	2	2		1	1	1	6	1	2		2	2		3
Castings						1	1	3			1	1	1	1
Consultancies	2	9	3			2	7	6	1	7	1	2		4
Cylinder Head & Block														
Telemetry		4					3	2				1		1
Designers		7			1	2	6	4		2	6	3		5
Differentials	1				1		1	1			2		1	1
Dynamometers				1	1	1	1	1			1	4	1	1
Engine Components	1	6			3	3	4	1	2	2	5	3	1	4
Engine Management	1													
Engine Manufacturers		9	3		3	4	12	10	1	3	8	4	2	4
Engineering Components		1			1		4	1		2	3	1	2	2
Engineering Services		5		3	1		5	3		1	5	3	2	5
Exhausts	3	4		2	1		4		1	3	1	2		3
Foundries						1					1	1		1
Fuel Injection		2				1	2				1			2
Fuel Tanks	2	1					3							
Gearbox Specialists	2	3	1	1	2		1	3		1		1	2	5
Glass / Carbon Fibre	3						4	2				1	1	2
Hoses and Fittings	1	1					2		2	1	3		3	1
Ignition Systems		1				1	3				1			1
Lamps and Lights		1		1	1		1			1				1
Oil and Fuel	2	1					1				1	3	2	2
Oil Tanks	2	2				1	2							
One Make Specialists	1	3		1		1	3	1		1	6	1	2	1
Propshafts		1			1						3			2
Quick Release Fittings		1	1		1		1				1			
Race and Rally Preparation	3	10	1	1	4	5	12	6	1	5	9	8	10	15
Race Car Construction	3	6			1		8	4		5	4	1	2	4
Radiators		1				1	1			1	1		1	
Rod Ends		1			1		2				2			
Roll Cages		2					2					1	1	1
Rolling Roads	1			1				1			2		1	1
Seat Belts and Harnesses	1	1		1			3	1		1	1	1		1
Seats			1	2	1	2	2	1				1		
Spherical Joints		1						3						
Suspension and Steering	2	5	2	2	2	1	9	7		1		2	1	6
Tyre Companies	1		1		1		2		1	1	7	1		
Wheel Manufacturers		1			1		1	2		2	4	3		1
Wind Tunnels								1		1				
Wings							1			1		1		
Wiring		2					3					1		
Totals	**34**	**101**	**17**	**18**	**34**	**29**	**140**	**70**	**12**	**47**	**89**	**54**	**45**	**88**
Percentage of Total	**1.6**	**4.7**	**0.8**	**0.8**	**1.6**	**1.4**	**6.5**	**3.3**	**3.6**	**2.2**	**4.2**	**2.5**	**2.1**	**4.1**

***Figure 9.2 Concentration of* Motor Sport Capability in Britain**

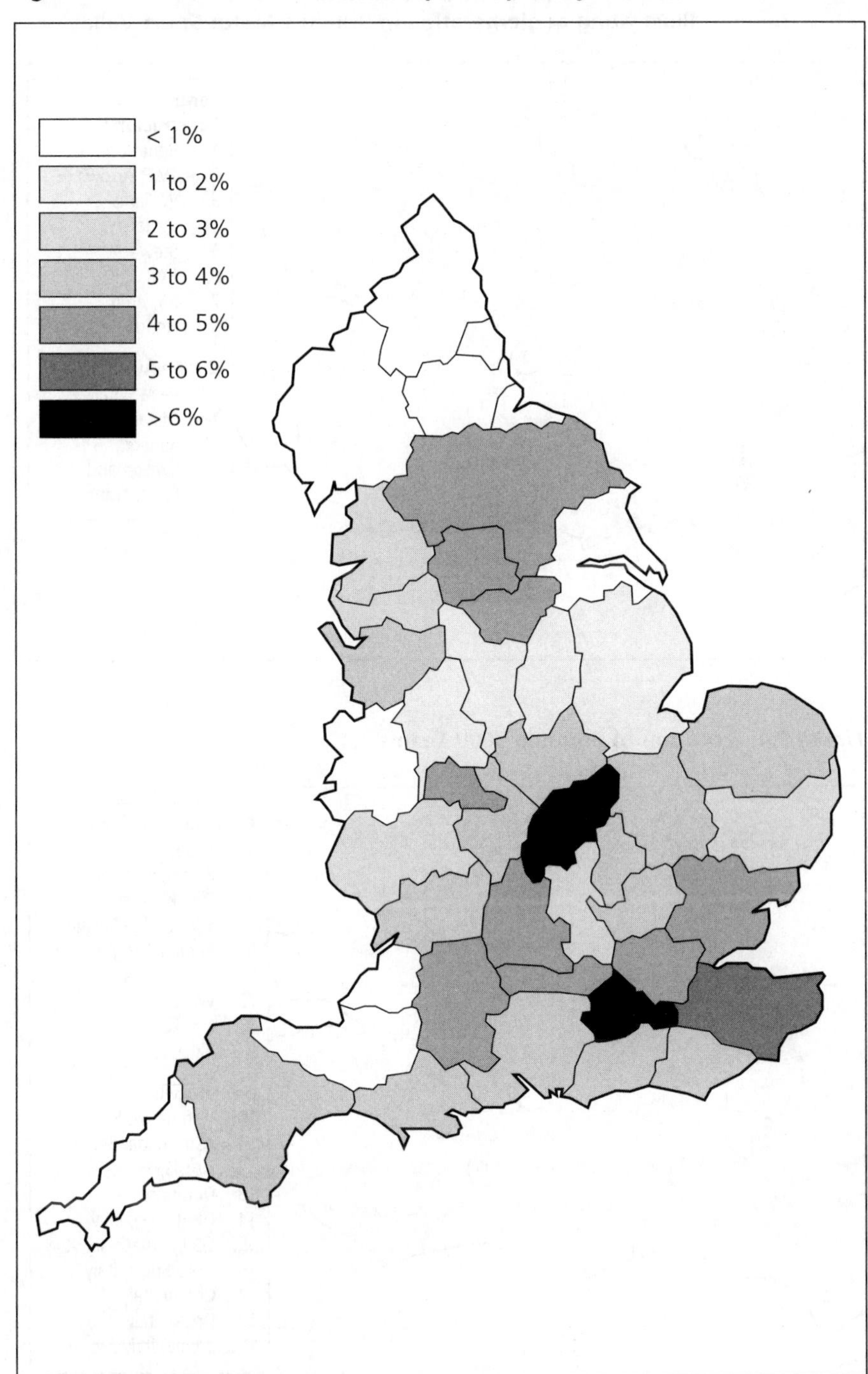

Figure 9.3 **Location of Formula One Constructors Illustrating agglomeration in Britain's Motor Sport Valley'**

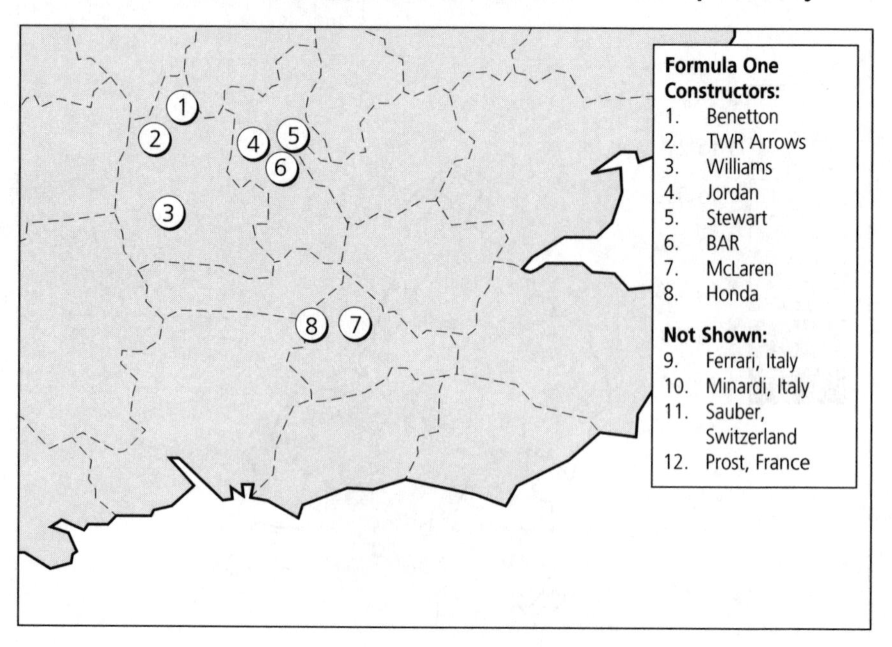

Figure 9.4 **Location of Formula 3000 Teams**

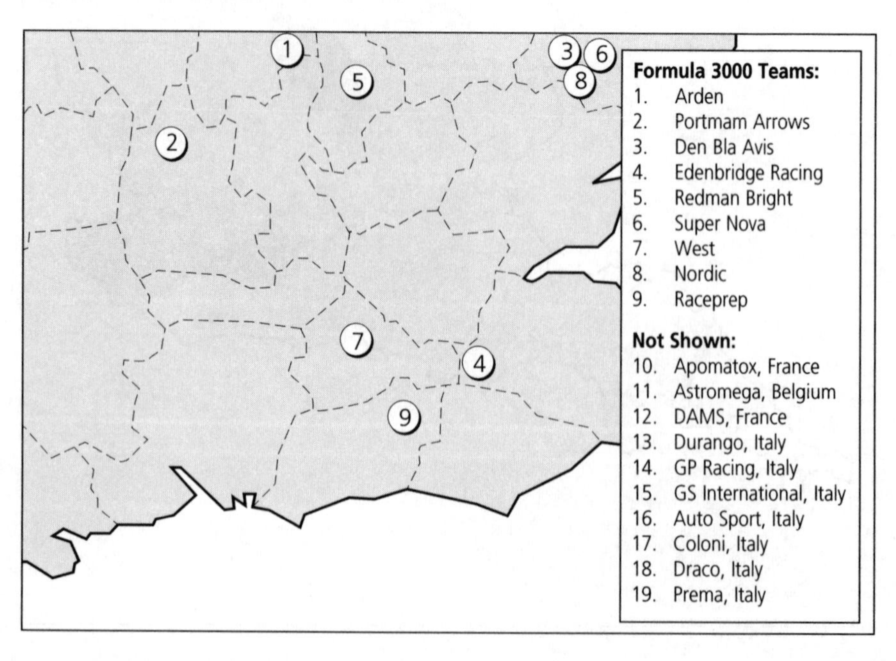

***Table 9.2* Suppliers to Formula One**

Team	Williams	Ferrari	Benetton	McLaren	Jordan	Prost	Sauber	TWR Arrows	Stewart	Tyrrell	Minardi
Engine	Mecachrome	Ferrari	Mecachrome	Mercedes	Mugen Honda	Peugeot	Sauber	Arrows	Ford	Ford	Ford
Dampers	Penske		Dynamics	Penske	Showa		Sachs	Dynamics	Penske	Koni	Dynamics
Steering	Williams	Ferrari	BFL		Jordan	Prost	Sauber	Arrows	Stewart	Tyrrell	Minardi
Gearbox	Williams	Ferrari	Benetton	McLaren	Jordan	Prost	Sauber	Arrows	Stewart	Tyrrell	Minardi
Clutch	AP Racing	AP Racing	AP Racing	AP Racing	AP Racing	AP Racing	Sachs	AP Racing	AP Racing	AP Racing	AP Racing
Brake Discs	Carbone Ind.	Brembo	Brembo	Carbone Ind.	Carbone Ind.	Carbone Ind.	Carbone Ind.	Carbone Ind.	Carbone Ind.	Hitco	Carbone Ind.
Brake Calipers	AP Racing	Brembo	Brembo	AP Racing	Brembo	AP Racing	Brembo	AP Racing	AP Racing		Brembo
Brake Pads	Carbone Ind.	Brembo	Brembo	Carbone Ind.	Carbone Ind.	Carbone Ind.	Carbone Ind.	Carbone Ind.	Carbone Ind.		Carbone Ind.
Seat Belts	Williams	TRW Sabet	TRW Sabet		Williana	TRW Sabet	TRW Sabet	TRW Sabet	TRW Sabet	Schroth	TRW Sabet
Wheels	OZ Racing	BBS	BBS	Enkel	OZ Racing	BBS	Speedline	BBS	BBS	BBS	Fondmetal
Tyres	Goodyear	Goodyear	Bridgestone	Bridgestone	Goodyear	Bridgestone	Goodyear	Bridgestone	Bridgestone	Goodyear	Bridgestone
Fuel Cell	ATL	ATL	ATL	ATL	ATL	ATL	ATL	ATL	ATL	ATL	ATL
Spark Plugs	Champion	Champion	Champion	NGK	NGK	NGK	Champion	Champion	Champion	Champion	Champion
Fuel	Petrobras	Shell	AGIP	Mobil	Repsol	Total	Petronas	Elf	Texaco	ELF	Elf
Lubricants	Petrobras	Shell	AGIP	Mobil	Repsol	Total	Petronas	Elf	Texaco	ELF	Elf
Number of Suppliers	11	8	11	9	11	9	9	9	10	10	11
Number based outside of Britain	5	3	4	3	5	4	6	4	4	5	5
Number based in 'Motor Valley'	2	2	2	2	1	2	1	2	2	2	2

Notes: *Suppliers with a significant British subsidiary or base are considered as supplying from within Britain e.g. Bridgestone. Information is collated from teams. Mnay suppliers of minor components (e.G. Xtrac who supply gears) are not listed* competence. He goes on to suggest that age and complexity will influence the proportion of tacit knowledge in technical knowledge. The newer or more sophisticated the knowledge or technique, the less likely it is to be documented or standardized.

Summarizing these definitions, we can derive a working definition of technology that groups under three primary headings.

- Materials and designs
- Techniques and processes, whether documented or embodied in tacit routines
- Knowledge, relating to the design, production or use of materials (often referred to in discussions about the 'learning curve'). As with techniques and processes, such technical knowledge can be explicit or tacit.

We can look to Freeman (1982) for a distinction between innovation and invention. He asserts that the process of innovation is concerned with turning an idea or an invention into a tangible product or service. Innovation, in the view of Slappendel (1996), is generally used in the context of describing high-technology equipment, such as a personal computer. Crucially, as he goes on to assert, innovation also refers to the process through which 'new ideas, objects and practices are created and developed or reinvented'. Schumpeter (1943) had a broader view of innovation, which included 'the new markets, the new forms of industrial organization that capitalist enterprise creates'.

There are a number of conclusions that are important here. Firstly, the literature and other empirical evidence established the general agreement that innovation is rarely the result of any one individual's work. Freeman (1990) provides the results of an extensive literature review, and notes that empirical studies of technological innovation have demonstrated 'the importance of both formal and informal networks', suggesting that 'multiple sources of information and pluralistic patterns of collaboration were the rule rather than the exception'. As reported by Jones (1997), 'it is essential to analyse these networks and to examine their impact on particular technological trajectories'.

Information on innovations has been collated from various sources, including interviews, literature and the world-wide web. Technologies adopted by the Motor Sport Industry are dealt with separately – only technologies innovated within the Motor Sport Industry are listed in Table 9.3.

What drives this innovation? Aston and Williams (1996) conducted a limited survey to establish the stimulus; their findings suggest that the majority of innovation is customer driven (32 per cent), or the result of In-house R&D (33 per cent).

But how are these innovations then adopted by associated industries? Most,

Table 9.3 **Technologies innovated within the Motor Sports Industry**

TECHNOLOGY
Continuous Variable Transmission (not used at senior level)
Accelerator control by Wire
Active Suspension
Traction Control
Sliding Skirts
Pneumatic valve gear

including pneumatic valve gear and sliding skirts, have found limited applications outside of motor sport. However, two technologies amongst a number of others have been adopted by the mainstream automotive industry:

- Lotus have developed active suspension technology, and introduced it in road going prototype vehicles. Through consultancy, this technology has also been made available to other manufacturers.
- Ford and Fiat have both introduced small passenger cars with Continuously Variable Transmission (CVT). This mechanically more efficient alternative to conventional torque converter automatic transmissions is still the subject of major manufacturer development programmes holding particular promise for smaller engine mass market designs. More glamorous transmission hardware from Grand Prix has been transferred in the principle of shifting gears from controls adjacent to/on the steering wheel. Later in this chapter we discuss this transfer further from the Grand Prix Ferraris of the past ten years to 1998–9 Fiat Group products, the Ferrari F50 and Alfa Romeo 156 Selespeed.

Technologies Exported

Motor racing has also exported a number of technologies that have been utilised by other industries (notably aerospace and its use of ultra lightweight materials) and companies within the mainstream automotive sector. Table 9.4 overleaf illustrates an extensive network of technologies that have flowed out of the motor sport industry into other areas and presents instances of technology transfer, found as a result of an extensive literature review, interviews and a search of the world-wide web.

Each row in the Table 9.4 records information relating to a single claimed instance of technology transfer. Such transfers may be to a recipient in a related industry, or to a competitor in the same industry.

Table 9.4 **Claimed Instances of Technology Transfer**

Provider	Recipient	Relationship	Power held by Provider?	Geographic Proximity of Provider and Recipient	Technology Transferred	Source of Information
Ferrari	Fiat	Intra-organizational	n/a	Close	Steering and suspension systems	Hotten (1998)
Ferrari F1	Ferrari Cars	Intra-organizational	n/a	Colocated	Chassis, suspension and gearbox operation	Various (1998)
McLaren International	McLaren Cars	Intra-organizational	n/a	Colocated	F1 road car	Hotten (1998)
F1 Constructors	Goodyear	Intra-organizational	n/a	National	Goodyear Eagle F1 Road Tyre	WWW
TAG McLaren	McLaren Audio	Intra-organizational	n/a	Colocated	Electronics	The *Sunday Times*, 13.9.98
McLaren	British Aerospace	Partnership	No	National	Just In Time manufacture and related processes	WWW
Stewart	Ford	Partnership	No	International	People, Preocess and Product	WWW
Prodrive	Caterham	Contractual	No	National	Suspension systems	Interview
Mike Pilbeam	Honda	Contractual	No	International	Suspension development	Interview
BMW Motorsport	BMW	Intra-organizational	n/a	Colocated	Multi-valve technology, six-speed gearbox, aerodynamics, brake technology, intelligent engine management	*BMW Club Magazine*, June 1998
Cosworth	Ford	Licensing	No	International	Cocast Casting Process	WWW
Hart	TWR	Vertical Integration	n/a	Close	F1 engine development	Interview
Williams	JCB	Contractual	No	National	Control technology	Interview
Williams	Unknown	Contractual	No	National	Development of 'leaning train' control technology	Interview
Cosworth	Illmor	Competitive	n/a	Close	Key personnel	Interview
Benetton	Ferrari	Competitive	n/a	International	Key Personnel	Interview
Tyrrell	Ferrari	Competitive	n/a	Close	Aerodynamic 'X Wings'	*Autosport*

Technologies Imported

Scholars such as Grant (1996) suggest that firm level knowledge is central to organizational performance. In order to develop and exploit firm level knowledge, Cohen and Levinthal (1990) argue that it is essential for firms to develop the ability to absorb knowledge from outside their boundaries. Of equal importance, in the authors' opinion, are the abilities to track technology trajectories, selecting appropriate technologies to absorb and securing a competitive advantage via the application of the selected technologies.

Key technologies adopted by Formula One constructors, along with their sources (based on unpublished research by Pinch and Henry, and information provided by Williams Grand Prix Engineering), are presented below in Table 9.5:

Motor sport companies, particularly those in Formula One, expend large proportions of their budgets on race driven research and development in the effort to develop race winning cars. As in almost all industries the costs of development are increasing as the increases in Formula One budgets shows. These rapidly rising costs and the fact that many companies in the mainstream industry are using their links with teams to adopt relevant developments, have led some Formula One teams to commercialize their developments, and expertise. Ohmae (1989) maintains that firms should look to amortize their fixed costs over a larger market base. This is fuelling the diversification of firms such as Prodrive, Williams, TWR, Ferrari and TAG McLaren.

But how are these innovations then adopted by associated industries? Patrick Head, Technical Director of Williams, comments' on the development within

Table 9.5 **Technologies Adopted by Formula One Constructors**

Technology Adopted	Source Industry
Active Suspension	Aerospace Industry/ Citroen practice-
Aerodynamics	Aerospace Industry/Pre-war record breaker practice
Wind Tunnel Testing	Aerospace Industry
Computational Flow Dynamics(CFD)	Aerospace Industry & Chemical Industry
Carbon Composites/ Kevlar	Aerospace Industry
Carbon brakes & clutches	Aerospace Industry
Telemetry	Aerospace Industry
Electronic controls	Aerospace Industry
Turbocharging	Aerospace Industry/ Commercial diesel practice
Four Wheel Drive	Automotive Industry
Mid-engine layouts	500cc Formula/Automotive Industry

motor sport and the process by which innovations are transferred to the mainstream automotive industry:

> 'The direct competitive status of motorsport provokes a development rate which does not occur within the production vehicle environment mostly due to the heavy investment in production tooling, but there is technology transfer to low volume performance vehicles and then across to the higher volume units.'

The Commercialization of Technology

Models of Intra-Organizational Transfers

Some of the major Formula One teams, including Williams and McLaren, TWR, Reynard and Prodrive, have transferred their technology and process expertise into other areas of industry. This trend towards diversification within the motor sport industry has taken a number of different forms, all of which are designed to enhance the returns the companies obtain from their technology and their process expertise. These 'transfers' also directly enhance the contribution of the motor sport industry to the UK economy and UK Plc.

Many of the companies now investing in the motor sport industry are aware not only of the extreme technological and process expertise the motor sport companies possess but are also of their value as brand names. In addition, companies outside the industry have transferred their technologies into the industry for reasons not simply connected with its direct utilization. These examples of the use of the motor sport industry and of its value take different forms. The McLaren organization is perhaps the most successful in this commercial environment.

This section explores how two benchmark organizations, TAG McLaren and Ferrari, are structured in order to facilitate, and benefit from, intra-organizational technology transfer.

The structure of the TAG Group is presented in Figure 9.5 based on information from the *The Sunday Times*, 13 September 1998.

TAG McLaren designs and produces complete electronic solutions for four Formula One Constructors, and supplies components to most of the others through one of its divisions, TAG Electronic Systems. This division also supplies to Porsche, BMW, Toyota and Peugeot. Ron Dennis, Managing Director of McLaren, quoted in Hotten (1998), stated 'We had the know-how in automotive electronics and other industries, so it made sense to exploit this ... We are a high-tech company. It is possible to have a series of satellite companies that supply Formula One, but also spin off commercially from Formula One'.

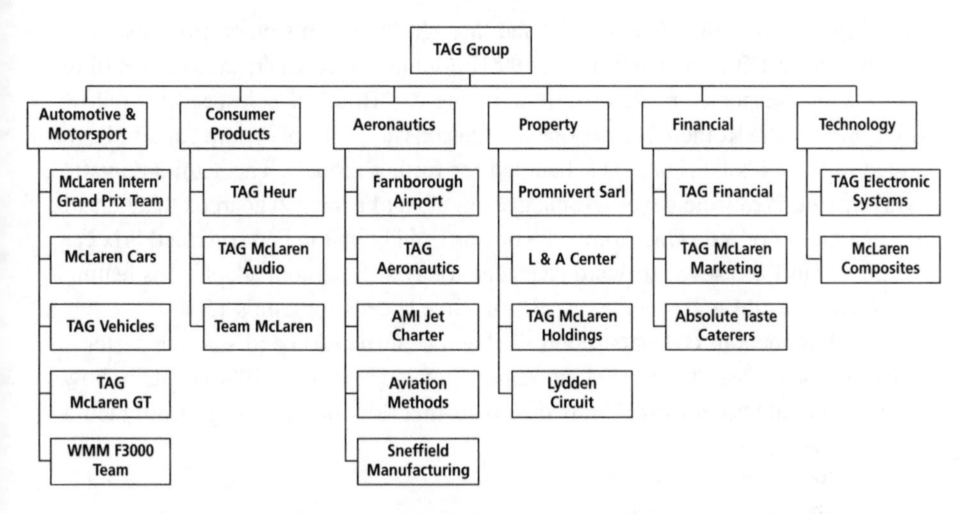

Figure 9.5 **Organizational Structure of the TAG Group**

The Sunday Times (13 September 1998) suggests that Mansour Ojjeh (an owner of TAG) and Ron Dennis are looking to develop TAG McLaren into a global consumer brand. The most recent step has been the formation of a new division, TAG McLaren Audio, through the acquisition of a separate company, Audiolab. Mansour Ojjeh states that 'We have become leading developers in technology and electronics through our success in Formula One and other businesses, and this gives us significant expertise that can be marketed in other fields'.

TAG McLaren Audio now markets high-end audio equipment that combines design experience garnered from Audiolab, with sophisticated electronics technology and production processes developed through involvement in Formula One.

Ferrari

Ferrari is unique amongst Formula One constructors in manufacturing its own Formula One engines and, of course, a range of high performance road cars. The company does the majority of its work in house, manufacturing approximately 75 per cent of components (Hotten, 1998). Ferrari is 90 per cent owned by, and accountable to, Fiat. However, the relationship is played down and the companies are marketed as separate entities to avoid weakening the image of the Ferrari brand. Ferrari now has a consultancy division, which works exclusively for Fiat.

According to Luca di Montezemolo, Ferrari's Chairman and Managing Director, technology and the computer are bringing uniformity to motor manufacturing. Therefore, as reported in Hotten (1998), Montezemolo believes that a critical success factor for companies in the future will be creativity, which he hopes will stem from the racing division. He points to a number of areas in which technology developed for Formula One has filtered through to Ferrari's other products:

The Ferrari F50, adapted from the 1990 Formula One race car, has a carbon fibre chassis and suspension lifted from the racing car. Branded Selespeed for fellow Fiat-owned Alfa Romeo, Ferrari's racing transmission control system has also been fitted to Ferrari's F355 and is scheduled for further models. The semi-automatic system is derived from the electronic management of a manual gearbox that Ferrari pioneered in Formula One from 1989 onward, although the Ferrari Grand Prix car originally utilized seven forward gears and today's showroom adaptations feature six forward ratios and reverse – at Ferrari, five speeds for Alfa's 156.

Developments in computer controlled active suspension and steering systems have also been passed to Fiat. Montezemolo, quoted in Hotten (1998) explains how organizational structure at Ferrari facilitates this flow of technology from racing cars to road cars:

> 'Our road cars have always been directly inspired by our racing cars in their technology, their dynamics and their appearance. Many times throughout our history they have even shared the same components. This close integration is possible because we are – and have been for some time – the only team in Formula One that makes the entire racing car in its own facilities. We manufacture the complete car, from the engine and the transmission to the frame and the suspension. This gives us complete control over every detail of the car and allows it to be fully integrated and optimised for best performance.'

He goes on to provide specific examples of technology transfer, and alludes to the importance of a strong corporate ethic:

> 'We were the first to fit a semi-automatic gearbox to a grand prix car, an advanced technology that we have just introduced on the F355 with great success. We have also been the first to introduce true ground-effects aerodynamics on our production cars, derived from Formula One. We have always challenged our engineers to do all they can to introduce features and technologies in our road cars that were derived from racing. This is a tradition to which we are wholeheartedly committed.'

Inter-organizational Technology Transfer Facilitated by Partnership

The initial but limited search for instances of recent inter-organizational transfer, facilitated by partnership agreements, threw up the following examples:

- Ford and Stewart Grand Prix
- British Aerospace and McLaren
- Hewlett Packard and Jordan Grand Prix

The following subsections tackle each case in turn.

Ford and Stewart Grand Prix

In 1996, Neil Ressler was responsible for forming the Motorsport Technology Department within Ford's Advanced Vehicle Technology structure. The remit of this department was 'to accelerate the pace of technology development, for the purpose of improving mainstream products'. In the first quarter of 1999, Ford has bought Cosworth Racing division from Audi, and Ressler has been appointed chairman of Cosworth Racing and joined the board of directors of Stewart Grand Prix. Events move rapidly in this industry and by June 1999 Ford had purchased Stewart Grand Prix and Ressler was Managing Director with a budget from Ford of £50 million per annum.

Ford is now not just the major stakeholder in Stewart Grand Prix, providing funding, engines and personnel, but the owner. In order to benefit from technology transfer, Ford are concentrating on three areas:

1. **Products:** Product improvement occurs by implementing rapid developments in technology innovation through motor sport. A product is exposed to the rigours of the racing environment, improved, and returned to mainstream production. Ford suggest, for example, that 'one weekend of off-road racing was comparable to 100,000 miles in fleet testing'.

   Examples cited include engine vibration dampers, valve lifters, lightweight starter motors, engines, brakes and bush materials. Testing the E40D automatic transmission in off-road racing led to 27 specific improvements in 8 months.
2. **Processes:** Processes and simulations are tested in racing, which allows for accelerated evaluation, before being applied to production programs. Racing offers a relatively controlled environment, ideal for this form of appraisal.

   Examples cited include use of the four-post road simulator for shock absorber and spring tuning and suspension geometry analysis procedure. Aerodynamics is also a growing focus for attention. Don Hayward, Ford's Indycar Car Program Manager and aerodynamics specialist, suggests: 'There may not be any production part you can point to and say "that was developed with racing aerodynamics". In this field, the technology transfer is through our engineering processes and our knowledge of the science.'
3. **People:** Working in a race program, Ford's engineers have to think on their feet and make decisions under pressure. Feedback is immediate. Ford's Motorsport Technology Department takes engineers on two-year rotations, to ensure that benefits are passed back to be realized in the mainstream environment. Ford has been particularly active in committing electronics engineers to Grand Prix engine programmes at Cosworth, a commitment that dates back more than ten years.

The importance of motor sport as a training ground is also recognized by other constructors. Patrick Head, speaking at a recent MIA conference, referred to the rate at which Honda's engineers were rotated when he quipped that 'As soon as you had got used to one set of engineers, a whole new wave of Zero pilots would be shipped in'.

British Aerospace and McLaren

Ron Dennis, quoted in Hotten (1998) suggests 'British Aerospace are quite interested in our management style and our mechanisms for motivating our workforce. They have some technology we are interested in, and we have some fast prototype strategies they are interested in, specifically, how we conceptualise an idea'. As part of this arrangement, staff have been seconded from British Aerospace to work with McLaren. The authors could find no evidence of tangible benefits from the programme to date.

Hewlett Packard and Jordan Grand Prix

Geoff Banks of Hewlett Packard is keen to stress that his company is partnering Jordan Grand Prix, not just sponsoring or supplying. The key difference, he suggests, being the extent to which both companies rely upon one another. Linkages exist between senior management in both companies, and Hewlett Packard have staff working on site with Jordan. Banks believes that Jordan benefits from having a tailored IT solution with worldwide support, and that Hewlett Packard benefit from using Jordan as a reference site. No new technology (as the term is now defined) has been innovated in the partnership, though Hewlett Packard has helped to introduce infrared links (for telemetry) and flat screen displays into Formula One.

More specifically, Hewlett Packard maintain that the partnership with Jordan provides them with an invaluable and unique environment for testing, developing and innovating both hardware and software.

Inter-organizational Technology Transfer Facilitated by Supplier-Consumer Relationships

All those interviewed agreed on the importance of choosing the correct business partner. Geoff Banks highlighted this issue when he mentioned, in passing, that Hewlett Packard had a difficult time achieving its requirements when working with Benetton. But then, Flavio Briatore, who ran the Benetton Formula One racing team at the time, cared little for the technology. Quoted in Hotten (1998), Briatore commented:

> 'I am not against technology. But in Benetton's philosophy, Formula One is an event. People don't come to the races to see our latest piston. They come to the races to see the fight. Benetton is in Formula One because it is about global communication. Noise and lifestyle, that is what Formula One is about.'

However, success for a Formula One team is winning and that depends on driver, race tactics and the car's speed. The latter is fundamentally a factor of technology; design processes and componentry.

The initial search for instances of technology transfer revealed the following examples, facilitated by a supplier consumer relationship:

- Goodyear, supplying tyres to several Formula One constructors
- AP Racing, supplying brake and clutch components to several Formula One constructors
- Fluent Europe, supplying software and support relating to computational fluid dynamics to several Formula One constructors
- An unnamed supplier of brake components to Ford

Each of these examples was researched further, and results are documented in the following subsections.

Goodyear

Goodyear has long been a major supplier of tyres to Formula One constructors, an arrangement that ceased at the close of 1998. In our interview, Dermot Bambridge (Public Relations Manager) made it clear that Goodyear had defined specific objectives for its involvement:

- To promote the product to major manufacturers and the end-consumer
- To foster a winning spirit and culture throughout the organization
- To improve the product through technology transfer
- To train engineers

Bambridge alludes to the tight time scales involved in motor sport, stating: 'developing a road tyre might take 18 months from conception to release. In Formula One, we can realise an opportunity on Wednesday, design a change on Thursday, produce 200 tyres over the weekend and be circuit testing on Tuesday'.

Motor sport also enables 'the use of new materials, which might be expensive or in short supply, and we can rapidly evaluate different compounds'.

Questioned on the transfer of technology to road tyres, Bambridge is confident that 'transfer occurs in the form of new compounds, constructions or mould shapes'. He believes that transfer occurs because 'the teams are constantly pushing us for improvements, and our racing division and road tyre research divisions communicate closely'.

Steve Myers, Goodyear's Director of Racing Tyre Sales and Marketing, is quoted as saying;

> 'Racing allows you to evaluate new products and new technology very quickly in the most demanding environment possible ... If you can develop a product that will withstand that environment, and is successful in it, it makes it very easy to transfer information and produce a better passenger tyre.'

This quote glosses over the process by which technology transfer occurs, or the benefits realised. Don Vera, Product Development Manager, provides more detail:

> 'Perhaps the area where consumers have benefited most is the technology gained from racing rain treads like the Formula One Aquatro. Generations of these treads have shown up in high-performance Eagle passenger tyres. Other passenger tyre innovations borne out of racing include low-profile sidewalls, wide treads, contoured tread shoulders and wraparound treads and tread compounds.'

However, such development is dependent on competition. In the 1998 Formula One championship, Goodyear and Bridgestone competed to provide the constructors that they supplied with a competitive advantage. With Goodyear withdrawing from Formula One at the end of 1998, there remains 'only one tyre supplier in Formula One and therefore no tyre development' (*Autosport*, 14 January 1999).

AP Racing

Norman Barker, Marketing Director of AP Racing, was interviewed specifically because AP Racing appeared to make no claims with regard to technology transfer. The company supplies brake callipers, carbon brake discs pads and carbon clutches to ten Formula One constructors. Only Sauber, of the 1998 Formula One constructors, did not source components from AP Racing.

Barker suggests that there is little ('practically none') technology transfer as far as AP Racing is concerned, though some constructors do push for product development. The firm supplies to the motor sport market because 'that's the core of our business', and '90 per cent of the firm's staff are working on motorsport projects'. He acknowledges that AP Racing does supply components (both original equipment and spares) to manufacturers of high performance road cars (TVR, Caterham and Ferrari), but notes that 'technology transfer just doesn't happen. In fact, the materials used and size of components are diverging'. However, involvement in Formula One does provide a marketing benefit – AP Racing uses its involvement to leverage sales to other niche sectors within motor sport.

Fluent Europe

Fluent Europe Ltd provides Computational Fluid Dynamics software and associated consultancy to six Formula One constructors. The service they provide enables constructors to simulate the performance of aerodynamic changes, cutting down on the necessity for wind tunnel testing and model making. Stewart Featherstone, Fluent's Commercial Director, suggests that Formula One constructors have benefited from the adoption of this technology, which was originally developed for aerospace and the chemical industry. He also admits that his people 'receive very little feedback from the teams' who he suggests 'worry when a supplier works for more than one team'.

Un-named Supplier to Ford

Phil Schilke is chairman of Ford's truck motor sport core group. He illustrates how motor sport led to Ford pushing back on one of its suppliers, to improve the brakes under development for the heavy [over 3500 lb./1750 kg] Ford Explorer Sports Utility Vehicle [SUV], a major sales success in the USA.

> 'Using the prototype brakes for the SCCA racing program, the materials analysis people found the material used in the fabrication of those brakes was too porous. Ford was then able to share the results with the brake supplier, and the supplier realised his casting process needed to be changed.'

Inter-organizational Technology Transfer via Consultancy or Contract

Several examples of technology transfer, via a contractual relationship, were established in the initial surveys presented in Table 9.4.

No further information could be established about Williams' contract work to develop control systems for JCB or the leaning train. However, an interview was conducted with Liam Clagger, Corporate Marketing Manager at Prodrive.

Clagger confirmed that Prodrive was looking to leverage competencies developed in their motor sport activities, which include competence in chassis development, control systems, and transmissions. This is being achieved by undertaking selected contractual assignments for clients in the automotive industry. Recent examples include:

- A contract undertaken for Caterham, to optimize ride and handling of a new model
- Consultancy undertaken for a motorbike manufacturer, to predict and improve handling characteristics across their range.
- Further projects are under way, including modifying Prodrive's simple semi-automatic transmission (developed for rallying) for use in HGVs. During development of this system Prodrive had used high pressure pneumatics to activate shift systems rather than the more widely used hydraulic activators with a potential for cost and weight savings. Originally featured in Subaru rally cars, Prodrive successfully transferred the steering wheel and central shift gearbox change system to a limited number of Ferrari Testarossas exported to the Middle East in the early nineties.

Inter-organizational Technology Transfer via Licensing

Through necessity, for its motor sport engines, Cosworth developed a new casting process for engine cylinder blocks and heads. This significantly improved machining tolerances, and minimized porosity in the heads. Having developed the Coscast casting process, Cosworth then implemented it within their foundry at Worcester in Britain, to meet the volume supply contracts with European manufacturers, including Mercedes in 1983-92. Cosworth Engineering also licensed the process to Ford, for use in the world's largest dedicated cylinder head and block foundry at Windsor, Ontario in Canada. This plant now produces 1.1 million castings per year.

Conclusions

The Motor Sport Industry in Britain is characterised by four key factors:

1 **Leading edge industrial organization:** At the heart of the industry is a network of small and medium enterprises, but the industry's network extends

to include some of the largest companies in the world. The network promotes innovation and flexibility, which can benefit those multi-nationals which maintain technological relationships with the motor sport industry.

2. **A community of knowledge:** Focused on superior ways to design and manufacture racing cars. Despite intense rivalry, the firms in Motor Sport Valley have developed a collaborative capacity to generate and disseminate knowledge. This capacity stems from high staff turnover, common suppliers and high rates of new firm formation and firm morbidity.
3. **An aerospace inspired technology trajectory:** As history demonstrates, a change in technology trajectory (perhaps precipitated by legislation or a change in technical regulations such as the introduction of electric powered engines) could prove a catalyst for the industry's relocation.
4. A cluster that comprises an engineering 'core' plus all the related employment, educational, financial, merchandising and marketing services.

According to Foxall and Johnston (1991), the transfer of technology between motor sport and the automotive industry is often presented as a dynamic process in which radical innovations are developed, win races for their innovators and are then introduced into the mainstream. Our research tends to suggest that such developments are normally incremental, as opposed to radical: developments and innovations rarely arise from motor sport itself, but result from the interaction of a complex network of companies, or from the adoption of technologies developed in other industries (notably the aerospace industry).

The actual processes of technology are numerous and require careful management. The technology transferred is frequently intangible, taking the form of processes, tacit knowledge and heightened competence. Goold and Campbell (1998) discuss the merits of exposing one set of people to another who have a different way of working. The Ford Motor Company is claiming benefits from just such an approach and will undoubtedly be using their ownership of the Stewart Grand Prix team to provide more such opportunities.

Other industries can learn from these findings. Technological progress is associated with market demand and progressive companies should seek out demanding markets. Association with entrepreneurial lead users, such as a Formula One constructor, can provide companies with the demand required to stimulate the innovation of new technologies and the rapid improvement of existing technologies.

Resources and Technical Infrastructures: From Motor Club to Race Circuit

Vital Beginnings

ASKED to nominate reasons for British pre-eminence in modern motorsports, overseas rivals usually begin with the variety of race tracks and test facilities that this small island possesses. In this chapter we explore this unique strength of the industry in mainland Britain in depth and some of the people who organize a plethora of weekend motor sport that is the envy of the competitive automotive world.

In the opening sections of this book we looked at the origins of Britain's motor sporting Grand Prix success in overthrowing entrenched Italian and French supremacy. Then the success of a small industry that succeeded in selling competition cars to the world, thanks to the efforts of some very hardy pioneers who were often laughed at by the establishment, for their grimy and obviously dangerous pursuits. Innovative, talented and brave though those men and women engineers, drivers and designers of the thirties and fifties were, none could have set a wheel on tarmacadam or muddy special stage had it not been for the organising motor clubs and the facilities that developed from fifties basics. The spectator of today demands a far higher standard of facilities and entertainment than previous generations of hardcore fanatics.

We have paid tribute to the Royal Automobile Club and traced its development through the RAC MSA, to today's professional Motor Sports Association (MSA). We have mentioned the re-establishment of a British Grand Prix at Silverstone in 1948, but we need to bring the story of the MSA to the brink of the Millennium. There were two major changes in the MSA's location and structure that conveniently spanned some ten years.

In 1988 the RAC MSA sold the remaining long lease to its prestigious offices at 31 Belgrave Square, London W1 and moved to modern offices in Colnbook, Slough, right on the London Heathrow flight paths; there were 38 employees as at May 1999. This move released a great deal of cash which has been reinvested and still accounts for one of the three primary sources of MSA revenue, that amounts to approximately £4 million annually. The other two MSA income streams are fees from competition and entrant's licences, plus sponsorship income for the biggest set pieces in British motorsport; the RAC British Grand Prix and the RAC Rally of Great Britain, actually referred to currently under Network Q Rally of Great Britain sponsorship title. In addition, there are many premier league motor racing and rally championships, including the British rally series and the British Touring Car or Formula 3 titles. There are many more within the MSA's gift to sell on to commercial sponsors, so this avenue, lined by blossoming TV interest, has most potential to boost future MSA earnings.

On 28 July 1998, the Motor Sport Association formally demerged from the division of the Royal Automobile Club that provides breakdown services. The organization retained links with some arms of the original RAC club, including access to the Pall Mall Club for prize giving ceremonies and other events. Publicly unused, but still part of their formal title is RAC MSA, the move to lose the RAC section being purely to distance themselves from the commercial interests that took over the RAC titles and brands. At press time it looked as though the RAC Club's assets have been secured by Lex after a measure of take-over offers that had seen Ford Motor Company bid. It was quite possible that Ford would then simply buy the Lex cross section of automotive holdings outright!

As if that was not all confusing enough the British Grand Prix has the RAC motoring services company as a title sponsor, paying the MSA to organize Britain's most prestigious motor race. Just remember that the MSA is a self-standing organization funded by investments, licence fees and sponsorship income to run motor sport in Britain and all remains almost clear. Then you find the MSA keeps the RAC section of their name when administering UK motorsport justice through their regular tribunals.

To amplify on those personnel and facility resources that make Britain's sporting business so viable in today's commercial climate, we subdivide this section into people the 'Big Three' Motor Clubs and organizational bodies and the track facilities they either rent, own or employ. Additionally we explore some of the technical resources such as wind tunnels and test tracks that were widely employed as the Millennium expired.

One of the oldest and reportedly the largest of the active racing clubs is the British Automobile Racing Club, BARC. They have over 4000 members and help in delivering motor sports to both armchair enthusiast and active competitors. Bigger one make car clubs in the USA such as BMW CCA and Britain's biggest MG club, attract over 50 000 enthusiasts apiece and will also get involved in race organization for events that cater for their preferred marque. Formed in 1912 as the Cyclecar Club, the BARC and its predecessors before

World War II staged both off road trials and rallies, as well as more glamorous racing events at Brooklands and Donington. Post-war the BARC became familiar through its events at the Goodwood race circuit (revived in 1998 for a single meeting per annum), but it's worth noting that the BARC grew dramatically when combined with the Brooklands Automobile Racing Club. Although Brooklands was never reopened for motor racing post-war, the BARC took on today's title in 1949.

When Goodwood was closed to regular race meetings in 1967, the BARC was left with a search to establish a new circuit for its most prestigious meetings. Thruxton airfield had been hosting endurance motorcycle races in the early sixties including the Thruxton 500 and from 1968 onward the BARC ran its major Easter meeting at this venue, regularly attracting more than 50 000 to the Bank Holiday Monday meeting. The BARC itself moved from a central London HQ out to the converted wartime airfield in the mid-seventies and remains based at the Hampshire track. Former competitions directors include Rick Gorne, interviewed for this book in his later director level status at Reynard and British American Racing.

Thruxton is not owned by the club as per BRDC and Silverstone, but leased from a commercial business consortium of owners. In 1989 the BARC redeveloped another airfield site, Pembrey on a South Wales peninsula and that is also leased on a long-term basis (50 years) by the BARC. By 1999 the BARC averaged 4500 members split over six UK regional centres and there is also an active BARC offshoot promoting ice racing and organising a premier league CART Fedex qualifying round based in Ontario, Canada. They contributed a basic £23.50 each (£105 750), those contesting one of the BARC's record 26 racing championships, which includes the prestigious *Autosport* Formula 3 title, at the 75 race meetings organized by the BARC pay a further racing membership fee of £55.50. The club estimates that 'about one third of the membership' (approximately 1485 people) are active racing contributors, which would allow over £82 000 revenue, so total membership income should exceed £188 000. Commercial sponsorship and popular test facilities at Pembrey (all such days sold in 1998) contributed to an October 31, 1998 record BARC surplus of £389 034 as reported by the chairman for 1997–98.

Of similar size to the BARC and one of the big three motor racing clubs organizing events in Britain is the post-war British Racing and Sports Car Club, which grew alongside the 500cc racing formula. Until 1954 the club's name was the 500 Club, to which we referred in our opening chapters. Formed in 1945, it had 250 members by 1946 many of them with links to the Bristol Aeroplane Company. The other BRSCC input to motorsport progress in Britain was to run the first meeting on the resurfaced one-mile layout that was Brands Hatch in 1950. The club grew by the promotion of sports car events and organization at other UK circuits through the early fifties. By September 1954 the name was changed to British Racing and Sports Car Club, reflecting this wider brief. Amongst others helping the club expand through that period was the energetic Ken Gregory, better known as the manager of Stirling Moss.

During the 1970s the club was steered by former BMC competition manager Peter Browning who moved them from their premises in Chiswick down to Brands Hatch. There was some controversy over how much independence it could maintain on the doorstep of the very powerfully managed Motor Circuit Developments Group and the influential John Webb. *See* the Brands Hatch circuit below.

By 1999 the BRSCC emerged as an independent club with separate Kentish premises occupied by six employees and a membership of 4000 that created an annual subscription income of £310 000. The BRSCC charged a £95 annual fee for racing membership in 1999, or £30 for non-racing enthusiasts, creating £120 000 in annual membership fees, plus another £190 000 from the racing membership, excluding individual motor race/championship registration fees. BRSCC personnel told the authors that racing versus non-racing memberships was approximately '50–50' in the summer of 1999. The racing members were involved in 65 meetings per annum with a total of 35 championships organized by the club.

BRDC, the British Racing Drivers Club is unique amongst motor racing clubs and circuit owners and likely to remain that way. Inextricably bound up with the fortunes of the Silverstone circuit(s) in Northamptonshire, the BRDC is the most exclusive motor racing club in Britain. The club has 755 full status members plus 73 honorary or associate members (a total membership of 828) all of whom are members through invitation only with an annual subscription in 1999 of £30.00. The BRDC club owns the Silverstone track freehold, along with substantial other chunks of local territory from a local public house to green fields.

Currently the BRDC remains the only British motor sport club with no outside owners, a 'quasi-charity' whose directors, including the Chairman Lord Hesketh, are trustees responsible for developing the varied business ventures housed within the 800 acre Silverstone estate. In popular parlance the BRDC Silverstone business is structured in the same way as many Golf clubs; 'a company limited by guarantee' was the phrase most often employed, without shareholders but with the club, rather than its individual members, owning the total assets.

Thus, in all the media quotes surrounding take over bids for the BRDC assets, it is worth remembering that no member can sell his shares individually. All offers, and there have many peaking at a headline £50 million for the total, were addressed to the club.

Another issue is that there has to be more than 75 per cent of the BRDC membership voting in favour of selling, and this they emphatically rejected in April 1999. Quotes of individual sums per member that were given as peaking at a reported and inaccurate £75 000, are the result of media friendly takeover talk, with a hefty degree of spin doctoring applied from the bidders. A computation based on membership numbers and the maximum figure per individual quoted in the press would have valued the club beyond £62.1 million, £19 million more than the actual best bid (43 million from Brands Hatch Leisure) received by September 1999.

The track and its facilities operate through Silverstone Circuits Ltd formed in 1966 and the club also owns Silverstone Estates Ltd, which operates the leases of industrial units located on the site. The majority of the industrial units are modern facilities; the last major expansion was during the winter of 1998–9, plus a few primitive conversions of earlier Nissen huts. The recent units are a favourite for racing and specialist fabrication teams to Formula Three level.

Future BRDC site development takes account of the local A43 bypass which is a vital link in connecting the M1 across country with the M40, being enhanced to a dual carriageway. The BRDC Silverstone organization did lose a few acres as land was purchased for this road programme, but the club has been purchasing more land parcels in the vicinity of Silverstone in 1999. The BRDC assured us that they had replaced the lost acreage and that we could accurately provide the figure of 800 acres for its land assets.

The BRDC structure of the mid-nineties was a much more complicated affair with defunct companies reflecting previous farming operations; even in 1996 there were nine BRDC owned companies. The BRDC did provide us with a list of dormant limited liability companies still owned, but advised 'all our business is conducted through Silverstone Circuit Ltd or Silverstone Estates and the latter is really only about the lease of industrial/business units'. Currently a BRDC director and official secretary to the club Howden Ganley revealed that the BRDC structure is now 'cleaned up considerably and the days of eight or nine companies and more being operated, are over'.

Very appropriately, BRDC's origins have a bloodline in British Racing Green, back to the Bentley Boys. Bentley racer Dr J.D. Benjafield conceived the idea of regular dinners in the company of fellow competitors during 1927. Brooklands habitués were soon included and by 1929 the BRDC's first working committee met. The result of their labours was a rather more than exceedingly good company as BRDC ran its first event that year, a serious 500-mile race on the banked Brooklands outer circuit, then one of the fastest contemporary race tracks in the world.

From the start the club invited only absolute top line drivers to be members, and that is true today for membership includes headline names such as Jackie Stewart, Stirling Moss, Damon Hill and others, although the club also extends its membership invitations beyond the traditional core of British and Commonwealth racing drivers implied in its title. Because of South Africa's varying Commonwealth status through its apartheid period, its leading drivers were not always automatically included, but more obvious contenders such as Jacques Villeneuve and Paul Tracy of Canada, along with Australia and New Zealand's high density of internationally successful drivers seem to automatically make BRDC status.

Overseas star drivers were invited to join in the thirties and included the leading Auto Union and Mercedes aces, their names erased by racing death or wartime patriotism. Today Michael Schumacher and other overseas world champions are invited to join.

Some of the more influential supporters and contributors to the world of motor racing, such as revered TV commentator Murray Walker OBE, have been offered Associate General Member status, as was the former Conservative Chancellor Kenneth Clarke. This category includes some of our outstanding engineer technicians, and the flamboyant Lord Hesketh. The local Lord led the BRDC with wit and style through a period of attempted takeovers and the anticipated loss of the British Grand Prix, although there were calls for his resignation and more radical BRDC restructuring.

The Independent of 19 May 1999 reported that BRDC members had been offered up to £75 000 each to sell to the Brands Hatch Leisure Group, valuing Silverstone and its BRDC resources at £62 550 000. As we have seen, the club constitution was not so simplistic as that, but it is worth noting that Silverstone last declared profits on 31 January 1999, at £2.8 million on a £26.2 million turnover. In broad terms, BRDC reported turnover tripling from £10 million to £30 million 'in the past five years', when we talked to the club in May 1999.

The Brands Hatch Leisure Group subsequently juggled their offers to buy out Silverstone's BRDC assets, believing they had secured the rights to stage the British Grand Prix from 2002 to 2007 by dealing directly with Bernie Ecclestone of the Formula One Association. The amount that BHL paid for this privilege has not been divulged. It appears that Mr Ecclestone has blocked the BRDC from making any comment to us or anyone else. The matter remains a large question mark.

The most complete reportage we could find in the sports and business press converged on a successful annual £11 million bid for the British GP rights for 2002–7. This is more than double the reported £5.5 million that Silverstone would have paid annually, until the expiry of their right to hold the premier British event in 2001. The BRDC President Lord Hesketh Silverstone clearly felt the price of continuing to stage the British GP was too high when he commented 'we are not going to commit the BRDC to financial suicide' *Autosport*, 20 May 1999.

What was the Grand Prix worth to the South Midlands economy? According to an FIA Report of 1996 quoted in the RAC British Grand Prix briefing of 1999, the answer was, 'a staggering £30 million annually'. The same source quoted over 90 per cent of that cash inflow from outside the local area and commented 'the average spectator spent £166 per day on tickets, parking, lodging, food, entertainment, and tourist purchases'.

As anticipated, regional hotels benefited with occupancy rates routinely set at 100 per cent. What has not been previously highlighted was that 'around 5000 temporary jobs were created during race week, with those local companies who most depend on GP business employing almost 45 000 people. In all, close to 15 000 people can be involved in staging a Grand Prix,' whilst 'at the GP itself a staff of 5000 will be on site, working an 18 hour day'. Such figures are an extremely rational reason why BHL and the BRDC fought their battles of the sixties, eighties and nineties to stage an attraction with spending power that has leapt spectacularly beyond inflation and any contemporary, alternative entertainment.

BHL's current determination to secure both the future rights to a British Grand Prix and (to a less obvious extent) the BRDC Silverstone holdings earned Mr Ecclestone's support. He commented to *Autosport* on 20 May 1999 that his objection to Silverstone and its running of the Grand Prix was, 'it's basically run like a big club race, I suppose. They've built new grandstands now, at last, but in general it looks a bit tired and "Battle of Britain". I could run it at Biggin Hill (the legendary British World War II base part-owned by Ecclestone in 1999) if we wanted that sort of factor'.

It is worth considering here a 1996 press statement made on behalf of the BRDC, which reported 'in the past ten years £88 million has been spent or invested locally from receipts of £104 million'. The BRDC is obviously no idle landlord and certainly not the province of geriatrics in blue blazers that its detractors and potential new owners insisted were the majority. The majority of the BRDC management are younger than the Formula One Association's boss Bernie Ecclestone, who is 69 years young when this was written. Mr Ecclestone since underwent open heart surgery and returned to work six weeks later fortified by the proceeds of the £875 million Eurobond flotation.. But none of the protagonists are as youthful as the BHL boss Nicola Foulston, at 31 years.

Silverstone has been substantially and extensively redeveloped since 1987, the year when it acquired exclusive rights to stage the British GP, an event that had alternated with Brands Hatch from 1964 to 1986. Amongst the more obvious and expensive changes were the introduction of gradients to the previous flat perimeter road layout instigated by Tom Walkinshaw of TWR and closed circuit TV to monitor activities around seven alternative race track layouts.

Other resources at the self-styled 'Home of British Motor Racing' include a driver associated school/driving experience operation that hosted more than 35 000 people in 1995, boosted to a staggering 50 000 in 1998–9. The growth was primarily though Silverstone absorbing the Donington-based Jim Russell race driving school and establishing a satellite operation at Croft, Darlington in North Eastern Britain.

In 1999 the company's customers were able to try driving experiences in over 200 assorted motorized machines, almost double the 112 Silverstone machines available in 1996. These were as varied as karting and 4×4 off-roaders, besides the traditional fleet of Formula Ford single seaters many now of later 1998 Van Diemen stock, saloons (Peugeots) and Caterham 7s, plus 1998's adoption of 12 Lotus Elises and assorted skid-control machines of devilish manners, mounted on electronically controlled rigs. An extremely significant by-product of this motorsport fleet was the BRDC fulfilling its stated mission to foster British driving talent. At Silverstone a youngster could begin Karting at eight and progress through the lower racing ladders through to in-house events using 1998 specification, Van Diemen Formula Fords.

The most public expression of such support for British drivers came through in the BRDC McLaren Autosport Awards, annually highlighting the best of British at a glamorous London prize giving sponsored by the leading weekly British motorsports magazine, *Autosport*. Both McLaren and the BRDC have devoted considerable resources to this scheme and some very promising drivers have been identified and given a chance to test drive premier league single seaters with a realistic cash award to further progress of one, from six annual finalists.

Demand for Silverstone track, pits and hospitality accommodation went far beyond racing weekends. Silverstone have also accommodated mini-sales conferences or dinner dances for up to 300 people and redeveloped its member's clubhouse accommodation in the 1998–9 winter. A regular revenue has been gathered from testing facilities during the week and a number of commercial shows picked Silverstone as their venue in the nineties, including BBC Top Gear and the annual Fleet Users' Show.

This commercial expansion has brought many major international companies into regular contact with Silverstone, with sponsorship often extended beyond racing weekends. Motor sport in the form of the second biggest spectator attraction to Grand Prix was the reason for Coys' auction house involvement in historic racing. Coys, having taken over from Christies in the late nineties with Chrysler, also drawn in by crowds exceeding 80 000 for the 'oldtimers'.

Although Ecclestone's political power over Formula One has been near absolute in this era, there were those who disagreed with criticisms of the way that the BRDC ran its unique business and the British Grand Prix. Some felt Brands Hatch might not be able to push through a £20 million Grand Prix redevelopment for planning and economic business reasons. Amongst such high profile critics were Ron Dennis of McLaren and 1979 World Champion Jody Scheckter.

The BRDC remained dedicated to the redistribution of 'all profits devoted to the development of British motorsport or donated to charity'. Doubtless such unfashionable and non-commercial aims and the BRDC's unique status amongst British sporting clubs and circuits, will continue to come under pressure into the New Millennium. The foresight of the BRDC's founding fathers in establishing the BRDC's quasi charity status could yet retain their independence from those whom Lord Hesketh memorably described as under the leadership of 'that temptress from Kent'. Hesketh summarized the pressures on the BRDC during the summer of 1999 equally memorably as 'the barbarians may not be quite at the gate, but they're in the park, looking at the buildings'.

Other Important Clubs and Organizations

Not so significant to the sporting contingent in Britain now as it was in the past, is the SMM&T, Society of Motor Manufacturers and Traders. Today there is a 20-man motorsport manufacturers committee that meets regularly at the SMM&T's London SWI headquarters in the magnificent Forbes House. The motorsport's committee consists of mass production vehicle and component manufacturers, rather than Formula Car constructors. It was not always so as it was hard to get a British sporting point of view across when men such as Colin Chapman and John Cooper sat on this committee.

Today the SMM&T role is primarily concerned with the problems of large-scale manufacturing and topics such as registration statistics. But they also have leading motorsport companies and small-scale manufacturers such as Caterham and Marcos, amongst the membership.

The British Motor Racing Marshals Club was established in 1957 and has become a great goodwill ambassador for British on track stage management, with a magnificent 'work force' that is entirely voluntary. Membership exceeded 1700 in 1980, with marshals attending more than 300 meetings. These could be at the very grass, and more often muddy, roots of motorsport or as part of the 1200 marshals needed at the British Grand Prix or the Rally of Great Britain which requires over 11 000 voluntary marshals to cope with crowds of up to two million. In the summer of 1999, the British Motor Racing Marshals Club could be contacted via Mr Peter Roberts, 22 Adlington Drive, Sandbach, Cheshire,CW11 1DX. (Tel.: 01270 768796).

The International Rally Drivers Club (IRDC), was established in 1969 and is the rallying equivalent of the BRDC, but without that club's enormous Silverstone assets. The IRDC provides a communications medium for current, future and retired rally crew who have qualified for an international licence. It issues a very useful annual directory, a regular large format magazine and was scheduled to operate an Internet site set from July 1999.

Membership is limited to around 500 and the annual fee is set at £19 per full member as at June 1999. That the club has withstood the pressures of more than thirty years motorsport membership is a credit to driving force and current Vice Chairman Rodney Spokes.

Further details? Contact membership and Directory editor Mr Spokes at 155 Scraptoft Lane, Leicester, LE5 2FF (Tel./Fax: 0116 243 1925. e-mail rbs@page-moy.co.uk).

Active British Motor Racing Circuits

There are 16 primary full-time British circuits that enable so much of Britain's motor racing wealth and technology to remain in such good health. There are many more karting, sprint and hillclimb venues in robust action, three-drag racing straight line strips and assorted circuits that cater for mixed surface rallycross and rallysprints, but the latter are usually adjuncts to an existing race circuit complex.

Aintree

Listed only as a racing driver's school trading from 1 Fairoak Court, Whitehouse, Runcorn, Cheshire WA7 3DX (Tel.: 01928 712877; Fax: 01928 790086). Aintree circuit has been a British Grand Prix venue in alternate years in 1955–61 and then in 1962, before Brands Hatch became the Silverstone alternative. Full of reminders of the adjacent Aintree Grand National course, it is now mainly used for race school instruction and timed sprints.

Brands Hatch

At Fawkham, Dartford, Kent DA3 8NG (Tel.: 01474 872331; Fax: 01474 874766). Flagship to the Brands Hatch Leisure Group (BHL) which also owns Cadwell Park, Oulton Park and Snetterton race circuits.

Always a controversial home to new ideas in motorsport since it was converted from an anti-clockwise grass track for motorcycles to an initial one-mile Tarmacadam layout for car racing in 1950 at a cost £17 000. It was further extended to 1.24 miles, and converted to clockwise operation in 1954 with a Grand Prix extension and a 2.65 mile lap circuit for 1960. The circuit hosted the British Grand Prix from 1964–86, on a rota with Silverstone for alternate years. Headline news at the moment is that the owners BHL have secured an agreement to stage the British Grand Prix from 2002–7. Major Brands Hatch track alterations amounting to £20 million are anticipated, although the basic theme of a challenging track over varying gradients, rare after the safety orientated layouts of the seventies, will remain.

Larger than life characters have always run Brands Hatch. Men such as John Webb ensuring that Brands Hatch was never far from the headlines when he ran it and acquired other circuits on behalf of Grovwood Securities and the combine, Motor Circuit Developments. In 1988 Brands Hatch was acquired by Atlantic Computers leasing magnate John Foulston, but he died in a motor racing testing accident at Silverstone the following year. The track became something of a backwater until Nicola Foulston, John's mercurial daughter, obtained the right from trustees to run the operation of the circuits. The BHL Company was floated as a public company in 1996 with backing from venture capitalists APAX. Since that time BHL, has outperformed the FTSE All Share index by 80 per cent and the successful and aggressive entrepreneur Nicola Foulston has won many business awards on the way.

Success has not come easily as Nicola has had a difficult and often traumatic time in achieving so much fighting her mother amongst many others for the right to run not just Brands Hatch but also its associated circuits and assets. But Nicola Foulston has shown grit and very considerable entrepreneurial flair in developing Brands Hatch marketing muscle and the facilities on the idyllic Kentish site. For example, a large hotel was built beside the entry gates and sold off, helping to finance other much-needed improvements to the circuit and its facilities, including the imposing John Foulston Centre.

Nicola Foulston now faces her greatest challenge in the Millennium, that of extracting profit from the estimated £30 million turnover annually generated by British Grand Prix, having spent at least £20 million on redevelopment initially. The City thinks she will succeed once again; when the six-year contract was announced BHL shares rose approximately 10 per cent. The question remains as to whether this formidable and impressive entrepreneur will out-manoeuvre the BRDC and the establishment.

Cadwell Park

At Brands Hatch Circuits Ltd, Cadwell Park Division, The Old Manor House, Cadwell Park Circuit, Louth, Lincs LN11 9SE (Tel.: 01507 343248; Fax: 01507 343519).

Rooted in a motorcycling past that stretches back to 1934, one that is evident in its generally narrow track width, Cadwell Park is respected as can be judged from its popular 'Mini Nurburgring' nickname. Catering for cars as well as motorcycles since 1960, the rural location delivers two challenging circuit layouts of 2.17 miles and 1.476 miles and offers natural viewing facilities. There are few permanent facilities on the site, which is under-developed by current standards and unlikely to grow much beyond its present pleasant club racing status owing to its distance from major population centres.

Castle Combe

At Castle Combe Circuit, Chippenham, Wilts SN14 7EY(Tel.: 01249 782417). Another former aerodrome site, but possibly the prettiest racing circuit location in the World, which has shaped its constricted public race meeting programme.

Opened in 1950 Castle Combe had a stop-go existence until 1976 when a consortium led by Howard Strawson of the local BRSCC, South Western Centre acquired the assets from AFN Ltd. As it was restricted to just five public race meetings a year few would have held out much hope for the track's commercial future. However, an individualistic approach by Mr Strawson ensured that there were large (10 000 to 15 000) crowds attracted whenever there was racing and they saw a wonderful variety of motorsport, a lot of different events on race day; at least double that offered by most contemporary rivals.

The track also attracted a few commercial enterprises to lease circuit buildings for racing car construction and parts sales. Castle Combe is easily accessible from the M4 motorway, which means it is a very popular midweek venue for business or club users who can meet the strict enforcement of local noise levels. There is also some extra weekend use for track action days, featuring cars silenced to normal public road standards, and this makes it a popular venue for clubs, classic car gatherings and motoring magazine supported shows, which can also feature track action as an added and comparatively low cost, attraction.

Croft

At Croft Circuit, CCHM Ltd, Vincemoor East, Croft on Tees, Nr Darlington DL2 2PN (Tel.: 01325 721815; Fax 01325 721819). Another redeveloped airfield track, Croft has not run continuously since its 1950 opening. Redeveloped in 1964, Croft hosted international status races and found fame as a television rallycross venue in the late sixties and through the seventies.

Neglected over the years, the circuit was comprehensively redeveloped again in 1996–7, hosting a premier league British Touring Car Round in June 1997.

It should have been a joyous occasion for the North East, but mud spoiled play along with controversy over the safety standards attained. However, Croft retained its place in the 1998–9 TOCA calendars and is praised by competitors who like its high speed layout. It remains privately owned through CCHM Ltd and is available to the public as a motor race facility, one that no longer runs rallycross events.

Donington Park

Operated by Two Four Sports Ltd, Donington Park, Castle Donington, Derby DE7 2RP (Tel.: 01332 810048; Fax: 01332 850422).

The most important UK race track in private hands, Donington also contains a unique formula car motor racing museum and advanced facilities. It is the venue for the annual British Motorcycle Grand Prix and has served as an occasional car racing Grand Prix venue when Britain was allocated the additional Grand Prix of Europe.

Donington Park opened to the public in 1931 as the first UK permanent road racing track. It was a venue for the British Grand Prix in the immediate pre-war years, but a revival after years of military neglect was out of the question. Then Tom Wheatcroft, a highly successful local developer and Grand Prix addict, acquired the circuit section of the Park (adjacent to Rolls Royce Aero Engines) in 1971. Even then the redoubtable 'Wheatie' fought strenuously for the right to stage motor racing once more, first moving his car collection onto the site in 1973. It was another three years before permission was granted to complete development of a two-mile track section.

In 1977 the first motorcycle and car races were staged and the track's natural attractions and central location have seen it attract enormous crowds [over 60 000 for the motorcycles] both for motorsports and occasional rock concerts [nearer 90 000].

Today Donington has two primary layouts (1.96 or 2.5 miles) but is surprisingly hampered in test or non-race weekend use by severe noise limits, surprising in view of the fact, that its lies next door to busy East Midlands Airport!

Nevertheless, Donington remains a testimony to one man's determination and his ability to find able people to run both the track and its many other activities, including a particularly adaptable conference/exhibitions hall and the unique attractions of the museum.

Bizarrely, the Silverstone takeover of Jim Russell Racing Driver School operations at Donington had led to the establishment of a Silverstone school at this site when we went to press.

There were motorsport insiders who wondered what Donington's financial fate would be beyond Mr Wheatcroft's working span? Some precautionary steps had been taken in the establishment of privately owned [not by Tom Wheatcroft] Donington Park Leisure Ltd, which held a 25-year lease to the circuit running from 1997 onward. The leisure company Managing Director was former *Autosport* journalist Robert Fearnell, who had run various aspects of Donington administration for many years.

Goodwood

And at the hillclimb course, Goodwood Motor Circuit, Chichester, West Sussex PO18 0PH (Tel.: 01243 789660; Fax: 01243 536497). Note that this facility is a widely used performance and race car venue but operates under the strictest noise regulations.

One of the most famous post-war tracks in southern Britain, Goodwood's glorious story apparently ended in 1967 when large scale public race meetings ceased. Meanwhile, horse racing flourishes on the Sussex Downs above the still very active light plane aerodrome and fast 2.4-mile circuit.

When Lord March took responsibility for the Goodwood Estates in the nineties, Goodwood's interest in mechanical horsepower accelerated again. First a hillclimb was formalized within the grounds of the house and an enormously successful June date for an annual retro meeting became a must in any classic car supporter's diary. It was not just a British affair and both German companies and personnel and their counterparts in America proved strong supporters to this most typically British weekend, which flowered into a separate September meeting at the reopened race track in 1998.

The race track had remained open for motor car and bike testing through the intervening thirty years (Bruce McLaren died testing his Can Am McLaren here in 1970), but it was popular wisdom that it would never open to the public again because of local resident and council opposition. This proved untrue, and shows that a persuasive landowner can still sway local opinion even in the most politically correct of times.

Consequent on the 1998 public opening, Goodwood facilities improved sharply over the previous trackside accommodation, particularly the pits. Otherwise, fixed facilities are more minimal than those of Thruxton, but conversion to public race day format provides more of the 'Right Crowd' pre-war aura than any venue in the world. Goodwood has thus become irresistible to marketing men and car enthusiasts of every persuasion. Deserves fuller recognition for the enormous local income generated and the amount of overseas support that benefits Britain.

Ingliston

At Ingliston Race Circuit, 40 Clydeford Road, Cambuslang, Glasgow G72 7JF. Tel.: 0141 641 2553; Fax: 0131 554 6993).

Handily located close to Edinburgh airport, Ingliston is also one of the most civilized circuits in the British Isles. Its facilities, such as restaurant and grandstands derive from its ownership as part of the Royal Highland and Agricultural Society showgrounds: in fact the race circuit was originally the golf course!

Knockhill

At Knockhill Racing Circuit Ltd, Dunfermline Fife KY 9TF (Tel.: 01383 723337; Fax: 01383 620167).

Packs an enormous number of gradient and corner changes into its 1.3 miles. Purpose built in 1976 via the efforts of Dennys Dobbie, Knockhill faded financially in its early days, but is now the annual Scottish date for the visiting TOCA 2 litres of the British Touring Car Championship, attracting thousands.

Also regularly used for tests and lower level club motorsports, Knockhill is privately owned by Derek Butcher.

Lydden Hill

At Lydden International Motor Racing Circuit, Wotton, Nr Canterbury, Kent CT4 6RX. Tel.: 01304 830557; Fax: 01304 831715). A unique operating structure, being owned by McLaren International but leased out to the BMCRC (British Motor Cycle Racing Club) to run its diet of weekend motorsports and occasional midweek testing.

Located minutes inland from Dover, Lydden was famous for providing the setting to TV rallycross meetings of the sixties and seventies that drew millions of BBC and ITV viewers. Its mixed surfaces, including notoriously slimy chalk sectors, were excellent for this branch of motorsport, but the conventional one-mile circuit is also a challenge to the teams of club car and motorcycle racers who descend on its natural hillside location today.

Owned and constructed by Bill Chesson in 1965, it stayed in Mr Chesson's hands until the nineties, when McLaren International acquired it. It was not developed into its intended McLaren test circuit and technical base role, as McLaren redeveloped a site two miles from their current Woking base over the spring 1999–2001 period to accommodate all their activities, including those of associated TAG McLaren Group, a car museum and a new full size wind tunnel.

Meanwhile, Lydden remained busy running club motorsport of all kinds during its restricted 52 days a year operation (as per local agreement to use) as the Millennium approached.

Mallory Park

At Mallory Park Motorsport Ltd, Mallory Park Circuit, Kirkby Mallory, Leicester LE9 7QE (Tel.: 01455 842931; Fax: 01455 848289).

This track famously combines the ultra fast Gerrards, one of Britain's fastest road racing corners, with the slowest hairpin in regular use, making it a superb test venue for all speeds. Founded as a pony-trotting track in the fifties, Mallory Park's 1.35-mile layout was established in 1956 and it remains in use, with minor modifications for both cars and motorcycles, with popular mid-week practice sessions usually split to accommodate two and four wheelers.

Mallory Park also has a shorter one-mile layout that can be used clockwise or counter, usually Eurocars and associates.

It is picturesque, having a lake with a private island base for track owner (since 1983) Chris Meek to keep wildfowl amused, and the assorted ducks and geese quite unfazed by the roar of 100-mph racing engines some 200 metres distant.

The circuit was formerly part of the Brands Hatch empire, but is now operated by Mallory Park Motorsport Ltd, who lease the track from former Leeds-based entrepreneur Meek and employ ten personnel. The company runs regular race meetings throughout the season, as well as midweek practice sessions. Mallory also hosts a number of commercial units including the Everyman racing school/driving experience and spares companies; these are individually leased from Chris Meek.

Its parkland location with beautiful Kirby Mallory would make it the perfect site for housing development. However, its continued motorsporting use over more than forty years must imply that such temptations have been rejected by both Brands Hatch groups and Mr Meek, whose business life involves knowing the value of property.

Oulton Park

At Brands Hatch Circuits Ltd, Oulton Park Division, Oulton Park Circuit, Little Budworth, Taporley, Cheshire CW6 9BW (Tel.: 01829 760301; Fax: 01829 760378).

Perhaps the most charismatic motor racing in Britain, the Oulton Park track swerves, jinks and climbs through gradients and dips that formed the original layout of 1953, when it measured 1.5 miles. There have been a number of track layouts to promote faster lap times and more public sightings of the vehicles, leaving a choice of three track layouts at 2.775 miles, 2.362 miles and 1.66 miles.

The track has been home to major sports and Formula One [non-championship] race meetings through the sixties but declined into little more than club use for much of the later seventies and early eighties. Always a popular touring car venue, its fortunes revived alongside those of the TOCA 2-litre SuperTouring Formula in the nineties, and the track became a regular date on the TOCA schedule at press time.

Open for midweek testing regularly, one of our authors used it to drive everything from 1998 Rolls Royce Seraph to 500 bhp Sierra RS Cosworth. The friendliest staff in the business and the nicest atmosphere, but facilities beginning to date and track accidents had tragic consequences, even in the safety-conscious nineties.

In need of major investment or disposal from a Brands Hatch Leisure commercial viewpoint.

Pembrey

At BARC Pembrey Ltd, Pembrey Circuit, Llanelli, Dyfed SA16 0HZ (Tel.: 01554 891042; Fax: 01554 891387).

Redeveloped by the BARC in 1989, Pembrey's peninsular location in South Wales brings a unique climate (it can be operable when the rest of Britain is under snow), a ready made band of local race and rally followers, and a technically extraordinarily demanding circuit on to one ex-airfield site.

In RAF circles Pembrey is best remembered as the June 1942 site where a World War II Focke Wolfe 190 mistakenly landed. That allowed the authorities a detailed early look at the fighter that was causing the legendary Spitfire significant operational losses.

Today Pembrey operates as a test circuit and BARC racing weekends, but these are well attended and included championship events to Formula 3 and TOCA Touring Car levels during the nineties. Pembrey was not high profile, being mainly used for testing and heavily subscribed club meetings. The track is also suitable for testing tarmac specification rally cars or for staging single venue rallies around the bewildering massed tyre walls. Facilities are basic by nineties' standards and include a control tower, cafe and limited under cover garaging. There are no formal pits.

The demand for motorsport facilities in Britain continues to grow and isolated locations such as Pembrey remain vital for test programmes outside the public eye (touring car or formula car). Pembrey is less than an hour from major population centres such as Swansea and Cardiff for well-attended racing weekends.

Thruxton

At Thruxton BARC Ltd, Thruxton Racing Circuit, Thruxton, Andover, Hampshire SP11 8PN (Tel.: 01264 772607; Fax: 01264 773794). Leased from a private company, Thruxton circuit also serves as headquarters to the British Automobile Racing Club (BARC) referred to earlier.

Also a converted wartime airfield, Thruxton begun to host car race meetings in 1952. The track catered mainly for motorcycles until the BARC were forced to stage their Easter 1968 major meeting at the Hampshire venue, following the closure of Goodwood. Thruxton was redeveloped in its present 2.53-mile format, perhaps the least changed active circuit in Britain over the past thirty years, and certainly one of the fastest in the country.

Squeezed between an operational quarry and busy light aircraft facilities, Thruxton has not developed the commercial activities that befit its respected and internationally recognized race track. Facilities, even basic toilets, were primitive for many years and the track remains pretty basic in respect of hospitality or workshop units.

The site accommodates a racing drivers' school (founded by the late Ian Taylor and now owned by the BARC) and has a few commercial lessees, but is most redolent of Silverstone in the sixties; no bad thing if you wear the motor racing faith on your sleeve, but lacking in facilities for families.

Ripe for further development.

Silverstone

At Silverstone Circuits, Silverstone, Nr Towcester, Northamptonshire NN12 8TN (Tel.: 01327 857271; Fax: 01327 857663). Also the headquarters for a major motor racing club (BRDC) and mentioned in our earlier section, Silverstone has apparently thrived on its unique constitution. Doubtless Brands Hatch Leisure Group (or any of the other 1999 bidders) would undoubtedly argue that it could be run as a far more commercial venture, returning spectacular profits to shareholders.

There are no less than seven motor racing track layouts within the complex, the longest 3.25 miles and the shortest 0.62 of a mile. More recently (1998) a rallysprint mixed surface track named after the late Roger Clark has opened for business. This has proved a popular public attraction in its own right, with frequent television coverage, the result of a carefully designed track that allows cars to literally fly.

Assuming Silverstone has lost the British Grand Prix between 2002–6, it will not be the end of the track's commercial appeal: it's too strong in depth to suffer the sort of decline that Brands Hatch suffered when the same fate befell it in 1986. We would compare Silverstone to Monza in Italy for the strength of its brand name in association with motorized speed, rather than its history and consider that the brand name was still an under-worked asset.

Snetterton

The Brands Hatch Circuits (Snetterton Division), Snetterton Circuit, Norwich, Norfolk NR16 2JU (Tel.: 01953 887303; Fax: 01953 888220).

Now a 1.95-mile single track, Snetterton has evolved from the traditional wartime air base role into a circuit with excellent motor racing unit facilities having housed such success stories as the David Sears SuperNova multiple Formula 3000 Championship winning team, before they migrated to nearby Thetford.

Snetterton has been through many stages since its discovery and initial operation at 2.7 miles by the Aston Martin Owners Club (AMOC). In the sixties it hosted international events and its main (Norwich) straight was renowned as a chance to run flat out. Unfortunately this rapid strip was deemed too dangerous from the seventies onward as it culminated in a 30-mph hairpin! But the track retains its challenge with a shorter (Revett) straight and standards that attract up to 20 000 for the TOCA touring car's annual visit, a unique night event in 1999.

Snetterton is also an outstanding and popular racecar test venue and its remote location bounded by agricultural land did allow a 24-hour and one 25-hour, race to be run annually from 1980 onward. That was the UK's only 24-hour event, but it had been defunct for more than five years. However a night race for British Touring Cars was staged in the summer of 1999 and this attracted 30 000 spectators.

Snetterton's future is naturally bound up with that of its owners at Brands Hatch Leisure, but if we were marking off a BHL site in their quartet of race tracks that might be a lot more financially rewarding as a housing/commercial development, Snetterton would come second only to Oulton Park in richly rural Cheshire as the most likely sell-off in the BHL portfolio.

Centres of Technological Excellence

The largest generally available technical facility to both motorsport and motor industry in Britain lies within the grounds of MIRA, the Motor Industry Research Association. Now based in the Midlands, MIRA grew from facilities such as state-funded pre-war research laboratories in Brentford, West London, into a seventies' awareness of commercial needs through wider ranging facilities that allow both dynamic and laboratory investigation of vehicle behaviour. By

1999 around 500 were employed at MIRA, which was funded both by individual projects from its customers and governmental money, which could just as easily come from Europe as Britain in the late nineties.

Funding is now commercial, as opposed to the original governmental backing, but MIRA remains a membership organization. The 50th birthday celebrations of 1996 highlighted how MIRA's financial status had altered. Finance Director Roger Barter recalled that in 1968 MIRA income was 'approximately £430 000 ' per annum. This was based on £90 000 received from the Ministry of Technology, £60 000 income from hire charges and fees received, and £40 000 from individual members. Yet the biggest single income source was a £240 000 block subscription collected via the SMM&T, the Society of Motor Manufacturers & Traders.

By 1994 MIRA had passed through its commercialization process of the seventies and eighties, Governmental funding was slashed through the Margaret Thatcher era and yet MIRA was still in receipt of more than £20 million annually. The 1968–94 comparison highlighted that the SMM&T block subscription had been annulled, whilst government grants were halved to approximately £50 000 per annum and membership subscriptions now accounted for £374 000 rather than £40 000. However, the gargantuan leap was *selling services commercially*, where income soared from that £60 000 of the sixties into *£19.8 million 26 years later*.

Operational from 1946 in their present Nuneaton, Hinckley, Leicestershire grounds, MIRA has accommodated the British motor industry, particularly Jaguar and other racing and rallying teams on a regular basis. It offers many circuit surfaces, but of particular interest to rallying teams are the ride handling and stability circuit with every blind brow, adverse camber trick in the book, to test a vehicle's on-limit reactions to the unexpected; whilst teams will also use the straight-line acceleration lanes to practically check out mechanical and aerodynamic drag statistics.

Other circuit layouts include a High-Mu (adhesion) figure-of-eight layout originally sponsored and nicknamed after Dunlop and a 2.82 mile high speed circuit with bankings that has been lapped at an average 161.65 mph/ 260.15 km/h. The circuit provides the opportunity for speeds close to 200 mph available on the straights that connect the bankings. For durability trials there are also pave block trails, but these are of more interest to the industry than motorsports. However, MIRA also offers vital wind tunnel facilities that are useful to British motorsport outside the Formula One ranks, where in-house or exclusive facilities are always sought in search of the ultimate edge.

MIRA has Britain's only full size wind tunnel with paying access. Although some of the Grand Prix teams were planning or had built such facilities for their own use by 1999, this is still a desirable asset. There is also a 40 per cent scale model tunnel that features a moving floor, and a facility of use to leading motorsport teams are Computational Fluid Dynamics (CFD) modelling using 'extremely powerful computers and the latest software available'.

Not of such obvious benefit, but used by Prodrive to ensure that Subarus were fit for the humid temperatures of Indonesia, are the climatic control tunnels, where harsh running under high ambient temperatures can be explored. Other leading rally teams to use MIRA facilities since the late Des O'Dell pioneered use of the facility in the late sixties for his Marathon winning Hillman Hunters, have included those representing Seat and multiple world champions, Ralliart-Mitsubishi, whose preparation premises are almost local, being located at Rugby.

MIRA has also played a strong part in improving motorsport safety with both side and frontal crash test rigs available within the HyGe Laboratory regularly employed to meet FIA international crash test standards. Even the suspension test rig has accommodated Grand Prix cars on occasion and most of the leading teams, certainly Benetton, Jordan, Williams and Reynard, have used some aspect of MIRA services. The earlier British arm of Ferrari R&D also paid to use facilities that have also been utilized by Penske from their Dorset construction base and the Thrust World land speed record team.

MIRA is located at Watling Street, Nuneaton, Warwickshire CV10 0TU (Tel.: 01203 355000; Fax: 0203 355355. The web site address is http://www.mira.co.uk).

The other large network of track facilities and more limited laboratory facilities used by both motorsport and industry is the GM site, Millbrook Proving Ground at Millbrook, Ampthill, Bedford Mk45 2JQ. Facilities are available by individual negotiation only. Telephone enquiries to Customer liaison man Colin Shurmer at 01525 404242; Fax: 01525 403420.

Opened in the eighties, Millbrook revolutionized vehicle testing and endurance trial in Britain, having a simple concrete speed bowl that allows sustained high speed. The site has been operated both by GM and its former acquisition Lotus, but other manufacturers flock to use its combination high speed bowl, internal handling tracks and unique dirt trails that are smooth enough for some rally car testing to be usefully undertaken. Unlike MIRA, there are no wind tunnels or access to CFD facilities.

Millbrook has been home to many exciting performance car developments including the Lotus Elise, TWR Jaguar XJ220, and is popular amongst car magazines for its straight line acceleration test facilities, plus the ability to accommodate most machines in flat out runs around the bowl. One of this title's authors arranged for Tom Walkinshaw's European Championship winning 1984 XJ-S to run at this venue in the high 170 mph bracket for an *Autocar* feature, but the effect of the bowl does slow absolute maximums appreciably. For example the lap record at this site is 186.97 mph/300.9 km/h. But the straight line speeds recorded were little above this mark, compared to MIRA where the record may be 'only' 161.6 mph, but the highest straight line speed between its tri-bankings was 196.2 mph /315.75 km/h.

More pertinent to our title is that winning World Rally Championship cars have been regular visitors to Millbrook, including both Ralliart Mitsubishi and M-Sport for Ford. In fact the Ford Focus was dynamically developed by a small unit of up to 20 engineers working at the Millbrook site prior to the public unveiling in November 1998. To our knowledge this was the first time that a competition car had been engineered as well as dynamically proven in this sub-contract manner.

Ford reported in 1998, 'the typical time to create an all new rally car is in the region of 18 months. Ford, M-Sport and their technical collaborators have almost halved that long haul to get the Focus WRC up and running just 317 days after top management gave the programme the green light'. The technical achievement of this all new car was doubled by the fact that the Focus WRC was competitive immediately and another 53 days saw it out on the Monte Carlo Rally. It also won events in its first season, including the incredibly demanding East African Safari of Easter 1999.

Maybe more top line competition cars will be developed this way? Certainly for Ford it was an eye opening performance after their 30-year tradition of developing competition machinery in-house, with full union manning from the eighties onward.

Bruntingthorpe

There are other track facilities in Britain that are not open to the public and one of the most interesting and commercially viable has been the conversion of an active Leicestershire airport. This has been adapted to a number of uses that include a 4.2 test track with a two-mile, the landing strip, straight. The 700-acre Bruntingthorpe Proving Ground is owned by the Walton family, based at Welford in Northamptonshire and no relation to one of our authors. Telephone queries should be addressed to the track staff at 01162 478040.

The Bruntingthorpe site also houses an aircraft museum and realistically open air stored obsolete craft, but interesting nonetheless. It also accommodates hundreds of manufacturer's oversell cars, usually of fleet model and offers off road facilities that are intended for 4×4 mud pluggers.

There is a noise limit of 87.5 Dba on drive by, but the track was recently used by the 1994 Indianapolis 500 winning Penske without upsetting the neighbours and has also been used for other single seater shakedowns, including Formula 3000. Bruntingthorpe is useful to shake down systems in reasonable privacy, but it is not a security-conscious site for mainly manufacturer use, as is the case for Millbrook or MIRA. This emphasized by the fact that the Jonathan Palmer Driving Experience is a regular feature at this track, renting garage space and 120 days a year in summer 1999.

The special merit of Bruntingthorpe is that two-mile straight, designed to accommodate the heaviest transporters and bombers. This is excellent for photography and is one of the few places in Britain delivering a flat-out run with an entry curve to launch on to that straight above 75 mph. Speeds brushing 200 mph at the close of the straight are not unknown.

The banked Chobham complex in Surrey with excellent in field 'Snake' course – was under temporary management and expected to close when this was written. Suffice it to say that it had served the military well for more than 40 years (the heart of Britain's tank-development proving grounds lay here and at the rough road complexes of Bagshot).

The majority of action pictures seen in motoring magazines were taken inside Chobham's high fences, which run adjacent to the M3. The McLaren factory at nearby Woking use the facility, mainly for low speed work on the 3-seater F1; and the Tyrrell Formula One team (when they were at Ripley in Surrey) used these facilities occasionally. They were best known as the backdrop to a thousand movie/TV car chases, the launch site for the original Mini and an occasional rally car début including the Triumph TR7 and Ford Escort. The opportunity for the public to use this track for single stage rallying was terminated in the nineties after an uninsured death.

Significant Technical Teaching/Further Education Resources

Motorsport's appetite for highly qualified technicians in many fields has prompted Britain's leading companies to implement a variety of schemes that lead students from theory to working practice. If you doubt the need for such liaisons, look at the jobs' pages in *Autosport* every week or the booming specialist motorsport recruitment business. Such jobs are not confined to Britain; advertisers come from all over the world, but regular opportunities occur in America, Germany, France, Belgium and Italy.

Just as Britain has become one recognized centre for automotive designers, thanks to the pioneering courses of the Royal College of Art in Kensington, so the authors can also foresee Britain benefiting from an influx of students interested in pursuing a professional career in motorsports.

Brooklands College, Heath Road, Weybridge, Surrey, Surrey KT13 8T. (Tel.: 01932 853300). Modular student courses in motorsport industry.

East Berkshire College, 36 St Leonard's Road, Windsor, Berks (Tel.: 01753 749000). National Diploma in motorsport engineering.

Farnborough College Of Technology, School of Automotive and Industrial Engineering, Farnborough, Hampshire GU11 6SB (Tel.: 01252 407113). General automobile engineering courses.

Highbury College, Cosham, Portsmouth, Hampshire, PO6 2SA (Tel.: 01705 383131). Paul Mackenzie (Motorsport Development Manager) runs NVQ courses.

Loughborough University, Department of Aeronautical and Automotive Engineering and Transport studies, Loughborough, Leicestershire LE11 3TU (Tel.: 01509 223449; Fax: 01509 223946). Undergraduate and graduate courses in specialist engineering.

Oxford Brookes University, School of Engineering, Gypsy Lane Campus, Headington, Oxfordshire OX3 0BP (Tel.: 01865 483938). BEng aimed at motorsport requirement, three or four year courses leading to Honours degree. This establishment is well supported by leading local motorsport industry including TWR, Prodrive and Reynard.

Swansea College of Higher Education, Mount Pleasant, Swansea SA1 6ED (Tel.: 01792 481168; Fax: 01792 481189). Degree courses in Automotive and Automotive Electronics Engineering. Motorsport degree course initiated 1998. By 1999 Swansea had attracted serious support from the business, Vauxhall and their touring car representatives, Triple 888 Engineering, forming a partnership with the South Welsh Institute to 'offer work placements to motorsport engineering and design students'. Participants were offered placements at Triple 888, lectures from professionals and the opportunity to participate in both test sessions and factory visits.

Key Company Profiles and Statistics

The Scale of the Industry

APPROPRIATELY the business of motorsport conducts itself at a pace that matches its racing raison d'être. As we closed for press some of the most significant deals of the century were proposed or enacted, and we were able to gather and statistically analyse a cross-section of the 150 firms questioned for this title with a low (15 per cent) response rate overall the survey was not infallible. However, as with many other surveys we concentrated on the engineering core of the industry but we consider that the scale and scope of the industry needs to be analysed under five major categories:

- The engineering and technological core; design, fabrication, engine technology, transmission, electronic systems, components and chassis.
- Engineering and manufacturing consultancy services; companies in the industry supply major mass manufacturers with design, concept manufacturing and engineering services.
- The oxygen of sponsorship; TV, media, advertising and other 'media' racing related activities.
- Races; the impact on the local economy of hospitality, expenditure on travel, ticket sales and other activities (*see* The Economic Impact of the European Grands Prix, FIA Brussels Office (Sport), Rue d'Arlon 50, B-1000 Brussels, Belgium).
- Merchandizing; marketing, manufacture and sales (from many companies separate from Grand Prix and other teams) worldwide.

The results of our survey and analyses of the 'engineering core' show a British Motorsport Industry that was even stronger in depth than our original predictions. The evidence from surveys suggests a total annual turnover of the race teams and engineering sector of the industry of approximately £1.8 billion, with up to 75 per cent exported. The engineering sector has an overall strength in depth which extends far beyond the Grand Prix summit of the UK motor racing colossus and the figure does not include related engineering consultancy and manufacturing services provided to the mass manufacturing industry. A recent survey by KPMG of the British music industry (another 'cool Britannia' industry) suggested that the industry's contribution to the UK's GDP was approximately £3.2 billion a year, with export sales of more than £1.3 billion, the latter figure exceeding Britain's steel exports. Our survey suggests that the total exports from Britain's motorsport industry would be in excess of the contribution made by the music industry, particularly if one took account of all the categories of expenditure related above, since many of the major teams and companies involved in the industry reported exports of up to 90 per cent of turnover in our survey.

There has as yet been no adequate survey of the total extent of Britain's motorsport industry, since almost all surveys (including the IPPR survey) have concentrated on the engineering core of the industry. The most recent survey (In Pole Position by Nick Henry, PhD, *Euro Motor Report* 1999) also appears to concentrate on the motorsport engineering core. In our own survey of the industry conducted in 1999, we also concentrated on the team's component suppliers who serve the industry in all categories and have only made very approximate assessments of the wider economic contribution the industry's related activities make to the economy and exports. In our view it is somewhat dubious to restrict one's analysis of the contribution that the industry makes to the economy to this engineering core since, as the KPMG study of Britain's music industry considered, there are the contributions to be made from live performances and other related activities. Therefore, whilst our survey indicated that the industry's engineering core was of approximately £1.8 billion in annual turnover and employs approximately 40–50 000 people, this takes no account of the total contribution. For example, a recent study by the FIA Brussels office suggested that more than $50 million is spent at the British Grand Prix alone (which would include some 'double counting' from the engineering core) and that total spectator spending at Europe's eleven Grands Prix amounted to in excess of $400 million. We have yet to assess the economic impact under all the categories related above, and no previous survey has included the extent of economic activity generated by companies such as the TWR Group. As with many companies in this sector, TWR, with a turnover of more than £370 million per annum and an employee count of over 2 400 worldwide, makes a major contribution to the global automobile industry at large, as a direct result of its race technology and heritage.

Motor racing deals exploded repeatedly into national headlines in the summer of 1999. Whilst Nicola Foulston of Brands Hatch Leisure Group continued her pursuit of Silverstone Circuit and Grand Prix glory with a formal offer amounting to £43 million (made after we closed our coverage of British race circuit resources in Chapter 10) the trend from tobacco finance to sponsorship and backing from many other sectors of the global industry for the Grand Prix équipes continued.

Amongst this trend towards 'new entrants' was the announcement that DaimlerChrysler, owner of the Mercedes brand, had purchased 40 per cent of the Tag McLaren Group for a reputed £150 million (*see* profile below for further details). In addition BMW were to absorb the financial shock of lost tobacco sponsorship in enhanced support of Williams Grand Prix, resulting in much greater visibility for that German company in the BMW Williams Formula One programme of Year 2000 onward. However, the significant deals were not confined to Formula One or Anglo-German teams.

For the long-term financial stability of Britain's formula car constructors, we would cite American Don Panoz (*see* also Chapter 7) and his Elan Motorsports Technology Group. Elan now own Van Diemen in Norfolk and G-Force's multiple enterprises in Sussex. True, ownership of vital British racing concerns passes out of UK hands, but the benefits should be enhanced access to American markets and output for Britain's biggest series race car constructors at Van Diemen, plus ready-made markets for even more of G-Force output in formula and sports car racing. Both should improve employment prospects and the economic contribution to Britain, if not immediate UK owners.

As a result of the July 1999 Panoz/Elan takeover, Don Panoz appointed Van Diemen founder Ralph Firman to become chief operating officer of the Elan Group. This group will look after G-Force, Van Diemen and also deal with previous Panoz co-operative racing programmes. These extended to Zytek (hybrid electric sports racing car: *see* Chapter 7) and DPS Composites, the David Price-established concern which has entered and prepared both Panoz and privateer BMW-powered sports racers. DPS also create and deliver high technology composites for many racing car categories in addition to constructing carbon fibre briefcases (vital when jostling for Paddock positions in the managerial pecking order) and ultra lightweight composite construction bicycles.

TAG McLaren Group

Based at Woking in Surrey, with plans to move to a purpose-built site just outside that Home Counties town, the TAG McLaren companies currently employ 400 staff and had a turnover reported as in excess of £60 million for 1998, in our 1999 survey. The parent TAG McLaren Group is owned 65 per cent by Mansour Ojjeh, the TAG founder, and 35 per cent by the man who made the McLaren Group the company it is today, former racing mechanic, Ron Dennis.

Established by leading New Zealand Grand Prix racer Bruce McLaren in 1963, the eponymous company survived the death of its multi-talented creator in a testing accident at Goodwood during 1970. By then McLaren was not just an established Grand Prix Constructor, but also produced brutally effective Can Am sports racing cars that dominated lucrative North American road races.

Bruce McLaren died when planning a venture into the most exotic of GT cars for public sale. It was therefore fitting that McLaren in the nineties manufactured the 1995 Le Mans winning adaptation of the Formula One tri-seater road car and were expected to manufacture another V12 supercar with Grand Prix partner and 40 per cent shareholder Mercedes early in the Millennium.

McLaren competed with Grand Prix distinction in the decade after Bruce McLaren's death, winning its first World FIA Constructors' title in 1974, but was probably remembered best for supplying the car in which James Hunt won the 1976 World title. Since then McLaren has drawn level with Ferrari in securing eight World Manufacturers FIA titles (1974, 1984–5, 1988–9, 1990–1, and 1998). In supplying the World Champion driver's car, McLaren was supreme at press time, taking ten such titles versus nine for Ferrari, seven for Williams and six for defunct Lotus. McLaren had already added to that score by August 1999, with Ferrari alone apparently able to stop further successes in 1999.

Many famous drivers, designers and engine partners have passed through the glass doors of that glossy Woking HQ, but the man who transformed McLaren from an able GP competitor into a dominant force was former Brabham mechanic and Project Four Formula 2 team leader, Ron Dennis.

McLaren International became the official title in 1980, representing an amalgamation of Team McLaren and Project Four Racing. Mr Dennis brought an amazing eye for detail and meticulous presentation to the new Grand Prix force and his network of contacts. These included former World Champion Niki Lauda, emerging from retirement to race for McLaren in 1982 and bringing McLaren new prominence.

In 1984 the TAG-financed Porsche turbo V6 motor became a McLaren power source and Alain Prost/Niki Lauda dominated the World Championship season with 12 wins recorded. In 1988 they would do even better, their fifteen victories marking wins in all but one Grand Prix that sledgehammer season. No wonder McLaren ranked with Ferrari (116 wins to 119) at the close of 1998, for McLaren's victorious strike rate was far higher than that of the Italian concern; McLaren had contested only 476 Grand Prix versus 603 of the longer-established Ferrari.

The authors have been privileged to visit McLaren at home on a number of occasions and found that, however the team was currently performing (and there have been some dismal times, even in the nineties), the will to win was equalled only by Williams. Of course TAG-McLaren had immense technical resources and motivated their key personnel through exceptional financial rewards and bonus schemes. Yet it was their restless desire for perfection, coupled with nothing less than an inward team outrage at anything less than total victory, race after race, that marks McLaren and its partners TAG, Ilmor and Mercedes as the likely dominant force in Grand Prix for the Millennium.

Ron Dennis set an example not designed to win personal popularity, just Grand Prix after Grand Prix win. Such leadership standards had indisputable impact on Grand Prix results from 1982–99. Without McLaren and Williams, Ferrari would have added to their tally of titles and the balance of motor racing supremacy could easily have shifted back to Italy, with consequent knock-on effects for our motorsport supplier industry.

Grand Prix racing is volatile and no race or season is won until it is over. Success is only transient and consistency always difficult and sometimes impossible, as we saw in the number of human errors that snagged McLaren's1999 technical supremacy.

Cosworth Racing

For such a cornerstone foundation to Britain's racing success, the Cosworth Group of companies has had a pretty chequered ownership record. This should now be behind them in the long term integration within Ford motor company's Racing-branded activities. Today Cosworth Racing at the St James Mill Road, Northampton address it has occupied since 1964 employs just over 500, with all but 50 of those in the UK and the remainder at its American race engineering facility at Torrance, California.

September 1958 was the foundation date for a then North London-based Cosworth to be created from the names of the founders, Mike COStin and Keith DuckWORTH. These gifted engineers, who had both survived the turmoil and inspiration that was daily life at Lotus, had some links with Ford engines from the start. They created the Cosworth Formula 3 engine of 1959 (a winner by 1960 for Jim Clark and Lotus) from the tough 4-cylinder, 1-litre Ford Anglia unit.

Early on Cosworth became involved in Ford performance work for their production-based cars, including camshaft and inlet manifolding suitable for Cortina power increases in road and motorsport applications. It is recorded that their first such consultancy fee was £750, a far cry from the £100 000 initial payment on the 1967 Ford-branded DFV V8 Grand Prix engine, or the millions (industry estimated at £35 million a year) required to develop, field and service a modern 10-cylinder Grand Prix engine.

By then Keith Duckworth was long retired from active engine design at Cosworth, with ill health in the later seventies also precluding piloting the helicopters he favoured for so many years. To assure the future of Cosworth it simply had to be sold, and at that time Ford Motor Company were not willing to bid. Despite the immense Ford presence in Cosworth history, Ford never did

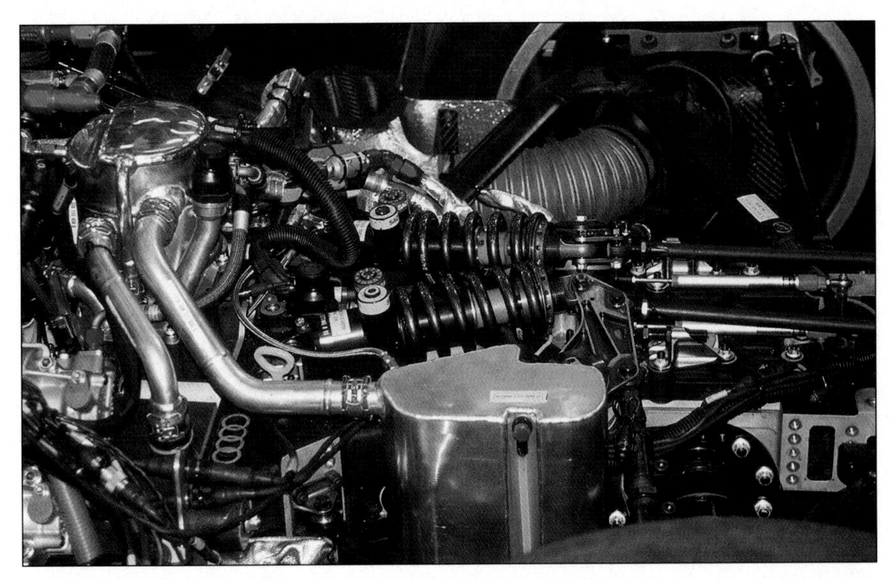

It goes in there and comes out here! The plumbing and electronics to a current turbocharged engine can be a maintenance nightmare: this is the 600 bhp twin turbo V8 created by Audi for British and American appearances in 1999. It utilised a British 6-speed gearbox. From Riccardo-FFD.

Surrey-based DPS Composites supplied the flyweight composite panels for Panoz in 1999. Best known for their serious racing technology, the David Price-founded company has also supplied carbon composite items from briefcases to mountain bikes.

Reynard's autoclaves at their new facilities at Brackley, Oxfordshire. As technology advances, the importance of carbon-fibre composites in the construction of race cars increases. Reynard are now the largest consumer of carbon-fibre composites outside the aerospace industry.

1999 BAR Formula One car with different livery. Banned by FIA, each car now has dual livery.

1999 BAR Formula One car with different livery. Banned by FIA, each car now has dual livery.

Formula One Williams, 1998 (Winfield).

Lotus 49 Gold Leaf. The engineering and commercial combination of Ford, Cosworth and Lotus.

TWR Virtual Reality Centre
Aston Martin DB7.

TWR Virtual Reality Centre
Airflow over Formula One car.

TWR Virtual Reality Centre
Aston Martin DB7.

Cosworth Engineering, Northants.

Cosworth Engineering, Northants.

Hewland Engineering Limited, Maidenhead.

Hewland Engineering Limited, Maidenhead.

Stewart Grand Prix at Milton Keynes.

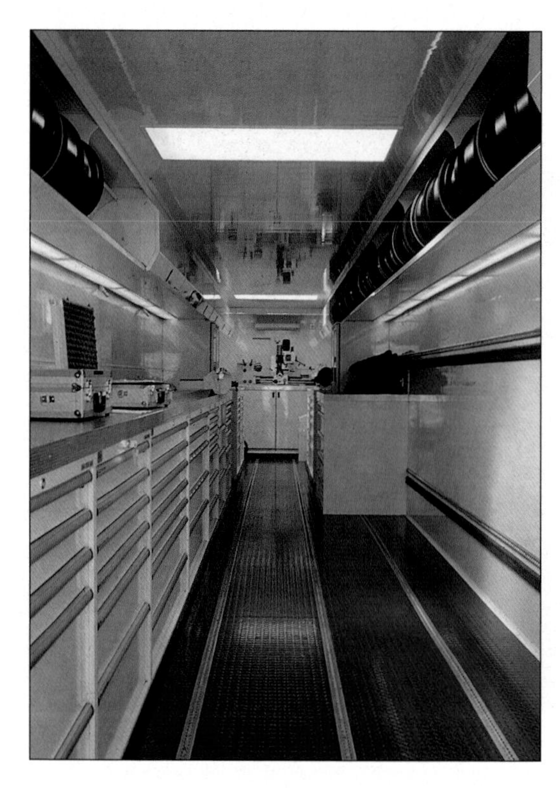

Stewart Grand Prix transporter interior.

acquire the company until an accidental blow-by of the Volkswagen Group purchase of Rolls Royce Bentley Motor Cars in 1998 from Vickers Plc, Cosworth's last long term owners prior to Ford.

Volkswagen initially passed on their purchase of all three Cosworth divisions (Racing, Casting, Production) to sibling Audi, who sold the racing business and its three Ford-contracted motorsport engine engineering programmes on to Ford for a rumoured £50 million. In 1999 Ford also acquired Stewart Grand Prix, and those two Ford-owned racing businesses will soon share premises. The current Cosworth premises are far from ideal, cramped after being carved up between Ford and Audi-owned divisions, right up to the point where temporary telephone, reception and other facilities had to be hastily incorporated.

By 1998 Cosworth had suffered a number of owners who were involved in non-engineering trading and therefore had no idea what the core Cosworth business was about. Investment often fell short of what was required to be as competition-competitive as the talent of their engineering staff would have otherwise attained.

There were, however, plenty of Cosworth achievements to celebrate. Ford are the most familiar amongst Cosworth contracts, but the sprawling Northampton and Worcestershire Cosworth premises have worked for arch rivals General Motors and delivered Mercedes an astonishingly effective road and race 16-valve aluminium cylinder head and casting, powering winning formula cars of every shape, size and origin.

Ford-branded products were headline news, however. One hundred and seventy four wins were scored by Cosworth-engineered V8 derivatives together with 139 pole positions, including at least one for the current V10 in 1999. Cosworth power had also brought Ford twelve Indianapolis 500 race wins and given Ford winning World Rally Championship Escorts over three generations. Other Cosworth-powered winners for Ford included Sierra RS Cosworth and Mondeo V6 Touring Cars. An insider reported to us that it costs more to engineer the complex production-based cylinder heads on the ex-Mazda V6 Ford Mondeo to yield over 315 bhp, than it does to manufacture the unrestricted racing cylinder head designs of the 800 bhp Ford-Cosworth Grand Prix V10!

Under Ford ownership Cosworth has expanded Research and Development (R&D) capabilities considerably and appears a much more committed Grand Prix contender. Key personnel included former Team Lotus racing mechanic Dick Scammel MBE as temporary Managing Director -- if it had not been for him Cosworth might not have survived to be taken over by Ford -- and Sales Manager Bernard Ferguson, who deserves the same accolade.

From 1 January 1999 Ford executive Neil Ressler became Chairman of Cosworth Racing with a Jaguar Chief Engineer Trevor Crisp, now Managing Director. Ressler was also appointed a non-executive director at Stewart Grand Prix.

Prodrive Group

Prodrive Limited is an unusual proposition, an immaculately presented engineering assembly and major manufacturer competition representative which grew to a turnover of more than £50 million in 1998, with 385 employees. It was all created out of a tobacco marketing agreement that originated with Rothmans. Founding partners David Richards and Ian Parry established Richards Autosport Ltd as a marketing consultancy in response to a request from Rothmans for a presence in motorsports during the 1979-80 winter. The pair had diverse backgrounds and are totally opposing characters; Richards is the epitome of the proverbial high achiever with his record as a World Rally Championship co-driver to prove his cool office management skills in the most hostile of environments. He has also been a successful helicopter precision flying competitor and in 1997 was the Bennetton Grand Prix racing director.

Parry, meanwhile, is the laid-back fellow who makes you laugh in the bar, but packs the shrewdest of insight into human nature alongside a natural charm that closes many of the deals Richards networks. Together they have built Prodrive from a 1995 turnover of £25.7 million to almost double that in 1997 (£42.5 million), with that growth sustained on past the £50 million mark in 1998. David Richards holds over 50 per cent of Prodrive Limited and there were three other directors at the time of our 1998–9 interviews, including Commercial Director Ian Parry and Technical Director Dave Lapworth.

The founding partners always wanted to campaign motorsport versions of major manufacturers' cars internationally, and the Rothmans branding bought in associations with just such corporations. In 1984 they had premises at Silverstone and fielded a brace of Rothmans-branded Porsche 911s internationally; they also used the tobacco company's ambition to support works Rover MG Metro rally cars in Britain the following season.

By 1986 they were ready to relaunch as Prodrive, an umbrella name for a marketing-orientated organization that uniquely packed a winning punch in both rallying and racing. The manufacturer and car that took them forward in both fields from 1987 onwards was BMW and its sporting M3. Prodrive enterprisingly sold BMW on the idea of venturing onto some of the smoother World Championship and European rallies. The results were spectacular, with a raft of European National titles gained. The more usual BMW racing role was (in Britain and some other Common Market countries) also shown to be within their competence, rewarded by extensive BBC TV coverage in the UK.

Post-BMW, who really did not want to go any further in rallying and sub-divided their British racing loyalties into the nineties (cutting Prodrive revenues), Prodrive selected Subaru as their major rallying partner. The company had not been effective previously but with first the Legacy and then the Imprezza range, Prodrive proved from 1989–99 that Subarus they created and entered could enjoy regular World

Championship success (three world titles for Subaru in the nineties), providing Britain en route with a World Champion rally driver for the first time.

The current Prodrive Subaru contract was set to run until 2001 and weathered the loss of principal tobacco sponsor BAT's 555 brand (who went Grand Prix racing with BAR-Reynard) at the close of 1998. The Subaru business has since been expanded both into the development of yet more rapid road cars and an 'Arrive and Drive' rally team which can charge more than £1 million a year to suitably qualified competitors – those wishing to concentrate on driving rather than the considerable organization required to prepare, ship and service a modern rally car on far-flung events. Prodrive is reported to have supported over 100 competition vehicles and sent crews to more than 70 international events in 1998, when they held both Subaru 555 World Rallying and Honda Motor Europe Touring Car contracts.

On the race tracks Prodrive were not so consistently successful. They played a support/host role to the works Alfa Romeo équipe during the Milan-based Fiat offshoot's domination of the 1994 BTCC title hunt, but the following year proved dismal for the red Alfa racers operated by Prodrive.

The company was absent from touring car racing before two years of Honda wins (1997–8) but gained no titles in the British and some selected European National Touring Car Championships with Honda. In 1999 Prodrive acquired the biggest spenders in the BTCC series, Ford Motor Company and their racing Cosworth-engined Mondeos.

In addition to its motorsport activities Prodrive has two other divisions Engineering and Sales. The Sales Division has two components, Motorsport and Performance Vehicle Products. The Motorsport section provides competition vehicles and components as well as management services for customers who compete world-wide. Prodrive customers have won over 100 rallies in 1999. The Performance Vehicle division markets components and bespoke vehicle enhancement packages from leading suppliers such as Bilstein, Speedline and Recaro as well as those designed and manufactured by Prodrive. This activity extends to the development and sales of high performance variants and limited editions of manufacturers' road cars. These activities now account for over 36 per cent of the compnay's total revenue. The company's current plans include further development of their road car engineering activities which will offer dramatic opportunities for growth. Prodrive will make an increasingly significant contribution to the revenue and profitability of Britain's motorsport industry.

To date the Fords have proved more competitive and there seems a distinct possibility that Richards will again be recruited back into the World of Formula One, this time to manage Ford's freshly acquired Stewart Jaguar GP operation while Prodrive continue with the Mondeo programme.

That Prodrive can and has operated without co-founder Richards, a fact it proved during his Benetton absence, shows how well the company has avoided the usual

British one-man entrepreneurial organization structure. Prodrive promise profitably increased turnover and much more work for its diverse divisions in engineering (some manufacturer consultancy here), motorsport operations and road car engineering in the new millennium.

Xtrac

Founded in 1984 and operational on an unofficial basis before that through the rallycross construction activities of founder and ex-Hewland employee Michael Endean, Xtrac at Wokingham in Berkshire is a brilliant example of the fact that the British can manufacture precision goods (in this case competition transmissions) and successfully export them, for more than 60 per cent of the gears, shafts and casings made by Xtrac are exported. It is also a company that displays continued expansion, despite Michael Endean's comparatively recent retirement and the management buyout headed by Henley Management College MBA, Peter Digby.

Cleverly managed by Digby and his team since Endean's amicable departure in February 1997 to the Channel Islands, Xtrac displays exceptional profit levels on a turnover that has risen from £28.7 million in 1997 to £31 million in 1998. Employment has remained static at some 170 to 176 over both those financial years.

Michael Endean was a second generation employee at Hewland Engineering (*see* accompanying company profile) and graduated from spare-time consultancy to creator of that multi-million pound Xtrac turnover in 13 years of consistent motorsport success. Endean led by example from such unpromising initial premises as those 'behind the local Chinese restaurant and Wokingham railway station', conceiving a 4×4 transmission layout that turned a privately campaigned Ford Escort into a regular leader (and 1984 victor) in the European FIA Rallycross Championship.

Such international success from a two and then five-man staff led to many other companies wanting Xtrac engineering expertise, but we must not forget that it was an approach from GM Opel Motorsport in Germany for Endean's consultancy that made such work practical.

A human tragedy unexpectedly catapulted the embryonic Xtrac into the single-seater and formula car limelight. Michael Endean recalled,

> 'a company called MEH over at Staines in Middlesex cut our racing gears and had the tooling to fabricate key racing car components. They had three directors and, tragically, the youngest died in his fifties. The two older guys simply wanted to sell, but one looked a bit further than that. We were able to negotiate a deal where he came along with the gear-cutting and fabrication tooling I had bought, and he taught my guys how to use that equipment'.
>
> This, completely by accident, was the cleverest thing we ever did. Shortly after

acquiring MEH and its assets, I started getting phone calls from leading race car manufacturers like Lola and McLaren. They wanted to know if we were going to carry on working for them as we had bought all the vital manufacturing equipment ...'

By April 1987 Xtrac had moved to its present modern industrial factory premises in a rather more salubrious Wokingham location. Today the company supplies not only its famous gearboxes (the majority of international touring and rally cars use Xtrac six-speed layouts, whatever the original maker's name) from Formula One to the World Rally Championship contenders and beyond, but also CAD with similarly computer-assisted R&D investigative services deployed in metallurgy and heat treatment process facilities. Xtrac also deliver rack and pinion steering mechanisms and many associated competition car transmission components, such as drive and propellor shafts or intelligent limited slip differentials.

Hewland Engineering Limited

As with many companies in this industry, there seem to have been three fundamental elements to success at Hewland; a unique personality, timing and a streak of genius. In this context Hewland Engineering at White Waltham in the pristine middle-class suburbs of Maidenhead is typical. Established in 1957 by a man who described himself as 'just a mechanic' at our interview in 1999, Michael Phillip Hewland (known as MPH), Hewland Engineering started in a very modest way in a small shed, undertaking odd engineering jobs. In 1960 Eric Broadley of Lola Cars enlisted Mike Hewland's help in building a modified transaxle for use in Formula Junior single-seat racing cars. All previous Formula Junior cars utilized Renault running gear and gearbox, which made ratio changes extremely difficult and complex, to say nothing of time-consuming.

Mike Hewland's Mk 1 gearbox utilized VW transmission with specially made Hewland gear ratios to make it more suitable for racing. Modified versions followed in rapid succession but the real breakthrough came with the Mk 4 gearbox which, whilst it retained the VW casing, contained a radical and innovative redesigned gearbox cluster and selection system. The Mk 4 was the basis for many future modifications and enabled race engineers to change the ratios by simply removing the rear plate of the gearbox. This made it possible for ratio changes to be executed extremely quickly during practice so the optimum ratio setup for each driver and track could be used. Amazingly, the innovation did not meet with universal acclaim and even the engineering genius Colin Chapman was initially unimpressed by the concept of interchangeable gear ratios. Needless to say, many later versions of Colin Chapman's single-seater designs utilized Hewland gearboxes with interchangeable ratios.

For more than thirty years Hewland Engineering designed and built gearboxes for almost all Formula single-seat racing cars: Formula One, Indycars, Formula Ford, Formula 3000 and Formula 2000, all supplied from a range of eight gearboxes. During the Ford Cosworth DFV engine era, when Britain's 'assemblatori' were beginning to dominate Formula One racing, Hewland supplied the transaxle assemblies for practically all the cars, with the exception of Ferrari and BRM. Companies from all over the world including America, Japan, France, Germany and Italy, beat a path to this company for innovative ideas and solutions to complex engineering problems involving transmitting horsepower to the road or track. Although in 1970 Mike Hewland received the prestigious Ferodo Trophy for his services to motorsports, by the mid 1980s the company had become complacent and was failing to recognize the changing rules of the game.

The financial revolution in motorsport, carried forward by one Bernie Eccleston, and the departure of an employee of Hewland called Mike Endean in the late 1980s, spelt potential disaster for the company. As MPH recounted to the authors, 'the company had lost its way' for the following reasons. Firstly, the company had failed to comprehend the huge impact that sponsorship, particularly tobacco sponsorship, had made on the resources available to the teams. Secondly, technological change in all areas of motor sport had quickened beyond recognition as teams strove to extract the best possible performance from their cars. Finally, the commercial pressures meant that teams demanded individual service and speed of response rather than 'off the shelf' solutions.

Mike Endean's new company, Xtrac, started to compete head to head with his old employers, offering the individual service and technological solutions the industry demanded. Hewland considered selling the company in 1984 and shortly after that Mike Hewland's son William, then aged just nineteen, declined to take over the business as he felt he lacked sufficient experience.

The increase in competition, particularly from Xtrac, forced the company to embark on a massive development programme and to make sweeping changes to its pricing structure, generating increased turnover but resulting in the first losses in the company's history. William Hewland was entrusted with the running of the company, assumed a majority shareholding, and in 1992 appointed Harry Sparrow as General Manager. They have engineered a turnaround in culture, technological development and, most importantly, profitability. By 1997 the company moved into a new high-tech factory, providing an ideal environment for future growth, and turnover for 1999 is projected to be over £12 million, with over 80 per cent exported.

Hewland's is an extraordinary success story that deserves future analysis. The young and innovative spirit of William Hewland has, helped by the experience and business acumen of Sparrow, transformed disaster into success.

Jordan Grand Prix

In the early 1990s the 'new kid on the Formula One grid' was Eddie Jordan, the impish Irish ex-banker. Moving into the most competitive (and expensive) Formula in world motorsport, the Jordan team has brought a unique approach to many facets of the business. Perhaps the most important of these is the sheer drive and obvious enjoyment that Jordan instils throughout the team. 'I don't think you have to go through life with a sour face to reflect a serious image.'

By 1998 the team's apprenticeship had been served and organization and funding were now in place to make the push up the grid. Their new Technical Director, Gary Anderson, now found himself with sufficiently deep funds available to embark on a development programme for the new car. From only 53 people in 1994, the company employed over 160 people in 1998 and was now housed in its new four-acre site at Silverstone, across the road from Britain's famous motor-racing circuit and home of the British Grand Prix. The team's new headquarters, complete with purpose-built factory, boasts a technological package appropriate to a Formula One team, including a 40 per cent wind tunnel and a seven-post rig. New offices alongside the team's headquarters house the engine suppliers, Mugen-Honda, ensuring the close integration of chassis and engine development. From running at the back of the grid in 1991 the team scored its first championship points in its first season at the Canadian Grand Prix in Montreal.

Throughout the following seasons the team made steady progress but this was often marred by a string of retirements between 1993 and 1997. Success does not come easily or cheaply in Formula One and by the end of the 1997 season the team was in fifth place in the Formula One World Constructors' Championship. 1998 was to be the take-off year, when the team appointed Damon Hill as Number One driver, backed up by Ralph Schumacher, and had in place an appropriate budget which funded all the necessary technological efforts. The highlight of that season was the team's first and second place at Spa-Francorchamps. This season's achievements were remarkable as it propelled Jordan into the top four in the World Constructors' Championship and paved the way for future sponsorship acquisition and race success.

As with so many teams and companies in this industry, it is difficult to underestimate the impact of the leadership and determination contributed by the team owner, Eddie Jordan. Jordan is now a serious player in the Formula One game (war?), sponsored by an impressive list of major companies including Benson & Hedges, their principal sponsor for 1999. The team has in addition made use of co-sponsors such as Hewlett Packard, who provide technical expertise, as do Intercond and Lucent Technologies. The team has retained its particular atmosphere and dedicated approach together with a remarkably innovative and creative pursuit of sponsors. Eddie Jordan negotiated a large equity investment from Warburg Pincus at the beginning of the 1999 season, the third such investment by a banking group in Formula One. There seems little doubt that the team's success will continue as Eddie Jordan pursues his dream.

Reynard Motorsport Limited

Reynard displayed its first car at the 1975 Racing Car Show in London. Established in 1973 as Sabre Automotive, the company has an extraordinary record of success in designing and building racing cars and is now arguably the world's most successful racing car manufacture. 'The first time a Reynard Formula Ford car raced, it won. The first time a Reynard Formula 3 car raced, it won. The first time a Reynard Formula 3000 car raced, it won. The first time a Reynard sports car raced, it won. The first time a Reynard Indy car raced, it won. The first time a Reynard-designed touring car raced, it won.' (*The Reynard Story* by Mike Lawrence, 1997.)

For the last twenty-five years Reynard Motorsport has developed through the energy, vision and creativity of Adrian Reynard, backed by his partner Rick Gorne, and transformed from a tiny garagiste into a group with a multi-million pound turnover and division specializing in design, computational fluid dynamics, composites, manufacturing, customer sales, service and support. The group currently employs over 260 personnel in the United Kingdom and the United States of America. The group's rise, from the small shed at 20–22 St John's Street in Bicester to their stunning new premises alongside British American Racing at Brackley in Northamptonshire, has been a story of continued success on the track and in the business of the sport. The company is now the world's largest manufacturer of carbon composite chassis and probably the world's largest user of composite material outside the aerospace industry.

Since his days as a student at the then Oxford Polytechnic, Adrian Reynard has always taken an unconventional line. His final year project on the degree course was supposed to be the development of a lateral strain-gauge accelerometer but instead he presented the first Reynard racing car, the 73F-001. He failed! The lack of convention continued when the now Oxford Brookes University presented (for the first and last time) a failed student with an honorary PhD in automotive engineering.

Reynard are now on another phase of expansion and development with the establishment of specialist divisions at their new Brackley facility; in particular, the innovations generated in computational flow dynamics and composites are leading edge. The group's order book for 1999 is exceptionally healthy, although both Swift and Lola have generated recent successes in North American racing. The group also supplies Nippon Racing in Japan with the 99L chassis, and delivery was followed by Reynard Cars recording the top ten fastest times in early testing. The 99L went on to win its first race of the season in true Reynard style, followed by five other Reynard Nippons.

As with many other high profile organizations in this industry, Reynard Motorsport succeeds because of the 'less visible' side of the group's activities in the new and emerging technologies of electronics and composite materials. With companies such as Stewart Grand Prix still waiting for their own wind tunnel facility (sure to come with Ford money), Reynard Motorsport has two wind tunnel facilities, one in the United Kingdom and one in the United States of America at Indianapolis. The latter, known as the Automobile Research Centre, is a joint venture with Pacwest Racing Group and Honda and is available not only to Champ Car Teams but also to other clients. In this way Reynard is typical of other organizations such as TWR Group, Williams Grand Prix Engineering and McLaren International in selling its expertise and leading edge technology outside of the motorsport industry as well as to racing clients. The extent of this company's research facilities includes its shared facility at Shrivenham and the group's computational fluid dynamics division at Brackley led by Dr Robert Lewis.

As Rick Gorne pointed out in our interview in 1999, the group's technologies are not exclusively devoted or indeed applicable to motor racing or automotive design, having other as yet untapped applications. CFD, which provides the ability not only to look at the effect of air flow but also to know the cause of airflow patterns inside and outside the car, probably gives Reynard's design teams a unique advantage. However, this technology could also be applied to environmental issues, and the use of composite materials will undoubtedly be applied in other fields.

In the last decade Reynard Motorsport has won the Queen's Award to Industry for Export Achievement on two occasions, in 1990 and 1996. The company has a current annual turnover of £33 million and employs over 250 people, with more than 90 per cent of its turnover exported. The Reynard philosophy is not only to seek excellence in its own field of activity, motor racing, but also to offer its expertise and experience to the automotive industry at large. Solutions have to be simple, cost effective and produced in the minimum time scale. Reynard's achievements derive from the concept that there is a science to winning.

TWR Group

This is the largest company in Britain's motorsport industry by a factor of approximately 3.5 times. Owned and run by Tom Walkinshaw, the company's record of growth and success is unparalleled. In just twenty-one years the group has established itself as one of the leading, if not the leading, supplier of race-bred technology and automotive skills to the mass manufacturing industry worldwide. Although born out of Tom Walkinshaw's racing activities when he established a touring car team, only 15 per cent of the Group's £370 million a year turnover is now a function of purely motor racing activities. The group was established in 1975 with Mazda and BMW as the first of their clients, and six years later TWR started a Sportpart programme for Mazda. In the TWR Group newsletter Walkinshaw has summed up the group's attributes as 'Speed, secrecy and skill'.

Since its much heralded activities with Jaguar (JaguarSport) and General Motors in Australia (Holden Special Vehicles), TWR has continued to guide the design, engineering and manufacturing activities in order to enhance the mass manufacturers' products. The group's racing heritage is extensive, covering Touring cars, Sports Racing cars and Rally cars. In 1988 TWR established their first joint venture with Jaguar and this collaboration resulted in the Silk Cut Jaguar winning the 1988 24-hour race at Le Mans. This race success has continued with three world sports car championships, further Le Mans victories in 1990 and race victories in the British Touring Car Championship with Volvo. In 1996 Walkinshaw acquired the Arrows Grand Prix team and signed the then world champion driver, Damon Hill. The same year TWR's Holden Racing Team won the Australian Touring Car and a TWR designed Porsche won at Le Mans.

These successes illustrate the wide range of companies that have beaten a path to TWR's door. On the road, as on the track, this company's record of innovation and success ranges from their extensive collaboration with Volvo and the transformation of the Volvo image, to the design and production of many concept cars for manufacturers whose names will never be divulged. More publicly, TWR collaborated with Jaguar in the design, engineering and manufacture of the Jaguar XJ220, and in 1992 Aston Martin and TWR joined forces to produce the DB7. This collaboration with these Ford-owned specialist car manufacturers continues to this day with the DB7 production taking over from the XJ220. Indeed, the Aston Martin car is truly a product of TWR, who were responsible for the engine design and production as well as the outstanding concept designed by Tan Callum. The success of the XJ220, the DB7, the Volvo C70 and many other design studies undertaken for unnamed companies, must place TWR Group within the forefront of the world's most famous design groups.

In 1996 TWR Group opened their new headquarters and research and development centre at Leafield in Oxfordshire on the site of a British Telecom facility. This impressive facility is but one of TWR's bases within the UK and the company has also opened offices in Japan and Brazil, plus of course its extensive operations in Australia. Whilst the Arrows facility at Leafield has failed to produce any impressive results, the extent of new technology within the complex is on a par with any of the major Grand Prix teams, and the road car facilities are outstanding. In 1999 the company entered into a collaboration with an American electronics firm called Silicon Graphics (SGI) to develop the 'first curved-screen immersive virtual reality environment' to be built in the United Kingdom. This impressive facility offers designers the opportunity to design car shapes, assess their aerodynamic qualities, model the airflow and view the shape in a special light tunnel giving the opportunity to assess the integrity of the curves and lines of the design. Engineers can also view their work in 3D and assess the compatibility of components as they are assembled, in 'virtual reality'. Currently the plan is that the facility will be extensively used for road car development and will be available for other manufacturers to hire. This facility will enable groups of designers to analyse and review projects before any tooling is committed, thus saving huge amounts of money and scarce resources, inlcuding time.

The breadth and depth of this company's technological applications were extended in 1998 when TWR Group produced the Astec Sulky, pulled by a more natural form of horse power, from their composites company based in Derbyshire. The Astec Sulky set a new world record in June of that year when John Campbell, its American driver, and his filly Armbro Romance raced the fastest ever mile for a horse of that gender.

In April 1998 the company opened a new division entitled TWR Technical Services, based in Heybridge, Essex. This part of the group will provide contract manpower support to all the TWR Group programmes and customers, as well as supplying design, engineering and training support to automotive suppliers throughout Europe.

The TWR Group is the largest company within this dynamic and fast-moving industry sector. It is still owned and run by one man, who controls the empire from the headquarters at Leafield and whose Broadstone Estates Trust still maintains control of 100 per cent of the company as there are no outside shareholders. In August 1999 TWR sold their Ixion motor group to Frank System Plc.

Since 1993 the company's turnover has grown by in excess of 20 per cent per annum and it has more than doubled its employees worldwide. The company has established facilities in England, Sweden, the United States of America, Brazil, Australia and Japan and has recently announced a new arrangement with Renault which will involve the company in the design and production of the specialist Renault Clio V6. The company's technical achievements have included all the aforementioned road and racing vehicles plus the Formula One Benetton B194 racing car, the Jaguar XJR14 sports car and its own Arrows Formula One cars, whose success on the track has yet to live up to the outstanding performance of this motorsport bred group.

Williams Grand Prix Engineering

The story of Frank Williams and motor racing has been recorded in many publications and certainly reads as a titanic business struggle. As we have already said, in this business there seems to be a fundamental necessary condition for success which is almost always related to the drive, ambition and tenacity of a single person; Frank Williams is the eponymous example. In the late 1960s Frank Williams entered motor racing and formed a close relationship with one Piers Courage, subsequently suffering the loss of this very close friend in the appalling crash of 1970 at Zandvoort.

In 1967, after many years of wheeling and dealing, Frank Williams established Frank Williams Racing Cars Ltd in a small workship with a flat overhead at 361 Bath Road, Chippenham. Success did not come and disaster struck repeatedly, but giving up was never an option. In 1975, after a great deal of consideration, Williams accepted an offer from Walter Wolf, an Austrian oil magnate, to fund his team and purchase the assets of the Hesketh Formula One team, all for the purpose of building a new Formula One enterprise. The reality was that Williams would no longer be the only voice and that as Wolf would be funding most of it his contribution was authoritative. Untypically, Frank Williams made an error of judgement since this mercurial and extraordinary character could not possibly work for someone else, and the Wolf/Williams relationship foundered two years later. In 1977 he decided to go his own way and thus started a journey during which he has created the world's most successful Formula One team.

Williams Grand Prix Engineering Ltd was founded in 1977 and based at 10 Station Road, Didcot. Frank's previous business record was one of hand to mouth struggles involving many brushes with creditors and bailiffs, but he always maintained a strong determination to succeed and in spite of everything maintained the affection and respect of most people in the industry. In retrospect 1978 can be seen as the turning point, as three elements established the foundations of the Williams Grand Prix team's future success. The first came in the guise of an unlikely gentleman in view of Frank's previous brushes with the banking world, as it was the local Barclays Bank Manager, Mr John Makepeace, who turned up at Station Road asking if he could help! Within a few days WGPE found itself with a £30 000 overdraft limit. Earlier Frank Williams had persuaded Patrick Head to join him and this partnership was to prove by far the most important element of the foundation, since the two men have continued to build success in business and engineering terms. The last element was Frank Williams' success in gaining his initial sponsorship from Saudia Airlines as a result of, as usual, dogged persistence and a modicum of luck. Finally, along came Alan Jones.

From these small beginnings WGPE rapidly moved to the forefront of the grid and, more importantly, within their first season as a Grand Prix team, in spite of being able to contest only ten rounds of the championship, they were being courted by Goodyear as a team to watch. In 1979 Clay Regazzoni won the British Grand Prix at Silverstone on 14 July in the FWO6 and, for a time, Alan Jones was leading the race with Regazzoni in second place. From then on success built on success, culminating in the team winning their first World Formula One Drivers' and Constructors' Championship in 1980. The lessons Frank Williams had learned from the thirteen years he had run Frank Williams Racing and then Williams Grand Prix Engineering were beginning to pay off. Persistence pays.

In the early 1980s the team's budget was approximately £500 000, including the purchase of the Ford Cosworth DFV engines. The team had none of the facilities they now have at their impressive and superbly organized headquarters in Oxfordshire. In spite of the continuing success during the 1980s, disaster was still waiting. In March 1986, returning from testing in the South of France and driving a hired car, Frank Williams suffered massive spinal injuries and is now a quadraplegic. This happened when the team was at the height of its success and had amassed more Drivers' and Constructors' World Championships. The implications of the accident were farreaching and at the end of that season Honda withdrew their engines. Within six months of the crash Frank Williams was back at the then Didcot headquarters and within twelve months the team had started to climb back to further World Championship success.

The team now enjoys a reputation second to none in Formula One and nobody can equal WGPE's record of nine Formula One World Constructors' Championships, which has been achieved in twenty-two seasons. Ferrari, who have raced for twenty-five years more than Williams, currently have eight. The team's budget is now nearly £100 million per annum and it employs approximately 200 people. Technical facilities include a wind tunnel, state of the art machining and tooling equipment, carbon composite fabrication facilities and sophisticated electronic CADCAM systems. In 2000 the team will use BMW Formula One engines which are currently being developed and, as with McLaren and DaimlerChrysler, there is the distinct probability of a strong relationship developing between these two organizations. Already BMW are using Williams Formula One in establishing a new brand and it seems inevitable that the cars and the products will recognize this close relationship. Formula One teams themselves are now being recognized as 'brands'.

The spirit of teamwork and leadership that this most extraordinary man (now Sir Frank Williams) and his designer and partner Patrick Head have created in Williams Grand Prix Engineering can be summed up in the quotation from Patrick Head to one of the authors several years ago 'Winning isn't everything but it sure as hell beats the ... out of coming second'.

Stewart Grand Prix

Grand Prix teams can no longer be set up in the manner in which Frank Williams went about creating Williams Grand Prix Engineering. The evolution of Jordan through the ranks of lesser formulae is one route and the purchase of Tyrrell by British American Racing is another. Stewart Grand Prix was established on the partnership of Jackie Stewart and his son Paul. The three times World Formula One Drivers Champion (1969, 1971 and 1973), was backed by the financial might of the Hong Kong and Shanghai Banking Corporation, Ford Motor Company, Hewlett Packard, the Lear Corporation and Bridgestone, to name but a few. The first car was launched in 1996 and their first season commenced in 1997. Jackie Stewart himself stated that winning was out of the question in 1997; survival was the objective. The team was founded on the business acumen and persuasive manner of this canny, intelligent and obsessive Scot in partnership with his son Paul; not the first such partnership in Formula One.

In spite of the advantages that Jackie Stewart's huge range of contacts in the business were able to offer and of the immense drawing power of his name, the launch and the birth of Stewart Grand Prix was no easy business. During the 1995–6 period when the financial backing of the team was being put in place, Paul Stewart Racing was still contesting the Formula 3 Championship. A crucial turning point occurred when Jackie Stewart contacted Sir William Purves, Chairman of the HSBC Group, with a view to developing a sponsorship relationship. This was to be the first banking foray into Formula One and it was a crucial element in ensuring that the Stewart Grand Prix project went ahead, as even the massive Ford Corporation required additional sponsors to be alongside them. The £25 million that HSBC eventually committed over a five-year period was a major coup and the very first time that any blue-chip financial company had ever invested in Formula One racing. The search for further sponsorship continued throughout 1995 and 1996 and eventually the team was launched.

The team now operates from a major facility at Milton Keynes opened in June 1998. Covering some 80 000 square feet, this state of the art facility is amongst the most modern in Formula One, although the team does not yet possess the technical facilities enjoyed by McLaren and Williams. The first SF1 car, launched in 1997, took just nine months to create and was designed entirely using a sophisticated CAD system supplied by Hewlett Packard. After just two seasons of racing, Stewart were beginning to make their mark in the Formula One circus when it was announced that Ford were to purchase the company for £100 million in June 1999. From the time the team made its debut in the Australian Grand Prix in 1997 and scored its first podium position in Monaco that year, Stewart Grand Prix has come together as a force to be reckoned with as a result of an extraordinary number of far-sighted partnerships.

The first is undoubtedly Jackie Stewart's long-term relationship with Ford, which has continued since he retired from Formula One racing in 1973. When Ford agreed to be the first major sponsor of Stewart Grand Prix it was not because of any long-term sentiment for Jackie Stewart, but because the company was looking for a new direction in its motorsport activities. Over the next three years a number of fortunate occurrences strengthened the link and made the logic of the partnership more obvious. During Summer 1998 Cosworth Racing Ltd was purchased, along with Rolls Royce and Bentley motorcars, by the German automobile company Volkswagen from the defence conglomerate Vickers. Volkswagen (through Audi) sold Cosworth Racing to Ford, who strengthened the company's links with Stewart Grand Prix and increased the technical collaboration, resulting in a dramatic improvement in the performance of the team's engines. Ford's subsequent purchase of Stewart Grand Prix is therefore probably but the first of many future acquisitions by major mass automobile manufacturers. The purchase gives Stewart Grand Prix major financial backing, which should enable them to move up the grid during the latter part of the 1999 season as they build on the firm foundations laid before. However, it also raises questions about the future control, name and direction of the still fledgling Formula One team. Ford will use it to enhance their brands, especially Jaguar.

The Future?

The business of Formula One racing is undoubtedly the pinnacle of all motorsport, both technologically and potentially in terms of global coverage. Whilst Indycar is still the dominant force in North American motorsport, the extension of the Formula One season to include a United States Grand Prix at Indianapolis in Year 2000, and further Grands Prix planned for Malaysia and China, assures the global march of Formula One. However, many of the major teams within the United Kingdom are reaching significant stages in their development, with control passing from the owner-managers to corporations. The future pattern of development of motorsport in general and Formula One in particular seems to be inextricably linked, not just with the technology of automotive engineering but with the billion-dollar advertising, merchandising and entertainment industries. It is this element of motorsport that attracts the mass manufacturers who are increasingly searching for brand differentiation in a market with considerable excess supply and many similar products.

The global technological, managerial and business leadership that the British Cluster possesses in motorsport provides a much larger advantage to the UK economy. Without this motorsport supremacy the authors consider that the UK would lose the much wider and larger contribution of companies such as TWR, TAG McLaren, Williams, Reynold, Hewland and Cosworth to name but a few. In addition, we would be at severe risk of losing much of the plethora of vital ancillary services that are too often ignored but directly serve this industry and market. It is the race based attitudes, managerial and technical culture as much as the technology that provides the UK with this unique industry that is much greater and more important to the UK economy than just its racing activities.

Philosophy for 2000: Why is Britain Good at Motorsport Engineering and Management?

Introduction

'It's difficult to analyse why we are so good at design and development. Britain tends to underestimate itself, but car racing is like being at war. It concentrates the mind.'

Gordon Murray, *Car Magazine*, August 1995

'In Italy we are cut away from the Silicon Valley of Formula One that has sprung up in England.'

Luca di Montezemolo, President of Ferrari,
The Sunday Times, 6 September 1992

THERE are two distinct questions that are important to an understanding of Britain's current, and (potentially) future, dominance of the world's motorsport industry. Firstly, why are the majority of companies and technologies currently based in Britain? Secondly, why are so many of the engineers, designers, mechanics and entrepreneurs in the industry British? It is the answers to these questions that will explain why the British element of the world's motorsport industry is so dominant.

The answer to the question why it is based in a specific area of the United Kingdom cannot be explained by a single set of causes. The answers to the two questions are complex, part of history as well as more theoretical factors and accident, chance and economics have all played their part. The process of design and development, alluded to above, has never been the work of any one company but now includes companies that specialize in using their race-bred expertise to supply the mainstream manufacturers. These are often ignored in analyses of the industry's economic and technological importance.

Before the Second World War and in the immediate post-war period until the mid-1950s the world's mass manufacturers, particularly the Italians, French and Germans who used racing as an extension of their research and development effort, dominated motorsport. However, in the 1960s the market became more complex, characterized by relationships between constructors, suppliers, sponsors and manufacturers. It was in this period that 'the centre of the motor racing world shifted from Italy to Britain, where specialist chassis-building teams used off-the-shelf engines and transmissions supplied by specialists' (Setright, 1973).

Ignoring Murray's warning, it is important that we explore the reasons why Luca di Montezelomo's words are so accurate and why the motorsport industry in Britain is currently so dominant. If for no other reason than the avoidance of the aphorism: 'Nothing fails so dramatically or successfully, as success.'

Why should the current performance and future of such a relatively small sector of the United Kingdom economy matter? The question is relevant with regard to the scope of this industry, since it has many links with other sectors but most notably the large scale vehicle manufacturers (*see* particularly Chapters 9, 11 and 14). Moreover, many firms in the sector apply their sport based or learned skills and technologies in the main automotive sectors. We shall examine the impact of this industry to the UK economy in a later chapter, meanwhile let us try and answer, why Britain?

The Development of Britain's Motorsport Industry

In Chapters 9, 11 and 13 we explore the current size, scope and structure of the Motorsport Industry in Britain. A number of points come across clearly from this analysis.

- The agglomeration of constructors in Motorsport Valley, although the spread of suppliers is geographically wider than the Thames Valley.
- High turnover of staff within the motorsport industry, and the 'musical chairs' that typifies that process.
- High rate of new firm formation and the rapid decline/demise of existing firms.
- The wide extent of technological links within the industry and to outside industries, particularly the mass manufacturers.
- The extent of the services upon which the industry depends that have been established in the 'cluster'.

The historical factors underpinning Britain's dominance contribute to the continuing success of the industry in Britain. A historical investigation appears necessary in order to understand how the current structure and dominance evolved? How can associated industries leverage this competence? Plus, an understanding of the factors that might lead to the erosion or loss of Britain's current dominance.

Records reveal the dominance of Italian manufacturers in motorsport during the early post-war years. From 1947 to 1954 Alfa Romeo, Ferrari, Maserati and Lancia all competed, successfully, with the common commercial intent of increasing their road car sales. In the latter part of the 1950s, continuing in the 1960s, this dominance switched to British constructors. There are, however, several conflicting views as to why dominance shifted to Britain in the latter 1950s and early 1960s.

The 'Series of Accidents' Theory

Ascribing Britain's dominance in motorsport to coincidence and accidents (both literal and metaphorical) may appear to lack academic rigour. However, the role of accidental factors was central to much of the respected work of influential economist Paul Krugman. Krugman (1990, 1991) theorized that national industrial specialities often result from accidental factors, but that once these industries are established the nation can gain a head start on its competitors.

Aston and Williams (1996) suggest that in the late 40s and early 50s, 'Italy did not dominate motor racing because it was better than Britain; rather it was better than Britain because it dominated racing and Italian personnel had built up skills and experience through years of racing success'. Subscribing to the view that the growth of the motorsport industry in Britain can be traced back to a combination of accidental factors, Aston and Williams go on to highlight the importance of the following factors:

A spate of major accidents

At Le Mans in 1955, a Mercedes crashed killing 83 spectators and injuring many more. A similar accident marred the Italian Mille Miglia road race in 1957. In the backlash, the dominant Mercedes team withdrew from motor racing. Other major motor manufacturers followed suit, leaving the specialist builders to continue with less competition. Political pressure forced road racing into decline which reduced the number of continental races, the effect being to promote racing at designated circuits. Switzerland went so far as to ban all motor racing on its territory.

The popularity of club racing in the UK

Amateur racing was becoming increasingly popular in Britain, and such races centred on the available surplus of disused airfields. Such popularity led to a dense network of local clubs, along with a growing number of enthusiasts and specialist engineering companies. With road racing denigrated, the British affinity for racing on airfield tracks gained relevance. Many of these airfield tracks (such as Silverstone, Thruxton, Snetterton and Goodwood) went on to become motor racing circuits.

The commercial intent of British racing car manufacturers

In contrast to vertically integrated constructors such as Ferrari and Porsche, which built racing cars for their own factory teams, British manufacturers were happy to sell a racing car to anyone who would buy them. This led to British cars dominating the starting grid, even if their drivers didn't make the podium.

A ban on cigarette advertising on television

This led to tobacco manufacturers sponsoring racing cars in order to maintain visibility for their products. British teams proved adept at securing this valuable commercial sponsorship, with Lotus securing the first major Grand Prix contract in 1968.

This argument, proposed by Aston and Williams (1996), suggests that once British manufacturers started, they gained an advantage through the development of external economies of scale in the dense network of specialist suppliers that grew up to service the industry. (It was Marshall [1949] who first investigated external economies of scale and scope, when analysing 'industrial districts' such as the steel industry of Sheffield. He defined economies of scale as factors that cause the average cost of a commodity to fall, as the volume of output of the commodity increases.)

Technology Based Theories

However, the fortuitous accident theory has its detractors. Pinch and Henry, economic geographers working on a paper to be published in 1999, contend that greater insight can be gained by considering the role of rapid and radical technological change. They believe that such technological change can provide a catalyst for the relocation of the industry supporting the technology.

This belief is not new; Scott and Storper (1987) record that this happened in the case of electronics, with the shift from valves to transistors and then on to semi-conductors. Both texts submit that the relocation of manufacturing capacity is possible because new supply chains and new forms of knowledge are required to support a radically new technology, a view also supported by Dosi (1984).

While continental racing car constructors relied on powerful engines, which being large and heavy required the support of a sturdy chassis, British constructors took a lead from technology developed within the aircraft industry and emerged with a radically different approach. It was Charles Cooper who is widely credited with first considering the impact of aerodynamics, size, new materials and weight distribution. The result was a small mid-engined racing car that achieved considerable success at an affordable customer price.

These small, lightweight, mid-engined racing cars required new supply chains. The preferred engine to power the car was a lightweight aluminium engine, commercially available from Coventry Climax (who designed the engine to be used as a water pump). An understanding of aerodynamics and materials technology was also required.

The British government had invested massively in the aircraft industry in the 1920s and 1930s, creating research facilities such as Farnborough. Britain's strength in the design and manufacture of aircraft, supported by skilled labour and specialist engineering companies, left the country ideally placed to fulfil the requirements of the new supply chain. Hebb (1993) reports that by the mid-1950s over 16 per cent of Britain's engineers were engaged in research and development relating to aviation.

As Pinch and Henry conclude, 'the ultimate result of this shift in technological trajectory was that the locus (location/focus) of the industry shifted away very rapidly from northern Italy to southern England'.

The Industry Cluster Theory

Generations of economists and geographers have concentrated upon the concept of location in terms of the development of economies. The theory had a great deal of relevance when the location and price of the inputs to the firm's productive activity dominated the geographic concentration of industries. The proximity of raw materials, climatic conditions or the supply of labour often determined the location of these early economic clusters. In a modern global economy companies can source goods, services and technology around the world, but there are still major examples of the importance of location. The clusters of companies that work in the same or a related activity serve to illustrate the continued importance of location.

The argument put forward by Michael Porter in an article in the Harvard Business Review suggests that the modern cluster that links an array of related companies and institutions has become a powerful force in determining the productivity of industries. He suggests that the cluster affects competition in three primary ways:

1 They increase the productivity of companies based in the area, since they

allow companies to source inputs, access information, technology and required institutions.
2 They maximize their access to the pool of intellectual capital that builds up around the companies. This is the essential ingredient that drives the pace and direction of innovation, reduces the costs of recruitment and ensures more direct flows of information.
3 The proximity of the people and businesses stimulates the formation of new companies and new groups of technologists and entrepreneurs. This formation and reformation ensures that existing companies have new sources of specialist suppliers.

There is a singular concentration of the related skills in the motorsport industry within the United Kingdom. Not only does this cluster benefit the economy directly through the increase in exports, value added activity and employment but benefits accrue both from the transfer of skills and technologies into the industry and from the motorsport industry to other industries. In Chapter 9 we detailed the extent and significance of the geographical location of the teams, suppliers and related companies that form the technological and entrepreneurial heart of Britain's motor sport industry.

A Critique of Documented Theories

The role of accidental factors appears important, but insufficient to fully explain the evolution of the motorsport industry in Britain. Is it fair to write off an enthusiasm for club racing as an accident? Or can this be attributed to engineers from Britain's burgeoning aerospace industry looking for an exhilarating sport that exercized their talents? Why wasn't Italy's intense interest in motor sport enough to preserve their domination?

Taking an eclectic view, embracing elements of both theories, the authors contend that happenstance set the scene, creating an environment in which the motor sport industry in Britain could begin to develop. Against this backdrop, a change in technology trajectory instigated by British engineers provided the necessary catalyst for relocation of the industry. As Britain could provide a pool of skilled engineers from the aircraft industry, and Italy's aircraft industry was relatively small, a new motor sport industry was rapidly established in Britain.

Subsequently, as the cluster of companies and organizations developed in the Thames Valley and in other UK areas, the reality of the reinforcing network of relationships that Porter defines played a major role in the development of the industry. The cluster theory is certainly a persuasive element in the overall picture of Britain's current dominance of the industry.

The Rise and Dominance of Britain's Motorsport Industry: a Further Explanation

Whilst the 'series of accidents' theory explains the initial location of the industry in Britain and the other theories provide extensions of that explanation, there are still gaps. The continued growth and durability of the industry in Britain, along with the reported concentration of teams and suppliers in motorsports Thames Valley, still require explanation. The vision and entrepreneurial ability of those involved often derived advantage from the 'accidents'. However, the technological 'step change' prompted by Coventry Climax and Cooper was a crucial factor earler, followed much later by the collaboration between Ford, Cosworth and Lotus.

In February 1965, amid concerns over escalating development costs caused by a regulatory change that would require the development of 3 litre engines for 1966, Coventry Climax announced their withdrawal from Formula One engine production. British constructors needed a new engine, but lacked the funds to develop one. With funding amounting to £100 000 from Ford, Cosworth Engineering (formed by Keith Duckworth and Mike Costin, who trained at De Havilland) were able to develop the Cosworth DFV Formula One engine.

This was a major commercial breakthrough and the partnership between Walter Hayes of Ford in Britain, Colin Chapman of Lotus and Mike (brother of Frank) Costin and Keith Duckworth of Cosworth (whose Racing division has recently been sold to Ford), Duckworth and the Cosworth team at Northampton created the Ford DFV (Double Four Valve) V8 engine and the Lotus 49. Not only the most successful racing engine ever built (Ford and Cosworth V8s of varying specifications won 174 Grand Prix 1967–94), but also the most widely available, at a profitable price, to all comers.

Deleting the headache of providing a competitive engine from the constructor along with the gearbox, which increasingly came from proprietary suppliers such as Hewland at Maidenhead, Britain had rapidly developed into purveyors of bespoke components of unmatched quality for Grand Prix and allied trades.

Engineering genius Colin Chapman brought non-motor-trade sponsorship to motor sport in 1968 with John Player Team Lotus, a direct result of lifting restrictions on sponsorship in the same year. A noble enthusiast Lord Hesketh, provided a great boost to the confidence of the UK motorsport industry in the mid-seventies, and amazingly risked several million sterling to manufacture and develop the Hesketh Grand Prix car; a platform that gave James Hunt the experience to win his World Driver' Championship with McLaren in 1976.

The phenomenal success of the Cosworth DFV might have led to the unassailable superiority of a single team (Lotus, for whom the engine was initially developed), had Ford not taken the decision to make the engine commercially available after one year of competition. The DFV became the standard Formula One engine of its time, winning every world championship from 1968 to 1974, and pioneering the use of the engine as a load-bearing element in the chassis. With Cosworth, based in Northampton, providing fresh engines and handling a significant workload in terms of overhauls and servicing, local suppliers were treated to levels of demand that led to economies of scale being realized.

The growth and success of Cosworth also spawned new motorsport companies, key examples are Ilmor the engine designers and constructors in the same Northamptonshire region as Cosworth. Another newcomer was the March Grand Prix Team (now defunct) established by Robin Herd and Max Mosley at Bicester, Oxfordshire. Information about this company, derived from an interview with Robin Herd along with information from Henry and Pinch (1997), is used to investigate:

- The mechanism of formation of SMEs active in the motorsport market
- The rate of new firm formations
- Business failures within the industry and the redeployment of key staff.

Robin Herd describes the process that Mosley and he used, in order to establish an initial location for March, as a mixture of compromise and chance:

> 'I was working for Cosworth in Northampton at the time, so we looked at a map and said we're both going to have to travel. Oxfordshire was reasonable, and we both knew Oxfordshire, so we went to an estate agent and they had a 3000 square foot factory warehouse available in Bicester. We rented and subsequently bought it.'

He goes on to describe how suppliers grew around March, which was 'the largest manufacturer of racing cars in the world at that period', and how this led to other racing teams being attracted to the area:

> 'We needed exhaust suppliers, welders, fabricators, fibre glass people, and so what happened was a whole cottage industry developed around the business. Then someone comes along and says "I am going to set up a racing team, where shall I go? Well, I can save myself a lot of aggravation by locating in Oxfordshire where I can already find exhaust manufacturers etc." and so the cottage industry attracts people … it developed a momentum of its own.'

These words echo those of Marshall (1890), who is worth quoting as he still provides possibly the best description of the advantages conveyed by such agglomeration:

'When an industry has thus chosen a locality for itself, it is likely to stay there long; so great are the advantages which people following the same skilled trade get from near neighbourhood to one another. The mysteries of the trade become no mysteries; but are as it were in the air, and children learn many of them unconsciously. Good work is rightly appreciated, inventions and improvements in machinery, processes and the general organisation of the business have their merits promptly discussed. If one person conceives a new idea, it is taken up by others and combined with suggestions of their own; and thus it becomes the source of further new ideas.'

However, Herd does not ascribe the success of March (which was, we should note, the first production race car constructor in what is now termed Motorsport Valley) to the company's location: 'We could have gone to Lancashire or Yorkshire, and it would still have been the same.'

As the area grew motorsport sub-contractors and suppliers, Herd was disinclined to relocate. He also came to appreciate the advantages of his chosen location:

'It was more convenient than we first realised. It's a fantastic venue with Silverstone, Cosworth, the airport and train journeys to London were easy. The fact that Cosworth was in Northampton was very useful, because that's actually an important link.'

With Cosworth supplying engines to March, who tested extensively at Silverstone, the benefits of proximity are compelling. Indeed, proximity of the supply base was later to become a tenet of 'Just In Time' manufacturing. The network of companies that were spun off from the March Company confirms the cluster theory's influence. This network is illustrated opposite (Figure 12.1).

Analysis Through Some Standard Techniques

This section explores the forces acting upon the motor sport industry and the market, illustrating the linkages that exist.

Pestle Analysis

Although technology is only one of the influences on the business environment, for many companies in the Motorsport Industry it is amongst the most important. However, it can only be assessed in relation to the other factors (political, economic *et al.*) with which it interacts. It is important to realize that trends influencing the industry will also influence consumers and the market, as illustrated in Figure 12.2:

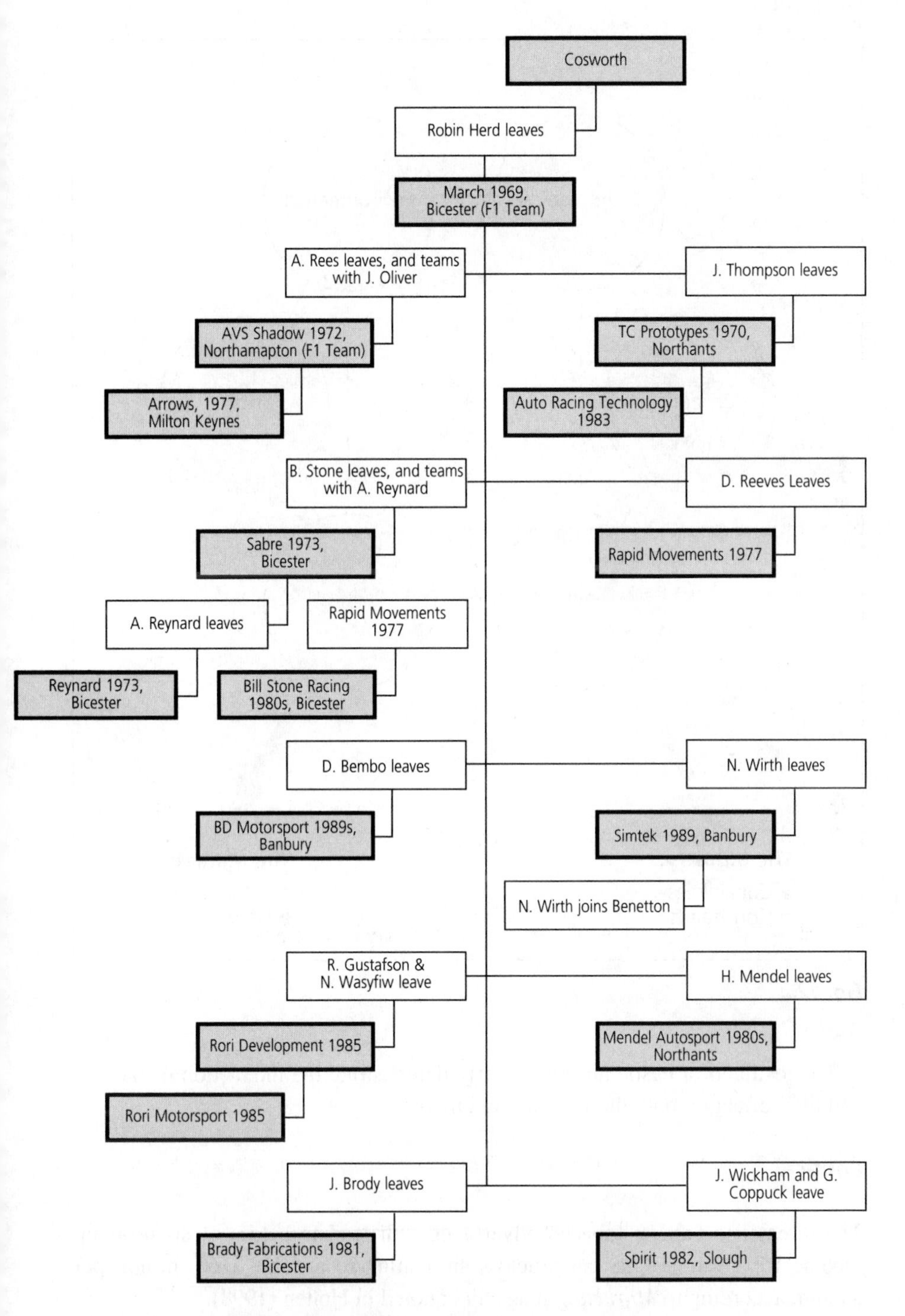

***Fig. 12.1* Companies spun off from March**

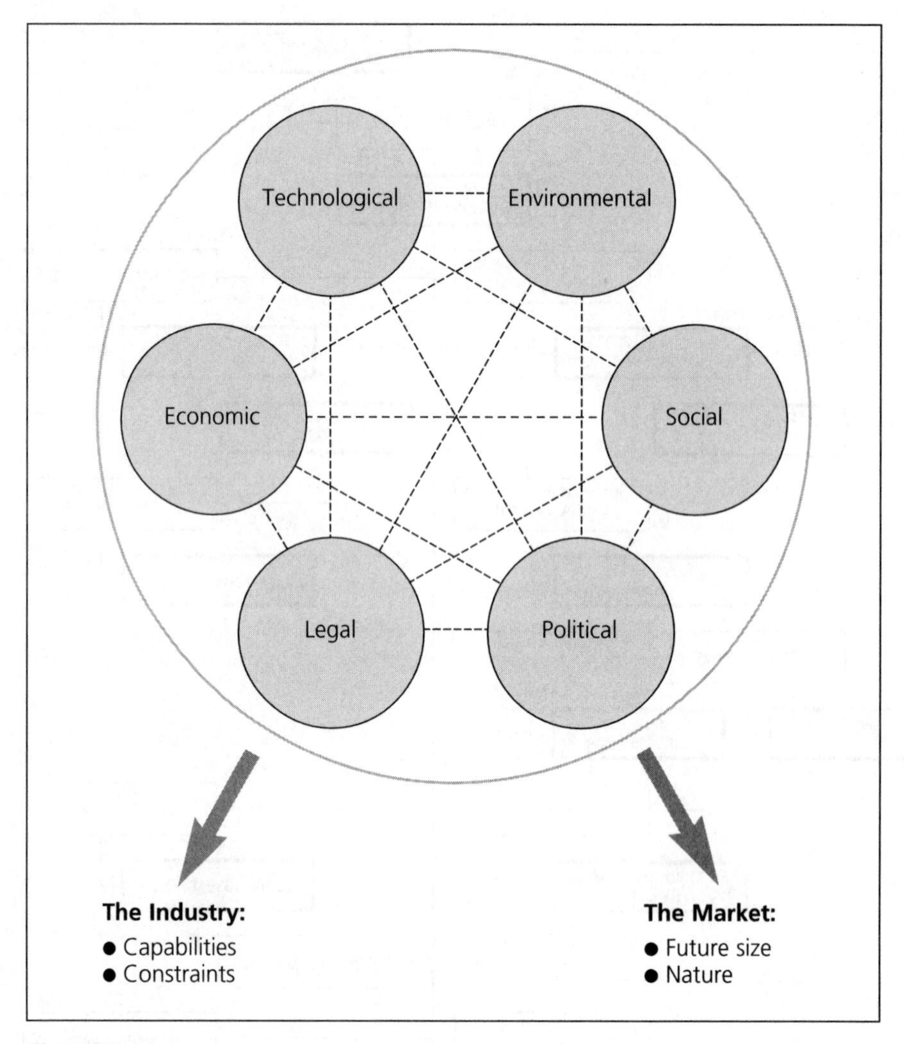

Fig. 12.2

The results of a Pestle analysis clearly demonstrate the interaction of factors, and their effect on both the industry and market:

Political

The threatened ban on tobacco advertising will lead to a loss of sponsorship income for Formula One constructors amounting to at least $160 million per annum, according to *Marketing* magazine quoted in Hotten (1998).

In an attempt to stall the ban, the FIA and Formula One have persuaded politicians that it could lead to the loss of 50 000 jobs and the decimation of Britain's Motorsport Industry (Hotten, 1998). However, this is something of an exaggeration – The FIA's President, Max Mosley, concedes that Formula One employs no more than 5000 people (Hotten, 1998).

Political pressures on Formula One are strengthening, as countries such as China, Indonesia, Malaysia and Korea contend for the right to host grand prix races. These Asian countries also represent the most important markets for Formula One's most powerful sponsors, the tobacco companies. In Britain, political awareness of the importance of the industry are growing, with Frank Williams being awarded a knighthood in the 1999 New Year's honours list.

Economic

If it proceeds, the flotation of Formula One may reduce the uncertainty about the economic environment felt by constructors, and improve the teams' stake in revenues accruing from broadcasting. As Ron Dennis, quoted in Hotten (1998), explains: 'A flotation may help the teams to come together in a more constructive way that allows them to understand and feel secure about their future'.

Major financial institutions are taking equity stakes in constructors, bringing City money into an industry traditionally financed by tobacco sponsorship. Warburg, Pincus, the venture capital firm, has taken a 40 per cent stake in Jordan for an investment of $60 million (*The Times*, 17 November 1998). Morgan Grenfell Private Equity has taken a major stake in TWR Arrows, valuing the company at £110 million, and relevant when considering the value to the UK economy of this sector.

Mergers and acquisitions, prevalent in many industries that sponsor motor sport (including petrochemicals, car manufacturing and the tobacco industry), are reducing the number of blue-chip companies interested in sponsoring motor sport. If Ford acquires BMW, then why should the two brands be seen to compete against each other on the Grand Prix circuit? Similarly, with BAT and Rothmans merging, 'it'd be relatively unlikely for the enlarged group to continue to sponsor two teams' according to a spokesman quoted in *Autosport* (14 January 1999).

Emerging economies are keen to avail themselves of the advantages of Formula One's global reach. By way of example, the Malaysian government sponsored Stewart Grand Prix, believing that 'the deal will spur our automobile industry to greater heights' according to the Malaysian Prime Minister Dr Mahathir Mohamad.

Social

The first Concorde agreement of 1981 between FOCA led by Bernie Ecclestone and FISA (now led by Max Mosley) sealed the involvement of worldwide television coverage, establishing huge commercial involvement and the immense, secretive, financial basis of motorsport as global entertainment. Ecclestone's foresight in recognizing the future potential of an international sport has yet to yield the billion dollar flotation that the architect of modern Grand Prix racing's commercial base seeks, partially because a European Commission is elaborately investigating possible Common Market regulation infringements. Already the major team owners receive an enormous sums from Bernie Ecclestone's management of TV rights, an income now estimated at £12 million per team per annum instead of £1.1 million just two seasons ago.

Interest in Formula One has intensified due to publicity surrounding a £1 million donation from Bernie Ecclestone to Britain's Labour Party, which was subsequently returned amid allegations relating to tobacco advertising and taxation.

The exposure received by Formula One is increasing. According to official figures from the FIA, the cumulative audience for the 1997 championship was 50.7 billion, up 20 per cent on the 1996 figure. This compares to a cumulative audience of 32 billion for the 1994 football World Cup.

Technological

Digital technology, allied to a revolution in television broadcasting, looks set to change the relationship between the industry's sponsors and the industry's ultimate consumers – the television audience. This will occur in two main ways:

1. Broadcasters will segment their audiences on behalf of sponsors. Sponsors and advertisers who do not require global coverage will be able to target specific countries
2. Advertisements will be superimposed on blank billboards, or added as a backdrop to the podium after a race. This technology already exists. According to Hotten (1998), Canadian viewers of an ice hockey match saw an advert for a tyre company in the middle of the pitch, while Swedish viewers saw one for Ikea.

However, sponsors are also wary of the potential downside of this new technology. Barry Gill of CSS International warns: 'Formula One should not be deluded by technology … Sport is about inspiration and participation … Mass audiences are essential for a healthy sport'. Subscription to Formula One channels in France and Germany has been slow to date.'

The FIA, with input from the Formula One teams, continues to regulate against the use of new technologies in Formula One and to introduce new regulations aimed at increasing competition and decreasing risk.

Legal

Karel van Miert, the European Competition Commissioner, launched an investigation in 1997 into the contracts that link Formula One, the FIA, the constructors and the broadcasting companies. This investigation caused the flotation of Formula One to be postponed.

The introduction of the Working Time Directive, on 1 October 1998, is causing concern among many of the larger motorsport companies (Willis, 1998). Motorsport traditionally pays high wages, to offset the long hours and intensive nature of such demanding work. If employees take up their legal option to refuse to sign a waiver, then the employment structure, and potentially the viability, of the industry in Britain will be compromized. In this event, the role of supplying SMEs and single employee companies may become more important, as these companies tend to do 'whatever it takes' to attract and retain business.

Environmental

Growing concern over the environmental impact of Formula One is influencing the FIA. Measures taken to date include:

1 Aligning the Formula One fuel regulations with regulations relating to future environmentally-friendly commercial fuels
2 Planting 25 000 trees in Mexico, to recycle the carbon dioxide generated by the sport.

Porter's Five Forces

The results of analysis using Porter's Five Forces framework are presented below (see Figure 12.3). Whilst, at first sight, this analysis does not appear to offer great insight, a couple of points are worthy of note:

- The industry is characterized by a relatively high level of contra-trade, where constructors provide advertising (via logos on the car) in return for goods and services. Determining the power held by suppliers and consumers is complicated by this type of arrangement, and best handled on a case- by -case basis.
- Barriers to entry may be low for suppliers, but for competing constructors the barriers are high. The size of the Formula One industry is limited, as the FIA regulate the maximum number of competitors. The FIA are also considering imposing a $25 million surety, to ensure that new constructors are able to meet the financial pressures of competition.

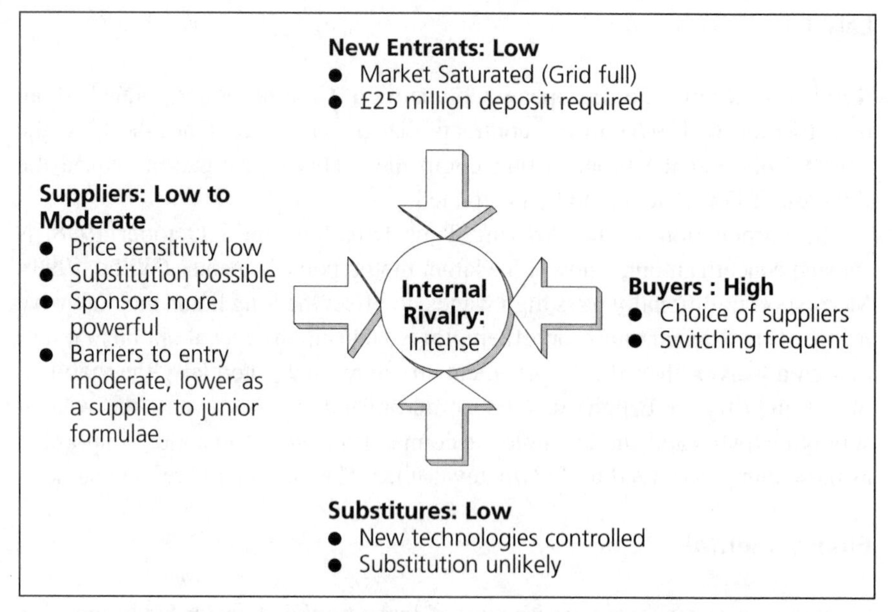

Fig. 12.3 **Application of Porter's Five Forces to Formula One Constructors**

Rapid Organic Growth from Excellence: The Industry Feeds on Itself.

The rewards are exceptionally high in Britain's motor racing business but the clients, especially in Japan and Germany, see anything less than winning as a failure to be punished. The honourable exception to prove the rule was the solid support Mercedes granted McLaren through uncharacteristic seasons without wins. McLaren-Mercedes are now rewarded by a dominance that has the opposition and media moaning that the silver and grey winners are 'boring' whilst a Ferrari Championship win would be seen as good for television and Grand Prix's image.

A TWR project was undertaken for Aston Martin Lagonda Limited, whose Chairman Walter Hayes was determined that a more affordable new Aston Martin would attract sufficient buyers, if it could be produced efficiently; increased volume was the key. Other TWR Group commercial connections today include racing and customizing road cars for General Motors in Australia and Volvo in the UK. But success means winning and a fabulously rewarding contract with Nissan to win Le Mans was terminated after two promising but not winning assaults on the French classic

This is not a level track and race/competition success does generate high quality, high profit business and global customers. TWR Group is now engaged in manufacturing high image Volvos in Sweden, such as the C70 coup. Alongside the leading TWR-Volvo British Touring Car Championship team, these moves have transformed Volvo's staid image in the marketplace. Ironically, the next public unveiling of a TWR-enhanced product for the showroom came from Volvo's domestic rivals, SAAB, who publicly joined the lengthening TWR client list in 1999 with the Viggen branded production SAAB.

Such specialist manufacturing is the first stage of a new trend in the motor industry, with motor sport based companies providing the design, development and manufacturing facilities for the production of specialist automobiles, concept cars and other marketing weapons. Speed of response, technological excellence, manufacturing flexibility, creative design and innovative flair are all part of the advantages that motorsport-related companies offer the giants. Such thinking also utilizes the motorsport industry that has built up around Formula One, providing another outlet for the advanced technology.

Britain's Silicone Valley of Motor Sport stretching approximately from Surrey in the South to Derby and west from Norfolk to Poole, is the primary region with the necessary range and depth of specialist designers, component suppliers, engineers and technicians able to support such an activity. That Ford found it more effective to sub-contract the design and development of a new Jaguar and Aston Martin to a relatively large race-based company (TWR), says a great deal about this industry.

Sadly, few British companies have used this pool of technological talent and expertise (British Aerospace being an exception) nor does British industry, with notable exceptions such as ICI and HSBC banking, fund UK motorsports through sponsorship. However, multi-national manufacturers use British racing teams and their related companies for competitive chassis design, affordable and rapid precision engineering, aggressive management, aerodynamic and design excellence.

The Way We Were or the Way We Are? Politics, Economics and Education

There is currently over-capacity in almost all of the world's major mass manufacturing or service industries certainly in Europe, including automobiles, food, clothing, banking, steel, chemicals, textiles and many others. The old production lines of the Ford factory style have seen their zenith and it is arguable that Britain does not have any comparative advantage in mass producing almost anything, unless the company is managed by foreigners as the Nissan factory in Sunderland has proved. That factory, which has recently been placed at the top of the European car productivity league, proves it can be done. The modern production processes pioneered by the Japanese and adopted by almost all manufacturers that currently survive, including Porsche, have sounded the death knell of the large car factory establishment as developed by the first Henry Ford.

The reasons for this decline of the importance of the mass manufacturing industries are still a matter of much research and analysis, but there are many indicators that help to show the path to the future. as manufacturing in general accounts for a smaller proportion of modern economic activity in the more advanced nations, the manner in which we produce services is changing.

Examples embrace call centres, dealing rooms, supermarket checkouts and telesales. In all of those examples the mass element has gone, individuals are undertaking specific tasks, often a complete task. The richer the more advanced nations become the more sophisticated and selective their consumer population is, requiring products that are differentiated and even bespoke, in the sense of having an element of scarcity.

Mass manufacturing is employing fewer and fewer people producing more and more products in more sophisticated ways. The simple fact of being the best in the world at mass manufacturing is no longer possible for a nation such as Britain; we probably have no sustainable advantages in that field.

This is an industry that is not only craft or bespoke dominated but is also an industry that is serving the mass manufacturing of other nations, providing them with the essential differentiating factors for their products. That the industry is based in the United Kingdom is no guarantee of its permanent residence. The advantage of a pool of talent and integrated supply base has been thrown away before in other industries. In the words of the Government White Paper on 'Our Competitive Future' (DTI 1998) a knowledge based industry is essentially a service industry in the widest sense of the word. The enormous advantage exists of the rich array of intellectual capital that is British, and British universities and colleges such as London's Imperial College, St Martin's School of Design, Cranfield and others are constantly adding to that distinct advantage.

The importance of industries that are rich in new technologies and the opportunities to apply them is probably exceptionally important for twenty-first century prosperity. There are already indications in many areas of massive incremental improvements in other industries that are possible with the technology and organization available in the motor sport industry sector.

The future of any industry is difficult to forecast but the knowledge industries are the more likely opportunities. Britain's record of invention and innovation is remarkable from specific artefacts such as the VTO aircraft, hovercraft, television, disc brakes, the computer and jet engine to name but a few. Add in the number of Nobel prizes won by Britain in the twentieth century and the record is remarkable. However, success shades into cataclusmic failure in the face of our relative lack of success in exploiting them.

The knowledge industries are our future, but that means industries that develop knowledge and actually apply it, to marketable products. Not just for the sake of ideas.

The Benefits to the United Kingdom Economy of the Motorsport Industry

Does Industry Matter?

PERHAPS the most fortunate aspect of governmental post-war policies towards the UK motorsport industry is that they have consistently displayed the kind of benign indifference under which this individual business has prospered. However, this cynical view must be modified as Britain comes under increasing overseas pressure in a business of such precious potential, one that governments will not be able to ignore for its profitable and technological value in the next Millennium. Meanwhile, a few home truths about Britain's manufacturing performance in recent years may surprise readers more used to receiving information with plenty of all-party political spin included.

Just mentioning Britain's economic, managerial, manufacturing or technological performance since the beginning of this century seems to elicit discursive heat and very little intellectual light. Concerning our overall economic performance, politicians of all parties are highly selective with the truth, making statements like 'We have never had it so good' (Harold Macmillan) and 'Britain is now the fastest growing economy in Europe' (John Major). Both actually true when they were said, but both less than a full picture of the situation of the time and less than revealing on our performance compared with major competitors.

The facts of Britain's economic performance during the post-war period are not too difficult to unravel. In 1950 the United Kingdom was, in spite of the war, a powerful economic force in the world with over 25 per cent of the world's trade in manufactured goods (near to the USA's share) and the highest GDP per head in Europe. Furthermore, our manufacturing capacity was heavily geared towards capital plant, potentially a high growth market in view of the need for reconstruction. In the early 1950s in foreign exchange terms the French economy was some 25 per cent of the United Kingdom economy, the German economy measured some 50 per cent of the United Kingdom's GDP and the Italian economy less than either.

In 1999 the German economy is, in foreign exchange terms, approximately 165% of the United Kingdom economy, France stands at some 115 per cent and the Italian figure is larger still if one includes their black economy. Since the population of all four economies has been similar (except after the re-unification of Germany), the league table in terms of Gross Domestic Product per head is the same, although the Republic of Germany's GDP per head was reduced by the unification with Eastern Germany. It is also true that the Italians are second only to the Swiss in terms of net personal wealth. As the table below shows, from the early 1950s to the late 1980s Britain's rate of real GDP growth has always been lower than that of Germany, France or Italy.

It is apparently extremely easy for politicians of all persuasions to ignore our long-term relative decline but the actual evidence of their success at managing the economy is somewhat limited. High growth industries such as the motorsport business have the potential to close that personal and national gap, but first we have to review the grim list of less successful manufacturing enterprises emanating from Great Britain Plc.

The United Kingdom economy has not only performed badly when compared to our major partners in the European Union, but the proportion of GDP that is accounted for by gross fixed investment is consistently lower. Throughout the period from 1950 to 1980 the UK invested less than any of our major competitor nations Germany, France or Italy and less than the United States. The current share of UK GDP accounted for by investment is about 16 per cent, which is historically lower than Germany (19–20 per cent) and lower than the EU average of 18–19 per cent.

The number of industries that have either left the shores of the United Kingdom, or industries in which we have failed is large, compounded by similar failures to maintain a lead or even a prominent position in the world league tables. Our list of industrial misery extends to textiles, automobiles, chemicals, heavy engineering and other areas of mass manufacturing. As a partial offset there are a number of smaller UK successes in other sectors. This record does at least throw doubts on the perverse and misleading philosophy that prevailed amongst UK commentators,

Table 13.1 **Average Annnual % Growth in GDP**

	1953–61	1961–73	1973–79	1979–89
Germany	7.2	4.5	2.4	2.1
France	4.9	5.6	3.0	2.3
Italy	5.8	5.1	2.6	2.9
United Kingdom	2.9	3.1	1.3	2.0

Source: EIU Country Profiles

particularly politicians, in the 1970s and 1980s that 'industry' was of a lesser importance than sectors such as financial services. They also made the point that the financial services sector would grow and make up for the continuing manufactured goods trade deficits.

Such antipathy towards industry and trade is not a new phenomenon in Britain. One such example is Sir Thomas Lipton, who was good enough to pay for and compete J class yachts against the Americans for the America's Cup, but not good enough to be a member of the Royal Yacht Squadron. Currently, industrialists are less respected or socially respectable than doctors, lawyers, accountants and many other occupations, including those in the City. Indeed, the latest (1998) social structure definitions demonstrate this, although the social nuances of the English class system are still deeply embedded and difficult to unravel. This has been referred to as the 'Arthur Daley School of Business' character.

There is compelling evidence that not only has Britain's overall economic performance been less successful than that of our (particularly Continental) major competitor economies, but that we have been singularly poor at manufacturing. Since the early 1980s the visible trade balance in goods has been in deficit every year; although it went into surplus in 1997 it is estimated to return to deficit in 1998. The country's manufacturing base has been in decline for many decades and it is likely that the erosion will continue. In 1997-8 Britain was a net importer of foodstuffs, raw materials other than fuels, clothing, footwear and motor vehicles. The main sources of export surpluses are financial services, mechanical machinery, petroleum and petroleum based products, chemicals, tobacco and whiskey.

Despite UK establishment antipathy towards industry and manufacturing, the structure and prosperity of the British economy today is still dominated by the returns, actual and potential, of our industrial base. The structure of the economy in 1998 taking the proportion of GDP by sector was as follows:

Table 13.2

TOTAL GDP	£766.3
Of Which	%
Manufacturing	21.1
Financial Services	18.1
Distribution & Catering	8.1
Education, Health & SS	12.7
Transport & Comms	8.4
Construction	5.3
Agriculture	1.8
Others	14.3

Source: EIU United Kingdom Country Profiles 1998

The stark feature of those percentages is that, despite a decline of the manufacturing sector since the end of the 19th Century, the sector still accounts for a large proportion of the economy (21.1 per cent) and for *the major* share (63.8 per cent) of exports. Definitions of 'services' can be misleading as they often includes activities such as Civil Aviation, Sea Transport, Travel, Communications and 'others'. All, especially the latter two, demand technological input (programming, IT, process skills). The latter also depend heavily upon human intellectual capital and the advantages derived from superiority in key technologies.

Therefore, manufacturing and technology certainly do matter to Britain's prosperity and in spite of the fact that many of the trends identified above have affected all mature economies, particularly the decline of heavy manufacturing as a proportion of GDP, Britain's performance has been relatively poor. It is true that the reasons for Britain's poor economic performance are very complex and certainly not attributable to such a simple cause. But it is the author's view that the overall position would be better had Britain's philosophical attitude and the UK's relationship with manufacturing not been dominated by the obsession with the 'Dark Satanic Mills' of manufacturing rather than the cleanliness and excitement of the high-technology industries.

Have UK Governments Helped?

There have been a number of studies that attempt to explain why Britain is so bad at mass manufacturing, and why we have failed to prevent the erosion of our industrial manufacturing base. Whilst it is not the object of this study to re-visit that extraordinarily rich field for analysis and argument, there are a number of factors that we should emphasize since the antithesis is perhaps the very reason why we are very good at other facets of 'creating things'. One of the most damaging notions that aided and abetted our complacency about manufacturing, was the 1970–89 political philosophy that 'industry' was of a lesser importance than sectors such as financial services. Commentators emphasized that the financial services sector would grow rapidly, making up for the continuing trade deficit on manufactured goods. In this dubious assertion they were no doubt comforted that 'something in the City' had a very non-industrial, non-engineering ring. Currently Britain's balance of trade deficit runs in excess of £20 billion, the highest of the EU and higher than France, Germany, and Italy who are all running strong surpluses.

Despite UK political and media hype, the reality is that the financial services sector has failed to deliver the politically promised level of surplus since the mid-1980s. Although the sector is undoubtedly successful, it has never been successful enough to counteract our trading deficits in manufactured goods.

Furthermore, it seems probable that financial services follow rather than lead industry.

First, we must exclude interest, profits and dividends from abroad, much of which remains private individuals' and British companies' strategic investments. Then we define the services sector to include government services, sea transport, civil aviation, travel, financial services and others in what is a pretty generously wide definition, so that the picture looks deceptively positive.

Between 1946 and 1983 the balance on services varied between a negative £292 million in 1946 to a maximum surplus of £4542 million in 1981. The subsequent picture to the present is similar, with the major credits coming from financial and other services amounting to a consistent UK surplus of between £5516 millions in 1993 and £9284 million in 1997. Such evidence supports the view that the financial services sector *will continue to fail* in replacing the deficit on manufactured goods, and is unlikely ever to do so.

For example, Britain's current deficits on road vehicles £7 billion, clothing and footwear £5 billion, plus food and live animals £6 billion, totalled £18 billion in 1997; nearly double the maximum surplus on financial services. Moreover, the surplus on Britain's overseas investment income has consistently exceeded the contribution from the financial services sector.

Additionally, neither the Labour policies of the 1970s, nor the Thatcherite policies of the 1980s contributed anything to the solution of this decline of our capacity to produce goods that we can consume and export. Even the second post-war wave of nationalization during the 1970s under both governments, failed to halt the decline in manufacturing capacity and appeared not to slow it appreciably. Despite successive governments and their officials (whether in Whitehall or Westminster) controlling the commanding heights of British industry in shipbuilding, steel, automobiles, aero engines, machine tools and airframe manufacture, Britain's share of these world markets continued to drop. The recent renaissance in the British motor industry's output has been due to inward direct investment from Japan and Germany and the application of their production and managerial processes.

Britain currently produces fewer ships than Croatia and the automobile industry is owned and run by Americans, Japanese, French and Germans. The indictment is fundamental in the case of the automobile industry since one company – Nissan – was able to establish a factory on a green field site that is now the most productive in Europe. Another company, the Blackpool-based sports car manufacturer TVR, makes desirable cars in small (around 2000 annually) but very profitable quantities: it also produces many of its own engines.

Why cannot other British companies manage to do the same as TVR, albeit on a large scale? Perhaps because TVR has not been the recipient of anything but the government's benign neglect?

Relationships between industry and the City are controversial. Britain's record of higher relative inflation and interest rates has failed to assist our manufacturers. Furthermore, medium and long-term capital availability in the United Kingdom is relatively poor when compared to the cost and opportunity for raising capital in the more competitive nations (see IMD World Competitiveness Report 1998).

Finally, the concerted efforts of governments since the Second World War appear to have had a somewhat mixed, possibly adverse, influence on the attitude and aptitude of Britain's industrial base. Even the current government's White Paper (DTI 1998 Competitiveness White Paper) only partially begins to address the problem of how government should support industries. The publication of the White Paper and Peter Mandelson's resignation (unconnected to the White Paper) in December 1998 were significant in so far as he had given this industry some clear support.

We shall examine the potential role of government policy in a later chapter, but it is important to state that no assumption can be made that previous failures of policies towards industry and technology mean that it is not possible for governments to help. What is important is that the assistance is specific and useful in the reality of the market.

Economic Benefits of Britain's Motorsport Industry

Identifying the financial and economic benefits of a specific industry or cluster of value adding activity is not an easy matter. Either such conclusions sound more like special pleading on behalf of the industry, or it leads to many false assumptions as to the importance of one industry over another.

According to Henry *et al.* (1996), the British Motorsport Industry 'displays many of the hallmarks of a new industrial space'. Production within the industry revolves around the design, construction and assembly of high performance one-off components. They note that 'it is a technologically advanced industry geared to small batch production at short notice such as between the roughly fortnightly race meetings of the Grand Prix circuit'.

However, such literature does not provide a clear definition of what is meant by the 'British Motorsport Industry'. Indeed, it is apparent from a study of existing literature that there is considerable confusion over what constitutes a market, as opposed to an industry. For instance, Milan (1995) makes reference to suppliers within the motor sport business sector that supply the more mainstream motor industry. Kay (1993) summarizes the confusion surrounding the definition of the term business:

> 'Sometimes the word business describes the market a firm serves – the needs of its customers and its potential customers. More often it relates to the industry a firm is in – a group of products associated by common technology or supply or distribution channels. Sometimes the business refers to the strategic group – those firms the company identifies as its primary competitors.'

Aston and Williams (1996) acknowledge that 'the distinction between markets and industries is one that we will need to bear in mind', but then go on to conclude simply 'motorsport is the market ñ not the industry'. They shy away from any reference to an industry, because 'the engineering involved in producing a Grand Prix car is different from that involved in the production of Touring and Rally cars'.

It is apparent that motor sport is a highly segmented market where segments are clearly defined by the sporting and technical regulations governing competition. However, if we follow Kay's definition of an industry as 'a group of firms producing technically related products' then it follows that, taken collectively, racing car constructors form an industry. Within this industry, where racing car constructors compete within a series (in other words, within a market segment), they form a strategic group.

Motorsport can best be viewed, therefore, as both a market and an industry. To illustrate by way of example, Formula One constructors form one strategic group within the race car construction industry and provide a market for suppliers from around the world.

Twiss and Goodridge (1989) assert that success in the mass market is typically associated with low-cost labour, *if* production is labour intensive. It becomes a manufacturing competence, *if* production is capital intensive.

Economists agree that both the relatively high cost of labour in Britain and our lack of productivity hinders our ability to succeed in labour intensive mass markets. Britain's economy, as with many advanced economies, relies more on the service sector, especially industries that add greater value, catering to specialist market segments and benefiting from exports as well as domestic sales. Motorsport manufacturing, as depicted in the previous section, fits this description.

This focus on adding value to increase profitability is prevalent. By way of example, Twiss and Goodridge cite ICI's move away from bulk chemical manufacture with low margins, to pharmaceuticals and speciality chemicals. Similarly, within the European motor industry, Mercedes and BMW are more profitable than mass-market manufacturers such as Renault, Fiat or the European subsidiaries of Ford and General Motors. Within such product ranges, the most profitable models are those that feature technological innovations, such as traction control or satellite navigation.

Twiss and Goodridge (1989) conclude that profitability is closely related to added value, and technology provides the basis for adding value. Accepting this conclusion, the importance of the motorsport industry to Britain's economy is likely to be a function of its added value, profitability and exports, rather than just employment. The idea that an industry is valued primarily for its contribution to the number of people employed in an economy is distinctly questionable because labour-intensive industries may be those that add the least economic value.

However, the financial contribution of the motorsport industry to the British economy is notoriously difficult to ascertain with accuracy since many of the companies involved are unquoted and privately owned. The extent of motorsport related employment created in ancillary industries such as marketing, television, safety, university based industrial research, entertainment/hospitality, travel and transportation and others so far defies conscientious research.

Certainly, the industry is volatile and company turnover is high. Nevertheless, the industry is an important sector of the United Kingdom's industrial and intellectual knowledge base for a number of reasons that follow.

NB. None of the following include the full contribution of companies such as TWR, Prodrive etc.

Turnover

Aston and Williams (1996) extrapolate the results of a small survey to estimate industry turnover at between £1 billion and £2 billion per annum.

Henry and Pinch (1997) reference Aston and Williams (1996), when they estimate industry turnover at £1.3 billion.

MILAN (1995) suggest industry turnover to be £1 billion, but offer no justification for this figure.

Dr. Mark Jenkins reported in *The Times* (22 January 1999), estimates industry turnover at £1.5 billion per annum.

Henley Centre for Automotive Studies, 1999, two surveys of over 150 companies in the engineering core of the industry suggests a turnover of £1.8 billion and employment of approximately 30 000 people. *See* Table 13.3 and Appendix 1. As we stated in Chapter 11, surveys of the sector including our own, fail to account for the full extent of the industry as defined in Chapter 11, page 196, and page 245.

Percentage Exported

Henry *et al.* (1996) report the results of a limited survey, which suggests that 90 per cent of firms had international sales accounting for over 75 per cent of their total sales.

Aston and Williams (1996) estimate that an average of 44 per cent of total turnover is generated by exports.

Milan (1995) states, simply, that much of the £1 billion annual turnover is derived from export business.

Williams Grand Prix, McLaren, Lola and Reynard have both won awards for export achievement

Value of Exports

Freeman (1992) estimates the industry's exports to be worth £600 million annually

Henley Centre for Automotive Studies, 1999, survey of over 150 companies in the industry suggests exports in excess of £1.3 billion. *See* Appendix 1.

Aston and Williams (1996) estimate the industry's exports to be worth between £440 million and £880 million per annum.

Turning to the value of British motorsport companies, a recent spate of acquisitions has provided some information. Major financial institutions are taking equity stakes in constructors, bringing City money into an industry traditionally financed by tobacco sponsorship. Warburg, Pincus, the venture capital firm, has taken a 40 per cent stake in Jordan for an investment of $60 million (*The Times*, 17 November 1998). Morgan Grenfell Private Equity has taken a major stake in TWR Arrows, valuing the company at £110 million (*Autosport* 14th January 1999).

Employment within the Industry

As there is evidence of confusion regarding what constitutes the motor sport industry in Britain, it is not surprising that there are conflicting views concerning how many people are employed within the industry. Sources often disagree not only on the number of people employed, but differ in their definition of the scope of the industrial sector that employs them:

- The Royal Automobile Club Motor Sports Association estimated employment at 50 000 in 1992 (Henry, 1994). This figure includes people associated with circuit management, racing schools, retail, publishing and journalism.
- Milan (1995) estimates that 50,000 people are employed 'within the motorsport sector of the automotive industry'.
- Henley Centre for Automotive Studies, 1999, two surveys of 150 companies in the engineering core of the industry suggests employment in excess of 50 000 people and up to 30 000 in the engineering core. *See* Table 13.3.
- Northamptonshire County Council (1997) reports that the 'performance automotive engineering and motor racing sector' employ 50 000 people.

***Table 13.3* Employment within the Motorsport Industry**

Expertise	No. of Companies		No. of Employees		Sensitivity Analysis		
	Min	Max	Min	Max	Min	Av	Max
Formula One	7	7	230	310	1610	1890	2170
F3000	8	8	25	40	200	260	320
BTCC, WRC	12	14	25	55	300	520	770
Other Constructors	60	90	25	40	1500	2438	3600
Fabricators	70	100	10	30	700	1700	3000
Major Engine Developer	4	4	300	450	1200	1500	1800
Engine Specialists	40	65	10	25	400	919	1625
Gearbox Specialists	20	30	20	40	400	750	1200
Electronics	25	40	15	30	375	731	1200
Others	450	600	15	25	6750	10500	15000
					13435	21208	30685

N.B. This does not include the full contribution of companies such as TWR, Prodrive etc.
Source: W. Betts unpublished MBA dissertation, Henley Management College 1998

As we have already mentioned, most of the surveys of the industry, including our own, have concentrated primarily on the 'engineering core' of the industry:

- Aston and Williams (1996) suggest 'there are between 25 000 and 30 000 people engaged in the engineering side of the industry'.
- Henry and Pinch (1997) consider a conservative estimate of engineering based employment in the industry to be 30 000 people.

Whatever the real number employed, and our studies certainly identified true employment in a microcosm of this fascinating business, rapid growth is evident. In a study showing the growth of the industry, Russell (1994) collected information about ten firms founded between 1958 and 1986. At start-up, these firms totalled 81 employees with eight of the firms employing fewer than 10 people. In 1998, employment in the firms had grown to 1063. By 1993, it had reached 1663.

Staff turnover is regularly cited as important to the dissemination of information and technology within the motorsport industry. Lisa Skaife of Race Relations, a firm specializing in recruitment within the motorsport industry, typifies the prevailing uncertainty over the size of the employed population within the industry. Estimates from the company vary from 30 000 to 50 000 engineers.

Furthermore, Lisa Skaife confirmed our understanding that, for mechanics and engineers, career advancement within the industry is often achieved by moving between teams. The intent, at each move, might be to:

1 Move to a more prestigious formula (e.g. from F3000 to Formula One).
2 Move to a better role within a different team competing in the same formula.
3 Move to an equivalent role in a more successful team.

Most job changes take place between November and February, when teams are not actively competing. Race team personnel have an opportunity to move each year, and Skaife reports that they experience a very high level of staff turnover, approximately '13 per cent to 17 per cent per annum'. She goes on to confirm that 'race teams have a higher turnover than engineering firms'. Tellingly, she also believes that 'very few people choose to leave motorsport to work in a different industry'.

In order to arrive at an independent assessment of the importance of staff turnover, with relation to the dissemination of knowledge within the industry, the authors researched the careers of the current chief designers within Formula One. The results, set out in Table 13.4, suggest that top designers will, on average, change job every four years. Of course, there are exceptions such as Patrick Head who has been with Williams Grand Prix Engineering since its inception, but if such exceptional cases were removed from the analysis, then the *average* tenure of other designers would be further reduced.

Whilst poaching and transfers within the industry are prevalent and often publicized, companies in related industries have not attempted, or been able, to attract key staff away from a career in motor sport. Robert Baldock, a senior partner with Andersen Consulting, has worked with Williams Grand Prix Engineering, Prodrive and Reynard. He simply suggests that 'after working in motor sport, any other job would seem pretty mundane'.

These comments, linked with the responses of other interviewees, suggest that staff turnover certainly contributes to the dissemination of technology within the industry, but that associated industries do not benefit from the experience amassed by key staff within the motor sport industry.

Summary of Economic Contribution

It has proved difficult to derive an adequate or definitive estimate of the turnover or of the economic contribution of the motorsport industry in Britain. Financial information is not publicly available and a substantial number of suppliers also act as contractors to other industries (notably the aerospace and defence industries). However, it is reasonable to assume that all Formula One

Table 13.4 **Career Progression of Formula One's Chief Designers**

Designer:	Gary Anderson	John Barnard	Ross Brawn	Gustav Brunner	Rory Byrne	Patrick Head	Alan Jenkins	Adrian Newey	Harvey Postlewaite	Pat Symonds	Nick Wirth
Started Motor Career:	1972	1980	1976	1980	1974	1970	1980	1980	1971	1976	1987
	Brabham	McLaren	Williams	Leyton Hse	Royale	Lola	McLaren	Fitipaldi	March	Hawke Racing	Leyton Hse
	McLaren	Ferrari	Force F1	Ferrari	Toleman	R. Scott Racing	Penske	March	Hesketh	Royale Racing	Simtek
	Anson Racing	Benetton	Arrows	Rial	Benetton	Williams	Onyx	Rahal	Wolf	Toleman	Benetton
	Galles Racing	Toyota	TWR	Zakspeed	Reyard		Footwork	Beatrice	Ferrari	Benetton	
	Bromley M'sport	Ferrari	Benetton	Minardi	Benetton		Stewart	Andretti	Tyrrell	Reynard	
	Reynard	TWR Arrows	Ferrari		Ferrari			Leyton Hse	Sauber	Benetton	
	Jordan	Prost						Williams	Ferrari		
	Stewart							McLaren	Tyrrell		
									Honda		
No. of Moves	8	8	6	5	6	3	5	8	9	6	3
Length of Career (yrs)	26	18	22	18	24	28	18	18	27	22	11
Average tenure (yrs)	3.3	2.3	3.7	3.6	4.0	9.3	3.6	2.3	3.0	3.7	3.7
Ave. of all Designers:	3.8 years										

Source: W. Betts unpublished MBA dissertation, Henley Management College 1998

constructors operate on an annual budget of between £30 million and £100 million (Ferrari's estimated budget for 1998, quoted in Hotten (1998)). Our own research in the form of a questionnaire (*see* Appendix 1) and visits over 30 years to both high profile figures within motorsport and small scale motorsport suppliers lead us to our own conclusions.

However, it is the authors' view that to concentrate upon the contribution of industries such as this towards employment is to miss the true importance of these industries. Their short and long term advantages are the high value added, technologically advanced knowledge, specialized services, the growth potential and export contribution of these industries to say nothing of unknown future technological transfers. Although the current concern with the level of unemployment in the economies of Europe is not misplaced, that concern should not be the only criterion (perhaps even not a major criterion) for assessing the importance of an industry. Their contribution is rather more important than simple numbers in employment, since the value added and the contributions to Britain's balance of payments is of greater advantage in the long run. Additionally, the growth opportunities of such industries and their future value as sources of technological advantage must not be ignored in spite of the fact that such advantages do not attract short-term political advantage.

There are a number of other major economic advantages that this industry/entertainment spectacle generates in the manner in which marketing, track and test facilities, hospitality and media coverage all feed off the technologically based entertainment. Additionally the contribution of the numerous tracks, related leisure facilities and the impact of major events such as Grand Prix are vital. The actual extent of this is extremely difficult to calculate but the survey the authors conducted in 1999 indicated that there is an extensive network of companies that are involved in supporting the industry and its media coverage. This is after all why sponsors ultimately fund the technology at all levels of the sport.

However, the authors believe there is a serious omission in all these surveys, including our own, in that they simply concentrate on engineering and racing core of this industry and not on the plethora of related activities, including the contribution these companies make to the global automobile industry. As Porter (*see* Chapters 12 and 14) indicates, it is essential that one considers the total cluster and its related activities rather than attempting to focus on the so-called core industry. Therefore, we suggest that any future analysis of the industry and its impact upon, and the benefits derived therefrom, need to be analysed under at least the following categories:

- The engineering and technological core; design, fabrication, engine technology, transmission, electronic systems, components and chassis.

- Engineering and manufacturing consultancy/services; companies in the industry supply major mass manufacturers with design, concept manufacturing and engineering services.
- The oxygen of sponsorship; TV, media, advertising and other 'e-media' racing related activities.
- Races; the impact on the local economy of hospitality, expenditure on travel, ticket sales and other activities (*see* The Economic Impact of the European Grands Prix, FIA Brussels Office (Sport), Rue d'Arlon 50, B-1000 Brussels, Belgium).
- Merchandizing; marketing, manufacture and sales (from many companies separate from Grand Prix and other teams) worldwide.

This industry and all its related activities amount to a major part of the world's global entertainment industry as well as an increasingly vital part of the world's automotive sector. It is a high speed sporting spectacular in which engineering is but a means to an end and in which the cars are but part of that means.

Technology Transfer, Innovation and Intellectual Capital

In Chapter 9 we discussed the considerable scope of the transfer of technologies from the industry, into the industry and between firms in the industry. The simple economic benefits, important as they are do not provide a sufficiently broad or realistic assessment of the important linkages between industries that help to drive economic development and growth.

Industries feed from one another and the extent to which this industry has spawned companies and growth is considerable. To repeat but one example the TWR Group with a turnover in excess of £370 million is a company that has its roots in motor racing and still earns approximately 15 per cent of its revenue from the sport or related activities. Furthermore, the company has transferred process, intellectual and technological knowledge derived from its motor sport involvement to the activities of volume manufacturers. In Chapter 9 we have also identified numerous technological transfers that take place between companies in this industry and other industries.

These activities suggest that clusters of excellence confer a number of important advantages to an economy. The magnitude of employment in the industry is perhaps the least important advantage, although politically important. It is perhaps worth emphasizing that there are currently more people in employment in the UK than at any time since 1945. The more mature economies such as that in Britain probably do not possess sustainable competitive advantage in mass manufacturing requiring high value added industries. This may eventually produce a problem of the redistribution of the wealth created but that appears inevitable as modern production processes make it possible to produce more with less. This is a high value added industry.

The technological transfers that the industry offers are important under all the categories identified in Chapter 9. However, the advantages of such clusters are that they also offer opportunities for the utilization of technologies and the development of new applications of existing technologies. It is exceptionally difficult to foresee the path that new technologies will take and the advantages to be derived from them. To possess a centre of excellence that serves a global industry is to have access to new opportunities to create wealth.

The pool of intellectual capital that has continuously developed in this industry is not only British, for opportunities the cluster offers tend to act as a magnet to talent from all over the world. As shown in Table 13.4 the most talented engineers move from team to team and provide the transfer of that intellectual capital and the constant improvement of the country's intellectual base.

The development of new processing technologies in the mass manufacturing industries is already raising questions about the future of large scale manufacturing as increasingly sophisticated consumers demand differentiated products. The processes employed by such companies as Williams Grand Prix Engineering, the TWR Group, McLaren International Prodrive Group and Reynard Motorsport Group also provide additional opportunities for the use of knowledge gained in the industry.

Finally, the importance of brands is being utilized by McLaren International in their partnership with the Tag Group and a range of branded audio equipment. Similarly, SAAB and Volvo publicly acknowledge TWR's important contribution to the development of their designs and technical partnerships just as the now Ford owned Aston Martin and Jaguar did in earlier liaisons.

Lotus pioneered such links in their Grand Prix days, from the Ford Cortina to the current UK Vauxhall Corsa with television acknowledgement of 'suspension by Lotus'. Other companies to include reference to Lotus' legendary ability to deliver technology and provide an after market glow to the broadest of brands include Isuzu, Toyota and Sunbeam/Talbot/Chrysler.

Note that in the recent takeover battles between BMW and Volkswagen for control of Rolls Royce Bentley, the fate of Cosworth went almost unnoticed. In the end Audi was handed or retained the two production divisions. Ford, through brilliant management or the Volkswagen Group's indifference, purchased Cosworth's race engine division. Thus they retained the right to continue their worldwide racing and rallying programmes through Cosworth and the exclusive rights to brand future road cars with a Cosworth badge; a marketing ploy Ford of Europe also employed from 1986–95 alongside the RS badge they used for competition-orientated product 1970–95. Further integration of Ford's racing programme was implemented when the company purchased the Stewart Grand Prix organisation in June 1999.

Conclusions: The Way We Were or the Way We Are? New Industrial Spaces

The extent of the benefits to the British economy of the motor sport industry do not need to be overstated, it is an important and vital industry for at least the following fundamental reasons:

The *economic benefits* although difficult to quantify accurately are clearly important in that they are in a high value added industry with a high export component. The industry places a great deal of its technology into other areas and acts as an increasing research base for the major mass volume manufacturers (*see* also Chapter 9).

The industry provides an arena for the development of human capital. It is a pure knowledge based industry.

There is currently over-capacity in almost all of the world's major mass manufacturing or service industries certainly in Europe, including automobiles, food, clothing, banking, steel, chemicals, textiles and many others. The modern production processes pioneered by the Japanese and adopted by almost all manufacturers that currently survive including Porsche have sounded the death knell of the large factory establishment. Motorsports give Britain a unique selling proposition for rich global manufacturers who wish to buy into an instant heritage to distinguish their mass production products from the ever more efficiently bland competition.

The reasons for this decline of the importance of the mass manufacturing industries in Britain are still a matter of much research and analysis, but there are many indicators that help to show the path to the future.

As manufacturing accounts for a smaller proportion of modern economic activity in the more advanced nations, the manner in which we produce services is changing. Furthermore, mass manufacturing is employing fewer, producing more products in increasingly sophisticated ways. The simple fact of being the best in the world at mass manufacturing is no longer possible for a nation such as Britain.

Motorsports depend on an industry that is not only craft or bespoke dominated but is also serving mass manufacturers overseas, providing them with the essential differentiating factors for their products. That the industry is based in the United Kingdom is no guarantee of its permanent residence.

The UK motorsports advantage of pool of talent and integrated supply base is unique, but such assets have been thrown away before in other industries. In the words of the government White Paper on 'Our Competitive Future' (DTI 1998) it is a knowledge-based industry and essentially a service industry in the widest sense of the word. The enormous advantage of the rich array of intellectual capital that is British plus that of British universities and colleges like London's Imperial College, St Martin's School of Design, Cranfield, Oxford Brookes and many others is a distinct advantage.

The importance of industries that are rich in new technologies and the opportunities to apply them should prove exceptionally important for twenty-first century prosperity. There are already indications in many areas of massive incremental improvements in other industries that are possible with the technology and organization available in the motor sport.

The message for competitive advantage is:

> 'The future path of any industry is difficult to forecast but the knowledge industries are the more likely opportunities for future growth and prosperity. Britain's record of invention and innovation is remarkable from the specific artefacts such as the VTO aircraft, hovercraft, disc brakes, the computer and jet engine to the number of Nobel prizes won in the twentieth century. Such knowledge industries as those that revolve around motor sports are probably our future staple industries.'

The Future of Britain's Motorsport Industry: National Pride Before a Fall?

The Way We Are

THE world of international motor racing is arguably one of the most intensively competitive fields of human activity and not just for the drivers. The level of technology, management expertise, team working and integration of different technologies is probably paralleled only by the aerospace industry. The industry's technological expertise also feeds the global car industry and the mass manufacturing organizations, providing them with services they apparently cannot replicate. The industry has an extraordinary level of international competitiveness and is probably the only industry in which Britain leads the world.

During the past century Britain has lost the lead, and in many cases the industry, in cotton manufacturing, steel, shipbuilding and other industries whilst we no longer own a mass manufacturing car company. Even in the aircraft industry, the huge cost of product development and the need to access world markets, has led to intense collaborations and alliances such that the ability of many of the major manufacturers (even in the USA) to work independently is now in the past. The demands of global markets and the scale of research and investment costs required to compete within them, are forcing new industrial organizations upon many industries.

We have examined the reasons as to why this cluster exists in the United Kingdom, its size and scale, the extent of its geographical spread and the variety of companies involved. In this context we have shown that the 'motorsport industry' is certainly rather more than the Formula One business, important as that is in the overall size of the industry and market. The companies within the cluster supply many different formulae worldwide with everything from chassis, transmissions and drive trains to race engines. We have also shown that the geographical dispersion of the industry's suppliers is wider than many studies show. Finally, and perhaps most importantly, in at least one important respect the industry is not simply the business of motorsport, but also the provision of specialist engineering and consultancy services to the world's mass manufacturers from Tokyo to Detroit, from Paris to Bavaria and Stuttgart. These organizations continue to beat a path to the doors of companies within this sector that are capable of providing rapid, innovative and creative solutions.

A number of papers have analysed the scale, geographic scope and linkages in the industry but many have tended to concentrate upon the Formula One industry[1]. In their analysis as we have concluded, they rightly emphasize the role of the sport/spectacle implying that the motorsport industry feeds off two related and very interdependent streams of financial resources, television and sponsorship. The huge quantities of cash that are derived from world-wide television provides the first source of funding that is fed to the teams and subsequently to their suppliers. In addition, the television coverage that is organized worldwide provides the two essential products, exposure to a global audience and the relationship with a high-tech sporting spectacle, that attracts a second source of funding, the sponsorship of teams by the industrial and commercial companies.

Therefore, one model describing the industry describes the edifice as founded upon two pillars that are not tied to or part of the cluster. The first is global television and the second the sport itself, the spectacle that television buys. The spectacle, the argument goes, is the reason for the income streams, the spectacle is not part of the cluster but it is the reason for the cluster's existence[1,2].

This argument then continues that the reasons for the cluster's existence are stated to be determined by the spectacle and sport driven by global television, rather than by any technological expertise or other inherent competitive advantage in the industry. The argument continues 'The business of the sport itself precedes the business of building cars for the sport. For the latter to be a success – and confer upon Britain the benefits it does – the former must be an even larger success[1]'. The reports also emphasize the role of the tobacco companies in financing the industry and conclude that the whole structure would be imperilled by the decline in tobacco sponsorship.

This argument therefore leads to the logical conclusion that the industry is dependent upon the money of global TV and on the continued popularity of the worldwide sporting spectacle. Whilst accepting part of this argument the authors argue that there is a rather more complex set of relationships between the companies in the sector and the worldwide mass manufacturing industry that is important.

The Role of The Cluster

Porter defines a 'cluster' (Clusters and the New Economics of Competition, *Harvard Business Review*, November 1st 1998) as;

> 'Geographic concentrations of interconnected companies and institutions in a particular field. Clusters encompass an array of linked industries and other entities important to competition. They include, for example, suppliers of specialised inputs such as components, machinery, services and providers of specialised infrastructure. Clusters also often extend downstream to channels and customers and laterally to manufacturers of complementary products and to companies in industries related by skills, technologies, or common inputs. Finally, clusters include governmental and other institutions – such as universities, standards-setting agencies, think tanks, vocational training providers, and trade associations – that provide specialised training, education, information and technical support.'

The United Kingdom motorsport industry satisfies the criteria that it is a 'cluster' in the sense that Michael Porter defines them. In that article he refers to the paradox of the importance of location in a world of global organizations, markets and industries. In this context it is vitally important ask the question that Porter puts in that article;

> 'But if location matters less, why then, is it true that the odds of finding a world class mutual fund in Boston are much higher than in most any other place? Why could the same be said of textile-related companies in North Carolina and South Carolina, of high-performance auto companies in southern Germany, or of fashion shoe companies in northern Italy?'

We have examined some of these reasons in Chapters 9 and 11 and conclude that certainly history did play its part but that the continuing dominance of the sector in world-wide motorsport has more to do with the development of the cluster than history. The cluster still remains relatively unknown and Porter does not mention the cluster of motorsport based racing car fabricators, component engineering companies, transmission and engine specialists, in Middle England.

Porter argues that clusters actually alter the economics of competition within industries in three ways;

- By increasing the productivity of companies based in the area
- By driving the direction and pace of innovation, which underpins future productivity and growth
- By stimulating the formation of new businesses, which expands and strengthens the cluster itself.

Clusters provide a number of distinct advantages that are clearly demonstrated in the motorsport industry. However, to analyse this industry that is based in the UK exclusively in terms of the motorsport industry is, in our view, to misrepresent the industry itself, the skills and unique attributes that it possesses and to fail to understand the nature of its competitive advantage. There are two key ways in which this cluster is unique.

The first key is the relationship that the cluster has formed with other industries and their marketing efforts. The rules of the game of motorsport changed in the 1960s and 1970s with the desire of tobacco companies to place their products before a worldwide audience. The spectacle was then organized and developed by a group of ancillary service organizations central to the industry, including the Royal Automobile Club, the Formula One Constructors Association and others, that had been founded and developed in the United Kingdom, is another example of how clusters develop. It has strengthened not detracted from the cluster and led to the development of many related services. *See* Chapters 1, 2, 9 and 11.

The second key relationship is the manner in which this industry has responded to the changes in the world's largest mass manufacturing industry, the automobile industry. The rules of the game in the worldwide automobile industry have also been transformed and these have also been fundamentally important to the cluster's development. The 'leaning' of the industry during the past twenty years and chronicled in books such as *The Machine that Changed the World* (by James G. Womak, Daniel T. Jones, Daniel Roos and Donna Sammons Carpenter, Macmillan 1990) has led to massive improvements in quality, productivity and value that are now common throughout the industry worldwide. These impacts, plus the fact that technological advantage is 'less and less of a brand differentiator' in this as in many other industries (Wolfgang Reitzle, Chairman of Jaguar Cars, *The Sunday Times*, 4 July 1999) has driven companies to seek new techniques and means to differentiate their products.

In the early part of this, the century of the automobile, motor racing was dominated by factory based teams who used motor racing to develop the market for their products. Companies such as Renault, Citroën, Mercedes to name but a few who still survive, took part in road races as advertising and marketing exercises. By the 1930s the teams that dominated racing were the tools of nation states that used motor racing as they used other sports, to demonstrate national superiority. In the period after the Second World War motor racing rapidly changed to a sport dominated by small entrepreneurial groups of skilled engineers who took advantage of the particular facilities and interest in the United Kingdom.

The organization of the teams in the United Kingdom was fundamentally different from the other continental teams like Ferrari who accused the British teams of being mere 'assemblatori'. British teams such as Lotus, Cooper, BRM, McLaren, Williams, Hesketh, Tyrell, Brabham, March all depended upon the numerous suppliers of components and large scale manufacturer's engines, to produce and develop their cars. Even BRM had an extensive list of suppliers who provide the components to original designs. The manner in which this part of the industry developed assisted the growth of the infrastructure of suppliers, component manufacturers, engine developers and specialist materials companies as well as services such as marketing and advertising specialist. This structure has continued to develop.

Within the past decade many of the mass manufacturers have sponsored teams or allied themselves to teams by supplying engines. Examples are the Lotus/Ford, Repco/Brabham, Brabham/Ford, Tyrrell/Ford and more recently TAG/McLaren with a Porsche engine, Renault Williams, Mercedes McLaren with BRM/Williams in the future and many others. The car industry is using the worldwide marketing tool of Grand Prix motor racing and motorsport to differentiate its products and to develop their brands. But it is not only the F1 part of the industry that benefits from the injections of TV cash, but an increasingly wide circle of companies.

The mass manufacturers are using the expertise of companies in this sector to differentiate their products, not only by association but by the development of special brands that differentiate particular models. Companies such as Prodrive involved in Rallying, teams involved in Touring Cars and other formulae, are all gaining ground in terms of the sponsorship and advertising spend from commercial and industrial companies as well as developing special models for them.

These global companies use the skills of organizations in this sector because of the rich pool of component suppliers, skills, technologies, ancillary services, technical and testing facilities that have been developed in the United Kingdom. Furthermore, the organization of the sport worldwide was developed in the United Kingdom and the impact of television harnessed by various organizations based in the UK.

The cluster is highly competitive and has developed a number of intrinsic advantages in addition to the simple concept of technological advantage (*see* Chapters 8, 9 and 10). This cluster has developed at least as much because it has organized the basis of motorsport's presentation to the world, as on the basis of the technological expertise of the teams, companies and firms involved. The cluster is also far wider than simply Formula One and many, including the authors, would argue that there is a huge potential in the development of other Formulae, Touring Cars, Rallying and other race categories (*see* Chapters 4, 5, 6 and 7). Furthermore, the further global development of Formula One, Rallying, Touring Cars and other Formulae is already assured, with the extension of tracks and races in the Pacific Rim, Malaysia and China as well as the United States of America.

The argument that this cluster is fragile simply because of its dependence upon the success of the sporting spectacle of Formula One in terms of future location, is one which, in the view of the authors, can be disputed because the industry is much more than Formula One. However, it must be emphasized for the following reasons that in spite of the strength of the cluster and its wide attractions apart from televised sport, any diminution in the scale of that sport would have a dramatic effect upon the industry. The question is how rapidly will the other areas of motorsport develop their international attraction? The main reasons why we consider the industry to be more than just the sport are as follows.

Firstly, the cluster provides an efficient and effective means of satisfying the main customers who are worldwide television, the mass automobile manufacturers (for both marketing opportunity and technological expertise) and the commercial and industrial sponsors including banks who fund the teams. The maximization of the potential advantage of worldwide television requires the ability to manage the spectacle on a worldwide basis and this exists in the cluster.

Secondly, a large number of the global mass manufacturers of automobiles have already recognized that it is better to move their own racing and specialist engineering efforts to this cluster, than to try and locate at their 'home' location. This includes Ford, who have regained control of Cosworth Racing and companies such as Volvo and Aston Martin. Renault, Subaru, Toyota, Honda, General Motors and others rely upon organizations within this cluster to supply them with racing know-how and engineering expertise that helps to improve their road products. The industry is used to differentiate their products and to supply design and development changes at a pace and level of excellence that the mass production manufacturers cannot match.

These mass manufacturers and many companies who assist teams with technological support, do so in order to provide a testing, demanding rapid response, environment to train their employees. This means that the large companies see advantages in this training environment and many of them quote the importance of the very early responsibility that the race environment offers (*see* Chapter 9).

Finally, the mass manufacturers are beginning to move towards ownership, or at least part ownership of some of the teams and companies in the motorsport cluster. Ford announced in June 1999 that they had purchased outright control of Stewart Grand Prix and speculation surrounds the future entry of Toyota into the Grand Prix circus; will they purchase an existing team or establish a new one? There is officially only one place left of the twelve-car grid. So far the signs are that the mass manufacturers recognize the considerable advantages of using firms like the TWR Group who announced a deal with Renault in July 1999 to design and produce a new Clio. Other collaborations that are going beyond racing are Mercedes and McLaren, TAG and McLaren, BMW and Williams, to name but some. The formula is certainly winning at the moment, on and off the track, in road cars as well as racing cars.

So what are the risks?

Future Risks: The Dangers of Decline

Nothing is more certain than change and this industry/market and the customers who utilize its expertise at all levels, has changed out of all recognition since the first days of motorsport in the early part of this century. The level of adaptation and evolution of technology and management is considerable and the organizations are exceptionally able to take advantage of new developments. But there are dangers.

The first risk is that government decides that the industry requires regulation and control so that the flexibility, speed of response and creativity of the industry is stifled. It may well be that this industry has been successful for the reason that it has suffered from nothing but the benign neglect of governments. But as we write it is not simply the United Kingdom Government that is the only source of potential problems, as the European Commission on Competition has announced its opposition to the current television contracts.

Secondly, the participants in the industry become too focused upon a small sector of the current wide range of commercial and industrial sponsors that feed their voracious appetites for cash to develop their rapid, promotional billboards. There is a potential danger that if the mass manufacturing automobile companies dominate the ownership of the teams they could, in one context, be a source of loss of advantage as they attempt to retain exclusive use of the television opportunities.

Thirdly, globalization of the locations for races and the huge attraction of the massive potential of markets in the Pacific Rim, India and China may refocus owners' and sponsors' attention on those regions. This may well lead to a relocation of many teams and suppliers as has occurred in the past. The mere possession of technological advantage is probably not a long-term source of competitive advantage. The essential aspect of the industries' current advantage lies not simply in technology but also in the productivity advantages that these companies offer their customers; speed and flexibility, time to market and the accessibility to the 'total' cluster.

Finally, extremely determined, exceptionally successful and entrepreneurial owner managers run most of the companies in the industry. They are, with few exceptions, first generation owner managers and one of the primary sources of the competitive advantages that their companies offer. If the ownership and executive control passes from these entrepreneurs to large scale, corporate committees, many of the advantages of their organizations will be lost. The TWR Group has a turnover in excess of £370 million per annum and is still able to provide companies such as Volvo and Renault with speed of response and quality beyond the mass manufacturers' abilities. To quote an Formula One figure on a major manufacturer 'They would discuss the design of a wheel over three months and still reach no conclusion. We'd design and make it in a few days'.

A set of scenarios involving all or one of these events would probably spell disaster for this industry although it has to be said that there are a number of alternative views as to the outcomes depicted. The authors consider that the industry is facing a particularly crucial period as the people who have been involved in the creation of this industry since the early 1950s, reach an age where they will be considering retirement. Whilst there has been an enormous pool of talent that has come forward, it is essential that that pool continues to be developed.

The Way We Might Be?

Porter suggests a number of factors that relate to clusters and which should influence the way in which strategic thinking develops in those companies concerned with the cluster. In many cases these aspects of cluster thinking are functions of the relationships and pools of knowledge that are built up over time. They often relate to the intersections of different industries or parts of the same industry. Alternatively, they may be a function of the entrepreneurial attitude of people in the industry and their ability to see new applications for their technologically advanced capabilities. The aspects of cluster thinking add a number of factors to the manner in which organizations that wish to take advantage of a cluster as well as organizations within the cluster should consider their future strategies.

Choosing Locations

There is already strong evidence that companies are choosing to locate the relevant parts of their organizations within this cluster. It is vital that the cluster continues to provide the incentives to location in terms of the interconnections of sophisticated suppliers. There are many examples of organizations in the cluster that have encouraged the relocation of partners. British American Racing located their new Formula One team at Brackley in Oxfordshire and Reynard, their technical partner located on the same site. In addition Honda are locating a new engine development facility within the cluster and Toyota are almost certain to locate their new Formula One team within the cluster.

Engaging Locally

The high degree of interpersonal relationships with this industry is crucially important as the people and organizations feed off one another. As companies grow and expand they tend to spawn other related companies and develop further pools of skills and intellectual capital. Reynard and other companies have long supported several locally based universities and colleges within the cluster in efforts to relate engineering training to the needs of the industry. Again, in Reynard's case an extremely important relationship with Oxford Brooks University developed out of Adrian Reynard's contact with the then Oxford Polytechnic.

Upgrading the Cluster

The health of the local business environment is vital to a clusters' economic and intellectual vigour. Companies within the cluster should consider developing relationships with organizations in complimentary fields to enhance their competitive advantage. A classic example of this is the relationship established by the TWR Group with the American Company Silicon Graphics, to provide a virtual reality centre at TWR's Leafield facility. This is similar to collaborations between other companies in the cluster, but in this case it is to be used primarily for developing road cars.

Working Collectively

Companies within the cluster literally benefit from the proximity of their activities and the collaboration that it encourages. The Motorsport Industry Association is an encouraging sign that the organizations within the industry are collaborating as well as competing. In this instance it is vital that the MIA concentrates on supporting collaborations across the industry and even outside the industry where the technologies of the industry are applicable to other industries. The importance is the support of the cluster not simply of the industry.

There is considerable evidence that the organizations within the industry do collaborate extensively, in spite of the intensely competitive nature of the relationships between, for example, the Formula One teams.

In addition there are three crucial aspects of policy that the government can influence.

The first relates to the status of engineering and technologists (*see Playing to Win* by Beverly Aston and Mark Williams, IPPR 1996). Since the beginnings of the post-war period there has been a steady decline in the status and numbers of able students going into engineering and technology. There are arguments that there has been an improvement in the position since the mid 1980s although the facts are somewhat less than conclusive. Universities still report a declining number of students undertaking engineering and technology degrees and the latest income and salary tables do not suggest a large change in the status and salaries of engineers, technologists and scientists. Furthermore in the survey that we conducted (*see* Chapter 13 and Table 13.3) many companies reported that they were concerned about the supply of fabrication skills, rather more than about the supply of engineers and technologists.

Since the industry requires a high level of engineering and technological skill there seems to be a strong argument for the government to continue in their attempts to improve the level of technology based education and their related skills. In particular some of the traditional skills in metal fabrication, machining and using sophisticated machine tools and composite fabricators are in particularly short supply, according to our survey. There is also the issue of the developments in computer-based technology that is increasingly driving the sport, and the industry that provides services to the mass manufacturers. This is another area where the assistance of government in developing and encouraging higher education to provide places and to develop the skill base. Companies such as TWR Group are able to supply a seamless concept, design and manufacturing process utilizing computer based virtual reality through to CADCAM. Whilst the technology is developed in the United States the applications are being led in this sector.

The second relates to the benign neglect point made earlier and also to the relationship between regulations governing the various formulae. Regulation in many forms has had a beneficial influence upon societies' relationship with industry and also a cost influence upon the industry. The role of the race regulators in the FIA and the related committees has had an enormous influence upon the safety measures at tracks, some of which have spun off into the design of the barriers that are now used on motorways all over Europe. Designers have continually stretched the regulations to gain competitive advantage and some of the improvements have (and continue to) been applied to road cars. This adds to the competitive advantage that companies such as Williams Grand Prix, McLaren International, Porsche, Jaguar, Ford and others are able to gain from motorsport. Basically, it would probably be a good thing if the sports regulators continued to influence the regulations so as to further the development of safety.

The one thing that governments should not do is to interfere in the regulatory process or in the competitive basis of the industry.

The third issue is one, which Rick Gorne of Reynard Racing mentioned to the authors in an interview in May 1999. The industry is at the forefront in developing and applying advanced technology that may have many applications to other sectors. The wide range of abilities from complex aerodynamics analysis, materials development and fabrication, lightweight/high strength constructions, high fuel efficiency/lightweight engines and constantly variable transmissions systems are but a few of the technologies involved.

The argument that this industry and the market of this sport/spectacle feeds off two related and very interdependent streams of financial resources alone, television and sponsorship, is a very narrow one. Whilst it is true that the huge quantities of cash that are derived from worldwide television provides the first source of funding that is fed to the teams and subsequently to their suppliers the fact is that, without the technological advantage the industry would not exist. The neglected and largely hidden part of the industry that provides the concept cars, design studies and ultimately the differentiated products for the mass market are a vital and growing element of Britain's motorsport activities.

The industry is therefore not simply a worldwide spectacle and a televised sport but a supporting act to one of the largest industries in the world. In this context it forms part of the group of high-tech industries that adds exceptional levels of value to its customers and may provide the answers to some of the current and future problems the human race will continue to grapple with to say nothing of its immense economic advantage to Britain Plc. We repeat:

Vision without Action is a Daydream
Action Without Vision is a Nightmare

JAPANESE PROVERB

Appendix 1: Bibliography

Chapter 1

1 Aston, B. and Williams, M., *Playing to Win*, Institute of Public Policy Research, 1996.
2 Williams, K., Williams, J. and Thomas D., *Why are the British Bad at Manufacturing,* Routledge & Keegan Paul, 1983.
3 Economist Intelligence Unit, *World Model Production Forecasts 1999.*
4 SMMT, Motor Industry of Great Britain 1986, *World Automotive Statistics*, London.
5 Maxton, G. P. and Wormald, J., *Driving Over a Cliff?*, EIU Series, Addison-Wesley, 1994.
6 Turner, G., *The Leyland Papers*, Eyre & Spottiswoode, 1971.
7 *World Economic Development Review*, Kline Publishing/McGraw Hill, 1994.
8 *United Kingdom Balance of Payments*, Office for National Statistics, 1998.
9 Court, W., *A History of Grand Prix Motor Racing 1906–1951*, Macdonald, 1966.
10 Crombac, G., *Colin Chapman*, Patrick Stephens, 1986.
11 Garrett, R., *The Motor Racing Story*, Stanley Paul & Co Ltd, 1969.
12 Jenkinson, D., and Posthumus, C., *Vanwall*, Patrick Stephens, 1975.
13 Hamilton, M., *Frank Williams*, Macmillan, 1998.
14 Mays, R., and Roberts, P., *BRM*, Cassell & Company, 1962.
15 Rendall, I., *The Power and the Glory*, BBC Books, 1991.
16 Underwood, J., *The Will to Win. John Egan and Jaguar*, W.H.Allen & Co. Ltd, 1989.
17 Henry, A., *March, The Grand Prix & Indy Cars*, Hazleton Publishing, 1989.

Chapter 2

1 Motor Sports Association, The, *British Motorsports Yearbooks*, Motor Sports Association [MSA], 1997–9.
2 David Hodges, David Burgess-Wise, John Davenport and Anthony Harding, *The Guinness Book of Car Facts and Feats*, Guinness Publishing, 4th edn, 1994.
3 Ian Morrison, *Guinness Motor Racing Records, Facts and Champions*, Guinness Publishing, 1989.
4 Uncredited authors, reproduction of 1948 Silverstone Grand Prix Programme, released at Christies Silverstone Festival 1998.
5 C. Clutton, C. Posthumus & Denis Jenkinson [1962] The Racing Car, R.T. Batsford, 1962.
6 Bruce Jones, (ed.), *The Ultimate Encylopedia of Formula 1*, Hodder & Stoughton (a Carlton imprint), 1996.

Chapter 3

1 Rex Hays, *The Vanishing Litres*, Macgibbon & Kee, 1957.
2. The staff of Motor Sport & Motoring News, *Castrol Guide to Motoring Sport*, Patrick Stephens, London [PSL], 1971.
3 Denis Jenkison and Cyril Posthumus, *Vanwall, the story of Tony Vasndervell and his racing cars*, Patrick Stephens Ltd, 1975.
4. Doug Nye with Geoffrey Goddard, *Great Racing Cars of the Donington Collection*, 1974.
5 Jacques Desenaux, *Grand Prix Guide, Marlboro*, with Charles Stewart & Co [Kirkaldy] Ltd, 1998.
6 Francois Michel Gregoire and Genevieve Farez, *Who Works in Formula 1?*, Starting Blocks Sprl, Belgium, 1993.

Chapter 4

1 Martin Holmes, Annual editions of *Rallying* or *World Rallying with Rothmans*, Audi or Pirelli backing, assorted publishers, 1978–91.
2 David Williams (ed.), Annual editions of *Rallycourse*, Hazleton Publishing, 1997–8.
3. Nick Brittan and John Davenport, *Safari Fever, the story of a car rally they said no European could win*, Motor Racing Publications, 1972.

Chapter 4

1 Authors and Editors various, Annual, *The Guild of Motoring Writers' Yearbooks*, Guild of Motoring Writers, 1975–98.

2 Mike Kettlewell, *Motor Racing Directory, Mike Kettlewell's guide to British motor racing*, Kettlewell Transport Information Trade Services, 1979.
3 NASCAR Inc., *NASCAR 1948–98, The Thunder of America*, HarperHorizon imprint, 1998.
4 Jonathan Gill/ Alan Gow and contributors, *The World is Watching*, TOCA information brochure. Information also drawn from annual TOCA diary and more than 20 TOCA/BTCC team interviews and UK weekly magazine, *Autosport*, 1998.
6 Arno Schmitt, *Handbuch der Deutschen Rennsport Meisterschaft*, Copress Verlag, 1981.

Chapter 5

1 Jeremy Shaw (ed.), *Autocourse Official Yearbook*, CART World Series, Hazleton Publishing, 1997–8.
2 Mike Lawrence, *The Reynard Story, from Formula Ford to Indycar Champions*, PSL [imprint of Haynes publishing], 1997.
3 Mike Kettlewell, *The Pace Motor Racing Directory*, Kettlewell Transport & Trade Information Services Ltd, 1981.
4 Contributors, various, *Pole Position, celebrating the Diamond Jubilee of the British Racing Drivers Club*, Motor Racing Publications, 1987.

Chapter 7

1 No books or annuals were used in the research of this chapter, but some dates were cross-checked with the Guinness Publishing titles quoted in 2 and 3 notes to Chapter 2.

Chapter 8

1 Rendall, I., *The Power and the Glory*, BBC Books, 1991.
2 Crombac, G., *Colin Chapman*, Patrick Stephens, 1986.
3 Stanley, Louis T., *Behind the Scenes*, Queen Anne Press, 1985.
4 Aston, B. & Williams, M., *Playing to Win*, Institute of Public Policy Research, 1996.
5 Garfield, A., '$1.4bn Bernie Bond', (*The Times* 29 May 1999).
6 *Business Outlook*, (*The Independent* 29 May 1999).
7 *Business Age*, 'Bernie Ecclestone and Max Mosley', (January 1999) pp. 54-70.
8 Author's Interview with Max Mosley, April 1999.
9 Levy, M., 'Winning Formula' (*The Director*, July 1999) pp. 44–8.

10 Steiner, R., 'Pole Position' (*The Sunday Times* 22 November 1998).
11 Hamel, G. and Prahalad, C.K., *Competing for the Future*, Harvard Business School Press, 1994.
12 Allsop, D., *Formula One Uncovered*, Headline Book Publishing, 1998.
13 Crombac, G., *Colin Chapman, The Man and his Cars*, Patrick Stephens Limited, 1986.
14 Henry, A., *Williams, The Business of Grand Prix Racing*, Patrick Stephens Limited, 1991.
15 Henry, A., *March, The Grand Prix and Indy Cars*, Hazleton Publishing, 1989.
16 Statistics and Figures from 'Sports Marketing Surveys' 1999.

Chapter 9

1 Betts, W.E., 'Technology Transfer and Britain's Motor Sport Industry' Unpublished MBA Dissertation, Henley Management College, 1999.
2 Henry, N. and Pinch, S., 'A Regional Formula for Success? The Innovation of Motor Sport Valley' The University of Birmingham, School of Geography, 1997.
3 Twiss, B. and Goodridge, G., *Managing Technology for Competitive Advantage*, Pitman, London, 1989.
4 Foxall, G., Fawn, J. and Johnston, B. (1992) 'Innovation in Grand Prix Motor Racing. II Extension of the Population Ecology Model' *Technovation* 12, pp. 1–14.
5 Kay, J., *Foundations of Corporate Success*, Oxford University Press, 1993.
6 Porter, M. 'Clusters and the New Economics of Competition', *Harvard Business Review,* 1 November 1998, p.77.
7 MILAN, 'The Performance Car Industry in the United Kingdom' National Network Office, 1995.
8 Henry, N., Pinch, S. and Russell, S. (1996) 'In Pole Position? Untraded Interdependencies, New Industrial Spaces and the British Motor Sport Industry' *Area, 1*, 1996, pp. 25–36.
9 Hotten, R., *Formula 1. The Business of Winning*, Orion, 1998.
10 Slappendel, C. (1996) 'Perspectives on Innovation in Organisations' *Organisation Studies*, 1996, **17.1**, pp. 107–129.
11. Aston, B. and Williams, M., *Playing to Win. The Success of UK Motorsport Engineering*, IPPR, London, 1996.
12 Jones, O., 'The Structuration of Technology Transfer: Towards a Social Theory of Innovation' Aston Business School Research Paper RP9704, 1997.

13 Jenkins, M., 'The Formula One Constructors', Cranfield School of Management, Case Study, 1998.

Chapter 10

1 Motor Sports Association, the, *British Motorsports Yearbooks*, Motor Sports Association [MSA], 1997–9.
2 Nick Brittan, *How to go Saloon Car Racing*, PSL, 1967.
3 The authors also acknowledge the provision of several publicity brochures from Motor Industry Research Association [MIRA] at Nuneaton. Most of the chapter material was gathered by original interviews.

Chapter 11

1 KPMG, 'A Sound of Performance' published by National Music Council, 1999.
2 Aston, B and Williams, M., *Playing to Win. The Success of UK Motorsport Engineering*, IPPR, London, 1996.
3 Henry, N., 'In Pole Position' *European Motor Report*, 1999.
4 McLaren International, Annual Report 1997.
5 Nye, D., *McLaren. The Grand Prix, Can-Am and Indy Cars*, Hazleton Securities Limited, 1988.
6 Nicholson, J. and Hamilton, M., *Against the Odds. Jordan's Drive to Win*, Macmillan, 1999.
7 Lawrence, M., *The Reynard Story. From Formula Ford to Indycar Champions*, Patrick Stephens Limited, 1997.
8 Henry, A., *Williams, The Business of Grand Prix Racing*, Patrick Stephens Limited, 1991.
9 Hamilton, M. and Nicholson, J., *Racing Stewart*, Macmillan, 1997.
10 DTI, The 1998 Competitiveness White Paper, 'Our Competitive Future. Building the Knowledge Driven Economy'.
11 Hamilton, M., *Frank Williams*, Macmillan, 1998.
12 *World Economic Development Review*, Kline Publishing/McGraw Hill, 1994.
13 *IMD International Competitiveness Report*, 1999.

Chapter 12

1 Henry, N. and Pinch, S., 'A Regional Formula for Success? The Innovation of Motor Sport Valley', The University of Birmingham, School of Geography, 1997.

2 DTI, The 1998 Competitiveness White Paper, 'Our Competitive Future. Building the Knowledge Driven Economy'.
3 Betts, W.E, 'Technology Transfer and Britain's Motor Sport Industry', Unpublished MBA Dissertation, Henley Management College, 1999.
4 Aston, B. and Williams, M., 'Playing to Win', Institute of Public Policy Research, 1996.
5 Porter, M. (1998) 'Clusters and the New Economics of Competition', 1 November 1998, pp. 77.
6 Williams, K., Williams, J. and Thomas D., *Why are the British Bad at Manufacturing?*, Routledge & Keegan Paul, 1983.
7 Henry, A., *March, The Grand Prix and Indy Cars*, Hazleton Publishing, 1989.
8 Hotten, R., *Formula 1. The Business of Winning,* Orion, 1998.
9 Hassan, W. and Robson, G., *Climax in Coventry*, Motor Racing Publications Limited and Mercian Manuals Coopers, 1975, reprinted 1997.
10 Henry, A., (1989) *March, The Grand Prix & Indy Cars*, Hazleton Publishing, 1989.
11 Rosenberg, N., *Inside the Black Box: Technology & Economics*, Cambridge University Press, 1982.
12 MILAN, 'The Performance Car Industry in the United Kingdom' National Network Office, 1995.

Chapter 13

1 Porter, M., *The Competitive Advantage of Nations*, Macmillan, 1998.
2 Porter, M., (1998) 'Clusters and the New Economics of Competition' *Harvard Business Review*, 1 November 1998, p. 77.
3 EIU Country Report 1999–2000, *The United Kingdom*.
4 *IMD International Competitiveness Report*, 1999.
5 Landes, D., *The Wealth and Poverty of Nations*, Little Brown, 1998.
6 Kay, J., *Foundations of Corporate Success*, Oxford University Press, 1993.
7 Aston, B. and Williams, M., 'Playing to Win', Institute of Public Policy Research, 1996.
8 Henry, N., Pinch, S. and Russell, S., (1996) 'In Pole Position? Untraded Interdependencies, New Industrial Spaces and the British Motor Sport Industry' *Area, 1*, 1996, pp. 25–36.
9 Twiss, B. and Goodridge, G., *Managing Technology for Competitive Advantage*, Pitman, London, 1989.

10 MILAN, 'The Performance Car Industry in the United Kingdom' National Network Office, 1995.
11 DTI, The 1998 Competitiveness White Paper, 'Our Competitive Future. Building the Knowledge Driven Economy'.
12 London Business School, 'Advanced Auto-Engineering: A Technology-Led UK Cluster', *Business Strategy Review*, 1998.

Chapter 14

1 Lilley, W. and De Franco, L., 'Great Britain's Grand Prix Fertile Valley. The Economic and Political Significance of World Leadership in High Design Auto Engineering', 1998, from *Incontext*, 1615 L Street NW, Suite 560, Washington DC 20036.
2 London Business School, 'Advanced Auto-Engineering: A Technology-Led UK Cluster', *Business Strategy Review*, 1998.
3 Porter, M, 'Clusters and the New Economics of Competition' *Harvard Business Review*, 1 November 1998 pp. 77.
4 DTI, The 1998 Competitiveness White Paper, 'Our Competitive Future. Building the Knowledge Driven Economy'.
5 KPMG, *A Sound of Performance*, published by National Music Council, 1999.

Appendix 2: Motorsport companies in the UK

Component suppliers

Activa Technology Roebuck House, Cox Lane, Chessington, Surrey KT9 1DG Tel: 0181 974 1907

Aztek 33 Brookfield Avenue, Loughborough, Leicestershire LE11 3LN Tel: 01509 261299

FF Developments Wolston Business Park, Main St, Wolston, Coventry, W. Midlands CV8 3LR Tel: 01203 544051

Gearace Ltd Unit 7, Field Farm Business Centre, Nr Launton, Bicester, Oxfordshire OX6 0EL Tel: 01869 277563

Icore International Leigh Road, Slough, Berkshire SL1 4BB Tel: 01753 823674

Accralite Spon Lane South, Smethwick, W. Midlands B66 1QJ Tel: 0121 552 5951 (pistons)

Active Sensors Ltd Unit 12, Wilverley Road, Christchurch, Dorset BH23 3RU Tel: 01202 480664 (Sensors)

Aero Tech Laboratories Inc 40 Clarke Road, Mount Farm Industrial Estate, Bletchley, Milton Keynes, Bucks MK1 1LG Tel: 01908 270591 (Fuel tanks)

Aeroform Ltd Dawkins Road, Hamworthy, Poole, Dorset BH15 4JW Tel: 01202 675957 (Autoclaves)

Aeroquip 292 Worton Road, Isleworth, Middlesex TW7 6EL Tel: 0181 847 5338 (Hoses)

Alcon Components Ltd Concentric Park, Apollo, Tamworth, Staffs. B79 7TN Tel: 01827 312800 (Brakes, Clutches)

AP Racing Wheeler Road, Seven Stars Industrial Estate, Coventry, Warks CV3 4LB Tel: 01203 639559 (Brakes, Clutches)

Astratech Spring Show, Church Road, Sunbridge, Sevenoaks, Kent TN14 6AT Tel: 01959 561865

AWF Gratton House, Gratton St, Cheltenham, Gloucestershire GL50 2AS Tel: 01242 222676

Bilstein UK Motorsport Service, Pilot Brands International Ltd, Unit 5 Swannington Road, Cottage Lane Industrial Estate, Broughton Astley, Leicestershire LE9 6TU Tel: 01455 285853 (Shock absorbers)

Brembo EC Unit C2 Lincoln Park, Borough Road, Buckingham Road Industrial Estate, Brackley, Northamptonshire NN13 7BE Tel: 01280 701728 (Brakes)

Bridgestone Bridgestone Corp Motorsport Branch (UK), Unit 1, Century Point, Halifax Road, Cressex Business Park, High Wycombe, Bucks. HP12 3SL Tel: 01494 478720 (Tyres)

BTB Exhausts Unit 3–5, The Beaver Centre, Great Central Way, Woodford Halse, Daventry, Northamptonshire NN11 3DP Tel: 01327 263577

Burmah Castrol Plc Castrol House, Pipers Way, Swindon, Wiltshire SN3 1RE Tel: 01793 430743 (Lubricants)

Champion Champion Automotive Products, Cooper Ltd, Arrowebrook Road, Upton Wirral Merseyside L49 0UQ Tel: 0151 5223123 (Spark Plugs, Coils, Cables)

Composite Wings Unit 23, Norwich Road Industrial Estate, Watton, Thetford, Norfolk IP25 6DR Tel: 01953 885479

Corbeau Seats 17 Wainwright Close, Churchfield Industrial Estate, St Leonards on Sea, East Sussex TN38 9PP Tel: 01424 854488

DPS Composites 18–21 Bookham Industrial Estate, Church Road, Great Bookham, Surrey KT23 3EU Tel: 01372 459437

Dynamic Suspensions 20 Fison Way, Thetford, Norfolk IP24 1HJ Tel: 01842 752626

Eibach Springs Eibach Suspension Technology Ltd, Unit 5 Swannington Road, Cottage Lane Industrial Estate, Broughton Astley, Leicestershire LE9 6TU Tel: 01455 285853 (Springs)

Elf Olympic Office Centre, 8 Fulton Road, Wembley, London HA9 0ND Tel: 0181 9020448 (Fuel and Lubricants)

Flexible Hose Supplies Race Division 140 Edinburgh Avenue, Slough, Berkshire SL1 4UA Tel: 01753 513050

HJS Motorsport Catalysts JE Developments, Claybrook Mill, Claybrooke Magna, Nr Lutterworth, Leicestershire LE17 5DB

K&N Air Filters John Street, Warrington, Cheshire WA2 7UB Tel: 01925 418948 (Air Filters)

Leda Suspension Unit 1, Park Drive Industrial Estate, Braintree, Essex CM7 1AP Tel: 01376 326530

Lifeline Fire and Safety Systems 1 Portway Close, Coventry, W. Midlands CV4 9UY Tel: 01203 474777

Magnecor UK Summerfield House, Station Road, Coleshill, Birmingham W. Midlands B46 1JG Tel: 01675 466329

Mobil Mobil House, 54–60 Victoria Street, London SW1E 6QB Tel: 0171 8302549 (Fuel and Lubricants)

Omega Pistons Oakbarn Road, Halesowen, W. Midlands B62 9DW Tel: 0121 559 6779 (Pistons)

PetroScience Ltd Tanglewood House, Aston Tirrold, Nr Didcot, Oxon. OX11 9DJ Tel: 01235 850724 (Fuel)

Pi Research Ltd Milton Hall, Church Lane, Milton Lane, Cambridge, Cambridgeshire CB4 6AB Tel: 01223 441219 (Data Acquisition)

PIAA (UK) Ltd Unit 4 Locking Farm Industrial Estate, Locking Moor Road, Weston-Super-Mare, N. Somerset BS22 8PJ Tel: 01934 820201 (Halogen lamps)

Poeton (Gloucestershire) Ltd Eastern Avenue, Gloucester, Gloucestershire GL4 7DN Tel: 01452 300050 (Low friction coatings)

R&D Motor Sport Siddeley Way, Royal Oak Industrial Estate, Daventry, Northamptonshire NN11 5PA Tel: 01327 300758 (Roll cages)

Race Engine Components 37 Beeches Road, West Bromwich, W. Midlands B70 6HN Tel: 0121 5855177 (Valves)

Racelogic 6 Little Balmer, Buckingham Industrial Park, Buckingham, Bucks. MK18 1TF Tel: 01280 823595 (Engine Management)

Scheroadel GB Fobello, Station Road, Claverdon, Warwick, Warks. CV35 8PH Tel: 01926 842858 (Valve Springs)

Shell Shell Centre, York Road, London SE1 7NA Tel: 0171 934 2044 (Fuel and Lubricants)

Stack Ltd Wedgewood Road, Bicester, Oxon OX6 7UL Tel: 01869 240500

TAG Electronic Systems Ltd Genesis Business Park, Albert Drive, Woking, Surrey GU21 5R Tel: 01483 750249 (Electronics)

Texaco Ltd 1 Westferry Circus, Canary Wharf, London E14 4HA Tel: 0171 7195180 (Fuel and Lubricants)

Tony James Component Wiring EIO Speedwell Way, Harleston Industrial Estate, Harleston, Norfolk IP20 9EH Tel: 01379 852718

Turbo Technics 17 Gallowhill Road, Blackmills, Northamptonshire NN4 0EE Tel: 01604 769668 (Turbochargers)

Willans Racing Harnesses Grosvenor Garage, High St, Stockbridge Hampshire SO20 6HE Tel: 01264 810247

Xtrac Ltd Hogwood Lane, Finchampstead, Wokingham, Berkshire RG40 4QW Tel: 01189 328257 (Gearboxes)

Consultancies

Automotive Developments 49 Welbeck Avenue, Tunbridge Wells, Kent TN4 9BD

C&B Consultants Unit 2B, 8 Cowley Road, Nuffield Industrial Estate, Poole, Dorset BH17 7RA Tel: 01202 661707 (Aerodynamics)

Cranfield Impact Centre Wharley End, Cranfield, Bedforoadshire MK43 0AL Tel: 01234 750944

Engine and Dynamometer Services Arisdale House, Arisdale Avenue, South Ockendon, Essex RM15 5AS Tel: 01708 855917

Induction Technology Group Ltd Unit 5 Fairfield Court, Seven Stars Industrial Estate, Whitley, Coventry, W. Midlands CV3 4IJ Tel: 01203 307999 (Air Filters)

Janus Technology 69 Burfield Road, Old Windsor, Berkshire SL4 2LN Tel: 01753 863534

MIRA Watling St, Nuneaton, Warks. CV10 0TU Tel: 01203 350311

Petbourne Ltd Unit 2, Murdock Road, Bicester, Oxon OX6 7PP Tel: 01869 253024 (Project Management)

Random Computing Ltd 29 Grand Union Centre, West Row, London W10 5AS Tel: 0181 9643994 (Aerodynamics)

Ricardo Bridge Works, Shoreham-by-Sea, W. Sussex BN43 5FG Tel: 01273 464124

Rollcentre Somersham Road, St Ives, Cambridgeshire PE17 4LY Tel: 01480 494547

Steve Bunkhall 72 Hurst Park Avenue, Cambridge, Cambridgeshire CB4 2AF Tel: 01223 303025

TC Prototypes Unit 5, Deningston Road, Deninston Trading Estate, Wellingborough, Northamptonshire NN8 2QH Tel: 01933 277399

Warrior Automotive Research Ltd 7 Bell Lane, Bellbrook Industrial Estate, Uckfield, East Sussex TN22 1QL Tel: 01825 769132

Engine specialists

AES Engines Unit 2, Rash's Green Industrial Estate, East Dereham Norfolk NR19 1JG Tel: 01362 696685 (Engine Specialist)

Connaught Competition Engines Unit 8, Newington Enterprise Centre, Wardwell Lane, Newington, Kent ME9 7ER Tel: 07070 500040 (Engine Specialist)

Dunnell Engines Unit 10, Tomo Business Park, Creeting Road, Stowmarket, Suffolk IP14 5AY Tel: 01449 770539 (Engine Specialist)

Mountune Racing Ltd The Causeway, Maldon, Essex CM9 7L Tel: 01621 856517 (Engine Specialist)

Swindon Racing Engines Ltd Crampton Road, Greenbridge Estate, Swindon, Wiltshire SN3 3JJ Tel: 01793 528484 (Engine Specialist)

Engineering companies

Bob Sparshott Engineering Unit 74, Tanners Drive, Blakelands, Milton Keynes, Bucks. MK14 5BP Tel: 01908 612609 (Engineering)
Composite Developments 2 Tannery Lane, Northleach, Gloucestershire GL54 3ES Tel: 01451 861176 (Engineering Composites)
Cronin Engineering Unit 6A, Silverstone Circuit, Silverstone, Northamptonshire NN12 8TN Tel: 01327 857423 (Engineering)
Famdon Engineering Bayton Road, Exhall, Coventry, W. Midlands CV7 9EJ Tel: 01203 644698 (Engineering)
Galmer Engineering Ltd Unit 4, Murdock Road, Bicester, Oxon. OX6 7PP Tel: 01869 248200 (Engineering)
Gomm Metal Developments 10 Manor Way, Old Woking, Surrey GU22 9JX Tel: 01483 764876 (Engineering)
Hewland Engineering Boyn Valley Road, Maidenhead, Berkshire SL6 4EQ Tel: 01628 39013 (Engineering Gearboxes)
Jack Knight Developments Woking Business Park, Albert Drive, Woking, Surrey (Engineering)
Kent Aerospace Eurolink Way, Sittingbourne, Kent ME10 3RN Tel: 01795 473438 (Engineering Castings)
Langford Performance Engineering Ltd Unit 17, Bradfield Close, Finedon Road Industrial Estate, Wellingborough, Northamptonshire NN8 4RQ 01933 Tel: 441549 (Engineering)
Metal Technology Ltd 49 Wedgewood Road, Bicester, Oxon. OX6 7UL Tel: 01869 324416 (Engineering)
MSD Ltd 12 Maryland Road, Tongwell, Milton Keynes, Bucks MK15 8HF Tel: 01908 216686 (Engineering)
Racam Precision Unit 3a, Silverstone Circuit, Silverstone, Northamptonshire NN12 8TN Tel: 01327 858537 (Engineering)
Ralt Engineering Sutton Farmhouse, Sutton, Nr Witney, Oxon OX8 1RY Tel: 01865 883789 (Engineering)
Stone Foundries Woolwich Road, Charlton, London SE7 8SL Tel: 0181 3051934 (Engineering)

Formula One constructors

Benetton Formula Ltd Whiteways Technical Centre, Enstone, Chipping Norton, Oxon OX7 4EE Tel: 01608 678800

British American Racing Operations Centre, Brackley, Northamptonshire NN13 7BD Tel: 01280 84400

Jordan Grand Prix Ltd Buckingham Road, Silverstone Northamptonshire NN12 8TJ Tel: 01327 858120

McLaren International Ltd Woking Business Park, Albert Drive, Woking, Surrey GU21 5JY Tel: 01483 720157

Stewart Grand Prix 16 Tanners Drive, Blakelands, Milton Keynes, Bucks. MK14 5BW Tel: 01908 216892

TWR Arrows Leafield Technical Centre, Leafield, Witney, Oxon OX8 5PF Tel: 01993 871100

Williams GP Engineering Ltd Grove, Wantage, Oxon OX12 0DQ Tel: 01235 764705

F3000 teams

Apomatox F3000 Magny Cours, France

Aroaden The Manor House, Bishop's Itchington, Warwickshire CV33 0QG Tel: 01926 613978

Auto Sport Racing Vedano al Lambro, Italy

Auto Sport Racing/GS Vedano al Lambro, Italy

Coloni Motorsport Tuoro sul Trasimeno, Italy

Dams Paris, France

Draco Engineering Massa Carrara, Italy

Durango Formula Mellaredo di Pianiga, Italy

Edenbridge Racing Station Road, Edenbridge, Kent TN8 6EY Tel: 01732 865443

G.S. International Team F3000 Padova, Italy

GP Racing Orgiano, Italy

Nordic Racing 5/6 Brunel Business Court, Thetford, Norfolk IP24 1HP Tel: 01842 755728

Prema Powerteam Cartigliano, Italy

Raceprep Motorsports Unit W, Riverside Industrial Estate, Little Hampton, W. Sussex BN17 5DF Tel: 01903 733321

Redman Bright F3000 28 Swannington Road, Broughton Astley, Leicester LE9 6PD Tel: 01455 285323

RTL Team Oreca F3000 Toulon Cedex, France

Super Nova Racing Church Road, Griston, Thetford, Norfolk IP25 6PY Tel: 01953 883308

Team Astromega Heist-Op-Den-Berg, Belgium

Team Den Bla Avis Church Road, Griston, Thetford, Norfolk IP25 6PY Tel: 01953 883308

West Competition Unit 13, Woking Business Park, Woking, Surrey GU21 5JY Tel: 01483 776110

Indycar constructors

Lola Cars Glebe Road, St Peters Hill, Huntingdon ,Cambridgeshire PE18 7DS Tel: 01480 456722

Penske Cars Ltd 4 Factory Road, Upton Industrial Estate, Poole, Dorset BH16 5SJ Tel: 01202 631728

Reynard Racing Cars Reynard Centre, Telford, Bicester Oxon OX6 0UY Tel: 01869 244786

Other major companies

Brian Hart Ltd Unit 5, Roydonbury Industrial Estate, The Pinnacles, Harlow, Essex CM19 5BZ Tel: 01279 635258

Cosworth Engineering St James Mill Road, Northampton, Northamptonshire NN5 5JJ Tel: 01604 758862

Ilmor Engineering Ltd Quarry Road, Brixworth, Northamptonshire NN6 9UB Tel: 01604 882056

Prodrive Ltd Acorn Way, Banbury, Oxon OX16 7XS Tel: 01295 271188

Zytec Automotive Ltd London Road, Bassetts Pole, Sutton Coldfield, West Midlands B75 5SA Tel: 0121 3232210

Manufacturer motorsport divisions

Ford Motorsport Boreham Airfield, Boreham, Chelmsford, Essex CM3 3DG Tel: 01245 234283

Peugeot Sport PO Box 25, Humber Road, Coventry, W. Midlands CV3 1BD Tel: 01203 884633

Renault UK Motorsport Denham Lock, Widewater Place, Moorhall Road, Harefield, Middlesex U9 6NS Tel: 01895 827683

Volkswagen Motorsport VAG (UK) Ltd, Yeomans Drive, Blakelands, Milton Keynes, Bucks MK14 Tel: 01908 601184

Other formulae

Argo Racing Cars Ltd Church Road, Griston, Watton, Norfolk IP25 6PY Tel: 01953 883308

Bowman Racecars 2 Harper Lane, Shenley, Radlett, Herts WD7 9HE Tel: 01727 826935

Caterham Cars Station Road, Caterham, Surrey CR3 6LB
Tel: 07000 646086
Elden Racing Cars Unit 7, Gasoline Alley, London Road, Wrotham, Kent
TN15 7RR Tel: 01732 887202
Jedi Racing Cars 36a Stanley Road, Wellingborough, Northamptonshire
NN18 1DY Tel: 01933 442778
Lyncar 311 Bath Road, Slough, Berkshire SL1 5PR Tel: 01628 667535
Mallock Racing Rowley Wood Lane, Hartwell, Northamptonshire
NN7 2QT Tel: 01604 863807
Pilbeam Racing Design Ltd Graham Hill Way, Cherry Holt Road, Bourne,
Lincolnshire PE10 0HH Tel: 01778 393032
Prosport Granville Road, Melton Mowbray, Leicestershire LE13 0SN
Tel: 01664 501762
Ray Mallock Whittle Close, Park Farm Industrial Estate, Wellingborough,
Northamptonshire NN8 6TY Tel: 01933 676519
Scarab High House, Kirton Road, Egmanton, Newark, Nottinghamshire
NG22 0HF Tel: 01636 822033
Swift Racing Car Constructors Unit 21 Bell Park, Newnham Industrial
Estate, Plympton, Plymouth, Devon PL7 4JH Tel: 01752 201780
Vector Racing Cars Ltd The Hollows, Hyde Lane, Kings Langley, Herts.
HP3 8RY Tel: 01923 291617

Race preparation

555 Subaru World Rally Team Prodrive, Acorn Way, Banbury, Oxon.
OX16 7XS Tel: 01295 266480
Andy Rouse Engineering 38 Herald Way, Binley, Coventry, W. Midlands
CV3 2RQ Tel: 01203 443054
Arrowstar Racing Centremead, Osney Mead Industrial Estate, Oxford
Oxon. OX2 0ES Tel: 01865 201177
Avon Racing Bath Road, Melksham, Wiltshire SN12 8AA
Tel: 01225 707443
BM Motorsport Ltd Unit 33, Silverstone, Towcester, Northamptonshire
NN12 8TN Tel: 01327 857653
Dawson Auto Developments Unit 23, Silverstone Circuit, Silverstone,
Northamptonshire NN12 8TL Tel: 01327 857737
Fred Goddard Racing Ltd Unit 21, Silverstone Circuit, Silverstone,
Northamptonshire NN12 8TL Tel: 01327 858304
Graham Goode Racing Lutterworth Road, Leicester, Leicestershire LE2
8PH Tel: 01162 440140

Griffin Motorsport Unit 1, Bagbury Park, The Street, Lydiard Millicent, Swindon, Wiltshire SN5 9LU Tel: 01793 772531

Guy Croft Tuning Unit 2, Keel Court, Enterprise Close, Rochester, Kent ME2 4LY Tel: 01634 290283

Hi-tech Motorsport Ashmores Industrial Estate, Tipton Road, Dudley, West Midlands DY1 4SA Tel: 01384 254489

Janspeed Castle Road, Salisbury, Wiltshire, SP1 3SQ Tel: 01722 415836

Madgwick International Unit 3 Farm Road, Brackley, Northamptonshire NN13 7BQ Tel: 01280 702793

Mardi Gras Motorsport Ltd Unit 9, Silverstone Circuit, Silverstone, Northamptonshire NN12 8TL Tel: 01327 858006

Mark Dunham Racing Stretham Station Road, Wilburton, Ely, Cambridgeshire CB6 3QD Tel: 01353 648208

Mitsubishi Ralliart Leigh Road, Swift Valley, Rugby, Warks. CV21 1JJ Tel: 01788 537588

Nissan Motorsport Europe Units 4–6, Moorbrook, Southmead Park, Didcot, Oxon. OX11 7HR Tel: 01235 819295

Think Automotive 292 Worton Road, Isleworth, Middlesex TW7 6EL Tel: 0181 8475338

Tickford Tickford House, Tanners Drive, Blakelands, Milton Keynes, Bucks. MK14 5BN Tel: 01908 618233

Triple Eight Race Engineering Greatworth Park, Greatworth, Banbury, Oxon. OX17 2HB Tel: 01295 768881

Zeus Motorsport Unit 6G/H, Silverstone Circuit, Silverstone, Northamptonshire NN12 8TN Tel: 01327 858266

Retailers/Various Suppliers

Aldon Automotive Ltd Breener Industrial Estate, Station Drive, Brierley, Hill, W. Midlands DY5 3JZ Tel: 01384 480418

Earl's Performance Products UK Ltd Unit 17, Silverstone Circuit, Silverstone, Northamptonshire NN12 8TL Tel: 01327 858473

International Spares Omega Way, Thorpe Industrial Estate, Egham, Surrey TW20 8RD Tel: 01784 477907

Race Products (Anglia) Ltd Bury Road, Chedburgh, Bury St Edmunds, Suffolk IP29 4UQ Tel: 01284 850959 (Fabrication)

Raceparts UK Unit 3, Rockfort Industrial Estate, Wallingford, Oxon. OX10 9DA Tel: 01491 836689

Trident Racing Supplies Unit 31, Silverstone Circuit, Towcester, Northamptonshire NN12 8TN Tel: 01327 858096

Appendix 3: Motorsport Industry Questionnaire

-1-

Company name:

1. When was your company established?

2. How many people does your company employ?

   .... full-time

   .... seasonal/contract

   .... part-time

3. What is your company's annual turnover?

   £ ....

4. What growth targets do you have for your company over the next five years?

5. What approximate proportion (%) of your company's annual turnover is attributable to motorsports?

6. If less than 100%, please broadly specify the activities of other customers.

7. What approximate proportion (%) of your company's annual turnover is exported?

8. Number the following major foreign markets in order of importance to your company (insert 0 where your company does not export):

- ☐ Europe
- ☐ North America
- ☐ South America
- ☐ Australasia
- ☐ South Africa
- ☐ Far East
- ☐ Middle East
- ☐ Rest of World

–2–

9. Tick motorsports categories in which your company or (its customers) participate:

- ☐ Formula One
- ☐ Formula 3000
- ☐ Indycar/CART
- ☐ Indy Lights
- ☐ Formula 3
- ☐ One-Make Formulae
- ☐ Other Single-Seater
- ☐ Class 1 Touring
- ☐ Super Touring
- ☐ Oval Touring
- ☐ One-Make Touring
- ☐ Other (please specify):
- ☐ Other Touring
- ☐ Sports-Prototype
- ☐ International GT
- ☐ National Sports or GT
- ☐ Group A Rallying
- ☐ Formula 2 Rallying
- ☐ Other Rallying
- ☐ Club Racing
- ☐ Hillclimbs & Sprints
- ☐ Rallycross
- ☐ Other Off-Track

10. Did access to any of the following influence your company's location decision. Please list in order of importance:

- ☐ Skilled Labour
- ☐ Customers
- ☐ Suppliers
- ☐ Test facilities
- ☐ Rivals
- ☐ Other reasons (specify)

11. Which companies do you consider are your major competitors?

In the UK? ....

Outside UK? ....

12. What approximate proportion of turnover (%) does your firm commit to its own R&D?

–3–

13. Is innovation by your company mainly:

☐ Customer-driven?
☐ Supplier-driven?
☐ In-house R&D?

14. Does your firm engage in collaborative R & D with:

☐ Customers?
☐ Suppliers?
☐ Neither?

15. What form does this collaboration take? (e.g. financial support, exchange of technical data, personnel)

16. Does your company ever collaborate with firms outside motorsports engineering (e.g. aerospace, chemical, electronic)? If yes, please specify.

17. Does your company seek technical help from universities?

☐ Often ☐ Sometimes ☐ Never

18. What distinctive/unique capability, does your company have relative to its rivals?

19. What significant product/process innovations has your company developed?

-4-

20. How does your company protect ideas and technology from imitation by rivals?

21. What approximate proportion (%) of your company's staff are recruited direct from:

.... Universities

.... Rival motorsport companies

.... Other motorsport companies

.... Other industries

22. How much of a problem for your company is the poaching of key technical staff?

☐ Major ☐ Insignificant
☐ Significant ☐ Not at all

23. Finally, please summarize which industries and technologies benefit from your company's technological area of motorsports engineering – and what do they get out of it?

Appendix 4: Motorsport Industry Questionnaire – Results

Category	Q. Issued	Replies with info	Category Employees	Sales (£m)	Sales/ Employee
Formula One	7	4	1000	290.0	290,000
Formula 3000	20	2	302	0.73	
Indy Cars	4	1	230	33.0	143,000
Other Majors	5	3	1002	101.0	100,000
Other Formula	13	1	110	6.0	54,000
Preparation	21	1	15	1.5	100,000
Components and Suppliers	55	7	668	61.7	92,000
Consultants	14	2	18	1.0	52,000
Engines	5	0			
Engineering	15	3	310	18.5	60,000
Totals	**159**	**24**	**3655**	**513.43**	

30 June 1999

N.B. We consider these survey results to be very limited and the totals do not include the firms in all the categories identified in the text. A further survey is required.

Index